I0893172

THE NORTH AMERICAN AUTO INDUSTRY SINCE NAFTA

Edited by Greig Mordue and Dimitry Anastakis

The auto sector is North America's most iconic of industries. Since the North American Free Trade Agreement came into existence in 1994, the sector has undergone tremendous change: escalating concerns around climate change, advances in electric and automated vehicles, deindustrialization/reindustrialization, and the rise of low-cost locations as hubs for manufacturing.

The North American Auto Industry since NAFTA examines the issues that have preoccupied the development of policy associated with the manufacture of automobiles in North America. The collection addresses the punctuations that have afflicted the industry since NAFTA's implementation as well as the slower, incremental evolutions that have also occurred. Several aspects of automobility and the industry are explored, including but not limited to the Canadian, American, and Mexican automotive sectors and their evolution and interaction under evolving trade regimes. The book analyses issues surrounding labour, technology, trade policy, regional development, the environment, and broader societal impacts of the automobile. It also draws on the expertise of a wide cross-section of industry experts and scholars to provide readers with a deeper understanding of the automotive industry and its central role in North America's economic, business, and political landscape.

GREIG MORDUE is an associate professor and the ArcelorMittal Dofasco Chair in Advanced Manufacturing Policy in the W Booth School of Engineering Practice and Technology in the Faculty of Engineering at McMaster University.

DIMITRY ANASTAKIS is a professor and the L.R. Wilson and R.J. Currie Chair in Canadian Business History in the Department of History and the Rotman School of Management at the University of Toronto.

Themes in Business and Society

Edited by Dimitry Anastakis

Themes in Business and Society explores new issues in Canadian and international business history. The series advances Canadian business history in a global context by publishing studies that examine firms, entrepreneurs, consumers, industries, the evolution of capitalism, business-government relations, the role of the state and regulation, and the changing environment of national and international business. Supported by the L.R. Wilson/R.J. Currie Chair in Canadian Business History at the University of Toronto and the Rotman School of Management, Themes in Business and Society provides new perspectives on how business impacts ordinary people, both in Canada and around the world.

THE NORTH AMERICAN AUTO INDUSTRY SINCE NAFTA

EDITED BY GREIG MORDUE AND DIMITRY ANASTAKIS

UNIVERSITY OF TORONTO PRESS
Toronto Buffalo London

Toronto Buffalo London
utorontopress.com
Printed in the USA

ISBN 978-1-4875-2736-5 (cloth)
ISBN 978-1-4875-2737-2 (paper)
ISBN 978-1-4875-2739-6 (EPUB)
ISBN 978-1-4875-2738-9 (PDF)

Themes in Business and Society

Library and Archives Canada Cataloguing in Publication

Title: The North American auto industry since NAFTA / edited by Greig Mordue and Dimitry Anastakis.
Names: Mordue, Greig, editor. | Anastakis, Dimitry, 1970– editor.
Series: Themes in business and society.
Description: Series statement: Themes in business and society | Includes bibliographical references and index.
Identifiers: Canadiana (print) 20240366956 | Canadiana (ebook) 20240367006 | ISBN 9781487527372 (paper) | ISBN 9781487527365 (cloth) | ISBN 9781487527396 (EPUB) | ISBN 9781487527389 (PDF)
Subjects: LCSH: Automobile industry and trade — North America. | LCSH: North American Free Trade Agreement (1992 December 17) | LCSH: United States-Mexico-Canada Agreement (2018 November 30)
Classification: LCC HD9710.N672 N67 2024 | DDC 338.4/76292097—dc23

Cover illustration: SK Lafoca / iStockphoto.com
Cover design: John Beadle

We wish to acknowledge the land on which the University of Toronto Press operates. This land is the traditional territory of the Wendat, the Anishnaabeg, the Haudenosaunee, the Métis, and the Mississaugas of the Credit First Nation.

University of Toronto Press acknowledges the financial support of the Government of Canada, the Canada Council for the Arts, and the Ontario Arts Council, an agency of the Government of Ontario, for its publishing activities.

Canada Council for the Arts | Conseil des Arts du Canada

ONTARIO ARTS COUNCIL
CONSEIL DES ARTS DE L'ONTARIO
an Ontario government agency
un organisme du gouvernement de l'Ontario

Funded by the Government of Canada | Financé par le gouvernement du Canada | Canada

Contents

List of Figures and Tables

Figures

Introduction

Chapter 1

Chapter 3

Chapter 4

Tables

Chapter 2

Chapter 3

Chapter 4

Chapter 6

THE NORTH AMERICAN AUTO INDUSTRY SINCE NAFTA

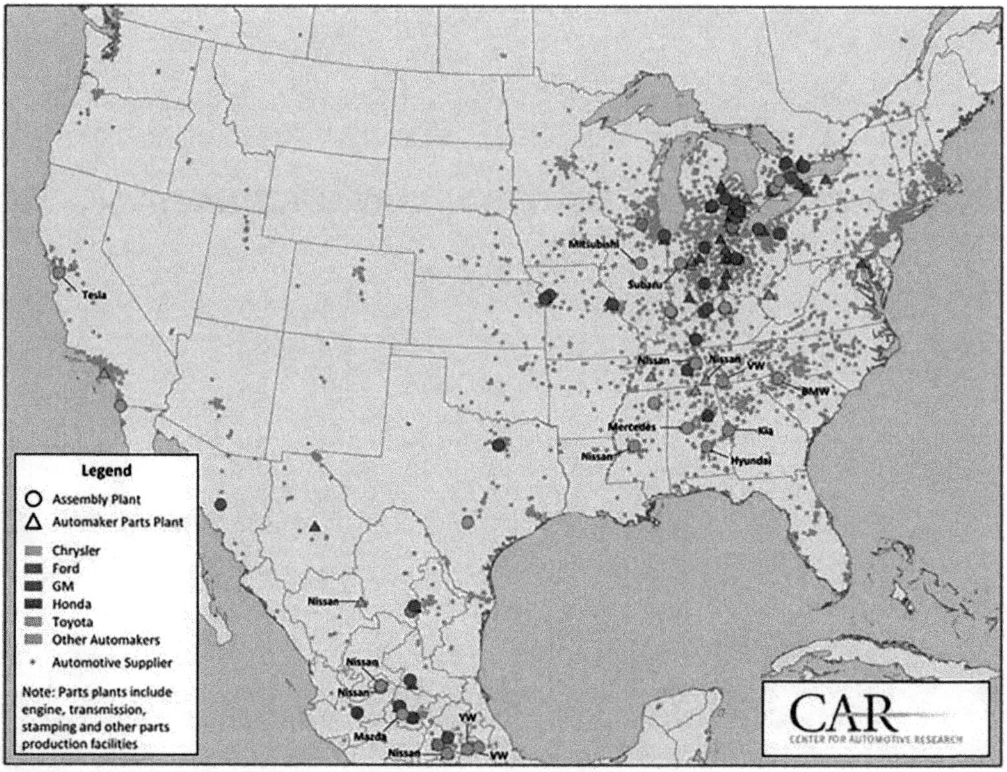

Location of Parts-Producing Facilities in Relation to Assembly Plants
Source: Centre for Automotive Research, https://www.azeconomy.org/2017/03/border-economy/arizona-mexico-and-north-americas-auto-alley/.

Introduction: The North American Automotive Industry from NAFTA to USMCA and Beyond

Greig Mordue and Dimitry Anastakis

On most basic measures, it seems that little has changed in the North American auto industry in the nearly three decades between the enactment of the 1994 North American Free Trade Agreement and the passage of the 2020 United States-Mexico-Canada Agreement (USMCA). That suggests the present North American automotive industry presents a profile similar to the one it had in the early 1990s. In the early 2020s, for example, automotive manufacturing employed about 1.5 million workers across the three countries, about the same number of people as it did at NAFTA's outset. Similarly, the sector was churning out vehicles in comparable volumes to the early 1990s, about 16 million a year. Moreover, key aspects of the operational composition of the North American industry were also relatively unchanged. In 1994, for example, about 26% of the industry's workers were employed in final assembly, with the remainder in upstream parts operations. Today, even after three decades of structural change, productive innovation, and regulatory evolution affecting the industry, about 23% of autoworkers continue to work in final assembly.

Yet this veneer of permanence does not stand up to closer scrutiny. Despite surface similarities, the North American auto sector underwent tremendous change during the almost three decades of the NAFTA's existence. Since 1994, the geographic profile of the North American automotive manufacturing industry has been transformed. Brands have died and new firms have emerged, mostly from the ashes of old ones. Awareness and understanding of the environmental, safety, and social policy implications of automobiles, their use, and the infrastructure necessary to support them have also matured and evolved. This has caused policymakers and industry actors to more urgently seek and invoke measures to contend with some of automobility's most deleterious effects. Indeed, those aspects – and others – have also caused the products autoworkers manufacture and the technologies and systems underpinning that production to be overhauled. Flowing from these changes, expectations and standards attached to automotive workplaces have likewise evolved. While most attention has been devoted to the product changes, the post-NAFTA period has also given rise to automakers and suppliers establishing targets and plans to limit and eventually eliminate the carbon footprint of their manufacturing operations.

All of this is to say that the appearance of relative stability masks a period of profound transformation. This collection aims to explore these adjustments, understand how and why they have occurred, and explain their implications not only for the auto industry itself, but for the broader economic, political, environmental, and social landscape of North America.

Unsurprisingly, despite the transformations it is clear that many of the issues and themes that dominated research and debate surrounding the North American automotive industry in the 1990s endure, albeit in slightly altered forms. In 1994, discussions about industrial policy as it affects the automotive industry hinged on its capacity to impact two foundational elements: investment and jobs. From that core issue of industrial policy, debates about the necessity or efficacy of investment incentives persist, including their effects upon – predictably – investment and jobs. Researchers, policymakers, and other industry actors continue to analyse and debate the effects of evolving – sometimes, devolving – rules affecting global and regional trade, typically through the lens of investment and jobs. That said, the intervening years have given rise to substantial nuance in that underlying preoccupation. Mere "investment and jobs" have given way to "green investment" and "green jobs." Meanwhile, aspects of 1990s-era deliberations about the implementation of lean production (see Womack, Jones, and Roos 1990) have given way to similar discussions about "Industry 4.0," a term encompassing a range of technologies including digital technology, the Internet of Things, cloud computing, and machine learning to support the automation and connection of manufacturing ecosystems. Discussion and debate surrounding Industry 4.0 also includes consideration of those technologies' impacts on the volume and nature of employment. Finally, industrial policymakers and researchers remain gripped by efforts to define and refine individual jurisdictions' unique competitive advantages, with, again, the underlying purpose being their own jurisdictions' capacity to generate or sustain investment and jobs. Moreover, even though the spoils – investment and jobs – are similar, the competitors are much altered.

In the face of the enduring but still relevant issues surrounding the manufacture of automobiles in North America, a primary aim of this collection is to address the sharp punctuations that have occasionally buffeted the industry post-NAFTA implementation, as well as the slower, incremental evolutions that occurred. While this is not the first compilation to adopt a pan–North American approach, it is the first significant collection to do so in more than two decades. Maureen Appel Molot's 1993 book *Driving Continentally: National Policies and the North American Auto Industry*, was released one year prior to NAFTA's enactment. Another continental analysis, *The North American Auto Industry under NAFTA*, edited by Sidney Weintraub and Christopher Sands, was published in 1998. While those compilations do contemplate Mexico's entry into the integrated North American automotive landscape, their analysis of Mexico's influence and impact was largely ancillary to material focused on North America's two national auto-producing incumbents at the time, the United States and Canada.

Thus, an update of the automotive industry and its central role in the now expanded North American economic, business, and political landscape is as timely as it is overdue. In the three decades since Mexico's entry into the integrated North American economy, the auto sector has proven to be the most economically important and politically contentious aspect of one of the world's largest and most dynamic trading blocs. For that reason, the chapters that follow examine several aspects of automobility and the industry itself, including, but not limited to, the Canadian, American, and Mexican automotive sectors and their evolution and interaction under evolving trade regimes from the 1989 Canada-United States Free Trade Agreement (CUSFTA) to the USMCA of 2020. They include analysis of issues surrounding labour, technology, trade policy, regional development, the environment, and broader societal impacts of the automobile and its industry.

While the chapters contained in this collection capture key, individual facets of the transformations that have occurred, a common theme binding much of the collection – and an unending issue in the auto sector – is the seemingly puerile, yet unambiguous, notion of "fair share." Indeed, the objective of acquiring a country's fair share of the bounty of the auto sector – demanded by national politicians and policymakers, workers, and advocates – is apparent throughout the history of the North American automotive industry. The term appeared in the 1961 report of the Royal Commission on the Automotive Industry authored by economist Vincent Bladen (Canada 1961) that gave rise to the continentalizing Canada-US Auto Pact of 1965, which itself became the fount of North America's integrated, managed auto sector. "Fair share" also appeared in subsequent reports, commentaries, and parliamentary debates (see Anastakis 2005, chap. 3; Mordue 2007, chap. 6), particularly in Canada but in US texts as well. In the end, the most basic manifestation of fair share materializes in each national jurisdiction's vehicle production volume relative to the size of its market, often expressed as a simple ratio. In fact, the Auto Pact specified a 1:1 production-to-sales ratio for both cars and trucks in Canada as one of two foundational requirements automakers were to meet in order to benefit from the duty-free movement of vehicles and parts across the Canada-US border (the other being a minimum 50% North American content requirement of parts or vehicles). Along with the terms of the treaty, the Auto Pact's other principal element was a requirement, agreed to in "Letters of Undertaking" between the government and manufacturers, including the Big Three auto producers of General Motors, Ford, and Chrysler, that the firms conduct significant levels of value added in Canada, defined as a ratio of Canadian value added to sales in Canada of 60%. This feature was designed to address a fear that US-headquartered automakers, also known as original equipment manufacturers (OEMs) would subsequently limit Canadian value added to perfunctory, yet modest, final assembly processes. Through the Letters of Undertaking, policymakers sought to encourage OEMs to integrate Canadian operations more deeply with US functions, elevating Canada's contributions by, for example, sourcing parts from Canadian suppliers or undertaking research or product development activities there. While the Auto Pact and its primary covenants have long been supplanted by evolving, less equivocal rules governing international trade (including bilateral and multilateral trade conventions), and the agreement itself was invalidated by the World Trade Organization (WTO) in 2001, the underlying objectives embedded in the Auto Pact endure. Indeed, the indirect legacies of the Auto Pact's managed trade regime are also visible in the USMCA, including content requirements, specific rules of origin, and minimal labour expenditures.

The idea of "fair share" provides a rudimentary way of keeping score of which country benefits most within the integrated North American auto sector. Thus, employing the unadorned standard of fair share as described above – that is, the ratio of production to sales – figure 1 shows that the United States' automotive industry has consistently underperformed (i.e., it has not gotten its fair share of North American automotive production), generally manufacturing about seven vehicles for every ten cars or trucks Americans have purchased since NAFTA's implementation. In fact, the last time American factories made more vehicles than Americans bought was in 1965, not coincidentally the year automotive tariff walls were eradicated between Canada and the United States. Additional context is provided via figure 2. Data from figure 2 show that in 1994 the United States built 12.25 million vehicles, 78% of the Canada-US-Mexico total. However, by 2021 United States vehicle production had dropped to 9.2 million, 68.3% of the NAFTA partners' overall volume.

Relative to the United States, Canada's automotive manufacturing industry experienced a more precipitous fall post-NAFTA. Data from figure 2 show that in 1994 Canada made 2.3 million vehicles, 14.8% of the NAFTA region's total. By the very elemental standard of "fair share" described above, figure 1 shows that at the outset of NAFTA, Canadian assembly plants made 1.85 vehicles for every vehicle Canadians bought. Then, after climbing to production of three million cars and trucks in 1999 and 1.99 vehicles made for every vehicle sold, Canada's automotive manufacturing industry commenced a now two-decade period of decline. By 2021 Canadian vehicle production had dropped to 1.1 million, 8.3% of the NAFTA region total. Moreover, starting with 1965, the year the Auto Pact came into force, Canadian assembly plants achieved an unbroken string of building more vehicles than Canadians bought for fifty-four years. That record ceased in 2019 and has not resumed. Accordingly, Canada's long-standing objective of receiving its fair share of the automotive industry's substantial spoils has, to a significant degree, evaporated.

As for NAFTA's third partner, Mexico, its output as a location for vehicle manufacturing has long outpaced its status as an automotive market. Prior to NAFTA, Mexico's policy of import substitution had the effect that vehicles sold in Mexico were, with few exceptions, made in Mexico. However, a primary consequence of Mexico's developing its industry premised on import substitution was that exports proved largely uneconomic. For those reasons, for generations production and sales remained largely in sync, consistently hewing to a 1:1 ratio. However, Mexico's maquiladora program, introduced in the mid-1960s, provided the

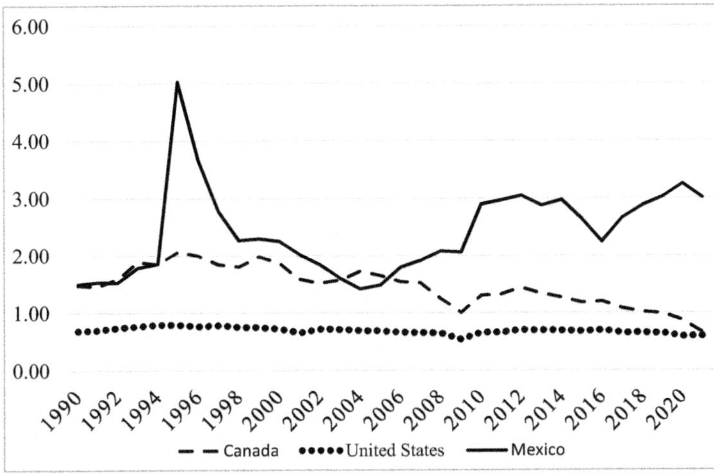

Figure 1. Vehicle Production-to-Sales Ratio for NAFTA Member Countries, 1990–2021
Source: Sales and production figures for Canada, US, and Mexico for 1990–2000 from DesRosiers (2002); for 2001–15 from DesRosiers (2017). Production figures for Canada, US, and Mexico for 2016–21 from OICA (2022a). Sales figures for Canada and US for 2016–18 from DesRosiers (2021); for Mexico for 2016–18 from INEGI (2021); for Canada, US, and Mexico for 2019–2021 from OICA (2022b).

basis for an eventual shift for the Mexican industry. The maquiladora program allows for the duty-free importation of raw materials and components for processing and final assembly in Mexico, provided those goods are eventually exported. Although it was established in the 1960s, it was not until the early 1980s, following a devaluation of the peso in 1982, that the program's use proliferated, particularly in the auto sector (see DuBois 1991). When the peso was devalued, Mexico's production-to-sales ratio jumped from 1.03:1 in 1982 to 1.86:1 by the time NAFTA came into effect in 1994. After NAFTA's implementation an even more rapid transformation of Mexico's automotive industry took hold. The chapters that follow provide details and nuance associated with that change, but the essence is clear: NAFTA provided the basis for deeper integration of Mexico's automotive industry with the North American automotive industry in general, and with the US industry in particular. Mexico became the North American region's hub for low-cost automotive manufacturing. Ultimately, data from figure 1 show that by 2021 Mexico's production-to-sales ratio had grown to 3.01:1, this despite the fact that data upon which figure 2 is based show that vehicle sales in Mexico more than doubled during the post-NAFTA period.

Explaining the emergence of Mexico's auto industry as the main beneficiary of the NAFTA regime is one aspect of this volume, but not the only compelling element of change and consequence in the story of NAFTA's impact upon the sector. The chapters consider a host of

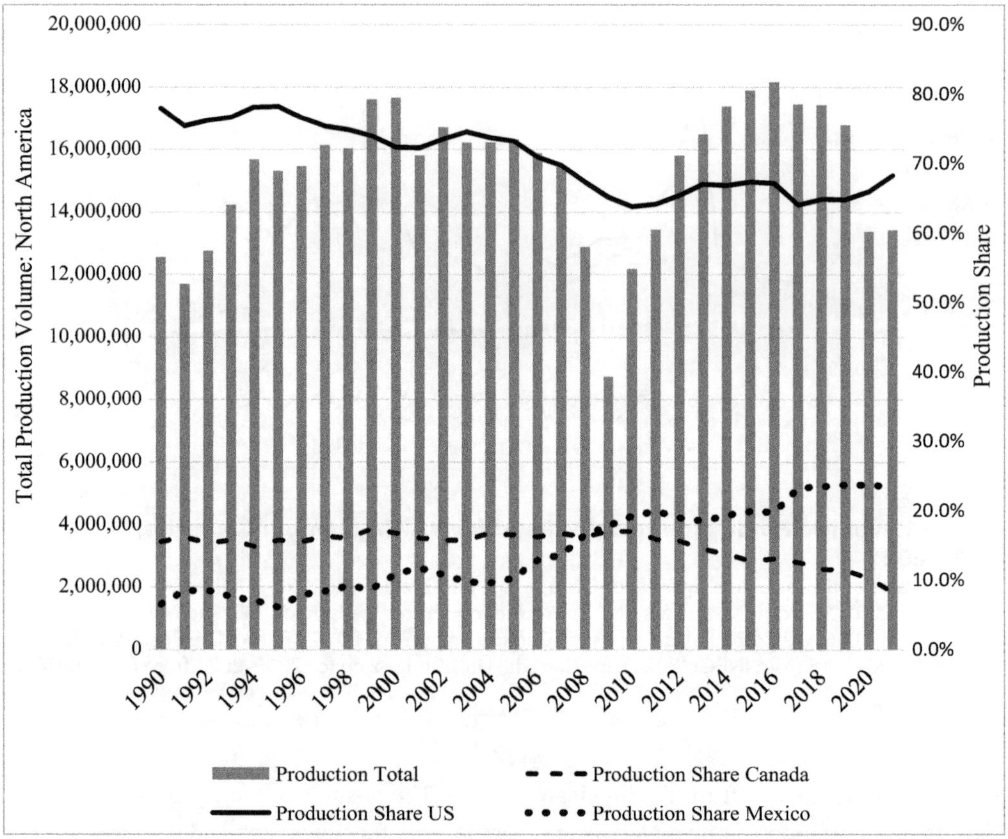

Figure 2. North American Production Volume and Share, 1990-2021
Source: Production figures for 1990–2000 from DesRosiers (2002); for 2001–15 from DesRosiers (2017); for 2016–21 from OICA (2022a).

diverse issues and themes that help us to better understand the evolution of this foundational sector of the integrated North American economy. For example, the first four chapters offer broad global, continental, and national overviews of the industry, providing overarching narratives and supplying context for the development of the integrated industry and its constituent national sectors. From there, the collection delves into more specific aspects of the industry's performance, operation, and evolution since 1994. This includes discussion of the USMCA's likely effect upon investment decisions as well as analysis of regional and national supply chains, labour issues, and the interdependence of the environment, regional economic development, and automotive technology.

To set the stage and frame for the collection, chapter 1, "The Stratification of the Global Auto Industry: North America as the Archetype" by Mordue and Sweeney, provides a helpful lens through which to view the post-1994 evolution of the region's automotive industry. The authors present a framework for capturing and categorizing the unique attributes of automotive-producing countries globally, including those comprising the NAFTA region. As such, the chapter furnishes context for specific themes that subsequent chapters explore. Mordue and Sweeney argue that the global and North American automotive industry comprises three distinct tiers: automotive core, semi-periphery, and integrated periphery countries. Core countries (in North America, the United States) derive power and competitive advantage by hosting the headquarters of automakers. They retain most research and development (R&D) functions and also keep for themselves high levels of production. At the other end of the continuum are integrated peripheries (in North America, that is Mexico). Those countries' main source of competitive advantage is their offer of low-cost labour. Nestled between core and integrated periphery countries are automotive semi-peripheries (represented in North America by Canada). Semi-peripheral countries have neither a home-grown automaker nor do they offer low-cost labour. However, they do possess other attributes that suggest potential for gaining mandates within automotive value chains: they offer well-educated workforces; they host the headquarters of some large Tier 1 suppliers (companies that directly supply parts, components, and systems to automotive OEMs, typically playing a critical role in the design, development, and production of vehicles); they are geographically proximate to core markets; and they retain a base of automotive assembly.

Indeed, the sources of power and competitive advantage wielded by North America's core and integrated periphery countries (the United States and Mexico, respectively) are well understood by those engaged in the process of dispensing mandates for automotive development or manufacturing. In short, the United States retains a stable base of automotive production and performs the preponderance of the automotive industry's most knowledge-intensive and value-added functions. Meanwhile, Mexico is recognized as the low-cost hub for manufacturing. By contrast, the sources of competitive advantage relevant to the automotive semi-periphery, Canada, while seemingly evident to policymakers and other industry actors in Canada, tend to be discounted by automotive investment decision makers outside of Canada. Mordue and Sweeney demonstrate that semi-peripheral auto-producing countries (including but not restricted to Canada) have struggled to either gain mandates for R&D or maintain production. In Canada's case, the authors document a range of often expensive industrial policy programs and narratives that the post-NAFTA implementation period has engendered – all with similar, tepid results.

In the end, Mordue and Sweeney suggest that the trifurcated core/semi-periphery/integrated periphery (US/Canada/Mexico) framework that has arisen in North America and around the world during the post-NAFTA period will eventually give way to a bifurcated model composed of countries demonstrating attributes of either the core or integrated periphery. They suggest that countries comprising the current semi-periphery will continue to wither, their manufacturing mandates ultimately absorbed by current integrated peripheries, their overtures to secure significant higher-value, knowledge-intensive mandates rebuffed by the core.

The pressures, influences, opportunities, and priorities suggested in chapter 1's framework coalesce in chapter 2, "Foreign Auto Transplants in the Age of NAFTA: Some Revealing Trends," by A.J. Jacobs, who documents the reallocation and reordering of production and investment post-NAFTA. In addition to the rise of Mexico as a hub for automotive manufacturing, Jacobs describes how various aspects of the profile of North America's automotive manufacturing base have changed since NAFTA, reviewing factory openings and closings, including the rise of Japanese-owned manufacturers and the relative decline of the Detroit Three incumbents. He also ponders the rise of new entrants, including those from China and India, portending the larger effect these new entrants may eventually have on North America's automotive manufacturing footprint.

Like Jacobs, Clemente Ruiz Durán also considers the reorganization and reallocation of vehicle production in chapter 3, "Mexico's Auto Industry: Its Role in the Construction of North American Global Value Chains." While Jacobs offers a pan–North American perspective, Ruiz Durán's assessment is restricted to the significant and enduring effect NAFTA has had on key, visible aspects of Mexico's automotive manufacturing industry: production levels and employment volume. Ruiz Durán also chronicles the Mexican auto sector's underperformance in other aspects. Key in that regard has been NAFTA's failure to engender wage growth for Mexico's automotive workers. (By contrast, he suggests, autoworkers in the United States and Canada experienced real increases in income over the course of the NAFTA.) Ruiz Durán also addresses the failure of the automotive industries in both Mexico and Canada to upgrade their participation in automotive value chains, an issue that is endemic to integrated periphery and semi-periphery automotive countries and can be explained by the framework provided in chapter 1. Ruiz Durán acknowledges that the USMCA contains provisions to address Mexico's stagnant automotive wage growth. However, he is doubtful about its capacity to address Mexico's under-participation in more knowledge-intensive aspects of global automotive value chains.

The examination of NAFTA-inspired decisions affecting the allocation of production mandates continues in the fourth chapter, "Spatial Integration of the North American Auto Industry under NAFTA," in which Klier and Rubenstein assess the extent to which NAFTA has engendered regional integration of automotive manufacturing in North America. They do so by focusing on two vehicle components the USMCA designates as "core": engines and transmissions. They confirm that most vehicles assembled in North America source engines and transmissions from within that region (i.e., engines and transmissions for vehicles assembled in North America are sourced from North America), a pattern that predates NAFTA. However, they also explain that automotive manufacturing *within* North America is highly integrated and became even more integrated during NAFTA. For example, less than one-third of the vehicles assembled in North America trace engine production, transmission production, and final assembly as occurring in the same country. Looking ahead, they argue that elevated regional content provisions for these USMCA-designated core products will persist.

In contrast with the first four chapters, which focus on the outcomes of the NAFTA regime, Michael Smitka's "Reorganization and Restructuring in the North American Automotive Industry" provides a summary of the NAFTA-inspired current state of affairs and a transition to analysis of the new USMCA regime. He documents consequential developments the US automotive manufacturing industry – a proxy for the North American industry overall – has orchestrated or endured during the post-NAFTA implementation period. Among the most notable transformations – the origins of which predate the NAFTA – he registers the termination of the Big Three/Detroit Three domination and the concomitant rise of new entrants, a trend that has manifest in uneven regional development within and across NAFTA's partner jurisdictions. This has also had effects on labour and its proxies. As well, Smitka points to the decline of vertical integration and the rise of globally oriented, technology-intensive automotive suppliers as a major source of post-NAFTA change, a phenomenon he describes as being an outcome of myriad elements: corroding profitability of the industry's global lead firms, rapid introduction of regulations that have triggered OEMs to source solutions from non-traditional (i.e., external) sources, the emergence of global platforms, and the ensuing practicality of awarding global contracts for large global platforms to single suppliers. Smitka argues that these and other factors (e.g., automation, lean manufacturing, the introduction of new materials, heightened global and regional trade) have given rise to steady increases in labour productivity, which has in turn led to fewer total manufacturing jobs across the US region and the emergence of a narrative of the industry as being "in decline," even though North American automotive output has climbed and the automotive industry's contribution to manufacturing and productivity has also increased.

Smitka's chapter focuses on the NAFTA region's dominant partner, the United States, and its industry. Certainly, the patterns that characterize the US industry's post-NAFTA evolution are also germane to Canada and Mexico, but these patterns do not apply with uniformity across all regions within the United States, and certainly not across all NAFTA-partner jurisdictions. For example, the trend of increasing productivity that Smitka reports within the US industry contradicts the North America–wide top-line results provided at this introductory chapter's outset. Those numbers, devoid of context, suggest relative stagnation of productivity, despite the NAFTA era's near-universal adoption of lean manufacturing and its various iterations, the introduction of Industry 4.0, and organized labour's acceptance of the inevitability of such tools. Our intention, therefore, is to bring nuance to these and other issues affecting the development of the North American automotive industry during the post-NAFTA period: across data sources, between regions, within firms, among stakeholders, over time.

The starting point for the next chapter is the USMCA. Dziczek and Swiecki's "NAFTA vs. USMCA Content Rules Comparison with Evidence from Automakers' Investment Strategies" considers automotive investments that were announced in the immediate aftermath of the USMCA. They thus begin the process of dissecting the potential effect of the USMCA on automotive manufacturing investment in the United States, Canada, and Mexico. They emphasize that the USMCA should only be considered the most recent iteration of a decades-long evolution and accumulation of trade-related policy across the three partners. Beyond that, a variety of additional influences have also coalesced to influence automotive investment decisions. As such, even though Dziczek and Swiecki explain the nuance of the USMCA in areas like rules of origin (ROO) and regional value content (RVC), they stress that it is not possible to isolate the effect of a single measure influencing automotive investment decisions, either before the USMCA or after. That said, Dziczek and Swiecki conclude that while the USMCA is proving to be an important consideration insofar as investment decisions are concerned, it is not in itself determinative.

Building from the categorization of automotive-producing countries expored by Mordue and Sweeney in chapter 1, Elena Goracinova in chapter 7, "From Automotive to Mobility Value Chains: Variety of Embeddedness and Regional Value Capture in Baden-Wurttemberg, Michigan, and Ontario," draws from evolutionary economic geography to assess the capacity of places possessing robust automotive and information and communications technology (ICT) sectors to promote new path development. She presents an analytical framework for doing so and then applies it to two automotive core locations, Baden-Wurttemberg in Germany and Michigan in the United States, and one semi-periphery, Ontario, Canada. Through this, she explains how the primacy of lead OEM automotive firms in core regions contributes to those firms leading (and dominating) cross-sectoral innovation. Meanwhile, she explains that an automotive semi-periphery location like Ontario experiences a different phenomenon. In the end, Goracinova offers a more optimistic prognosis for the automotive semi-periphery than that described by Mordue and Sweeney. She argues that because it lacks a home-grown automaker, a key differentiating attribute of the automotive semi-periphery, Ontario has engendered increased levels of innovation among new and often smaller entrants. She suggests that even though core regions continue to be the epicentre of automotive innovation, semi-peripheral jurisdictions like Ontario have an opportunity to build capabilities, particularly in emerging areas at the intersection of automotive industry and ICT.

Like Goracinova, Wolfe and Lemphers explore issues at the intersection of technology and the automotive industry. The focus of their work in "The Political Economy of Energy Transitions in Canada: Implications for the Auto Industry" provides a basis for the next section of this collection: the electrification of mobility. Wolfe and Lemphers's chapter considers the consequences of the transition away from carbon-based mobility and the effect that adjustment will have on two regions and two industries in Canada: Ontario's automotive manufacturing industry and Alberta's large oil and gas sector. They argue that though Ontario and Alberta have long been viewed as holding divergent and often-fractious political and economic interests, the fact that their two major industries – automotive manufacturing and oil and gas production, respectively – are centred on carbon-based industrial development has locked them into mutually dependent paths.

Notwithstanding the parallel ties, Wolfe and Lemphers acknowledge that the assets, technologies, and social and political institutions buttressing each province suggests divergent post-carbon restructuring. They maintain that while Alberta's key actors remain bound to its carbon-based economic model, Ontario – including its policymakers, automotive industry, and labour – has accepted the necessity of the transition to decarbonization. Even so, Wolfe and Lemphers caution that Ontario's path will be difficult. Those challenges include ensuring that Battery Electric Vehicle (BEV) mandates already granted are executed by the firms that announced them; that its automotive supply base also transitions to post-carbon mobility; and that batteries and other unique-to-BEV technology are developed *and* commercialized within Ontario. They also caution that the uneven pace of each province's post-carbon transition will challenge the Canadian federation in manners analogous to those experienced generations prior.

The challenges and opportunities associated with the transition from the internal combustion engine (ICE) to BEVs are further examined by Kazzaz, Greene, and Yates in chapter 9, "A North American EV Supply Chain: What It Means for Canada's Vehicle Parts Manufacturing Industry." They argue that Canada possesses a range of attributes that suggest it is well-positioned for BEV-supported investment in its supply chain: technological capabilities, resource availability, a well-established automotive manufacturing infrastructure located primarily in southern Ontario in proximity to American-based OEM headquarters. That said, they also acknowledge that large questions and significant hurdles linger. The chapter inventories many of the obstacles that Canada's regionally based automotive manufacturing industry can expect to encounter as the transition to BEVs unfolds. Moreover, the complications that Canada's automotive industry will experience can be anticipated in other regions of North America and in other segments of the industry. This contribution reminds the reader that the transition will manifest in challenges for regions, firms, workers, and policymakers that will be more substantive, more disruptive, and more vexing than anything those engaged in automotive policy or strategy have previously encountered.

The conditions and complications associated with the transition to EVs are further explored by Vallejo, Carrillo, Cabral, and Jimenez in chapter 10, "The Automobile Industry in Mexico and the Challenges of a New Era: A Perspective on Electric Vehicles and Green Technologies." Drawing from a combination of literature and data, Vallejo et al. argue that the paths integrated periphery countries have taken towards electrification – Mexico being a case study – will be rife with contradiction. They argue, for example, that Mexico has been slow to adopt EVs and that local and national policies have been at best indifferent to the transition. They suggest policymakers' lack of interest is rooted in their support for PEMEX, the state-owned petroleum company. Notwithstanding policymakers' equivocality and local consumer reluctance, they acknowledge that Mexico's automotive manufacturing industry will prosper, as its low-cost integrated periphery status will eclipse the influence of this reticence and ambivalence.

In the next segment of the collection, the post-NAFTA evolution of issues affecting labour is considered over the course of three chapters. The first is Mathieu Dupuis's "Collective Bargaining and Employment Relations in the North American Auto Industry: From Convergence to Marginalization?" Dupuis provides an overview of the post- NAFTA influences and pressures confronting autoworkers and their employers in both Canada and the US. He acknowledges the common narrative: the American United Auto Workers (UAW) union responded to plant closures and threats to their employers' market positions with cooperation and concessions; the Canadian Auto Workers (CAW) and its successor, UNIFOR, countered with heightened obduracy and a rejection of concessions. Ultimately, however, Dupuis shows that a confluence of factors, including the creation of NAFTA, the long-term contraction of Canada's auto manufacturing base, and the interventions of government have engendered a convergence of labour practices and outcomes in the United States and Canada. This has also given rise to increased stratification of autoworkers in both Canada and the United States, with those layers demarcated by inconsistent benefits, wage rates that employees "grow" into over several years, and contract workers performing similar functions alongside permanent employees.

The Dupuis chapter provides a valuable base for the following chapter, Tod Rutherford's "Prometheus Bound? Technology and Labour in the North American Automotive Industry." While Dupuis charts the sometimes-divergent paths of organized labour in Canada and the United States in the post-NAFTA period, Rutherford concentrates on a single theme: technological innovation and its effects upon labour. Rutherford reminds us that the global automotive industry has long been at the vanguard of emerging technology. This includes innovation related to the processes and practices associated with vehicle manufacturing (e.g., Fordist mass production and lean production). He also acknowledges that technological adoption associated with automotive manufacturing has never been about simply suppressing labour costs or curbing labour's power. That said, the introduction of new technologies or production practices has important implications for labour. Rutherford's analysis of the effect on labour of the suite of tools known as Industry 4.0 is thus timely. Like Dupuis's contribution, Rutherford explains that acceptance and adoption of technological innovation, including Industry 4.0, has been uneven across the United States, Canada, and Mexico. Ultimately, he argues that labour's current relative weakness – whether in achieving wage growth or in prioritizing a role for unions to influence technology decisions – has caused adoption of Industry 4.0 tools to be muted.

The focus of the third labour-based chapter is Mexico. In "The USMCA and Third-Generation Labour Arrangements: From Previous Experience in Latin America to Probable Scenarios in Mexico" Covarrubias V. and Dufour-Poirier trace several Latin American and Caribbean countries' trade pacts with the United States, starting with the original NAFTA and culminating with the USMCA. Drawing primarily from data and case studies of the automotive industry in Mexico, they demonstrate how evolving trade regimes have affected the efforts of some – but not all – actors in Mexico (as well as the US and Canada) to support wage growth, legitimize collective bargaining, and instil workplace democracy. Ultimately, they argue that though trade pacts *have* contributed to change, improvements have been limited, focused primarily on a limited collection of strategic transnational industries, the automotive industry being the most visible.

As said above, the thirteen chapters contained in this collection are centred on understanding the adjustments that have ensued since the implementation of NAFTA. They also provoke questions and debates about the trajectory of various aspects of the North American automotive sector going forward, whether those adjustments occur as a consequence of trade related measures or otherwise. For those reasons, the context provided in the chapters that follow is helpful, providing a tool for understanding the automotive industry's most important issues and developments as those matters have evolved during a period of substantial transformation. They are aimed not only at those interested in the auto sector, including academics and practitioners, but also at scholars and students interested in the operation of the North American polity and economy. Accordingly, research and researchers have been brought together from a range of disciplines, including economics, business history, economic geography, and engineering. We have also drawn from scholars across the NAFTA's partner countries with expertise in public policy, labour studies, industrial policy, and trade. The research they have provided explores a range of issues at the intersection of the automotive industry, technology, labour, and trade that cut across the strata of core, semi-periphery and integrated periphery automotive manufacturing countries that constitute the NAFTA – now USMCA – region. Ultimately, the authors provide explanations for the patterns and trends as they have emerged surrounding the shared and enduring objective of policymakers, labour, and industry: the preservation and growth of automotive investment and jobs. While the authors do not provide a blueprint for the challenges that lie ahead, they do portend continued and justifiable preoccupation with this, North America's most iconic of industries.

REFERENCES

Anastakis, D. 2005. *Auto Pact: Creating a Borderless North American Auto Industry, 1960–1971*. Toronto: University of Toronto Press.

Canada. 1961. *Report, Royal Commission on the Automotive Industry* (Chair: V.W. Bladen). Ottawa: Queen's Printer.

DesRosiers, D. 2002. *DesRosiers Automotive Yearbook: 2002 Edition*. Toronto: DesRosiers Automotive Consultants.

– 2017. *DesRosiers Automotive Yearbook: 2017 Edition*. Toronto: DesRosiers Automotive Consultants.

– 2021. *DesRosiers Automotive Yearbook: 2020 Edition*. Toronto: DesRosiers Automotive Consultants.

DuBois, F. 1991. "The Maquiladora Industry: Economic Solution or Problem?" *Journal of International Business Studies* 22: 738–41.

INEGI (Instituto Nacional de Estadística, Geografía e Informática). 2021. "Retail Sale and Production of Light Vehicles by Make, Model, Segment and Country of Origin." [In Spanish).]http://en.www .inegi.org.mx/app/tabulados/pxwebv2/pxweb/es/RAIAVL/RAIAVL/RAIAVL_8_9.px/.

Molot, M.A., ed. 1993. *Driving Continentally: National Policies and the North American Auto Industry*. Kingston/Montreal: McGill-Queen's Press.

Mordue, G. 2007. "Government, Foreign Direct Investment and the Canadian Automotive Industry, 1977–1987." PhD diss., University of Strathclyde.

OICA (International Organization of Motor Vehicle Manufacturers). 2022a. *Production Statistics*. http://www.OICA.net/production-statistics.

– 2022b. *Sales Statistics*. https://www.oica.net/category/sales-statistics/.

Weintraub, Sidney, and Christopher Sands, eds. 1998. *The North American Auto Industry Under NAFTA*. Washington, DC: Center for Strategic and International Studies.

Womack, J., D. Jones, and D. Roos. 1990. *The Machine That Changed the World*. New York: Rawsoin.

PART 1

The Post-NAFTA Integration of the North America Auto Industry

1

The Stratification of the Global Auto Industry: North America as the Archetype

Greig Mordue and Brendan Sweeney

The post-2000 period has coincided with significant restructuring of the global automotive industry. Building on the work of Pavlínek (2018), Mordue and Sweeney (2020) explain that this process is an outcome of the emergence of a global automotive industry comprised of three distinct tiers. In it, core automotive countries derive power and competitive advantage by hosting the headquarters of automakers. Those countries include the US, Germany, and Japan. They retain most R&D and high levels of production. At the other end of the continuum are integrated peripheries, their main source of competitive advantage residing in their offer of low-cost labour. That category consists of Mexico as well as countries in central and eastern Europe. While the period following the North American Free Trade Agreement (NAFTA) has given rise to integrated peripheries earning increasing levels of vehicle production, those countries have been unable to attract knowledge-intensive portions of the automotive value chain (Sweeney et al. 2020). Between core automotive countries and integrated peripheries are automotive semi-periphery countries. These neither have a homegrown automaker nor offer low-cost labour. Consequently, they have struggled to gain mandates for R&D or maintain production. That category of automotive countries includes Canada, Spain, the United Kingdom, Belgium, Austria, and Sweden.

In this chapter, we examine how this process of restructuring occurred in North America. In doing so, we demonstrate that the North American automotive industry is the archetype of the post-2000 global process of automotive-producing countries' "trifurcation." We also discuss how the path that industry has taken is a manifestation of both global trends and regional developments, the latter in part a consequence of the NAFTA in 1994.

In North America, the competitive advantages held by countries at the tails of the continuum, represented by the US (core) and Mexico (integrated periphery) are engrained. As such, the industrial policy actions undertaken by those categories of automotive-producing countries are more evident and more permanently affixed. However, for countries comprising the automotive semi-periphery, the sources of competitive advantage are more ambiguous, a condition that makes the process of identifying and implementing industrial policy measures there more enigmatic. For that reason, our analysis focuses on North America's automotive semi-periphery, Canada. We assess Canada's purported competitive advantages and the policy levers it has implemented in the post-NAFTA period to sustain or win investment. We juxtapose Canada's approach with those of the US and Mexico, seeking to understand if the post-2000 trifurcated model of the global automotive industry into core, semi-periphery, and integrated periphery automotive countries – a pattern reinforced by the NAFTA – is sustainable. Alternatively, we consider if the trifurcation of the global automotive industry is merely a transitional state until such time as the industry reverts to a more traditional bifurcated/binary model, one where the primary actors are countries demonstrating the attributes of automotive core countries and automotive peripheries.

The chapter is organized as follows. We first review global trends with respect to the location of automotive manufacturing and R&D during the post-NAFTA period, placing particular emphasis on the period between 2000 and 2021. The framework for our analysis is the strata of three automotive jurisdictions – core, semi-periphery, and integrated periphery – introduced by Pavlínek (2018) and more thoroughly developed by Mordue and Sweeney (2020). We draw from this framework to demonstrate how the three countries comprising continental North America represent the archetype for global trends during the post-2000 period, also discussing how the location of production has changed and how long-established patterns shaping the location of automotive R&D have endured. We focus on the automotive industry in Canada, a consequence of the unique and significant challenges that jurisdictions comprising the automotive semi-periphery encounter whether they are in North America or elsewhere, as they seek to enhance or merely maintain their precarious position in global or regional automotive value chains. From there, we discuss Canada's policy responses to these post-2000 transformations and classify the measures Canada has taken into two categories: industrial policy measures and industrial narratives. This chapter concludes with a discussion of our findings, including an explanation of why and how the semi-periphery constitutes the most diverse, nuanced, and confounding category of automotive manufacturing locations in the context of debates related to industrial policy.

THE TRIFURCATION OF THE GLOBAL AUTOMOTIVE INDUSTRY

Almost three decades have passed since the implementation of NAFTA. During that time, a series of significant and enduring adjustments have buffeted the global automotive industry. These include flashpoints like the recession of 2008–9 and the COVID-19 pandemic. In recent years, discourse related to the automotive industry has centred on issues related to connectivity, autonomy, the sharing of vehicles, and electrification (the so-called CASE). While the anticipated effects of these technological adjustments, both individually and combined, are profound, their ultimate effects have yet to be fully absorbed by consumers or

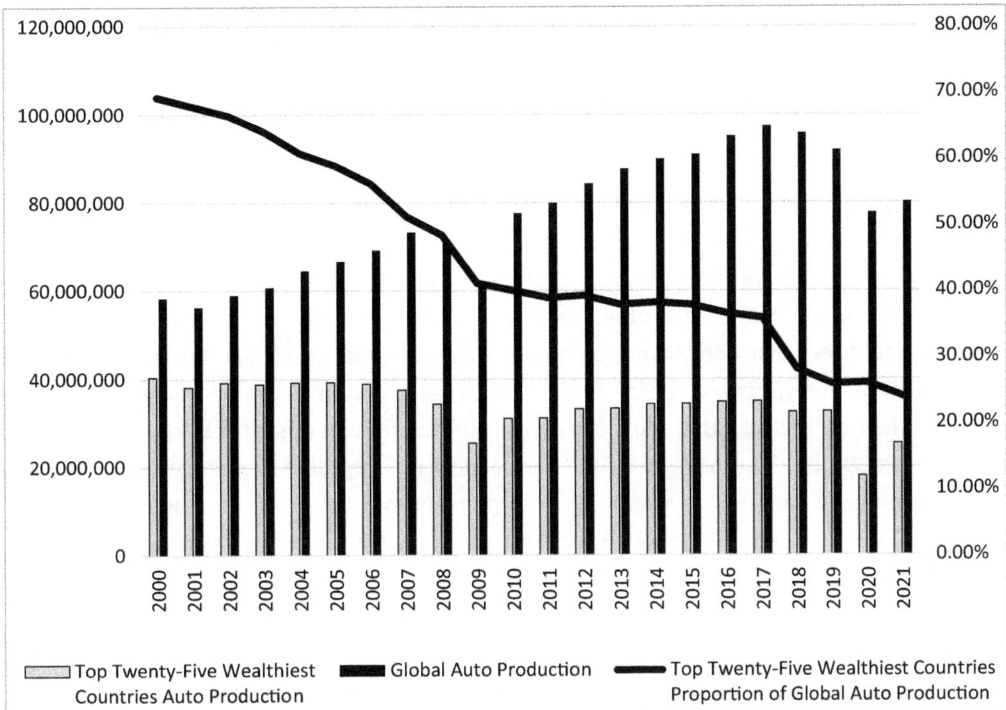

Figure 1. Automotive Production in the Twenty-Five Wealthiest Countries, 2000–21
Source: Year-by-year vehicle production from OICA (2022); gross national income (GNI) per capita from World Bank (2022).

policymakers. Indeed, we argue that the most profound vicissitudes that many stakeholders – including policymakers, auto workers, and communities – have experienced since the mid-1990s arose out of a shift in automotive production to less affluent countries. One of the consequences of this shift is a "trifurcation" of automotive-manufacturing countries.

Throughout the first century of the automotive industry, the process of conceiving, developing, and assembling vehicles was the preserve of the most economically advanced countries. Figure 1, for example, shows that as recently as 2000, 69.3% of global vehicle production occurred in the twenty-five wealthiest countries. However, after 2000, the tendency to locate automotive manufacturing in the wealthiest countries declined. Figure 1 shows that by 2021 just 24% of vehicles were made in the twenty-five wealthiest countries. Today, the preponderance of the world's automotive manufacturing occurs in less developed countries with lower labour costs. This includes China and India, whose automotive industries have grown by factors of thirteen and five respectively between 2000 and 2021 (OICA 2022).

The dimming profile of wealthier countries as automotive manufacturing hubs and the rise of automotive production in less affluent ones occurred in increments. Consequently, the trend has been largely obscured, particularly when compared to the more dramatic but still largely anticipatory effects of CASE. Even so, the post-2000 geographic transformation of automotive manufacturing (see Brincks et al. 2018; Pavlínek 2020) has been investigated through several theoretical lenses, including global value chains, global production networks, uneven development, and the international division of labour (Domański, Guzik, and Gwosdz 2017; Lampón, Lago-Peñas, and Cabanelas 2016; Pavlínek 2018, 2020; Sturgeon et al. 2009). Out of this has emerged a framework that labels automotive-producing countries as occupying one of three categories: "core," "semi-periphery," or "integrated periphery" (Pavlínek 2018; Mordue and Sweeney 2020). This trifurcation of automotive-producing countries is captured in figure 2.

Figure 2 shows that core countries host the headquarters of global automotive original equipment manufacturers (OEMs) (e.g., Volkswagen, General Motors, Toyota) and are distinguished by the fact that they engage in both manufacturing and R&D (Mordue and Sweeney 2020). At the other end of the continuum are integrated periphery countries, their primary source of competitive advantage resting in their offer of low-cost labour (Mordue and Sweeney 2020). In the post-2000 period, integrated peripheries have assumed increasingly elevated roles as nuclei for automotive manufacturing (Pavlínek 2020; Sturgeon and Van Biesebroeck 2011). Large automotive-manufacturing footprints have emerged in automotive integrated periphery countries in central and eastern Europe as well as in North Africa, Mexico, and Thailand. Between core and integrated periphery categories is the automotive semi-periphery. Lacking the domestic ownership of an OEM as characterized by the core or the cost-competitiveness of the integrated periphery, semi-periphery countries face major challenges. They are unable to attract significant levels of the automotive industry's knowledge-based activities – the preserve of the core – nor are they gaining major new manufacturing mandates – the domain of the rapidly emergent integrated peripheries (Mordue and Sweeney 2020). Semi-peripheries include places that were formerly members of the automotive core, a function of their previous hosting of the headquarters of an automotive OEM (e.g., Sweden and the United Kingdom), as well as countries like Canada and Austria: places with a long history of automobile manufacturing and that are closely integrated with core countries like the US and Germany, respectively. Semi-peripheries possess neither the market power nor the residual power derived from the core's role of hosting the headquarters of a global product leader. Moreover, they now find themselves increasingly squeezed by the offer of low-cost labour associated with their emergent integrated periphery competitors.

The trifurcation of automotive-producing countries in general and the emergence and expansion of several low-cost automotive integrated periphery countries in particular are outcomes of a phenomenon that Mordue and Sweeney (2017) call the "commoditization" of automotive assembly. This term suggests that the process of assembling vehicles has become sufficiently indistinguishable that competitor locations, regardless of their economic strata, are able to perform the function. Its advent creates the condition for OEMs to tilt investment location decisions to locations offering the lowest-cost labour. Previously, the process

Category	Core	Semi-Periphery	Integrated Periphery
Countries	United States Germany Japan South Korea France Italy	UK Canada Spain Austria Belgium Sweden Finland	Mexico, Slovakia, Poland, Indonesia Iran, Czech Republic, Turkey, Russia, Thailand, South Africa, Malaysia, Romania, Argentina, Brazil, Slovenia, Morocco, Hungary Uzbekistan, Taiwan, Portugal
	China India		China India
Primary Source of Competitive Advantage Recognized by Automotive Industry	**Power**	**?**	**Low Cost**
Key Attributes			
Homegrown Automakers	Yes	No	No
Automotive R&D Spending	High	Low–Medium	None–Low
Labour Costs	High	High	Low
Foreign Ownership	Low–Medium	Medium–High	High
Homegrown Top 100 Suppliers	High	Low–Medium	None–Low

Figure 2. The Trifurcated Framework for the Largest Auto-Producing Nations (>100,000 Units Annually)

Source: Adapted from Pavlínek (2018) and Mordue and Sweeney (2020).

of making vehicles was considered to be sufficiently complex that less developed countries – many comprising the newly emergent integrated periphery – were restricted to limited or truncated mandates for automotive production (see, for example, Wilkins and Hill 1964; Wilkins 1974; Baranson 1969; Dassbach 1989). However, the post-2000 advent of low-cost, economically less developed countries like the Czech Republic, Hungary, Mexico, Morocco, Slovakia, and Turkey as significant destinations for automotive investment has rendered that description obsolete. According to Mordue and Sweeney (2017), the commoditization of automotive assembly is the result of the standardization of processes and practices within firms and of the automotive industry's ability to recruit top-tier talent, particularly in less developed jurisdictions. Beyond mere production growth, the emergence of integrated periphery countries as foci for automotive manufacturing is evident in the convergence of quality results (see J.D. Power 2011, 2020), in capital intensity across geographic boundaries and economic strata, and in the emergence of luxury vehicle production in those countries (e.g., luxury brands BMW, Audi, and Infiniti make vehicles in Mexico). Ultimately, this has manifested in stagnation of final assembly production in more developed countries (as captured in figure 1).

While the placement of countries along the core–semi-periphery–integrated periphery continuum tends to be static over the short to intermediate term, the status of several locations demonstrates dynamism over the longer term. This pattern is especially evident in the category of countries comprising the automotive semi-periphery. As said above, some semi-peripheries were previously members of the automotive core but now find themselves relegated to the semi-periphery, an outcome of the sale or closure of their resident global lead firm (e.g., Volvo in Sweden, Jaguar Land Rover in the United Kingdom, SEAT in Spain). Other semi-peripheries occupy that status because of the arrival of the category "integrated periphery." In other words, their status as semi-peripheries is the result of the global industry transformation from a binary framework (core and periphery only) to a three-stage continuum (containing the core at one end, the newly created integrated periphery at the other, and semi-peripheries in between). Thus, the semi-periphery exists *today* because most of the countries comprising the newly emergent automotive integrated periphery were previously inconsequential. Moreover, two countries, China and India, demonstrate attributes of both the core and integrated periphery, an outcome of the fact that their competitive advantage stems from the defining characteristic of integrated peripheries: low production costs, *and* core country's primary sources of competitive power: their hosting of global lead firm (OEM) headquarters combined with large domestic markets.

NORTH AMERICA AS THE ARCHETYPE OF THE TRIFURCATION OF THE AUTOMOTIVE INDUSTRY

The preceding section describes a global experience: the post-2000 stratification of automotive-producing countries to the statuses of core, semi-periphery, and integrated periphery. However, of greater consequence than the global trend is the impact the trend has on regions and communities, their automotive ecosystems, and the compatibility of industrial policy measures with each category of countries' underlying characteristics. In this section we begin to examine the phenomenon as it has emerged in North America. We demonstrate that the North American automotive industry is the archetype of trifurcation as we understand it. We will also explain how its manifestation is a consequence of both global trends and regional developments, the latter related in large part to the implementation of the NAFTA in 1994.

Even though the NAFTA integrated the automotive industries in its three member countries, it did not cause the automotive industries of those countries to develop in comparable manners. Subsequent to NAFTA's implementation, the development of the automotive industry in the US reinforced the attributes associated with core automotive countries as captured in figure 2. Meanwhile, Mexico emerged as the model for an automotive integrated periphery. However, like many other automotive semi-peripheries, Canada struggled: no longer the lower-cost production option in an integrated North American automotive industry that before NAFTA had been restricted to the US and Canada, and unable to earn mandates for more knowledge-intensive portions of the automotive value chain that are persistently located near the corporate headquarters of OEMs in places like Detroit, Stuttgart, and Tokyo (Mordue and Sweeney 2020).

In this section we argue that the transition(s) experienced by automotive semi-peripheries are vexing and nuanced in manners and to degrees experienced by neither core nor integrated peripheries. The competitive advantages held by automotive countries at opposite ends of the continuum, represented by the US (core) and Mexico (integrated periphery) are deeply rooted. Core automotive countries derive power, competitive advantage, and benefits from the historical advantage conferred on locations hosting the headquarters of product lead firms (OEMs like Toyota, General Motors, or Volkswagen). Integrated peripheries gain competitive advantage and production mandates from their offer of low-cost labour. As such, the industrial policy actions undertaken by both core and integrated periphery countries are more evident and more permanently affixed. However, for countries comprising the automotive semi-periphery, the sources of competitive advantage are indistinct, making the challenge of devising industrial policy unclear. It is for that reason that this analysis focuses on North America's automotive semi-periphery, Canada.

The trifurcation of the North American automotive industry is most evident in vehicle production trends. Figure 3 shows that prior to the 1994 NAFTA, Mexico's automotive industry was small in nominal terms and relative to its population. For example, in 1994 Mexico vehicle production was less than half that of Canada. However, within two years of NAFTA's implementation, vehicle production in Mexico commenced a prolonged ascent. For the first few years following that implementation, the rise of Mexico as an automotive-manufacturing nation could be ignored by countries like Canada and the US. Data from figure 3 show that Mexico's production rose by 38.3% between 1994 and 1999, but the market for vehicles throughout North America was also expanding rapidly. As a result, US and Canadian vehicle production continued to rise. Figure 3 shows that between 1994 and 1999, vehicle

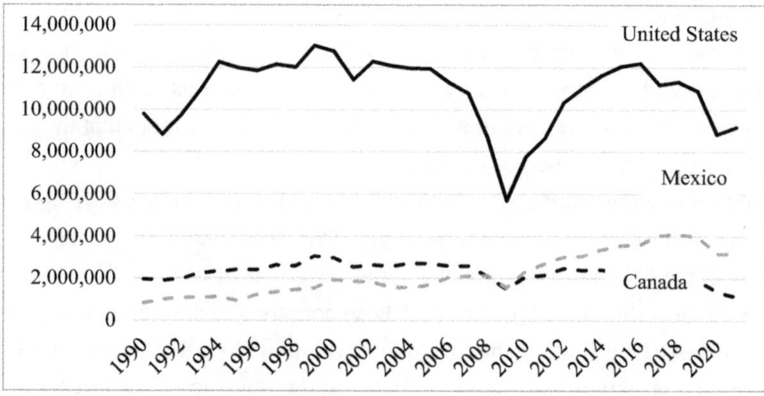

Figure 3. Vehicle Production in US, Mexico, and Canada, 1990–2021
Source: Production data for 1990–9 from DesRosiers (2017), for 2000–21 from OICA (2022).

production in the US and Canada rose by 6.3% and 31.7%, respectively. However, after 2000, production levels in the two countries started to diverge from their NAFTA partner, Mexico. As figure 3 shows, by 2008 – on the eve of the recession, rather than a consequence of it – vehicle production in Mexico eclipsed vehicle production in Canada. By 2021, Mexico's share of North American production was three times that of Canada. Thus, during the post-2000 period, Mexico absorbed virtually all of the vehicle production losses experienced by its northern neighbours. During that time, the effect on Canada was disproportionate to that experienced by the US. In effect, Mexico dislodged Canada as the North American automotive industry's low-cost non-core location.

The challenges experienced by North America's automotive semi-periphery, Canada, are contextualized in table 1, which captures vehicle production in the world's current or previously significant automotive semi-peripheries in 2000 and 2021 ("significant" defined as countries currently or previously producing 100,000 vehicles annually). As recently as 2000, Canada, with production of 2,961,636 vehicles, was the world's seventh-largest producer by volume (OICA 2022), and its share of global production was 5.1%. On a regional basis, Canadian vehicle production in the year 2000 accounted for 16.7% of the volume generated in Canada, the US, and Mexico. By 2021, production volume in Canada had dropped by more than 60% vis-à-vis 2000 and its global ranking among vehicle-producing nations had deteriorated to sixteenth. Table 1 also shows that during that period, Canada's share of global production sunk from over 5% to 1.4%, and on a regional basis (i.e., North America) its share slipped from almost 17% to 11.4%.

Before NAFTA, the North American automotive industry was bifurcated. The US operated as the core and Canada occupied a role similar to that of the current members of the integrated periphery (i.e., it was the lower-cost regional alternative). The subsequent emergence of Mexico dislodged Canada from its pre-NAFTA role. The pattern exhibited in North America

Table 1. Vehicle Production in the Semi-Periphery, 2000 and 2021

		2000			2021		
Region	Country	Vehicle Production	Share of Global Production (%)	Share of Regional Production (%)	Vehicle Production	Share of Global Production (%)	Share of Regional Production (%)
North America	Canada	2,961,636	5.08	16.73	1,115,002	1.39	11.42
Europe	UK	1,813,894	3.11	8.95	932,488	1.16	6.48
	Austria	141,026	0.24	0.70	136,700	0.17	0.84
	Spain	3,032,874	5.20	14.96	2,098,133	2.62	13.24
	Sweden	301,343	0.52	1.49	258,000	0.32	1.31
	Belgium	1,033,294	1.77	5.10	261,038	0.33	1.34
	Finland	38,926	0.07	0.19	93,172	0.12	0.54
European Semi-Periphery		6,361,357	10.91	32.05	3,779,531	4.72	28.82
Total Semi-Periphery		9,322,993	15.99	-	4,894,533	6.11	-

Source: Aggregate global, North American, and European production data for 2000 and 2021 from OICA (2022).
Notes: European data include countries comprising the European Union and the United Kingdom plus those in central and eastern Europe. (Russia, Uzbekistan, Belarus, Turkey, and Ukraine are not included.)

in general and Canada in particular is not unique, particularly among countries occupying the status of semi-periphery. For example, Canada, North America's sole semi-periphery country, experienced a 31.7% drop in its share of regional production between 2000 and 2021. The six countries comprising Europe's automotive semi-periphery also witnessed their share of regional vehicle production drop, albeit their decline was less acute. Table 1 shows that in Europe's case, semi-peripheries' share of regional production dropped from 32% in 2000 to 28.8% in 2021.

That the profiles of the member countries of North America's automotive industry transformed following implementation of the NAFTA was predictable. After all, one need only consider the effects of the 1965 Canada-US Automotive Products Trade Agreement (better known as the Auto Pact) to anticipate reorganization. The Auto Pact – the forerunner to the Canada-US Free Trade Agreement of 1989 and the NAFTA of 1994 – launched the process of intra-continental integration of the North American automotive industry. The agreement provided for the duty-free trade of vehicles and automotive parts within Canada and the US so long as (1) member automakers assembled one vehicle in Canada for every vehicle they sold, and (2) those automakers met rigid domestic value-added requirements (see Dykes 1970; Lyndon B. Johnson School of Public Affairs 1985; Anastakis 2005). After its implementation, Canada's vehicle-manufacturing incumbents (GM, Ford, Chrysler, and AMC) made significant investments in Canadian manufacturing facilities. Accordingly, vehicle production climbed and plants achieved improved economies of scale (see Science Council of Canada 1980; Mordue 2007). These investments occurred as a consequence of the threat of tariffs that governments could impose on non-compliant companies, as well as lower Canadian labour costs vis-à-vis the US (see Beigie 1970; Emerson 1975; Wilton 1976; Flynn 1979). Mordue (2007) shows that following the implementation of the Auto Pact there were several occasions when US-owned Auto Pact–eligible automakers did not comply with one or both of the Auto Pact's requirements related to production and value-added. However, rather than impose tariffs (then approximately 12.5%), the Canadian government leveraged individual automaker's shortcomings to generate additional investment.

Notably, even though the Auto Pact *did* cause the industries in the two countries to integrate, its implementation did *not* cause the automotive industries to evolve in duplicative manners. Indeed, the trifurcation of the automotive industries in the US, Canada, and Mexico to which the NAFTA contributed in 1994 (captured, in part, via figure 2) was preceded by a distinct Auto Pact–initiated bifurcation in 1965. As described, the Auto Pact prompted significant investment in Canadian operations by the incumbent vehicle-making firms. However, the benefits of elevated production came at a price. Before the Auto Pact, Canadian subsidiaries of US-owned automobile manufacturers operated as near-separate entities. In fact, the pre-Auto Pact, less integrated nature of the North American automotive industry engendered an automotive ecosystem in Canada with several unique-to-Canada features. These included the existence of flexible manufacturing lines capable of producing low volumes with a wide product mix; the design, adaptation, purchasing, and logistics of parts to support manufacturing at lower volumes; and more sophisticated, stand-alone marketing and product-planning activities (see Canada 1978; MacDonald 1980). Many of these features disappeared in the new, post-Auto Pact integrated environment, a turn of events that caused significant consternation among policymakers (see Canada 1978) and spawned a series of forceful policy measures in the 1980s (see Lavelle and White 1983; Pringsheim 1983; Mordue 2020).

Reflecting on the 1965 Auto Pact and the bifurcation it engendered is instructive. It informs our understanding of the development of the automotive industry following implementation of the next continental restructuring, NAFTA, almost thirty years later. The outcome of the Auto Pact was that the automotive industries of its member countries – the US and Canada – evolved (and in Canada's case, it has been argued, devolved) in an identifiable, dualistic pattern. The effect of NAFTA was different. If the Auto Pact caused bifurcation, NAFTA provoked polarization. Located at either end of the continuum, automotive core and integrated periphery countries established clear sources of competitive advantage, an outcome that parallels the roles established by the US and Canada following the Auto Pact. The effect of the NAFTA, however, has been that one of the Auto Pact's founding member nations, Canada, was relegated to a location between the continuum's poles, an outcome that limited its prospects and confounded its policymakers. We consider these challenges in the next section, by exploring the post-NAFTA industrial policy paths adopted by North America's automotive semi-periphery, Canada.

THE POST-NAFTA EVOLUTION OF AUTOMOTIVE INDUSTRIAL POLICY IN THE NORTH AMERICAN SEMI-PERIPHERY

Until 1994, the policy instruments that linked the North American automotive industry were confined to Canada and the US, an outcome of the Auto Pact of 1965 and reinforced by the Canada-US Free Trade Agreement of 1989. However, the inclusion of Mexico in the NAFTA in 1994 altered the competitive calculus for Canadian automobile production.

The post-2000 emergence of a trifurcated global automotive industry caused policymakers to rethink, reposition, and refine their approach to industrial policy as it affected the industry. This tendency was most evident among the newly emergent integrated peripheries on one hand and the previous low-cost champion, semi-peripheries, on the other. Put simply, the integrated periphery (in North America's case, Mexico) started to assume the role and earn the mandates previously dispensed to countries like Canada. Key features of the policies and procedures associated with the expansion of automotive production in Mexico are captured elsewhere in this collection. For example, notwithstanding Mexico's ascendancy as North American's low-cost vehicle manufacturing hub, Clemente Ruiz Durán in chapter 3 explains the country's concurrent failure to transition to more knowledge-intensive aspects of global automotive value chains. Vallejo et al. delve deeper in chapter 10, focusing their assessment on the transition to electric vehicles. These chapters represent useful extensions of earlier research documenting Mexico's ascendancy as North America's low-cost automotive manufacturing choice, the simultaneous decline of Canada's automotive industry (see Mordue 2020), and the role of Mexican policymakers in triggering that country's transition (see Rothstein 2005; Gereffi and Sturgeon 2013; Martínez-Martínez and Carrillo-Viveros 2019).

Thus, the post-NAFTA automotive industries of Mexico and Canada have taken disparate paths. While the industrial policy strategy of the former has been well defined and its trajectory mostly unimpeded, the latter has adopted an equivocated approach and its outcomes have been, at best, modest. Subsequently, its capacity to identify a clear, sustainable source of competitive advantage has suffered, a condition that that has provoked a quixotic approach to the strategies it has deployed and the industrial policy measures it has adopted. The effect: almost three decades after the implementation of the NAFTA, Canada's automotive industry fumbles for regional relevance.

During this post-NAFTA implementation period, Canada has leaned on two policy measures to supports its automotive industry. The first represents a distinct and recognizable form of industrial *policy*: incentives for large-scale automotive manufacturing investments. The second is more aptly described as industrial *narratives*: a series of government-led campaigns to promote Canada as a location for investments in an evolving series of emerging automotive technologies, narratives that promote existing and latent capabilities and are quite often not automotive-specific. The efficacy of both measures – Canada's automotive industrial policy and its series of automotive industrial narratives – has been mixed, with the former proving insufficient to suspend Canada's decline as a vehicle manufacturer and the latter not yet provoking the transition its agents have foretold. Through the remainder of this section, we describe the measures Canada has taken in the post-2000 period, first exploring Canada's application of industrial policy as it applies to its automotive industry and then examining the succession of automotive industry narratives it has adopted.

AUTOMOTIVE INDUSTRY POLICY IN CANADA

The application of industrial policy in the form of direct financial incentives for large-scale automotive manufacturing investments in Canada began in the late 1970s. This occurred shortly after the US began incentivizing similar investments (e.g., VW Pennsylvania, Ford Avon Lake, Ohio) (Mordue 2007) and as inter-jurisdictional competition for such investments intensified. Consequently, since the late 1970s most major greenfield automotive investments in Canada have been supported by government financial assistance. This included Canada's first such dalliance: support to Ford for a greenfield engine plant in Windsor, Ontario, in 1978 (see Thomas 1996; Mordue 2010) as well as subsequent packages for new assembly plant investments in Quebec and Ontario in the 1980s by Honda, Toyota, Hyundai, Suzuki (with GM), and Renault (with AMC) (see Mordue 2007). Table 2 presents significant automotive investments in Canada (of CDN $100 million or more) during the period 1980–2000. It shows that six projects met that criterion. Of those, five were for greenfield assembly plants and one for the refurbishment of an existing operation. Table 2 also shows that government funding was provided for five projects, representing 23.3% of the six investments' total cost. Most of those funds, $651 million representing 91.1% of total government support, took the form of interest-free loans. Outright grants, at $63.8 million and 8.9% of total spending, were less consequential.

Therefore, the practice of incentivizing greenfield automotive investments in Canada was well established by 2000. During the post-2000 period, policymakers at both the federal and provincial (Ontario) level continued to rely on this form of industrial policy. This occurred because after 2000, Canada's competition for final assembly investment intensified, a consequence of the rise of North America's new integrated periphery, Mexico. Mexico's ascent was most unambiguously demonstrated by the fact that between 2001 and 2021, six vehicle assembly plants in Canada closed (one of which re-opened in 2022) and only one new facility opened (Toyota in Woodstock, Ontario, in 2008). The net result was that by 2021 Canada hosted five fewer assembly plants than in 2000, vehicle production dropped to barely a third

Table 2. Large Automotive OEM Projects in Canada, 1980–2000 (>$100 million)

	Investments					Incentives						
		Purpose / Type of Investment										
Company	Year Announced	Sustain Existing Operations	Greenfield	Description/ Production Capacity Increase	Total Investment ($)	Total ($)	Govt. Support as % of total project(s)	Grant ($)	Grant as % of Govt. Support	Loan ($)	Loan as % of Govt. Support
Honda	1984		X	40,000-capacity assembly plant in Alliston, Ontario	100 million	0	0	0	0	0	0
AMC-Renault	1984		X	150,000-capacity assembly plant in Bramalea, Ontario	764 million	121 million	15.83	0	0	121 million (royalty payback)	100
Toyota	1985		X	50,000-capacity assembly plant in Cambridge, Ontario	400 million	50 million	12.5	15 million (training grant)	30	35 million	70
Hyundai	1985		X	100,000-capacity assembly plant in Bromont. Quebec	300 million	208.8 million	69.6	8.8 million (cash and land)	4.23	200 million	95.78
General Motors-Suzuki (CAMI)	1986		X	200,000-capacity assembly plant in Ingersoll, Ontario	650 million	85 million	13.07	40 million (training grant)	47.05	45 million	52.95
General Motors	1987	X		Refurbishments to support next-generation models at Ste. Therese, Quebec assembly plant	450 million	250 million	55.55	0	0	250 million	100
	SUMMARY	***1 project***	***5 projects***	***540,000***	***3.064 billion***	***714.8 million***	***23.32***	***63.8 million***	***8.93***	***651 million***	***91.07***

Source: AMC-Renault information from Partridge (1984); General Motors-Suzuki (CAMI) from *Ottawa Citizen* (1986) and *Globe and Mail* (1986); Honda from *Globe and Mail* (1984); Toyota from Milner (1985); Hyundai from Shalom (1985) and *Globe and Mail* (1985); General Motors from *New York Times* (1987).

of the level achieved in 2000 (see figure 3), automotive assembly employment fell by 20% from 53,204 to 44,277, and automotive parts employment fell by 33% from 98,869 to 74,297 (Statistics Canada, 2021).

In the face of these challenges, Canada's and Ontario's automotive industrial policymakers expanded their use of incentives for production. Here, two modifications are noteworthy. First, after 2000 interest-free loans, the currency of 1980s-era automotive investment attraction in Canada, drifted away. As table 3 shows, after 2000 loans began to be replaced by grants. Before 2000, as table 2 demonstrated, more than 90% of support provided by government came in the form of loans. After 2000, as table 3 reveals, outright grants became the primary instrument, representing 82.13% of government incentive packages.

As described, throughout most of the post-2000 period the main automotive industrial policy tool of the province of Ontario has been direct grants. During that time the federal government attempted to limit their involvement to interest-free loans (which they referred to as "repayable contributions"). While automakers expressed a preference for grants over loans (Keenan 2013), they also acknowledged that the long-term, multi-decade nature of the federal government's "repayable contributions" provided a net present value comparable to a grant. However, the government's argument that the interest-free loans they were extending were equivalent to a grant buckled in 2013 when the Canada Revenue Agency (which interprets and administers tax laws for the federal government and for most provinces and territories) ruled that "repayable contributions" must be recognized as income in the year received (Canadian Vehicle Manufacturers' Association 2014.) The effect: profitable firms – firms with income to recognize and taxes to pay – no longer considered the primary automotive industrial tool of the federal government to be beneficial. In 2016, the Government of Canada removed lingering dissatisfaction with their main automotive industrial tool, shifting subsequent federal infusions from "repayable contributions" to grants.

While the post-2000 shift from interest-free loans to outright grants was important, the second and more substantive adjustment was related to the types of projects and volume of applications governments would consider. Before 2000, government support for automotive production was focused on securing greenfield investment. For example, five of the six large projects captured in table 2 were for greenfield assembly plants. However, after 2000 Canada and Ontario expanded their application of an industrial policy tool that the federal government first experimented with in the 1980s: inducements to support periodic upgrades of already-established assembly plants. Such refurbishments typically occur every five to seven years, generally in conjunction with model or platform changes.

The first evidence of an incentive for an investment in an *existing* facility in Canada occurred in 1987 when the governments of Canada and Quebec provided General Motors with an interest-free loan of $220 million to help finance a $450 million modernization of that company's Sainte-Thérèse assembly plant. In return, General Motors agreed to operate the plant, which employed approximately 3,500 people, for a minimum of seven more years.

Table 3. Large Automotive OEM Projects (>$100 million) and Government Support, 2000–20

		Purpose/Type of Investment				Government Support					
Company	Date(s)	Sustain Existing Operations	Greenfield	Project(s) Description	Project Size ($)	Total: Canada and Ontario ($)	Govt. Support as % of total project(s)	Grant ($)	Grant as % of Govt. Support	Loan ($)	Loan as % of Govt. Support
Ford	2004	X		Upgrades to Oakville assembly plant; establishment of R&D centre for fuel cell technology	1 billion	200 million	20	100 million	50	100 million	50
	2008	X		Reopen an engine plant and create a powertrain research centre, both in Windsor, Ontario	700 million	110 million	15.71	30 million	27.27	80 million	72.72
	2013	X		Upgrade Oakville assembly plant	700 million	143.2 million	20.45	71.6 million	50	71.6 million	50
	2017	X		Upgrade engine plant (in Windsor, Ontario); R&D for advanced powertrains and vehicle connectivity	1.2 billion	204.8 million	17.06	204.8 million	100	0	0
	2020	X		Refurbishments to build electric vehicles in 2020	1.8 billion	590 million	32.77	590 million	100	0	0
				TOTAL (Ford)	***$5.4 billion***	***$1.238 billion***	***22.92***	***$986.4 million***	***79.67***	***$251.6 million***	***20.32***
General Motors	2005	X		Investments at GM plants in Oshawa, St. Catharines, and Ingersoll, Ontario (Most aspects subsequently collapsed, a victim of GM's financial pressures during the early 2000s)	2.5 billion	435 million	17.4	235 million	54.02	200 million	45.97

(Continued)

Table 3. Continued

Company	Date(s)	Purpose/Type of Investment: Sustain Existing Operations	Purpose/Type of Investment: Greenfield	Project(s) Description	Project Size ($)	Government Support: Total: Canada and Ontario ($)	Govt. Support as % of total project(s)	Grant ($)	Grant as % of Govt. Support	Loan ($)	Loan as % of Govt. Support
	2020	X		Reopening of Oshawa, Ontario, assembly plant; electric van production in Ingersoll, Ontario, assembly plant; and investment in St. Catharines, Ontario, engine and transmission plant	2.3 billion	Government support yet to be announced. We assume support for this project at the same rate as Ford's 2020 project listed above (32.77%). Therefore 753.71 million	Assume 32.77 (see 2020 Ford project above)	Assume $753.71 million (see Ford 2020 project above)	100 (see Ford 2020 project above)	0 (see Ford 2020 project above)	0 (see Ford 2020 project above)
				TOTAL (General Motors)	***$4.8 billion***	***$1.18871 billion***	***24.76***	***$988.71 million***	***83.17***	***$200 million***	***16.82***
Honda	2006	X		Upgrades and more jobs at Alliston, Ontario, assembly plant	154 million	15.4 million	10	15.4 million	100	0	0
	2017	X		New paint shop and new models at Alliston Ontario, assembly plant	492 million	83.6 million	16.99	83.6 million	100	0	0
				TOTAL (Honda)	***$646 million***	***$99 million***	***15.32***	***$99 million***	***100***	***0***	***0***
Chrysler/ Daimler Chrysler/ fCA/Stellantis	2005	X		Upgrades to assembly plants in Windsor and Brampton, Ontario	768 million	122.8 million	15.98	76.8 million	62.54	46 million	37.45
	2014	X		Major refurbishments at Windsor, Ontario, assembly plant	1 billion	86 million (incentives not announced	8.6	86 million	100	0	0

Table 3. Continued

Company	Date(s)	Purpose/Type of Investment: Sustain Existing Operations	Purpose/Type of Investment: Greenfield	Project(s) Description	Project Size ($)	Government Support: Total: Canada and Ontario ($)	Govt. Support as % of total project(s)	Grant ($)	Grant as % of Govt. Support	Loan ($)	Loan as % of Govt. Support
	2020	X		$1.58 billion for Windsor, Ontario, plant to build electric and/or hybrid vehicles by 2024; $14.8 million for Etobicoke, Ontario, casting plant; $50 million for Brampton, Ontario, assembly plant	1.64 billion	Government support yet to be announced. We assume support for this project at the same rate as Ford's 2020 project listed above (32.77%). Therefore 537.428 million	Assume 32.77 (see 2020 Ford project above)	Assume $537.428 million (see Ford 2020 project above)	100 (see Ford 2020 project above)	0 (see Ford 2020 project above)	0 (see Ford 2020 project above)
		TOTAL (Chrysler, DaimlerChrysler, FCA, Stellantis)			***$3.408 billion***	***$746.228 million***	***21.89***	***$700.228***	***93.83***	***$46 million***	***6.16***
Toyota	2005		X	New assembly plant in Woodstock, Ontario	800 million	125 million	15.62	70 million	56	55 million	44
	2008			Additional spending on new Woodstock assembly plant (announced in 2005) plus training centre in Cambridge, Ontario	300 million	22.8 million	7.6	22.8 million	100	0	0
	2011			Plant upgrades and new model introduction at Cambridge and Woodstock, Ontario, assembly plants	545 million	141.6 million	25.87	70.8 million	50	70.8 million	50

(Continued)

Table 3. Continued

Company	Date(s)	Purpose/Type of Investment: Sustain Existing Operations	Purpose/Type of Investment: Greenfield	Project(s) Description	Project Size ($)	Government Support: Total: Canada and Ontario ($)	Govt. Support as % of total project(s)	Grant ($)	Grant as % of Govt. Support	Loan ($)	Loan as % of Govt. Support
	2013	X		Plant upgrades for Lexus model change and expansion of production at Cambridge, Ontario, assembly plant	125 million	34 million	27.2	17 million	50	17 million	50
	2015	X		New model launches and new stamping line in Cambridge, Ontario	421 million	101.1 million	23.99	42.1 million	41.64	59 million	58.35
	2018	X		Upgrades and model changes at assembly plants in Cambridge and Woodstock, Ontario;	1.4 billion	220 million	15.71	220 million	100	0	0
				TOTAL (Toyota)	***$3.591 billion***	***$644.5***	***17.93***	***$442.6***	***68.67***	***$201.8***	***31.18***
All OEMs	***Years (200–20)***	***16 refurbish-ments***	***1 greenfield***	***TOTAL: All companies, all projects (with assumptions for government support for 2020 GM and Stellantis projects)***	***$17.837 billion***	***$3.916438 billion***	***21.95***	***$3.216938 billion***	***82.13***	***$699.4 million***	***17.85***

Source: Information on Ford from Keenan and Tuck (2004), Tuck (2004), Chase, Howlett, and Keenan (2008), Keenan (2017a), Canadian Press (2014), Irwin (2020). Information on General Motors from Greenberg (2006), Keenan (2005), Irwin (2021). Information on Toyota from CaOntario(2008), Deveau (2011), Canadian Press (2013), Keenan (2013), Flavelle (2015), Yates and Lewchuk (2017), Canada (2018b). Information on DaimlerChrysler, FCA, and Stellantis from PR Newswire (2005), Keenan (2016), Tuck (2005), Cision (2020). Information on Honda from Ontario (2006), Owram (2017).

General Motors fulfilled its commitment but closed the plant in 2002. It finished repaying the loan in 2017 (Hutchins 2018).

After the Sainte-Thérèse interest-free loan, Canadian governments' use of such tools for the refurbishment of existing automotive facilities went dormant for several years, not re-emerging until the 2000s. When that occurred, two changes materialized: such packages became (1) commonplace and (2) more costly. Indeed, incentives for merely sustaining production shifted in the same manner as did incentives for greenfield investment: from comparatively modest loans to comparatively rich grants. Before 2000, the 1987 support for GM's Sainte-Thérèse plant was the only known example of government assistance for refurbishment. After 2000, table 3 shows, a flood of packages was sought by automakers and provided by the governments of Canada and Ontario. Table 3 catalogues seventeen different announcements by the five automakers with assembly operations in Canada in the post-2000 era for which government packages were extended. Sixteen of those projects were to support refurbishments of existing operations; only one was for a greenfield assembly plant, that one by Toyota in 2005 (and extended in 2008).

The data contained in tables 2 and 3 alongside other sources reveal four aspects of automotive industrial policy as it has evolved before the year 2000 and after.

First, policymakers have expanded and altered their use of incentives: from a focus on expanding the country's automotive manufacturing footprint via new greenfield plants prior to the year 2000 to merely retaining existing operations after.

Second, despite the more modest post-2000 goals, the shift has been costly. Canada and Ontario spent $714 million between 1980 and 2000 on six projects, five of which were new greenfield assembly plants. After 2000, table 3 shows, the seventeen projects announced during that period received $3.9 billion. Moreover, it must be emphasized that table 3 does not encompass the participation of the governments of Ontario and Canada in the 2009 bailouts of DaimlerChrysler and General Motors. For that, the two governments' involvement consisted of an initial commitment of $13.7 billion, comprised of a suite of loans. Those loans were eventually paid back, written off, or converted into equity and sold. Milke (2015) estimates that the ultimate cost to Canada and Ontario of the bailouts was $3.7 billion. The upshot is that the process of propping up General Motors and DaimlerChrysler in 2009 (cost: $3.7 billion) plus the grants and long-term interest-free loans (with a net present value we assume is equivalent to that of a grant) that are catalogued in table 3 (cost: $3.91 billion) mean that automakers in Canada have received incentive packages totalling $7.61 billion since 2000. Context for the extent of the spending is available in multiple manners: spending per vehicle, spending per direct final assembly job, per automotive manufacturing job, and per automotive manufacturing job including spin-offs.

Third, the practice has achieved limited success. Between 2000 and 2021, Canadian vehicle production dropped by more than 60% and Canada slipped from being the world's seventh-largest producer of vehicles to sixteenth (OICA 2022). During that period, five vehicle assembly

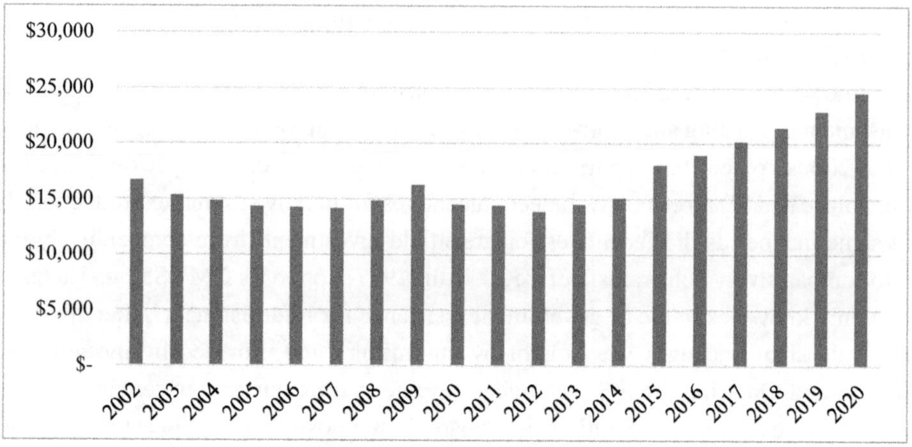

Figure 4. Imported Vehicle Content per Vehicle Made in Canada, 2002–19
Source: Annual vehicle production in Canada from OICA (2022); data on imported automotive parts from Innovation, Science and Economic Development Canada (2021).

plants closed, only one opened, and several currently operate below capacity. Of particular relevance: several assembly plants that received support to retain operations subsequently closed, thus calling into question the enduring effectiveness of the underlying strategy.

Fourth, despite the expanded spending during the post-2000 period, the economic benefits of automotive manufacturing in Canada and Ontario have diminished. This is a consequence of stagnating wages for autoworkers, particularly after 2005 (Sweeney, Holmes, and Miller 2017), and increasing imported content in Canadian-made vehicles. Data from figure 4 show that the value of imported parts in Canadian-made vehicles climbed by almost 50% between 2002 and 2019. The effect of these factors is that while one automotive assembly job in the US automotive industry creates or supports seven additional jobs in the economy (Hill, Cooper, and Menk 2015), the multiplier in Canada is estimated to be between four and six (see Tanguay 2018; Mordue and Sweeney 2019).

AUTOMOTIVE NARRATIVES IN CANADA

In addition to the tangible industrial policy tools described above, the post-2000 period has witnessed an evolving suite of industrial narratives, each designed to position Canada as a logical and preferred location for investment. These narratives have sought to promote the benefits of investing in automotive manufacturing and automotive R&D by articulating existing competitive advantages vis-à-vis other jurisdictions in the United States and Mexico.

The chosen narratives have centred on a combination of the benefits associated with Canada's highly educated workforce, its R&D capabilities, and its available natural resources. In the section that follows we present three industrial narratives that emerged during the post-2000 period, considering their viability, authenticity, and effect. The first two hinge on attributes of the Canadian workforce. The third represents a perceived opportunity to leverage unique-to-Canada resources, natural and otherwise, to establish standing in a key segment of the evolving global automotive industry.

Narrative 1: Leveraging Canada's High-Quality Workforce

Industry stakeholders have long touted Canada's workforce as one of the country's primary competitive advantages. There is some truth to this. Canada has a world-class public education system, and Canadian students have high rates of literacy and numeracy, especially when compared to the US South and Mexico. As a result, Canadian assembly plants enjoyed relatively high rates of productivity throughout much of the 1990s and were awarded an outsized number of J.D. Power awards for plant quality, a fact that is still mentioned by Canadian industry stakeholders and policymakers (see Tanguay 2018; Ontario 2019). Additionally, several Canadian colleges and universities are proximate to Canada's automotive manufacturing industry, a fact lauded by those engaged in automotive investment attraction (see Yates and Lewchuk 2017).

These long-touted advantages notwithstanding, Canadian vehicle manufacturing has declined steadily since 2000. Even plants that received J.D. Power awards for initial quality have closed.

Upon review, we suggest several flaws in the "quality workforce" narrative. First, as described earlier, the process of automotive manufacturing has become commoditized (Mordue and Sweeney 2017). Second, automakers tend to locate new assembly plants in regions – whether automotive core, semi-periphery, or integrated periphery – where they will occupy the role of "alpha" employer, offering better pay and working conditions than most other employers, manufacturing or otherwise. Such status allows them to recruit employees with above-average skills and talent, a process colloquially referred to as "creaming" or "high-grading" the labour market. Therefore, while the *average* Canadian may be more numerate, literate, or educated than the average person in the southern US or Mexico, automakers in the southern US or Mexico are not hiring the average person. This means that differences in worker quality among jurisdictions is of limited consequence, a condition that renders Canada's long-standing automotive investment-attraction narrative unconvincing. Third, in an effort to mitigate the labour cost advantages of places like the US South and Mexico, automakers in Canada have taken several measures to limit total compensation, effectively blunting the automotive industry's "alpha employer" strategy in Canada and reducing the Canadian automotive industry's capacity to attract the highest-quality candidates. Such measures include transitioning pension plans from defined benefit systems to defined contribution (see Martell and Taylor 2016; Unifor 2013), introducing increasing numbers of lower-wage, lower-benefit "temporary" workers (Dziczek 2011; MacDuffie and Pil 2018) and elongating the grow-in period for transition to upper-tier wages (Rutherford and Holmes 2013). This occurred as labour markets for manufacturers tightened in southern Ontario, particularly in the late 2010s, a confluence of trends and events that have further diminished the "exceptional labour" narrative. Fourth, while the Canadian workforce may be talented, they are increasingly choosing to work in industries other than automotive manufacturing (Auto Labour Market Information Project 2019). Therefore, the narrative that Canada's talented workforce is sufficient to attract investment does not reflect labour markets conditions in Canada, particularly vis-à-vis its competitor jurisdictions.

Narrative 2: Transitioning to a Knowledge-Intensive Profile

A second narrative that emerged in the mid-2010s touted Canada's capabilities in automotive R&D. This emerged as investments in greenfield automotive assembly appeared increasingly out of reach (as noted earlier). Encouraging R&D investments was perceived to be well aligned with Canada's profile. For starters, despite its challenges during the post-2000 era, the Province of Ontario rivals Michigan as the largest subnational automobile assembly jurisdiction in North America. Additionally, four of the world's largest one hundred suppliers are located there (*Automotive News* 2021) and its tax incentives for R&D are among the most generous in the world (Southwestern Ontario Marketing Alliance 2019). On top of that, its overall workforce is one of the most highly educated in the world, with nearly two-thirds of adults having post-secondary education (Canada 2021). A passage from a report by the Auto Advisor to the governments of Canada and Ontario captures governments' and industry's aspirations: "the (automotive) industry is undergoing massive change with new technologies on the horizon defining the car of the future. Thanks in part to our manufacturing base and our R&D capabilities, Canada is incredibly well-positioned" (Tanguay 2018, 5). During testimony to a parliamentary committee the director general of the Automotive and Transportation Industries Branch at Canada's Department of Innovation, Science and Economic Development (ISED) focused on Canada's capabilities in an emerging high-profile area: "Canada is uniquely positioned to play a leading role in the development of connected and autonomous vehicles. Not only do we have an established automotive manufacturing base, but Canada is also home to the largest IT cluster in North America outside of Silicon Valley, including world-renowned experts in technologies that will be key to the development of connected and autonomous vehicles" (Canada 2017).

The rise of the knowledge-intensive narrative has coincided with some notable investments. These include a 2017 announcement by Ford that it would establish a new software R&D centre in Ottawa and hire 295 persons (Keenan 2017b) and General Motors' intention to create one thousand engineering positions in active safety and autonomous vehicle development software (Canadian Vehicle Manufacturers' Association 2021). Governments also point to Canadian R&D investments by firms like Uber (Kalanick 2017), Linamar (Canada, 2018a), and Didi (*Financial Post* 2018) in autonomous-vehicle-related artificial intelligence.

Isolated announcements notwithstanding, the transition to a more knowledge-intensive Canadian automotive industry has been slow. In fact, the overriding trend conflicts with the narrative preferred and propagated by government and industry. Inputs to research, expressed by automotive R&D spending, have dropped from $407 million in 2001 to $313 million in 2010 and $329 million in 2019 (Statistics Canada, 2017, 2020a, 2020b). (For context, companies like General Motors, Toyota, and Volkswagen each spend more than US $10 billion annually on R&D.) Output has also slumped. Mordue and Sweeney (2019) show that Canada's share of global automotive patents has dropped from 0.84% in 2001 to 0.42% in 2016. This has occurred because automotive R&D concentrates in core automotive locations, near the headquarters of automotive OEMs in places like Detroit, Stuttgart, and Tokyo. In fact, Mordue and Sweeney (2020) also show that Canada's largest suppliers conduct the majority of their R&D not in proximity to their own headquarters (in Canada) but near the headquarters of their OEM customers.

Narrative 3: Canada as a Leader in Carbon-Free Mobility

More recently Canada has promoted itself as a jurisdiction capable of supporting electrified vehicle manufacturing and technology development. This came amid announcements in late 2020 by GM and Ford about plans to retool their Ingersoll and Oakville, Ontario, assembly plants (respectively) to assemble electric vehicles (see Irwin 2020, 2021). Additionally, Toyota and Stellantis confirmed they will continue production of hybrid and electrified vehicles in Canada. Beyond that, in an attempt to secure additional components of the electrified vehicle supply chain – namely battery manufacturing – Canadian stakeholders have promoted a "mines to mobility" narrative (see Bains 2020; Canada 2020). This narrative touts the potential to mine and refine minerals, such as lithium and cobalt – resources that Canada possesses – as a means by which to lever development of battery electric vehicle investments, not the least of which is battery cell manufacturing.

While the narrative is tempting in the abstract, practical implementation is problematic. First, with just 3% of global cobalt reserves, Canada's position is minor compared to the Democratic Republic of Congo (DRC), Australia, and others (Prause 2020). Canada's reserves of lithium are of similar consequence (see United States Geological Service 2021). Second, the long-term necessity of cobalt in batteries, the commodity the mines-to-mobility narrative promotes most frequently, is questionable. This is a consequence of cobalt content in lithium-ion batteries, the leading global use for cobalt, being reduced over time (United States Geological Service 2021). Third, the process of transitioning a known reserve to an operating mine is lengthy, typically ten years or more (International Council on Mining and Metals 2021). Fourth, the connection between commodity extraction and refining and eventual battery cell manufacturing is tenuous at best. There are no major lithium-ion battery producers headquartered in Canada (e.g., Panasonic, CATL, LG, BYD, Samsung). Contrary to the "mines-to-mobility" narrative, the existence of mines or refining capability does not guarantee further value-added production downstream. A case in point is Canada's nickel mining and refining industry. Canada is a substantial source of the world's raw and refined nickel. However, Canada has very little stainless steel manufacturing capacity (the primary use of nickel is the production of stainless steel). Moreover, international trade policy prohibits measures that compel higher-order processing with access to the underlying resource. As well, Canada has a long history of avoiding clashes with the expectations of global trade (see Hart 1998; Pomfret 2000, Krikorian 2012). Thus, while the data above suggest Canada *does* possess reserves of commodities necessary for battery production, there are several reasons why the underlying premise of the mines-to-mobility narrative is flawed.

DISCUSSION AND CONCLUSION

Three strata of automotive-producing countries have emerged during the post-NAFTA period and especially since 2000. The competitive advantages conferred upon two of those types, the automotive core (in North America, the US) and the integrated periphery (Mexico), are obvious. Moreover, the industrial policy instruments those countries have directed at their automotive industries have been orthodox and predictable, tailored to the recognizable sources of competitive advantage each country presents.

By contrast, the sources of competitive advantage relevant to automotive decision makers for the third type, the semi-periphery, which in North America's case is Canada, are not well defined. Consequently, automotive industries in such countries in the 2000s have languished. Canada, like other automotive semi-peripheries, has experienced a steady deterioration of its base of automotive manufacturing despite, in Canada's case, an aggressive albeit quixotic response by its policymakers. Indeed, analysis of the trajectory of the post-NAFTA automotive industry in Canada, in combination with the industrial policy tools and narratives the country has deployed to grow or simply sustain its automotive industry, affords improved understanding: about the efficacy of its tools, the logicality of its narratives, the prognosis for its automotive industry, and the prospects for automotive industries in other, similarly constructed countries. To be sure, clarity about the enduring relevancy of the trifurcated model upon which this chapter is premised is also possible.

This research has demonstrated that the mediocre results Canada has achieved in terms of vehicle production in the 2000s do not stem from a lack of interest by the governments of Canada or Ontario. We have shown that since 2000 those governments have expended

$7.6 billion to prop up final-assembly operations at the five automakers it hosts. However, we have also demonstrated that despite those investments, Canadian vehicle production has slipped to about a third of the level it reached in 2000, and many of the plants to which funds were directed have closed. We have also explained that during this period, the rationale for making such investments has dimmed, an outcome of weakened upstream and downstream economic benefits of automotive manufacturing in Canada caused by stagnant worker incomes and rising imports of parts.

As vehicle production slowed, Canada introduced a series of narratives to promote various aspects of its automotive industry, each focused on exploiting existing or latent capabilities. This chapter explored three. The first narrative, based on the quality of Canadian workers, has been shown to be ineffectual. Measures to limit labour cost gaps with key competitors have further diminished the merits of that claim. A second narrative centred on Canada's R&D capabilities has also proven futile. Isolated singular investments notwithstanding, Canada has not become a magnet for automotive R&D. For example, inputs, expressed by automotive R&D spending in Canada, have been consistently low throughout the 2000s. Outputs, expressed by automotive patents, have also flagged, from just under 1% of global output in the early 2000s to less than half that level today. A third narrative, this one designed to position Canada as a leader in electrification, was also shown to be weak: Canada's resources are unexceptional, timelines for resource development are long, and there are no lithium-ion battery producers headquartered in Canada. Additionally, the underlying premise, that the existence of mines or refining capability will provide a gateway to higher value-added production downstream, was shown to be flawed.

All of this – the overall spending, the shift in industrial policy targets from attracting greenfield investment to merely sustaining existing operations, the willingness to change from loans to grants, the carefully orchestrated and well-promoted narratives – have proven incapable of halting unrelenting deterioration of the industry in Canada. Vehicle production continues to track downward, and the transition to new revenue streams has proven elusive. Moreover, while Canada's challenges are significant, they are not exceptional, particularly amongst the global automotive semi-periphery.

From this, we make two summative observations. First, the post-2000s have caused Canada and automotive semi-periphery countries like Canada to undertake actions – industrial policy measures (specifically, incentives to support vehicle assembly) and industrial narratives (e.g., promotions about its research capabilities) – to gain rewards that integrated periphery and core automotive countries earn inherently. However, the objectives associated with the measures Canada has taken and the narratives it has promoted have been targeted at the rewards automotive core and integrated periphery countries earn, *not* those countries' defining sources of competitive advantage. For the integrated periphery, their defining source of competitive advantage is low-cost labour. For the core, it is their hosting the headquarters of automakers and the power it engenders. In the end, the practice of targeting the *rewards* of core and integrated periphery automotive countries rather than developing a compelling and meaningful-to-key actors source of competitive advantage has confined Canada and other semi-peripheries to limited and declining roles.

Second, the accumulation of these factors calls into question the long-term pertinence of the trifurcated framework of auto-producing nations upon which this chapter has been based. As described, the post-NAFTA/post-2000 emergence of ultra-low-cost integrated periphery automotive countries caused countries comprising the automotive semi-periphery to slowly withdraw as hubs for automobile assembly. Meanwhile, Canada's automotive R&D narrative notwithstanding, long-established patterns governing the location of automotive R&D have endured, the effect of which has been to preclude hopeful upstarts from semi-periphery countries like Canada from expanding their automotive R&D profiles. Consequently, with a low-cost labour source of competitive advantage unpalatable and the emergence of a home-grown automaker unlikely, semi-periphery countries like Canada are deprived of a source of competitive advantage that the automotive industry has been shown to value. As such, the drift that has characterized semi-peripheries' post-NAFTA/post-2000 history will endure.

In the end, the polarized bifurcated core and periphery framework is likely to return, not because countries comprising the current semi-periphery will graduate to the status of core or revert to integrated periphery. Rather, their manufacturing mandates will continue to be absorbed by current integrated peripheries and their overtures to secure significant higher-value, knowledge-interest mandates will be rebuffed by the core.

REFERENCES

Anastakis, D. 2005. *Auto Pact: Creating a Borderless North American Auto Industry, 1960–1971*. Toronto: University of Toronto Press.

Auto Labour Market Information Project. 2019. *Automotive Industry Labour Market Analysis: Preliminary Insights: Labour Market Challenges in Canada's Automotive Manufacturing Sector*. Toronto. https://automotivepolicy.ca/wp-content/uploads/2019/11/Preliminary-Insights-Labour-Market-Challenges-in-Canadas-Automotive-Manufacturing-Sector.pdf.

Automotive News. 2021. "Top 100 Global OEM Parts Suppliers." https://www.autonews.com/suppliers/heres-our-latest-list-biggest-parts-suppliers.

Bains, N. 2020. "Mining Gives Canada a Competitive Advantage in Electric Vehicle Market." *Policy Options*, 17 September 2020. https://policyoptions.irpp.org/magazines/september-2020/mining-gives-canada-a-competitive-advantage-in-electric-vehicle-market/.

Baranson, J. 1969. *Automotive Industries in Developing Countries*. Washington, DC: World Bank.

Beigie, C.E. 1970. *The Canada-US Automotive Agreement: An Evaluation*. Vol. 31. Washington, DC/Montreal: Canadian-American Committee.

Brincks, Corey, Bolesław Domański, Thomas Klier, and James Rubenstein. 2018. "Integrated Peripheral Markets in the Auto Industries of Europe and North America." *International Journal of Automotive Technology and Management* 18 (1): 1–28.

Canada. 1978. *The Canadian Automotive Industry: Performance and Proposals for Progress.* Ottawa: Queen's Printer.

– 2017. *Proceedings of the Standing Senate Committee on Transport and Communications.* Issue no. 11 – Evidence, 14 February 2017. https://sencanada.ca/en/Content/SEN/Committee/421/TRCM/11ev-53077-e.

– 2018a. "Federal Government Investment to Create 1,500 New Jobs and Secure More than 8,000 Others in Guelph." News release, 15 January 2018. https://www.canada.ca/en/innovation-science-economic-development/news/2018/01/federal_governmentinvestmenttocreate1500newjobsandsecuremorethan.html.

– 2018b. "Canada's Investment in Toyota Supports Thousands of Jobs in Ontario." 4 May 2018 https://www.pm.gc.ca/en/news/news-releases/2018/05/04/canadas-investment-toyota-supports-thousands-jobs-ontario.

– 2020. *From Mines to Mobility: Seizing Opportunities for Canada in the Global Battery Value Chain: What We Heard Report.* https://publications.gc.ca/site/eng/9.891985/publication.html.

– 2021. "Automotive Investment Attraction." https://www.ic.gc.ca/eic/site/auto-auto.nsf/eng/h_am02387.html.

*Cision*Canadian Press. 2013. "Toyota Lexus Plant in Cambridge, Ont., Gets $34 Million from Ottawa and Ontario." 23 January 2013. https://globalnews.ca/news/382418/toyota-lexus-plant-in-cambridge-ont-gets-34-million-from-ottawa-and-ontario/.–. 2014. "Ford Adding 1,000 Jobs to Oakville Plant, Union Hopes for Additions in Windsor." 1 October 2014. https://toronto.citynews.ca/2014/10/01/ford-adding-1000-jobs-to-oakville-plant-union-hopes-for-additions-in-windsor/.

Canadian Vehicle Manufacturers' Association. 2014. *Pre-budget Consultation Report & Recommendations: Submission to the Standing Committee on Finance by the Canadian Vehicle Manufacturers' Association.* 6 August 2014. https://www.ourcommons.ca/Content/Committee/412/FINA/WebDoc/WD6615327/412_FINA_PBC2014_Briefs/CanadianVehicleManufacturersAssociation-e.pdf.

– 2021. *What's Been Happening?* https://www.cvma.ca/priorities/innovation/research-and-development/.

Chase, S., K. Howlett, and G. Keenan. 2008. "Federal Politics, Listeriosis Outbreak: Harper Vows to Launch Tainted-Meat Inquiry." *Globe and Mail*, 4 September 2008. https://www.theglobeandmail.com/news/national/harper-vows-to-launch-tainted-meat-inquiry/article1060253/.

Cision. 2020. "Unifor Members Ratify New FCA Contract That Delivers New Jobs and Investment." 19 October 2020. https://www.newswire.ca/news-releases/unifor-members-ratify-new-fca-contract-that-delivers-new-jobs-and-investment-810118095.html

Dassbach, C.H. 1989. *Global Enterprises and the World Economy: Ford, General Motors, and IBM, the Emergence of the Transnational Enterprise*. New York: Garland.

DesRosiers, D. 2017. *DesRosiers Automotive Yearbook: 2016 Edition*. Toronto: DesRosiers Automotive Consultants.

Deveau, S. 2011. "Toyota Gets $142-Million from Ontario, Ottawa; Productivity Lift." *National Post,* 6 July 2011.

Domański, B., R. Guzik, and K. Gwosdz. 2017. "The New International Division of Labour and the Changing Role of the Periphery: The Case of the Polish Automotive Industry." In *Globalising Worlds and New Economic Configurations*, edited by M. Tamasy and M. Taylor, 85–99. London: Routledge.

Dykes, J. 1970. *Canada's Automotive Industry*. Toronto: McGraw-Hill.

Dziczek, K. 2011. "Economic Engines." *Community College Journal* 82 (3): 36.

Emerson, D. 1975. *Production, Location, and the Automotive Agreement*. Ottawa: Economic Council of Canada.

Financial Post. 2018. "DiDi Launches Labs in Toronto, Expanding Global Research Network to Canada." 19 November 2018. https://financialpost.com/pmn/press-releases-pmn/business-wire-news-releases-pmn/didi-launches-labs-in-toronto-expanding-global-research-network-to-canada.

Flavelle, Dana. 2015. "Toyota to Invest $421 Million in Cambridge." *Toronto Star*, 31 July 2015. https://www.thestar.com/business/toyota-to-invest-421-million-in-cambridge/article_354b0fba-6570-5f36-8926-d6313a683b0c.html.

Flynn, D.M. 1979. "The Rationalization of the United States and Canadian Automotive Industry: 1960–1975." Doctoral diss., University of Massachusetts.

Gereffi, G., and T. Sturgeon. 2013. "Global Value Chains and Industrial Policy: The Role of Emerging Economies." In *Global Value Chains in a Changing World*, edited by D.K. Elms and P. Low, 329-60. Geneva: World Trade Organization.

Globe and Mail. 1984. "Alliston Residents Excited about Honda Plant Plans." 7 June 1984.

Globe and Mail. 1985. "Quebec and Ottawa to Share Interest Cost of Hyundai Factory." 22 November 1985.

– 1986. "GM and Suzuki to Get $50 Million for New Car Plant." 7 August 1986.

Greenberg, L. 2006. "Camaro's Long-Anticipated Comeback Launched." *Edmonton Journal,* 22 August 2006.

Hart, M. 1998. *Fifty Years of Canadian Tradecraft: Canada at the GATT 1947–1997*. Ottawa: Centre for Trade Policy and Law.

Hill, Kim, Adam Cooper, and Debra Menk. 2015. *Contribution of the Automotive Industry to the Economies of All Fifty States and the United States*. Ann Arbor, MI: Center for Automotive Research. https://www.cargroup.org/publication/contribution-of-the-automotive-industry-to-the-economies-of-all-fifty-state-and-the-united-states/.

Hutchins, A. 2018. *"GM Canada: A 100-Year History of Benefitting from Taxpayer Dollars." Maclean's*, 29 November 2018. https://www.macleans.ca/economy/business/gm-canada-a-100-year-history-of-benefitting-from-taxpayer-dollars/.

Innovation, Science and Economic Development Canada. 2021. Trade Data Online Report - Trade Data Online - Import, Export and Investment - Innovation, Science and Economic Development Canada.

International Council on Mining and Metals. 2021. *Why We Need Mines*. https://www.icmm.com/en-gb/mining-metals/about-mining/operating-mines.

Irwin, J. 2020. "Government Incentives Seal Unifor, Ford Contract: Union Hopeful Leaders Will Step Up in FCA Talks." *Automotive News*, 5 October 2020.

– 2021. "Making a U-Turn: Investments in Canadian Plants Signal Stronger GM-Unifor Relations." *Automotive News*, 25 January 2021.

J.D. Power. 2011. "Initial Quality of Recent Vehicle Launches Is Considerably Lower than in 2010, while Carryover Model Quality Is Better than Ever." Press release. https://www.jdpower.com/business/press-releases/2011-initial-quality-study-iqs.

– 2020. "New-Vehicle Quality Mainly Dependent on Trouble-Free Technology, J.D. Power Finds." Press release. https://www.jdpower.com/business/press-releases/2020-initial-quality-study-iqs.

Kalanick, Travis. 2017. "Transforming Transportation in Toronto." Uber Newsroom. https://www.uber.com/en-CA/newsroom/atg-toronto-2/.

Keenan, G. 2005. "GM Goes to School with Investment: Universities to Share $2.5-Billion Outlay." *Globe and Mail*, 3 March 2005.

– 2013. "Auto Sector Gets Ottawa's Ear on Lagging Investment." *Globe and Mail*, 28 November 2013.
– 2016. "FCA Funding a Victory for Ontario Plant." *Globe and Mail*, 12 October 2016.
– 2017a. "Ford to Invest $1.2-Billion in Canada, Create Ottawa R&D Centre." *Globe and Mail*, 30 March 2017.
– 2017b. "Ford to Rev Up Autonomous Vehicle R&D in Ottawa." *Globe and Mail*, 31 March 2017.
Keenan, G., and S. Tuck. 2004. "Ottawa Shells Out $100-Million to Lock Up $L-Billion Ford Factory." *Globe and Mail*, 23 October 2004
Krikorian, J. 2012. *International Trade Law and Domestic Policy: Canada, the United States, and the WTO*. Vancouver: University of British Columbia Press.
Lampón, J., S. Lago-Peñas, and P. Cabanelas. 2016, "Can the Periphery Achieve Core? The Case of the Automobile Components Industry in Spain." *Papers in Regional Science* 95 (3): 595–612.
Lavelle, P., and R. White. 1983. *An Automotive Strategy for Canada: Report of the Federal Task Force on the Canadian Motor Vehicle and Automotive Parts Industries*. Ottawa: Ministry of Supply and Services.
Lyndon B. Johnson School of Public Affairs. 1985. *The U.S.-Canadian Automotive Products Agreement of 1985: An Evaluation for Its Twentieth Year*. Policy Research Project report no. 68. Austin: University of Texas at Austin.
MacDonald, N.B. 1980. *The Future of the Canadian Automotive Industry in the Context of the North American Industry*. Ottawa: Science Council of Canada.
MacDuffie, John Paul, and Frits K. Pil. "2018. "Changes in Auto Industry Employment Practices: An International Overview." In *After Lean Production*, edited by T. Kochan, R. Lansbury, and J.P. MacDuffie, 9–44. Ithaca: Cornell University Press.
Martell, A., and S. Taylor. 2016. "Unifor Faces Pension Pressure from Single-Plant Deal." *Automotive News*, 1 September 2016.
Martínez-Martínez, A., and J.H. Carrillo-Viveros. 2019. "Evolution of Industrial Policy in Emerging Regions: The Case of the Automotive Industry in Guanajuato, Mexico." *Estudios sociales. Revista de Alimentación Contemporánea y Desarrollo regional* 29 (54).
Milke, M. 2015. *How Much Did the 2009 Automotive Bailout Cost Taxpayers?* Regina: Canadian Taxpayers Federation
Milner, B. 1985. "Toyota to Begin Building Ontario Plant Ear'y in '86." *Globe and Mail*, 13 December 1985.
Mordue, G. 2007. "Government, Foreign Direct Investment and the Canadian Automotive Industry, 1977–1987." PhD diss., University of Strathclyde.
– 2010. "Unanticipated Outcomes: Lessons from Canadian Automotive FDI Attraction in the 1980s." *Canadian Public Policy* 36 (Suppl. 1): S1–S29.
– 2020. "Shifting Patterns in the Application of Industrial Policy." *International Journal of Automotive Technology and Policy* 20 (1): 50–75.
Mordue, G., and B. Sweeney. 2017. "The Commoditisation of Automotive Assembly: Canada as a Cautionary Tale." *International Journal of Automotive Technology and Management* 17 (2): 169–89.
– 2019. *The Economic Contributions of the Japanese-Brand Automotive Industry to the Canadian Economy, 2001–2018*. JAMA Canada.
– 2020. "Neither Core nor Periphery: The Search for Competitive Advantage in the Automotive Semi-Periphery." *Growth and Change* 51 (1): 34–57.
New York Times. 1987. "G.M. Receives Canada Loan." 1 April 1987.

OICA (International Organization of Motor Vehicle Manufacturers). 2022. "Production Statistics." https://www.oica.net/production-statistics/.

Ontario. 2006. "McGuinty Government Partners with Honda Canada to Bring Innovative Engine Facility to Ontario." 17 May 2006. https://news.ontario.ca/en/release/82234/mcguinty-government-partners-with-honda-canada-to-bring-innovative-engine-facility-to-ontario.

Ontario. 2008. "New Woodstock Toyota Plant Starts Production." 4 December 2008. https://news.ontario.ca/en/release/1653/new-woodstock-toyota-plant-starts-production.

Ontario. 2019. *Driving Prosperity: The Future of Ontario's Automotive Sector*. Toronto: Queen's Printer.

Ottawa Citizen. 1986. "Ontario Wins $650M Auto Plant." 7 August 1986.

Owram, K. 2017. "Honda to Invest $400M in Canada; Governments Add $80M for Ontario Plant." *National Post,* 10 January 2017.

Partridge, J. 1984. "New AMC Auto Plant to Create 1,800 Jobs." *Globe and Mail,* 12 June 1984.

Pavlínek, P. 2018. "Global Production Networks, Foreign Direct Investment, and Supplier Linkages in the Integrated Peripheries of the Automotive Industry." *Economic Geography* 94 (2): 141–65.

– 2020. "Restructuring and Internationalization of the European Automotive Industry." *Journal of Economic Geography* 20 (2): 509–41.

Pomfret, R. 2000. "Trade Policy in Canada and Australia in the Twentieth Century." *Australian Economic History Review* 40 (2): 114–26.

Prause, L. 2020. "Conflicts Related to Resources: The Case of Cobalt Mining in the Democratic Republic of Congo." In *The Material Basis of Energy Transitions*, edited by A. Bleicher and A. Pehlken, 153–67. London: Academic Press.

Pringsheim, K. 1983. *The Car Wars between Canada and Japan.* Working Paper no. 16. University of Toronto/York University Joint Centre on Modern East Asia. Toronto: Founders College, York University.

PR Newswire. 2005. "DaimlerChrysler to Invest CDN $768 Million in Canada." 21 November 2005.

Rothstein, J.S. 2005. "Economic Development Policymaking Down the Global Commodity Chain: Attracting an Auto Industry to Silao, Mexico." *Social Forces* 84 (1): 49–69.

Rutherford, T.D., and J. Holmes. 2013. "(Small) Differences That (Still) Matter? Cross-Border Regions and Work Place Governance in the Southern Ontario and US Great Lakes Automotive Industry." *Regional Studies* 47 (1): 116–27.

Science Council of Canada. 1980. *Multinationals and Industrial Strategy: The Role of World Product Mandates.* Ottawa: Minister of Supply and Services.

Shalom, F. 1985. "Hyundai Plant Called PQ Election Boost." *Globe and Mail*, 16 November 1985.

Southwestern Ontario Marketing Alliance. 2019. *Research and Development Cost Advantage*. https://canadasindustrialheartland.com/regional-profile/why-invest-here/research-a-development.

Statistics Canada. 2017. "Table 27-10-0002-01. Business Enterprise Research and Development Characteristics by Industry." https://www150.statcan.gc.ca/t1/tbl1/en/tv.action?pid=2710000201.

– 2020a. "Table 27-10-0001-01. Average Business Enterprise In-House Research and Development Expenditures, by Industry Group Based on the North American Industry Classification System (NAICS) and Country of Control (x 1,000)." Accessed 20 June 2021. https://www150.statcan.gc.ca/t1/tbl1/en/tv.action?pid=2710000101.

– 2020b. "Table 27-10-0333-01. Business Enterprise In-House Research and Development Expenditures, By Industry Group Based on the North American Industry Classification System (NAICS), Country of Control and Expenditure Types (x 1,000,000)." Accessed 20 June 2021. https://www150.statcan.gc.ca/t1/tbl1/en/tv.action?pid=2710033301.

– 2021. "Table 14-10-0202-01. Employment by Industry, Annual." Accessed 20 June 2021. https://www150.statcan.gc.ca/t1/tbl1/en/cv.action?pid=1410020201.

Sturgeon, T.J., O. Memedovic, J. Van Biesebroeck, and G. Gereffi. 2009. "Globalisation of the Automotive Industry: Main Features and Trends." *International Journal of Technological Learning, Innovation and Development* 2 (1/2): 7–24.

Sturgeon, T.J., and J. Van Biesebroeck. 2011. "Global Value Chains in the Automotive Industry: An Enhanced Role for Developing Countries?" *International Journal of Technological Learning, Innovation and Development* 4 (1/2/3): 181–205.

Sweeney, B., B. Holmes, and S. Miller. 2017. *Wages and Earnings in Ontario's Unionized Independent Automotive Parts Manufacturing Industry, 2007–2016*. Hamilton: Automotive Policy Research Centre. https://automotivepolicy.ca/wp-content/uploads/2018/05/wages-unionized-parts-industry-sweeney.pdf.

Sweeney, B., G. Mordue, and J. Carey. 2020. "Resilient or Resistant? Critical Reflections on Resilience in an Old Industrial Region." *Geoforum* 110: 125–35.

Tanguay, R. 2018. *Drive to Win: Automotive Advisor Report*. Toronto: Canadian Automotive Partnership Council.

Thomas, K.P. 1996. "Auto Bargaining in Canada, 1965–87." In *Foreign Direct Investment in a Changing Global Political Economy*, edited by S. Chan, 7–24. London: Palgrave Macmillan.

Tuck, S. 2004. "Ottawa Likely to Aid Ford's Oakville Overhaul with Loan from TPC Program, Ontario to Also Contribute $100-Million." *Globe and Mail*, 29 October 2004.

– 2005. "Daimler to Spend $768-Million to Upgrade Ontario Plants: Aimed at Boosting Manufacturing Flexibility, Adding Windsor Paint Shop." *Globe and Mail*, 22 November 2005.

Unifor. 2013. "Toyota Changes Pensions." 9 December 2013. https://www.unifor.org/news/all-news/toyota-changes-pensions.

United States Geological Service. 2021. *Mineral Commodity Summaries 2021*. https://pubs.usgs.gov/periodicals/mcs2021/mcs2021.pdf.

Wilkins, M. 1974. *The Maturing of Multinational Enterprise: American Business Abroad from 1914 to 1970*. Cambridge, MA: Harvard University Press.

Wilkins, M., and F. Hill. 1964. *American Business Abroad: Ford on Six Continents*. Detroit: Wayne State University Press.

Wilton, D. 1976. *An Econometric Analysis of the Canada-United States Automotive Agreement: The First Seven Years*. Ottawa: Minister of Supply and Services.

World Bank. 2022. "GNI Per Capita, Atlas Method (Current US $)." Accessed 15 November 2022. https://data.worldbank.org/indicator/NY.GDP.PCAP.CD.

Yates, C., and W. Lewchuk. 2017. "What Shapes Automotive Investment Decisions in a Contemporary Global Economy?" *Canadian Public Policy* 43 (S1): S16–S29.

2

Foreign Auto Transplants in the Age of NAFTA: Some Revealing Trends

A.J. Jacobs

The North American Free Trade Agreement (NAFTA) among the US, Canada, and Mexico went into effect on 1 January 1994. It was replaced on 1 July 2020, when the new United States-Mexico-Canada Agreement (USMCA) went into force. During the NAFTA's twenty-six-year tenure an amazing transformation took place in the North American automobile industry. In 1993, the last full year before NAFTA's promulgation, a combined 15.65 million light vehicles (cars and light trucks) were sold in the three nations. After years of peaks and valleys, this total had expanded to 20.19 million in 2019, the last full year of the trade pact. More specifically, light vehicle sales rose in the US during this period from 13.90 million in 1993 to 16.95 million in 2019. By comparison, deliveries increased in Canada from 1.16 million to 1.92 and in Mexico from 593,005 to 1.32 million after 1993.

To serve this rising demand, and to meet NAFTA's regional domestic content requirements, automakers from the US, Japan, Germany, Korea, and elsewhere raised their light vehicle production in the three-nation region from a combined 13.87 million in 1993 to 16.20 million in 2019. As part of this, non–North American automakers tripled their combined output in the NAFTA region from 2.58 million in 1993 to 7.93 million to 2019. In contrast, the "Detroit Three" American automakers, GM, Ford, and Chrysler, reduced their collective North American light vehicle assemblies by one-fourth after 1993, from 11.29 million to 8.27 million.

In the process, foreign transplants or "new domestic automakers" increased their share of NAFTA region light vehicle production from 18.59% in 1993 to 48.96% in 2019. This stunning growth was led by Japanese automakers, which collectively raised their output from 2.32 million to 5.55 million units during this period, and their share of regional production from 16.72% to 34.28%. This was a stunning contrast with the Detroit Three, whose contracting market share, constant restructuring, and shuttering of a net twenty-four assembly plants resulted in their percentage of the region's vehicle assemblies plunging from 81.41% prior to NAFTA to just 51.04% in its last full year.

This chapter chronicles this dramatic reshuffling in the North American automotive industry under NAFTA, focusing upon the assembly plants of foreign automakers, particularly from Japan. As such, the discussion is driven by factory openings and closings and light vehicle production data since 1 January 1994. To set the scene, however, in following sections I provide historical information on foreign automaker plants prior to NAFTA.

OVERVIEW OF LIGHT VEHICLE PRODUCTION IN THE THREE-NATION NAFTA REGION, 1993–2019

As table 1 shows, the US, Canada, and Mexico assembled 13,867,984 light vehicles in 1993. The category included passenger cars, sport/crossover utility vehicles (SUVs/CUVs), minivans, pickup trucks, and light-duty commercial vans. Combined light vehicle output in the three nations strongly grew to 15,285,289 in 1994, the first year of NAFTA, before gradually increasing to 17,056,849 in 1999. Regional production then plateaued in 2000 at 17,161,447 and tumbled to 15,477,481 in 2001 and 15,754,003 in 2004.

After hovering between 15.02 million and 15.75 million between 2005 and 2007, NAFTA region light vehicle production sank to 12,579,453 in 2008 and then to a twenty-seven-year low of 8,558,226 in 2009. The latter was provoked by the 2008–9 global financial crisis (see Minchin 2021). Output then recovered to 11,910,219 in 2010 before roaring back to 16,096,527 in 2012 and to 16,946,602 in 2014. Final light vehicle assemblies then advanced to 17,440,070 in 2015 before establishing its current all-time high of 17,732,798 in 2016. Over the next two years, production remained strong, at just under seventeen million units, before settling at 16,195,520 in 2019, the final full year of NAFTA.

In terms of the geographical distribution of output, as again shown in table 1, US factories built 10,590,137 light vehicles in 1993, or 76.36% of those produced in the NAFTA region during that year. By comparison, Canada built 2,223,501 units in 1993, for a 16.03% regional share, and Mexico produced 1,054,346 light vehicles for a 7.60% stake. This intraregional distribution then gradually recalibrated over the next five years, with America's share of NAFTA output contracting to 73.80% in 1999, despite assembling an a new all-time high of 12,588,268 light vehicles during that year. In contrast, Canadian factories produced a still all-time record 2,996,073 light vehicles in 1999, achieving a peak share of 17.57% for that year. Meanwhile, final assemblies at Mexican factories in 1999 jumped to 1,472,365 units and its regional stake to 8.63%.

As regional output declined after 1999, the regional breakdown essentially remained stagnant through 2005. Thereafter, America's share began to dramatically decline to 70.82% in 2006 and then to an all-time low of 65.17% during the Great Recession of 2009. In the latter year, US factories built just 5,577,148 of NAFTA's 8,558,226 cars and light trucks, their fewest unit total in sixty-one years. Similarly, Canada's output declined to 2,662,958 units and a

Table 1. NAFTA Light Vehicle Production, 1993–2019

	1993	1994	1999	2004	2009	2014	2019
NAFTA LV production	**13,867,984**	**15,285,289**	**17,056,849**	**15,754,003**	**8,558,226**	**16,946,602**	**16,195,520**
All US LVs – built	10,590,137	11,923,271	12,588,411	11,602,520	5,577,148	11,371,386	10,527,301
All Canada LVs – built	2,223,501	2,285,208	2,996,073	2,662,958	1,479,161	2,382,218	1,893,274
All Mexico LVs – built	1,054,346	1,076,810	1,472,365	1,488,525	1,501,917	3,192,998	3,774,945
% NAFTA LVs built in US	76.36	78.00	73.80	73.65	65.17	67.10	65.00
% NAFTA LVs built in Canada	16.03	14.95	17.57	16.90	17.28	14.06	11.69
% NAFTA LVs built in Mexico	7.60	7.04	8.63	9.45	17.55	18.84	23.31
Non-NA brand LVs built in NAFTA	**2,578,272**	**2,940,471**	**3,608,586**	**4,538,765**	**3,906,816**	**7,816,608**	**7,929,733**
Non-NA brand LV built in US	1,795,185	2,119,127	2,499,599	3,286,394	2,557,949	5,282,057	4,931,346
Non-NA brand LV built in Canada	359,328	370,846	501,069	680,413	583,227	868,356	875,766
Non-NA brand LV built in Mexico	423,759	450,498	607,918	571,958	765,640	1,666,195	2,122,621
% non-NA brand/NAFTA-built LVs	**18.59**	**19.24**	**21.16**	**28.81**	**45.65**	**46.12**	**48.96**
% Non-NA brand of US-built LVs	16.95	17.77	19.86	28.32	45.86	46.45	46.84
% Non-NA brand of Canada-built LVs	16.16	16.23	16.72	25.55	39.43	36.45	46.26
% Non-NA Brand of Mexico-built LVs	40.19	41.84	41.29	38.42	50.98	52.18	56.23
% non-NA NAFTA LVs built – total	**100.00**	**100.00**	**100.00**	**100.00**	**100.00**	**100.00**	**100.00**
% non-NA NAFTA LVs built in US	69.63	72.07	69.27	72.41	65.47	67.57	62.19
% non-NA NAFTA LVs built in Canada	13.94	12.61	13.89	14.99	14.93	11.11	11.04
% non-NA NAFTA LVs built in Mexico	16.44	15.32	16.85	12.60	19.60	21.32	26.77

(Continued)

Table 1. Continued

	1993	1994	1999	2004	2009	2014	2019
Detroit 3 brand LVs built in NAFTA	**11,289,712**	**12,344,818**	**13,448,263**	**11,215,238**	**4,651,410**	**9,129,994**	**8,265,787**
Detroit 3 brand LVs built in US	8,794,952	9,804,144	10,088,812	8,316,126	3,019,199	6,089,329	5,595,955
Detroit 3 brand LVs built in Canada	1,864,173	1,914,362	2,495,004	1,982,545	895,934	1,513,862	1,017,508
Detroit 3 brand LVs built in Mexico	630,587	626,312	864,447	916,567	736,277	1,526,803	1,652,324
% Detroit 3/NAFTA-built LVs	**81.41**	**80.76**	**78.84**	**71.19**	**54.35**	**53.88**	**51.04**
% Detroit 3 of all US-built LVs	83.05	82.23	80.14	71.68	54.14	53.55	53.16
% Detroit 3 of all Canada-built LVs	83.84	83.77	83.28	74.45	60.57	63.55	53.74
% Detroit 3 of all Mexico-built LVs	59.81	58.16	58.71	61.58	49.02	47.82	43.77
% Detroit 3 NAFTA LVs built - total	**100.00**	**100.00**	**100.00**	**100.00**	**100.00**	**100.00**	**100.00**
% Detroit 3 NAFTA LVs built in US	77.90	79.42	75.02	74.15	64.91	66.70	67.70
% Detroit 3 NAFTA LVs built in Canada	16.51	15.51	18.55	17.68	19.26	16.58	12.31
% Detroit 3 NAFTA LVs built in Mexico	5.59	5.07	6.43	8.17	15.83	16.72	19.99

Source: Compiled by the author from *Ward's Automotive Yearbook* (1968–2020) and VW (1968–2020).

16.90% share in 2004 before plunging to 2,047,022 in 2008 and then to a twenty-seven-year low of 1,491,161 during the 2009 economic meltdown. This gave NAFTA's northern nation a 17.28% share in the latter year. On the other hand, after backtracking to 1,488,525 units in 2004, final assemblies at Mexican factories soared to a then record 2,084,938 in 2008. This total plummeted to 1,501,917 in 2009. In the interim, the region's southernmost nation out-produced Canada for the very first time in 2008, while its share of NAFTA light vehicle output expanded from 9.45% in 2004 to 17.55% in 2009 (again, see table 1).

As mentioned earlier, NAFTA region production rebounded strongly after 2009. Whereas the US share of this output has somewhat stabilized since 2012, Mexico's plants have continued to expand at the expense of Canada. More specifically, final assemblies at US factories recovered to 7,597,147 in 2010, when American plants contributed their smallest share ever to North American light vehicle production at 63.79%. Output then bounced back to more than ten million in 2012 and 2013 before coming in at 11,371,386 in 2014, when American factories captured 67.10% of regional production. The situation improved further in 2015 and 2016, with US plants building 11,920,171 units in 2016, their highest total since 2002. It then reversed, with assemblies falling below eleven million thereafter, and to 10,527,301 in 2019. As a result, in the final full year of NAFTA, America produced just 65.00% of the region's light vehicles.

For its part, Canadian plants recovered to produce more than two million light vehicles in 2010 and 2011, before accelerating to 2,454,064 in 2012 and 2,382,218 in 2014. In contrast, regional share fell noticeably north of the border after 2010, to a new NAFTA low of 14.06% in 2014. Output then began to contract appreciably after 2016, coming in at 2,175,572 units in 2017 and finally at 1,893,274 in 2019. In the interim, Canada's regional share of light vehicle production declined to a forty-six-year low of 11.69% in the final year of NAFTA.

As for Mexico, its plants recovered quickly, building a then-record 2,250,313 light vehicles in 2010 before accelerating to 3,192,998 units in 2014, when the nation contributed a then unprecedented 18.84% of regional output. These trends continued through 2017, when Mexico built a record 3,906,676 light vehicles before retreating to 3,774,945 in 2019. Nonetheless, Mexican plants captured a record 23.31% of NAFTA regional production in the final full year of the trade pact.

NON-NORTH AMERICAN AUTOMAKER PLANTS JUST PRIOR TO NAFTA, 1993

Whereas Mexico increasingly became the site of choice for foreign light vehicle plants after the 2009 global financial crisis, the leading country of origin for these new domestic automakers during NAFTA's entire twenty-five-year run was Japan. As table 2 illustrates, a total of sixteen foreign-led light vehicle assembly plants existed in North America at the end of 1993:

Table 2. Non-North American Automaker Plants in the NAFTA Region, 1993 and 2019

				Production	Vehicle capacity		Light vehicle output		Employment
1993	2019	Automaker plant	Location	began	1993	2019	1993	2019	2019
NAFTA total				-	**3,440,000**	**10,423,500**	**2,578,272**	**7,929,733**	**147,243**
Canada				-	**450,000**	**1,040,000**	**359,328**	**875,766**	**13,200**
Japanese automaker plants									
1	1	Honda Alliston	New Tecumseth, ON	Nov-86	100,000	440,000	100,621	407,764	4,200
2	2	Toyota Cambridge	Cambridge, ON	Nov-88	70,000	350,000	79,219	246,138	9,000
-	3	Toyota Woodstock	Woodstock, ON	Nov-08	-	250,000	-	221,864	**
3	-	Suzuki-GM (CAMI)	Ingersoll, ON	Apr-89	240,000	-	159,399	Joint venture (JV) ended Dec-09	
Other automaker plants									
4	-	Volvo Bayers Lake	Halifax, NS	Jul-86	15,000	-	5,504	Closed Dec-98	
5	-	Hyundai Bromont	Bromont, QC	Jan-89	25,000	-	14,585	Closed Mar-94	
United States total					**2,440,000**	**6,155,000**	**1,795,185**	**4,931,346**	**82,363**
Japanese automaker plants									
1	1	Honda Marysville	Allen Twp, OH	Nov-82	370,000	440,000	283,038	385,761	4,200
2	2	Honda East Liberty	Perry Twp, OH	Dec-89	150,000	240,000	120,737	226,848	2,900
-	3	Honda Lincoln	Talladega Co., AL	Nov-01	-	340,000	-	351,874	4,900
-	4	Honda Greensburg	Greensburg, IN	Oct-08	-	250,000	-	240,561	2,500
3	5	Nissan Smyrna	Smyrna, TN	Jun-83	420,000	640,000	386,973	531,882	8,400
-	6	Nissan Canton	Canton, MS	May-03	-	500,000	-	231,154	5,250
-	-	Nissan at Ford	Avon Lake, OH	Apr-92	60,000	-	52,608	JV ended June-02	
4	-	Toyota-GM (NUMMI)	Freemont, CA	Dec-84	340,000	-	321,428	Closed Apr-10, sold	

(Continued)

Table 2. Continued

				Production	Vehicle capacity		Light vehicle output		Employment
1993	2019	Automaker plant	Location	began	1993	2019	1993	2019	2019
5	7	Toyota Georgetown	Georgetown, KY	May-88	440,000	550,000	234,060	444,334	8,059
-	8	Toyota Princeton	Union Twp, IN	Dec-98	-	420,000	-	362,222	7,296
-	9	Toyota San Antonio	San Antonio, TX	Nov-06	-	250,000	-	230,916	2,542
-	10	Toyota Blue Springs	Union County, MS	Nov-11	-	160,000	-	157,489	1,741
6	-	Mazda-Ford (AAI)	Flat Rock, MI	Sep-87	240,000	-	115,774	JV ended Aug-12	
-	-	Mazda at Ford Plants	Various	Aug-90	60,000	-	56,447	JV ended May-11	
-	-	Mazda Toyota*	Huntsville, AL	Late-2021	-	-	-	-	-
7	-	Mitsubishi[†]	Normal, IL	Sep-88	240,000	-	97,562	Closed Nov-15, sold	
8	11	Subaru Lafayette	Lafayette, IN	Sep-89	120,000	450,000	126,558	368,516	5,900
German automaker plants									
	12	BMW Spartanburg	Spartanburg Co., SC	Sep-94	-	450,000	-	411,620	11,000
	13	Mercedes Tuscaloosa	Vance, AL	Feb-97	-	300,000	-	212,118	4,200
	14	Mercedes-Benz Vans	Charleston Co., SC	Sep-18	-	15,000	-	15,090	1,600
	15	VW Chattanooga	Hamilton Co., TN	Apr-11	-	250,000	-	107,694	3,800
Korean automaker plants									
	16	Hyundai Montgomery	Montgomery, AL	Mar-05	-	390,000	-	336,000	3,000
	17	Kia West Point	West Point, GA	Nov-09	-	360,000	-	274,000	3,075
Other automaker plants									
	18	Volvo Car Charleston	Berkeley Co., SC	Aug-18	-	150,000	-	43,267	2,000
Mexico				-	**550,000**	**3,228,500**	**423,759**	**2,122,921**	**51,680**
Japanese automaker plants									
1	1	Nissan Cuernavaca	Jiutepec, Morelos	May-66	190,000	300,000	105,159	132,471	3,000

Table 2. Continued

				Production	Vehicle capacity		Light vehicle output		Employment
1993	2019	Automaker plant	Location	began	1993	2019	1993	2019	2019
2	2	Nissan Aguascalientes	Aguascalientes, AG	Dec-92	120,000	550,000	79,523	492,023	9,000
-	3	Honda El Salto	El Salto, Jalisco	Nov-95	-	63,000	-	36,066	850
-	4	Honda Celaya	Celaya, Guanajuato	Feb-14	-	200,000	-	168,349	4,100
-	5	Toyota Baja	Tecate, Baja Calif.	Sep-04	-	166,000	-	167,470	2,021
-	6	Toyota Guanajuato	Apaseo el Grande, GJ	Dec-19	-	100,000	-	785	1,073
-	7	Mazda Salamanca	Salamanca, GJ	Jan-14	-	250,000	0	116,527	5,200
-	8	Nissan-MB (Compas)	Aguascalientes, AG	Nov-17	-	230,000	-	90,408	3,600
German automaker plants									
3	9	VW Puebla	Cuautlancingo, Puebla	Oct-67	240,000	600,000	239,077	443,414	11,829
-	10	Audi San Jose Chiapa	San Jose Chiapa, PU	Sep-16	-	180,000	-	156,661	5,268
-	11	BMW San Luis Potosi	Villa de Reyes, SL	Apr-19	-	175,000	-	24,755	2,800
-	12	Kia Monterrey	Pesqueria, Nuevo Leon	May-16	-	400,000	-	286,600	2,339
Other automaker plants									
-	13	JAC/Giant Sahagun	Sahagun, Hidalgo	Mar-17	-	6,000	-	4,747	300
-	-	Fiat Toluca (FCA)	Toluca, MX	Dec-10	-	2,500	-	2,345	-
-	-	BAIC/AT Motors	Puente Nacional, VC	May-17[§]	-	6,000	-	NA	300
-	-	BAIC*	TBA	Planned '22					

Source: Compiled by the author from Wards (1968-2020) and Jacobs (2016).
Notes: * Announced in December 2018 but no location named. † The former joint venture with Chrysler known as Diamond Star. †† Fiat brand capacity only. Production ended in November 2019. § Claimed. No record of final assemblies according to *Ward's Automotive Yearbook* (1968–2020) and INEGI (2021).

eight in the US, five in Canada, and three in Mexico. The Canadian figure included, Hyundai Bromont in Quebec, which had been idled in September 1993 for retooling, but would ultimately permanently shutter on 18 March 1994 (see Jacobs 2016, 2021).

These sixteen facilities produced 2,578,272 light vehicles in 1993, for a combined 18.59% of North American output in the year prior to the trade pact's promulgation (see table 1). A total of 1,795,185 of these units or 69.63% were manufactured in the US, 359,328 or 13.94% were finished in Canada, and 423,759 or 16.44% were assembled in Mexico. On the other hand, this meant that foreign transplants produced 16.95% of all the light vehicles built in America, 16.16% of those finished in Canada, and 40.19% of those assembled in Mexico during 1993. In all cases, Japanese automakers were responsible for most of these vehicles.

JAPANESE AUTOMAKER PLANTS IN NORTH AMERICA PRIOR TO NAFTA, 1993

As shown in table 2, thirteen of the sixteen foreign-run plants operating in North America in 1993 were led by Japanese automakers. Among the thirteen, Honda, Nissan, and Toyota operated several plants. Joint vetures also existed between Japanese and American automakers (e.g., Toyota and GM, Suzuki and GM, Mazda and Ford, Mitsubishi and Chrysler) as well as between several Japanese-owned automakers (e.g., Subaru and Isuzu). Thirteen Japanese-led factories were situated in the US, three were in Canada, and two were in Mexico (see *Ward's Automotive Yearbook* [henceforth in this chapter *Ward's*] 1968–2020; Jacobs 2016).

Nissan Mexicana Cuernavaca Plant in Jiutepec, Morelos, was the first facility producing Japanese brand light vehicle models in North America, launching knockdown kit (KD) assembly of Datsun Bluebird 410/411-Series subcompacts in May 1966 (Nissan Global, 2021). A little more than a year later, in December 1967, Canadian Motor Industries (CMI) produced its first Japanese cars at its small warehouse in the Point Edward community of then Cape Breton County, Nova Scotia. CMI assembled KD kits of 7,975 Toyota Corolla and 1,328 Isuzu Bellet before ceasing operations in November 1975 (Jacobs 2016).

Although these plants were the first, the true launch of the Japanese automaker's North American invasion occurred in November 1982, when the Honda Marysville plant in Allen Township, Union County, Ohio, commenced production of Honda Accord. Nissan soon followed, inaugurating production of "Hardbody" pickups in Smyrna, Tennessee, in June 1983. Not to be outdone by its rivals, Toyota arrived next, launching output of a Toyota Corolla–derived Chevrolet Nova at its New United Motor Manufacturing, Inc. (NUMMI) joint venture with GM in Freemont, California, in December 1984 at a previously GM plant (see Jacobs 2016; Honda 2020; Nissan Global 2021).

The flurry of new plants was not a surprise, as they were provoked by Japan's May 1981 voluntary export restraint (VER) agreement with the US government. As part of this, Japanese automakers agreed to restrict their vehicle imports into America to 1.68 million in fiscal year 1981–82 (retroactive to 1 April 1981), and thereafter to no more than 17.5% of demand for automobiles in the US in any given year. In June 1982, similar measures capped the growth rate in Japanese vehicle imports into Canada at 10% above the previous year. The US quota was subsequently raised to 1.85 million on 1 April 1984, and then to 2.3 million between 1 April 1985 and 31 March 1989 (*Ward's* 1968–2020; JAMA Canada 2005; Jacobs 2016).

Honda also was the first Japanese automaker to set up an assembly plant in Canada, launching production of the Accord at its new Alliston Plant in New Tecumseth, Ontario, in November 1986. In the interim, Toyota simultaneously announced two North American plants in December 1985, one in Georgetown, Kentucky, which it inaugurated in May 1988, and one in Cambridge, Ontario, christened in November 1988. Meanwhile, Mazda's AutoAlliance International (AAI) joint venture revived a dormant Ford factory in Flat Rock, Michigan, in September 1987, and Mitsubishi Motors launched its Diamond Star collaboration with Chrysler in Normal, Illinois, in September 1988 (see Jacobs 2016).

The year 1989 proved equally busy for Japanese transplants, with Suzuki's Canadian Automotive Manufacturing, Inc. (CAMI) joint venture with GM in Ingersoll, Ontario, commencing output in April 1989; the Subaru-Isuzu Automotive (SIA) factory in Lafayette, Indiana, up and running in September 1989; and Honda's East Liberty, Ohio, plant opening in December 1989 (see Jacobs 2016; Honda 2020). Then, after a short break, Nissan closed out the pre-NAFTA Japanese invasion by inaugurating its second factory in Mexico in December 1992. The automaker accomplished this by transforming its eleven-year-old engine and stamping operations in Aguascalientes into a full-fledged vehicle assembly complex. Thereafter, Nissan decided to make Aguascalientes the host for US-bound output of the Nissan Sentra and to reduce output of the economy car at Smyrna (*Ward's* 1968–2020; Jacobs 2016; Nissan Global 2021).

As table 3 shows, a total of 2,319,106 Japanese brand light vehicles were produced in the US, Canada, and Mexico in 1993, or 16.72% of North American output for the year. Toyota produced the largest number of these light vehicles, with its US and Canadian factories building 634,707 Toyota brand and rebadged Geo vehicles. Nissan was second, producing 571,655 units at its own US and Mexican factories and having another 52,608 Nissan Quest minivans assembled on contract at Ford Motor Avon Lake Plant in Ohio. Honda was third at 504,396 units in 1993 and Mazda fourth at 172,221, with 115,774 Mazda brand cars produced at AAI and a combined 56,447 Mazda pickups assembled at its partner Ford Motor's plants in Edison, New Jersey, and Louisville, Kentucky.

As illustrated in table 4, a total of 1,795,185 Japanese models were built in the US in 1993, representing 100% of all foreign-brand light vehicles assembled in the country during that year. At the time, these factories were capable of building 2.32 million vehicles (see table 2). Again Toyota, Nissan, and Honda led the way. By comparison, and as presented in tables 5 and 6, Suzuki's CAMI venture built 159,399 of the total 339,239 Japanese-brand light vehicles produced in Canada (including Geo). and Nissan assembled all 184,682 of the Japanese

Table 3. New Domestic Automaker Brand Light Vehicle Production in NAFTA Region, 1993–2019

	1993	1994	1999	2004	2009	2014	2019
NAFTA light vehicle production	13,867,984	15,285,289	17,056,849	15,754,003	8,558,226	16,946,602	16,195,520
Non-NA brand LV built in NAFTA	***2,578,272***	***2,940,471***	***3,608,586***	***4,538,765***	***3,906,816***	***7,816,608***	***7,929,733***
Japanese brands	*2,319,106*	*2,676,743*	*3,067,981*	*4,084,965*	*3,157,487*	*5,801,276*	*5,551,054*
% of total NAFTA LV production	16.72	17.51	17.99	25.93	36.89	34.23	34.28
% of non-NA	89.95	91.03	85.02	90.00	80.82	74.22	70.00
Toyota-Lexus	634,707	724,589	1,068,049	1,443,805	1,256,370	1,881,253	1,855,915
Honda-Acura	504,396	607,018	971,049	1,217,755	1,030,958	1,807,124	1,817,223
Nissan-Infiniti	624,263	696,261	559,280	1,068,272	724,716	1,748,353	1,417,570
Subaru	47,117	54,002	93,070	105,541	82,953	193,022	368,516
Mazda	172,221	202,784	136,652	146,541	41,383	102,346	91,830
Mitsubishi	97,562	121,977	119,048	78,142	18,502	69,178	0
Suzuki-Geo	159,399	170,231	15,079	26	2,605	0	0
Isuzu	79,441	99,881	105,754	24,883	0	0	0
Korean brands	*14,585*	*0*	*0*	*0*	*211,061*	*768,361*	*896,600*
Hyundai-Kia	14,585	0	0	0	211,061	768,361	896,600
German brands	*239,077*	*257,292*	*540,605*	*442,758*	*535,870*	*1,175,410*	*1,431,439*
VW-Audi-Porsche	239,077	256,317	410,317	225,342	323,622	592,749	707,769
BMW	0	385	52,402	143,916	121,666	349,949	436,375
Mercedes	0	590	77,886	73,500	90,582	232,712	287,295
Other country brands	*5,504*	*6,436*	*0*	*11,042*	*2,398*	*71,561*	*50,640*
Sweden	5,504	6,436	0	0	2	0	43,267
France	0	0	0	11,042	2,396	0	281
Italy	0	0	0	0	0	71,561	2,345
China	0	0	0	0	0	0	4,747

Source: Compiled by the author from *Ward's* (1968–2020) and VW (1968–2020).

Table 4. New Domestic Automakers Brand Light Vehicle Production in the US, 1993–2019

	1993	1994	1999	2004	2009	2014	2019
Total US light vehicle production	10,590,137	11,923,271	12,588,411	11,602,520	5,577,148	11,371,386	10,527,301
Non-NA brand LV built in US	***1,795,185***	***2,119,127***	***2,499,599***	***3,286,394***	***2,557,949***	***5,282,057***	***4,931,346***
Japanese brands	*1,795,185*	*2,118,742*	*2,371,097*	*3,068,978*	*2,134,638*	*3,813,353*	*3,531,557*
Honda-Acura	403,775	498,710	685,900	803,403	723,375	1,268,904	1,205,044
Toyota-Lexus	555,488	638,718	856,967	1,155,708	894,127	1,334,691	1,194,961
Nissan-Infiniti	439,581	502,670	373,706	754,760	371,698	947,558	763,036
Subaru	47,117	54,002	93,070	105,541	82,953	193,022	368,516
Mazda	172,221	202,784	136,652	146,541	41,383	0	0
Mitsubishi	97,562	121,977	119,048	78,142	18,502	69,178	0
Isuzu	79,441	99,881	105,754	24,883	0	0	0
Suzuki	0	0	0	0	2,600	0	0
Korean brands	*0*	*0*	*0*	*0*	*211,061*	*768,361*	*610,000*
Hyundai	0	0	0	0	195,561	398,851	336,000
Kia	*0*	*0*	*0*	*0*	*15,500*	*369,510*	*274,000*
German brands	*0*	*385*	*128,502*	*217,416*	*212,248*	*700,289*	*746,522*
VW-Audi-Porsche	*0*	*0*	*0*	*0*	*0*	*117,628*	*107,694*
BMW	0	385	50,806	143,916	121,666	349,949	411,620
Mercedes	0	0	77,696	73,500	90,582	232,712	227,208
Other country brands	*0*	*0*	*0*	*0*	*2*	*54*	*43,267*
Swedish (Volvo-Saab)	0	0	0	0	2	0	43,267
Italian (Lancia)	0	0	0	0	0	54	0

Source: Compiled by the author from *Ward's* (1968–2020).

models completed in Mexico in 1993. Japanese automaker capacity at the time was 403,500 in Canada and 310,000 in Mexico (again, see table 2).

As will be discussed below, all three nations would experience significant growth in their Japanese brand output thereafter, although this growth would be considerably slower in Canada during the NAFTA era than in the US and Mexico.

GERMAN AUTOMAKER PLANTS IN NORTH AMERICA PRIOR TO NAFTA

As table 2 shows, the Volkswagen de Mexico Puebla Plant in Cuautlancingo, Puebla, was the only German car factory in operation in North America in 1993. It opened a little more than a year after Nissan Mexicana Cuernavaca Plant and built its first VW Beetle on 23 October 1967. Driven by exports of the popular subcompact to America, output at the then 2,619-worker factory grew steadily through the early 1970s. Following the shift from the original Beetle to the VW Rabbit (Golf) in 1974, annual vehicle capacity at Puebla expanded, reaching 100,000 in the late 1970s (see VW 1968–2020, 2020, 2021).

To rekindle stagnant demand for its cars in the US, the West German automaker launched production of the Rabbit at its brand new 240,000-capacity Westmoreland Plant in East Huntingdon township, Pennsylvania. in April 1978. This was not the Wolfsburg-based auto group's first attempt to build cars in North America. In fact, it investigated opening a facility in Canada as far back as 1952, before acquiring a Studebaker-Packard factory in North Brunswick township, NJ, in 1955. It hoped to commence Beetle output there in October 1956, but this plan never panned out (see Jacobs 2016).

After the company assembled a peak of 225,496 Rabbit and Rabbit pickups in 1980, sales flamed out in America. In response to massive losses, production at Westmoreland was cut back dramatically, and renovations to a recently acquired army factory in Sterling Heights, Michigan, were halted even though 80% of the project was completed. The almost rehabilitated, 200,000-capacity VW Sterling Heights Plant was then sold to Chrysler in 1983, and Westmoreland shuttered in July 1988. In addition to internal company problems, a major factor driving VW's American demise was the fuel-efficient and extremely reliable cars of Japanese automakers: the same factor culling market share from American automakers (Jacobs 2016).

Reseeded as the sole base for VW's North American production, the 10,000-worker, 240,000-capacity Puebla complex saw output surpass 200,000 in 1991 and nearly achieve a 100% utilization rate in 1993, when 239,077 Beetle Type 1, Jetta, Golf, and Eurovan/Caravelle were assembled (VW 1968–2020). Thereafter, Germany's largest auto group would have to navigate some steep terrain in North America, before finally regaining its footing in the late 2000s, buoyed by its Audi and Porsche luxury brands. Re-energized, VW would open a new factory in the US in 2011, but only after witnessing the successes of its national rivals, BMW and Mercedes-Benz.

OTHER AUTOMAKER PLANTS IN NORTH AMERICA PRE-NAFTA

By the early 1960s, Canada had accumulated a massive trade deficit, with the imbalance in the automotive sector accounting for $460 million and more than 90% of the national shortfall. In response, the federal government decided to take a more active role in industrial development by imposing tariffs on vehicle imports. With the dominant Big Three already operating in Canadian, these policies primarily affected European automakers, forcing them to consider opening their own assembly facilities in the country. With the implementation of the Canada-United States Automotive Products Trade Agreement (Canada-US Auto Pact) in 1965, such plants also gave the Europeans freer access to the much larger US market (Anastakis 2005, 2013).

To sweeten the pot, Canadian, provincial, and local policymakers offered construction subsidies, property and business tax abatements, and tariffs reductions on imported motor vehicle parts if manufacturers completed final assembly in Canada. Volvo of Sweden was the first to take the bait, opening a two-hundred-worker, 5,000-capacity plant in Dartmouth, Nova Scotia, and putting the finishing touches on its first imported Volvo 120-Series KD kits in June 1963 (Anastakis 2005, 2013; Jacobs 2016).

By 1964 France's Renault, Peugeot, and Citroen (then separate) were in discussions regarding plants in Quebec, and Daimler-Benz of Germany and Alfa-Romeo of Italy were linked to Ontario. Only the Renault came to fruition, with a third-sector firm connected to the province, General Investment Corporation (GIC), reaching a licensing agreement with Renault and Peugeot to produce a combined 6,000 to 8,000 cars annually at a fully subsidized plant in Saint-Bruno-de-Montarville near Montreal. The endeavour was then placed under the direction of GIC's newly created subsidiary, Societe de Montage Automobile (SOMA), and commenced production of Renault R8 subcompacts in November 1965 (see Anastakis 2005, 2013; Jacobs 2016).

Output at SOMA Saint-Bruno grew to 8,094 in 1968 and peaked at 11,980 in 1971. The operation was far from smooth, however; with constant shutdowns and threats of closure, it lasted only until January 1973. Renault again briefly built cars in North America in the early 1980s, this time at the American Motors Corporation (AMC) Kenosha Main Plant in Wisconsin. Renault took over the factory in 1982, before abandoning it and a newly built plant in the Bramalea section of Brampton, Ontario, when it unloaded the hemorrhaging AMC on Chrysler in 1987 (see *Ward's* 1968–2020; Jacobs 2016).

In the meantime, Volvo slowly trudged forward in Nova Scotia, shifting to a larger structure in Halifax in 1967, where it assembled 10,449 KD cars in 1973, rising to a high of 13,337 in

1975. Concurrent to this, the Swedish automaker commenced construction on a 3,500-worker, 100,000-capacity car factory in Chesapeake, Virginia. Completed in June 1976 and scheduled to launch in late 1976, the new plant was to have marked the end of the Halifax operations. Nonetheless, Volvo would never meet its sales targets in America, and after a second energy crisis and global recession that created excess capacity in Europe, the automaker abandoned its Chesapeake operations. The half-baked facility was eventually shuttered in 1986, after building only a handful of buses (see *Ward's* 1968–2020; Krampitz 2001; Anastakis 2004; Jacobs 2016).

Despite the last-minute stay, output at Volvo Halifax shrunk to 6,826 in 1977, before gradually rebounding to more than 10,000 annually in 1982 through 1986. The following October, Volvo moved into the new 15,000-capacity Bayers Lake Assembly at Point Edward in Cape Breton County. After a combined 8,523 vehicles were assembled in 1987, output flattened and contracted to just 5,504 in 1993 (see table 2). By then, the domestic content requirements proposed under NAFTA and lagging sales in America appeared to spell the end of Volvo Bayers Lake (see Krampitz 2001; Anastakis 2004, 2005; Jacobs 2016).

NAFTA would derail the short-lived first North American assembly plant of Hyundai Motors. The South Korean automaker first entered the market in February 1983, when it opened its Hyundai Auto Canada, Inc. (HACI) sales office in north Toronto. Its cars, however, lacked a catalytic converter, barring them from US market. This omission did not inhibit shipments to Canada, where the automaker registered its first Hyundai Pony sales in December 1983 and delivered 25,123 units of the car in 1984. Sales then soared to 79,072 in 1985, turning Hyundai into Canada's annual sales leader among non-North American automakers and the Pony into the nation's best-selling car among all models for the year (see *Ward's* 1968–2020; Chung 1998; Jacobs 2016, 2021; Hyundai 2021).

As this was playing out, in August 1985 Hyundai declared its intention to build a car factory in Canada. After scouting sites in Quebec, Ontario, British Columbia, and Nova Scotia, on 15 November 1985, it announced plans to build a 100,000-capacity plant in Bromont, Quebec, approximately fifty-five miles (eighty-eight kilometres) east of Montreal. The plant was scheduled to launch KD assembly of Pony and Stellar in 1988, and to reach full capacity by 1990, when it was to employ 1,200 workers. Quebec had been viewed as the favourite all along, as the Korean automaker's cars were most well received in the province (see *Ward's* 1968–2020; Hyun and Lee 1989; Jacobs 2016, 2021).

The timing of the announcement was no coincidence, as in January 1987 South Korea was set to lose its special classification in Canada as a developing economy. Under this status, Hyundai cars were not subjected the 10% federal excise tax levied on Japanese imports, saving the Korean automaker an estimated $140 million in tariffs in 1985 and 1986. The duty-free status also enabled Hyundai to sell its models at lower sticker prices than Japanese and American cars within the same segments. Lastly, Hyundai feared its continued growth would ultimately make it subject to American and Canadian import quotas similar to those forced on Japanese automakers under the VER. Ironically, the VER, along with a stronger yen versus the US dollar, helped create an opening for Hyundai cars (see *Ward's* 1968–2020; Hyun and Lee 1989; Jacobs 2016, 2022).

Galvanized by its announced project in Canada and a new 300,000-capacity car plant in Ulsan, the Korean automaker introduced its fully compliant, Mitsubishi Motors-derived Hyundai Excel to America in March 1986. The subcompact would take the continent by storm, registering US sales of 168,882 units and Canadian deliveries of 70,024 during that year. Thereafter, American purchases would jump to 263,610 in 1987 and 264,282 in 1988. Conversely, Hyundai sales in Canada would fall back to 50,646 and 31,013, respectively (see *Ward's* 1968–2020; Hyun and Lee 1989; McDermott 1995; Jacobs 2016, 2021).

As mentioned earlier and shown in table 2, HACI Bromont never reached its potential. Stalled by dumping complaints levelled by Ford and GM against its supposedly "underpriced" cars in Canada, social and labour unrest in Korea, and production problems, the first Hyundai Sonata mid-size sedan did not roll off the new plant's assembly line until 12 January 1989 (neither the Stellar nor Pony were ever built in Canada). By then, the automaker had already pushed back by a year its original plans for reaching full capacity, to 1991 (Jacobs 2016, 2021).

The beginning of the end for the plant came in July 1990, when Chrysler reneged on its preliminary agreement to purchase 30,000 Sonata and marketed them as the rebadged Chrysler's Eagle Premier. Output at Bromont peaked at 28,201 in 1991 and fell to near half that in 1992 and 1993, with the last Sonata assembled, the operations suspended, and most of its 841 workers furloughed on 17 September 1993. The idling was originally announced as a retooling, as part of a plan to relaunch output with the Hyundai Elantra in July 1995. The plant would never reopen, as $400 million in losses had made it more expensive to run than to shut down (McDermott 1995; Jacobs 2016, 2021).

HACI Bromont was doomed from the start by production flaws, vehicle quality problems, a related contraction in North American sales, a failure to secure a larger partner to jointly build vehicles, and, most prominently, by NAFTA. Company officials concluded that without major investments, such as erecting an engine plant, it would be impossible for the plant to achieve the trade pact's 62.5% regional content threshold by 2002, in order to ship duty-free in North America. By that time, they also believed Mexico would present a much cheaper option to serve the US market (Jacobs 2016, 2022).

Much would change for Hyundai, and its then rival Kia Motors, after 1993. As will be discussed in the next sections, the Korean automakers would follow a similar path to their Japanese competitors under NAFTA, first establishing factories in America before landing in Mexico. As was the case for all new domestic automakers during the NAFTA era, except for Toyota and Honda, this route would steer clear of Canada.

CHRONICLING THE SURGE OF NON-NORTH AMERICAN PLANTS DURING THE NAFTA ERA, 1994–2019

To serve rising demand and meet NAFTA's regional domestic content requirements, foreign automakers raised their combined light vehicle output in the region from 2,578,272 in 1993 to 2,940,471 in 1994 and then to 7,929,733 in 2019 (see tables 1 and 2). Transplant growth was not straight line, however, with output rising to 3,608,586 and then to 4,538,765 in 2004 before peaking at 5,608,865 in 2007. Final assemblies by the new domestics then shrunk to 3,906,816 in 2009 before rocketing forward to 7,793,366 in 2014. They have essentially remained flat ever since. Nonetheless, foreign automakers built 48.96% of the 16,195,520 light vehicles assembled in the NAFTA region in 2019. This represented a stunning increase from 18.59% of 13,867,984 units in 1993 and 19.24% of 15,285,289 in 1994. In contrast, the Detroit Three built 51.04% of the light vehicles assembled in the region in 2019, a conspicuous downward trajectory from 81.41% and 80.76%, respectively.

In other words, not only did new domestic automakers more than triple their light vehicle output under NAFTA, they also raised their share of regional production by more than 30%. In the process, they increased the number of factories they operated from sixteen to thirty-four and nearly tripled their combined annual vehicle capacity, from 3,440,000 in 1993 to 10,423,500 in 2019. Nonetheless, this evolution was far from evenly distributed across the trade pact's three nations (Jacobs 2016; *Ward's* 1968–2020).

As table 2 illustrates, whereas Mexico realized a net increase of ten foreign automaker plants under NAFTA, the US experienced a net gain of three and Canada suffered a net loss of two during the trade pact era. On the other hand, although annual light vehicle capacity in Mexico ballooned by 2,678,500 units and 487.00%, from 550,000 in 1993 to 3,228,500 in 2019, it increased by 3,715,000 and 152.23% in the US during this period, from 2,440,000 to 6,155,000. In contrast, transplant capacity rose by 590,000 units and 131.11% in Canada under NAFTA, from 450,000 to 1,040,000. Finally, after 1993 thirteen new foreign-run factories were constructed in America and ten in Mexico, but only one was built in Canada. Conversely, both the US and Canada lost two foreign assembly plants to closure and each had a joint venture dissolved, but no transplant factories were shuttered in Mexico during NAFTA (based on *Ward's* 1968–2020; Jacobs 2016).

Overall, the thirty-four light vehicle plants in the NAFTA region employed 147,243 people in 2019 (see table 2). Of this, the eighteen in the US engaged 82,363 workers, the ten in Mexico 51,680, and the three in Canada 13,200. Finally, two new factories were under construction during 2019, the final year of NAFTA, one in the US and one in Mexico. Again, in the face of these disparities, one fact held true before and after NAFTA: Japanese automakers blazed the trail for others to follow (data from *Ward's* 1968–2020; Jacobs 2016).

JAPANESE TRANSPLANTS EXPAND EVEN FASTER UNDER NAFTA, 1994–2019

As illustrated in table 2, Japanese firms operated twenty-one of the thirty-four foreign-run light vehicle plants in the NAFTA region in 2019: eleven in the US, all three in Canada, and seven in Mexico. In addition, in 2019 a Japanese-German joint venture was operating in Mexico and construction commenced on a twenty-second all-Japanese collaboration in America. If we incorporate the concurrent major expansions at Japanese transplant operations launched prior to 1994, Japanese automakers more than doubled their North American production capacity under NAFTA. Continued trade friction with the US, along with a desire to set up shop close to local sales markets, spurred this growth. The combined massive investment prompted Canadian local officials to begin calling these new-to-North America manufacturers the "new domestics" (Jacobs 2016).

As shown in tables 3 through 5, Japanese-brand light vehicle assemblies soared to 5,551,054 in 2019, an increase of 3,231,948 units and 139.36% compared to 1993. This included upsurges in output of 3,551,557 in America, 1,143,731 in Mexico, and 875,766 in Canada. As a result, Japanese transplants raised their share of all NAFTA region production, including the Detroit Three and Tesla, from 16.72% in 1993 to 34.28% in 2019. This growth was made possible by a 3,864,000-unit or 122.23% enlargement in Japanese transplant annual capacity, from 3,160,000 in 1993 to 7,024,000 in 2019. This enlarged capacity to 4,240,000 units in the US, to 1,744,000 in Mexico, and to 1,040,000 in Canada in the latter year. It also pushed combined employment at these factories to 90,932 in 2019, including 53,688 in America, 24,044 in Mexico, and 13,200 in Canada (*Ward's* 1968–2020; Jacobs 2016). (To clarify: the CAMI, NUMMI, AAI, and Diamond Star joint ventures in 1993 include only Japanese and Geo brand production capacity. The same was true for COMPAS for 2019.)

More specifically, the NAFTA era's Japanese automaker expansion drive began in El Salto, Jalisco, in November 1995, when Honda launched assembly of a small batch of Accord at its first Mexican vehicle plant (see table 2). Over the next five years, the automaker also expanded capacity at its Marysville, Ohio, operations from 370,000 to 440,000 units; at East Liberty to 240,000 units; and in Ontario from 100,000 to 400,000. The latter entailed an expansion of Allison #1 to 200,000 and the opening of the new 200,000-capacity Alliston #2 to build Odyssey minivans in September 1998 (*Ward's* 1968–2020; Jacobs 2016).

Toyota welcomed its first addition under NAFTA in December 1998, when it commenced output of Toyota Tundra pickups at its new 150,000-capacity Princeton Plant in Union Township, Indiana. In the interim, Japan's largest automaker also enlarged capacity at Toyota Georgetown in Kentucky from 440,000 to 500,000 and at Toyota Cambridge in Ontario from 70,000 to 200,000. The latter involved the construction of the 100,000-capacity Cambridge North plant, which launched production of Toyota Corolla in August 1997, and the

Table 5. New Domestic Automaker Brand Light Vehicle Production in Canada, 1993-2019

	1993	1994	1999	2004	2009	2014	2019
Total Canada light vehicle production	2,223,501	2,285,208	2,996,073	2,662,958	1,479,161	2,382,218	1,893,274
Non-NA brand LV built in Canada	***359,328***	***370,846***	***501,069***	***680,413***	***583,227***	***868,356***	***875,766***
Japanese brands	*339,239*	*364,410*	*501,069*	*680,413*	*579,348*	*868,170*	*875,766*
Toyota	79,219	85,871	211,082	287,859	319,547	475,163	468,002
Honda	100,621	108,308	274,908	392,528	259,796	393,007	407,764
Suzuki-Geo	159,399	170,231	15,079	26	5	0	0
Other country brands							
Korean (Hyundai)	14,585	0	0	0	0	0	0
Swedish (Volvo)	5,504	6,436	0	0	0	0	0
German (VW by Chrysler)	0	0	0	0	3,879	0	0
Italian (Fiat)	0	0	0	0	0	186	0

Source: Compiled by the author from *Ward's* (1968–2020).

enhancement of the original Cambridge factory, renamed Cambridge South, to 100,000 units, enabling it to begin assembling Camry-based Toyota Solara coupes in June 1998 (*Ward's* 1968–2020; Jacobs 2016).

During the 2000s, Honda cleared space for its Acura MDX mid-size luxury SUV at Alliston #2, by shifting output of the Odyssey to its new 340,000-capacity Lincoln plant in Talladega County, Alabama. The latter launched in November 2001. The company then inaugurated production of Honda Civic at its new 100,000-capacity Greensburg plant in Indiana in October 2008. Meanwhile, Toyota began assembling Toyota Tacoma pickups at a 30,000-capacity KD plant in Tecate, Baja California, Mexico, in September 2004. It followed its first Mexican endeavour by retooling Princeton in preparation for the Highlander mid-size SUV. To accommodate this transfer of the popular vehicle from Kyushu, Japan, Toyota reassigned output of the larger Tundra to its new 250,000-capacity San Antonio factory, which launched in November 2006 (Jacobs 2016).

Toyota followed its Texas plant with the construction of its 150,000-capacity Woodstock plant in Ontario, which began manufacturing the popular Toyota RAV4 compact SUV in

November 2008. In between, Toyota started contruction on its planned 160,000-capacity Blue Springs plant in Union County, Mississippi, in April 2007. Initially slated to build Highlander, the factory was delayed for eighteen months, its launch date pushed back until 2011, by (1) the progressive rise in American gasoline prices to four dollars per gallon by July 2008; (2) the world financial/economic crisis sparked by the 15–16 September failures of AIG and Lehman Brothers; and (3) the fallout from the recall of more than 5.5 million vehicles in the US in 2009 and 2010 and a related ten-month investigation by the US National Highway Traffic Safety Administration regarding the so-called "sudden unintended acceleration" of Toyota vehicles (Jacobs 2016).

While Honda and Toyota were significantly expanding their NAFTA footprint, the cash-strapped Nissan Motors was forced to sell a controlling 36.8% stake to Renault in 1999. After finalizing its alliance with the French firm, the Yokohama-based automaker joined its rivals by enlarging annual capacity at Nissan Smyrna from 420,000 to 500,000, constructing the 340,000-capacity Nissan Canton near Jackson, Mississippi, and improving utilization and then expanding its Cuernavaca and Aguascalientes complexes in Mexico to a combined 500,000 units. The new Canton factory launched output of Nissan Quest in May 2003, taking on the assignment from Ford Avon Lake, which had assembled the minivan on contract between April 1992 and June 2002 (Jacobs 2016).

As for Japan's smaller automakers, Subaru and Isuzu's alliance at the then 200,000-capacity SIA in Lafayette, Indiana, unravelled with the withdrawal of Isuzu in January 2003. Output of Isuzu Rodeo SUVs at the factory was then discontinued in July 2004. The decision allowed Subaru's parent Fuji Heavy Industry to retool SIA to build its new Subaru B9 Tribeca. On the other hand, plans to rebadge and sell a batch of the new SUV as the Saab 9-6X were abandoned in 2005, prompted by GM's decisions to divest its 20% stake in Subaru and to slash its 49% controlling interest in Isuzu to 12%. In its stead, the renamed Subaru of Indiana Automotive (also SIA) began building Toyota Camry in February 2007, under contract from its new minority partner, Toyota. This pushed capacity at SIA to 250,000 by 2010 (Jacobs 2016; Subaru 2021).

In contrast to Subaru's turnaround, Mazda, Mitsubishi Motors, and Suzuki all floundered during the NAFTA era after splitting up with their American partners over vehicle build quality, model offerings and badging, and factory assignments. After Mitsubishi bought out Chrysler's stake in their Diamond Star Motors joint venture in October 1991, a new accord entitled the American automaker to purchase half of the Mitsubishi vehicles built at the Normal, Illinois, plant through 2000. The arrangement actually lasted until February 2005, when the former 240,000-capacity factory produced its last 348 Chrysler Sebring and 1,427 Dodge Stratus mid-size coupes (Jacobs 2016).

Diamond Star assembled only 87,294 vehicles in 2005 and 92,499 in 2006. Thereafter, it was idled more frequently than it was running, and built just 18,501 Mitsubishi in 2009. By 2012, the end appeared near for the downsized 135,000-capacity Mitsubishi Normal factory, following the discontinuation of Mitsubishi Eclipse sports coupe production in August 2011, the Endeavor SUV that September, and the Gallant mid-size sedan in 2012. As a result, only 37,150 vehicles were completed in 2011 and 37,019 in 2012 (see *Ward's* 1968–2020; Jacobs 2016). (Note: the Chrysler Warren plant in Michigan also produced 22,388 Mitsubishi Raider pickups between August 2005 and February 2009.)

Nonetheless, propelled by the July 2012 launch of the Outlander Sport SUV, assemblies slightly recovered to a six-year high of 67,362 in 2013 and then 69,178 in 2014. Concurrently, new alliances with Renault-Nissan and Fiat Chrysler (FCA) suggested that the twenty-six-year-old Illinois factory would get a needed shot in the arm. This hope would prove illusionary, as production of a new Mitsubishi and Chrysler co-branded subcompact car model was instead assigned to Mitsubishi Thailand, a planned Renault-based Mitsubishi brand mid-size sedan was dropped, and a new Nissan-derived full-size car was awarded first to Renault-Samsung Busan in South Korea and then to Nissan's Infiniti factory in Kaminokawa, Tochigi, Japan. The fallout led to the shuttering of Mitsubishi Normal in November 2015 and the shifting of North American–bound output of Outlander Sport (RVR in Canada) to Okazaki, Japan. Mitsubishi Motors itself was then taken over by Nissan in May 2016, after which its American plant was sold to the startup electric truckmaker Rivian in January 2017 (see *Ward's* 1968–2020; Jacobs 2016; MMC 2019).

As for Suzuki, after battling over the quality of the vehicles assembled at CAMI, and thereby refusing to allow the plant to build its prized new Suzuki Kizashi sports sedan, management dissolved its partnership with the debt-ridden GM in December 2009. By that time, most Suzuki brand models sold in North America were already being assembled at GM's Daewoo Bupyeong in Incheon, South Korea. In fact, the 240,000-capacity CAMI in Ingersoll, Ontario, produced only 12,357 Suzuki-badged vehicles in 2008 and 5 in 2009 (all Subaru XL-7 SUVs). With American Suzuki Motor Corporation in receivership, the parent company announced it was withdrawing from the North American market in March 2013. The last recorded sale of a Suzuki, a Kizashi built at Suzuki's Sagara Plant in Makinohara, Japan, was then registered in Canada in December 2013 (see *Ward's* 1968–2020; Jacobs 2016, 2021).

The situation at Mazda-Ford's AAI plant in Flat Rock, Michigan, was somewhat similar. After Ford discontinued production of Mercury Cougar sports coupes that August, output at AAI sank to just 65,924 in 2002, including 47,603 Mazda. New life appeared, however, in October 2002 with the launch of Mazda 6 mid-size sedan, the remodelled and sporty replacement for the Mazda 626. This was followed in September 2004 by the newly redesigned Ford Mustang muscle car. As a result, assemblies at AAI rebounded to 133,264 in 2004 before doubling to an all-time high of 272,632 in 2005. The latter year included 91,339 Mazda 6 (see *Ward's* 1968–2020; Jacobs 2016).

Although Ford had derived its Mercury Milan, Lincoln Zephyr/MKZ, and original Ford Fusion from Mazda 626/6 designs, the two automakers were on their way to a divorce by 2008, when the hemorrhaging Ford gradually began divesting its 33.4% interest in Mazda.

By 2010 this stake had fallen to 3.5%, and output in Flat Rock to 122,754, including 45,168 Mazda 6. Related to this, assembly of Mazda pickups (rebadged Ford Ranger) was terminated at Ford's Twin Cities assembly plant in St. Paul, Minnesota, that July; it had shifted there upon the closing of Ford Edison in New Jersey in March 2004. This was followed by the discontinuation of Mazda Tribute SUV production at Ford Kansas City in May 2011 (aka Ford Escape and Mercury Mariner) (see *Ward's* 1968–2020; Jacobs 2016).

The final wheel in the partnership came off in June 2011, when Mazda announced that, beginning with the 2014 model, it would reassign manufacture of the Mazda 6 to its Hofu plant in Yamaguchi Prefecture, Japan. Concurrently, Ford acquired Mazda's stake in AAI, with the last of 37,566 Mazda 6 built that year rolling off the Flat Rock assembly line in August 2012. In contrast, on 17 June 2011 Mazda announced plans to erect a 250,000-capacity factory in Salamanca, Guanajuato, Mexico. Output of Mazda 3 commenced there in January 2014, followed by Mazda 2 that October, with 102,346 total cars produced in that year. Beginning in June 2015, and through a partnership with Toyota, the Salamanca factory began restamping and selling a batch of Mazda 2 and Scion iA. Two months later, a restyled variant of the car also was being assembled as the Toyota Yaris. A total of 116,527 cars were produced at Mazda Salamanca in 2019 (see table 2). This included 91,850 Mazda 2, 3, and CX-30, and 24,697 Toyota Yaris (see *Ward's* 1968–2020; Jacobs 2016; Mazda 2020).

Mazda's decision to launch a plant in Salamanca was not surprising, as four of the five new Japanese transplant factories opened in the NAFTA tegion since 2009 have been built in Mexico. Production at Toyota's Blue Spring Mississippi plant commenced in 2011. Eight years after that, Toyota Motor inaugurated its 100,000-capacity Guanajuato factory in Apaseo el Grande in December 2019. Japan's largest automaker also upgraded and expanded its Baja plant to enabled it to manufacture 166,000 pickups per year. By 2019 Toyota had also expanded capacity at Georgetown to 550,000, in order to introduce production of Lexus ES sedans; at Princeton to 420,000 to fill rising demand for the Highlander SUV; and at Cambridge and Woodstock to a combined 600,000 for the RAV4 and Lexus RX350 luxury crossover (see *Ward's* 1968–2020; Jacobs 2016).

For its part, Honda opened a 200,000-capacity plant in Celaya, Guanajuato, in February 2014 and enlarged El Salto to 63,000. Celaya built 168,349 Honda Fit subcompact hatchbacks and HRV crossovers in 2019 and El Salto assembled 36,066 HR-V. On the other hand, output at Alliston was restored to pre-2009 levels and then increased to all-time highs of 430,164 in 2017 and 432,771 in 2018 before producing 407,764 in 2019. The 2019 total included the automaker's two most popular models, the Civic at Alliston 1 and CRV crossover at Alliston 2 (Honda 2020).

As for Nissan, it expanded its Mexican footprint by enlarging capacity at Cuernavaca to 300,000 and at Aguascalientes to 550,000. The latter entailed the launch of Aguascalientes #2 in November 2013, situated just six miles (9.4 kilometres) south of the original factory. This enabled Nissan to centralize NAFTA production of its Sentra compact, Versa subcompact, and new Kicks CUV at the two Mexican factories. In the interim, the automaker enlarged US capacity at Smyrna to 640,000 and at Canton to 500,000, with output at both plants reaching or surpassing one million in 2016: 645,514 in Tennessee and 361,807 in Mississippi. Finally, Nissan's Infiniti luxury division opened a 230,000-capacity 50/50 joint venture with Daimler in Aguascalientes in November 2017. Announced in June 2014, the new Cooperation Manufacturing Plant Aguascalientes (COMPAS) was set two miles south-west of Nissan #2 and built 90,408 vehicles in 2019, including 30,321 Infiniti QX50 luxury crossovers. Originally based on the Nissan Skyline, the second generation QX50 now shares Daimler's MFA2 platform with the Mercedes-Benz GLB CUV and the A-Class compact car (see *Ward's* 1968–2020; Jacobs 2016; *MexicoNow* 2017; Nissan Global 2021).

As its rivals began relying more heavily on Mexico, Subaru ramped up capacity in Indiana from 300,000 in 2014 to 450,000 in 2019. This decision, along with the ending of its contract to assemble Toyota Camry, enabled the Japanese automaker to both meet growing American demand for its Outback mid-size wagon and launch two additional models at SIA: the Impreza compact and the Ascent three-row CUV. Including the Legacy mid-size sedan, the factory built 368,516 vehicles in 2019 and was expected to expand further, before being best by vehicle recalls and the outbreak of COVID-19 (Subaru 2021).

Finally, and also in contrast to the Japanese automakers' post-2009 focus on lower-cost Mexico, in January 2018 Mazda and Toyota announced plans for 300,000-capacity joint venture plant in Huntsville, Alabama. Scheduled to open in late 2021, the new factory represented the first new Japanese-led assembly plant built in America in ten years. Nonetheless, as the next sections chronicle, German and Korean automakers have followed a similar albeit smaller growth path as the Japanese under NAFTA: build in America first before expanding in Mexico. The only major exception to this was Volkswagen, whose locus for North American production has remained south of the border for more than fifty years.

GERMAN AUTOMAKER PLANTS IN NORTH AMERICA UNDER NAFTA, 1994–2019

German automakers operated six light vehicle plants in the NAFTA region in 2019, three in the US and three in Mexico. As mentioned above, Mexico's COMPAS joint venture between Daimler and Nissan in Mexico constituted a seventh factory. These complexes had a combined annual capacity of 2,085,000 units, built 1,431,439 light vehicles, and employed 42,297 people in 2019. Of this, 1,015,000 in capacity, 746,522 vehicles built, and 20,600 workers were situated in America; the remaining 1,070,000 in capacity, 715,238 vehicles assembled, and 21,232 employees were located in Mexico. By comparison, the 240,000-capacity VW Puebla was the only German automaker factory in the region pre-NAFTA, with its 14,209 workers assembling 239,077 cars and light vans in 1993 (see tables 3–5) (see *Ward's* 1968–2020; Jacobs 2016).

Import tariffs and a strong desire by management to avoid Germany's powerful labour unions (works councils) provoked this seven-fold growth. These factors also encouraged BMW and Daimler's Mercedes-Benz to make America their global export bases for SUVs. With the exception of Volkswagen, however, German producers did not begin their expansion into Mexico until 2016. Although the opposite initially appeared to the case at the start of NAFTA, when Daimler began assembling cars at its medium-duty truck plant in Santiago Tianguistenco, State of Mexico, in January 1994. Nevertheless, the Stuttgart-based automaker built only 4,314 C-, E-, and S-Class units at the facility between January 1994 and March 1999. By the latter year, Mercedes had established its NAFTA region base in Vance, Alabama, where in February 1997 it commenced production of M-Class SUVs at its 65,000-capacity Tuscaloosa plant. Output surpassed capacity in 1998 before seesawing to 73,500 at the enhanced 120,000-capacity plant in 2004 (see *Ward's* 1968–2020; Jacobs 2016).

In the meantime, Daimler-Benz assumed control of Chrysler in May 1998 before unloading it at nearly a $30 billion loss in August 2007. Unfortunately, this occurred before the merged DaimlerChrysler eliminated 13,000 Chrysler jobs in the US and Canada. In contrast, with the launch of the Mercedes-Benz R-Class passenger van in June 2005 and the GL-Class SUV in January 2006, final assemblies at Tuscaloosa jumped to 173,600 in 2006 before shrinking to 90,582 in 2009. Conversely, in response to rising demand, foreign exchange issues, and tariffs, in December 2009 Daimler revealed plans to expand its Alabama factory to incorporate North American-bound production of its C-Class car line. During the preparation process, output in Vance expanded to 185,146 and then 232,712 in 2014, with assembly of the C-Class commencing on 18 June of the latter year (see *Ward's* 1968–2020; Jacobs 2016).

Although Mercedes was the first German luxury carmaker to assemble cars in Mexico, BMW pre-empted its rival in America, launching output of BMW 3-Series sedans at its new 50,000-capacity Spartanburg factory near Greer, South Carolina, in September 1994. Seven months later, in April 1995, the Munich-based automaker also began assembling KD kits of 3-Series at its 28,000-capacity BMW Mexico Toluca plant in Lerma, State of Mexico. The automaker had originally considered constructing a large manufacturing complex at the site, but ultimately completed only 9,159 units of 3-, 5-, and 7-Series and 82 Porsche 911 before terminating its joint venture with local investors in March 2003 (*Ward's* 1968–2020; Jacobs 2016; BMW 2021).

In the meantime, Spartanburg ramped up to 50,278 vehicles in 1996, with the addition of the Z3 roadster that January. The factory's capacity then was expanded to 100,000 in September 1999 to accommodate the launch of the new BMW X5 sport activity vehicle (SAV) crossover. This increased to 160,000 in 2002 to meet a doubling in American sales to 256,622 for that year. Output then advanced to 166,090 in 2003 before retreating to 143,916 in 2004 and 104,632 in 2006. Buoyed by the March 2008 launch of the new X6 crossover coupe, output at Spartanburg increased to 170,739 during that year before contracting to 121,666 in 2009, in the midst of the financial crisis (see Jacobs 2016).

The global economic difficulties failed to slow down BMW's plans to turn its South Carolina operations into its largest worldwide production site, however; it launched its new X3 SAV there in September 2010, raising final assemblies to 276,065 in 2011. The X3's success prompted the automaker to commit to investing another $1.9 million at the plant between 2012 and 2016, in order to enlarge capacity to 450,000 and to accommodate two new vehicles, the X4 crossover coupe and the flagship X7 SAV. Output of the X4 commenced at Spartanburg in April 2014, pushing output at the 8,800-worker plant to 349,949 for that year. As this project was moving ahead full-steam, the Bavarian automaker announced plans to construct a 150,000-capacity assembly plant in Villa de Reyes, San Luis Potosi, in July 2014. Output of BMW and Mini brand subcompacts was expected by 2019, with lower production costs, particularly related to wages, considered the final decisive determinant driving the automaker's selection of Mexico over competing sites in America (see Jacobs 2016).

Whereas its luxury German rivals were expanding in the US, Volkswagen enlarged capacity to 440,000 in Puebla to accommodate further exports of the VW Jetta compact and the New Beetle subcompact cars. The latter was introduced in December 1997 and helped push output at the Mexican plant to 410,308 in 1999. The New Beetle's revival was short lived, however, in 2004 causing final assemblies at Puebla to plunge to 225,342 and VW's American market share to again tumble below 2.0% (see *Ward's* 1968–2020; Jacobs 2016; VW 1968–2020).

With the consolidation of North American and European production (from Wolfsburg) of the fifth-generation VW Jetta at Puebla in late 2005, vehicle output rebounded to 411,129 in 2007 and then to a record 449,096 in 2008. A unprecedented 394,103 of these were Jetta variants, including 26,507 stamped as Bora for Latin American markets. At the same time, and despite flattening American sales, VW announced plans to again build vehicles in America. Almost exactly twenty years after the closure of VW Westmoreland, the German automaker declared its plans in July 2008 to erect a 150,000-capacity assembly plant in Hamilton County, Tennessee (see Jacobs 2016; VW 1968–2020). In return for the plant, the automaker received a record $577 million in state and local incentives, or a whopping $172 million more than offered by Limestone County (near Huntsville) and Alabama for the project. The figure also was nearly double the $294 million granted Toyota in February 2007 for its Blue Springs, Mississippi, plant and $168 million more than the previous record gifted Kia Motors for its factory in West Point, Georgia.

Delayed by the 2009 global financial crisis, VW Chattanooga launched in April 2011 and built 152,543 VW Passat in 2012. Interestingly, in February 2011, before the plant was even opened, VW declared its intention to increase capacity at Chattanooga to 200,000. Rumours circulated that a second vehicle would be built at the factory, possibly the VW Phaeton flagship luxury sedan, the Tiguan CUV, or an Audi or Porsche luxury crossover. Some even suggested that VW would build a second plant at the site to manufacture Audi. This proved incorrect when in April 2012 the German automaker revealed that it would build its Audi Q5 CUVs at a new 150,000-capacity plant in San Jose Chiapa, Puebla, Mexico. Output was projected to launch at the site, located forty-three miles (sixty-nine kilometres) east of VW Puebla, in May 2016 (see *Ward's* 1968–2020; Jacobs 2016; VW 1968–2020).

Meanwhile, VW terminated its manufacturing contract with Chrysler, which had assembled 67,313 VW Routan between February 2008 and October 2013. Built at Chrysler's Windsor Assembly in Ontario, Canada, the large minivans were merely rebadged copies of the Chrysler Town & Country/Dodge Caravan. Thereafter, VW ceased selling minivans in the US and Canada and continued importing passenger variants of the VW Transporter light commercial van to Mexico from Hannover, Germany. VW had ended deliveries of the so-called Eurovan in the two advanced nations in 2003 (*Ward's* 1968–2020; Jacobs 2016).

The Jetta-powered VW Puebla increased production to a record 475,121 in 2014. In contrast, with American sales of the Passat falling well below expectations, output at Chattanooga backtracked to 117,628 for the year, sparking rumours that VW might close its three-year-old Tennessee factory. This gossip was put to rest in July 2014, when VW chair Martin Winterkorn announced that his group would invest another $900 million to enlarge capacity to 250,000 to accommodate the newly developed VW CrossBlue crossover coupe by late 2016. In exchange, the State of Tennessee and local governments provided the German automaker with an additional $274 million in tax breaks, worker training subsidies, and infrastructure improvements. This brought the complex's total incentive package to an inconceivable $851 million (Jacobs 2016).

Despite the massive subsidies, VW continued to concentrate its NAFTA region expansions in Mexico after 2014. In March 2015 VW revealed plans for a $1 billion expansion at Puebla, which was to take on North American–bound production of the Tiguan SUV from Wolfsburg. Launched in January 2017, this expansion raised annual capacity at the sprawling 11,829-worker factory to 600,000 in 2019. The automaker engaged another 1,233 persons at its engine plant in Silao, Guanajuato. Although assembly of the New Beetle ended at the plant on 10 July 2019, the complex in the Municipality of Cuautlancingo and the Puebla conurbation built 443,414 vehicles in 2019 (see table 2) (see *Ward's* 1968–2020; Jacobs 2016; VW 2020; INEGI 2021; VW Mexico, emails to author, 8–9 March 2021).

As for Audi San Jose Chiapa, it commenced output in September 2016, with the 180,000-capacity plant employing 5,268 and building 156,661 Q5 in 2019. In contrast, VW Chattanooga continued to flounder, with shrinking sales of the Passat dropping output to just 87,156 in 2015. Finally, the promised new hope came in December 2016, when production commenced of the newly developed VW Atlas. Known as the Teramont in Mexico (and when built in China), the Atlas was offered in two-row mid-size and three-row full-size SUVs, and as the Atlas Cross Sport coupe (i.e., the production version of the CrossBlue concept model). Nonetheless, due to a retooling for the November 2019 launch of the next-generation Passat, the 3,800-worker, 250,000-capacity Chattanooga produced only 107,684 vehicles in 2019 (see VW 1968–2020, 2021; Audi 2020).

As for Mercedes-Benz's activities in the NAFTA region, as mentioned earlier, its COMPAS joint venture with Nissan in Aguascalientes began manufacturing Infiniti QX50 in November 2017. Output of Mercedes GLB CUVs and A-Class sedans followed in July and September 2019, respectively, with the 3,600-worker, 230,000-capacity plant assembling 60,087 Mercedes-Benz among the 90,408 vehicles it built that year. In July 2020, however, production of the A-Class was reassigned to the firm's factory in Rastatt, Germany, in order to accommodate more GLB, QX50, and the new QX55 crossover coupe (*Ward's* 1968–202; Jacobs 2016; Karkaria 2020; Daimler 2021).

Meanwhile, in January 2015 Daimler revealed that it had signed an agreement with the former American Motors affiliate AM General to transfer Tuscaloosa's allotment of Mercedes-Benz R-Class to its 70,000-capacity plant in Mishawaka, Indiana. AM General assembled 26,912 R-Class between August 2015 and October 2017, when the vehicle was discontinued. The shift of the R-Class was made necessary by the impending May 2015 launch of the successor to the popular M-Class SUV, the Mercedes GLE. In response, Tuscaloosa output increased to 300,796 in 2015 before retreating to 212,118 in 2019. Despite the setback, Daimler indicated it intended to expand the factory's production and employment (see *Ward's* 1968–2020; Jacobs 2016; MBUSI 2021).

Finally, in March 2015 Daimler announced plans to invest $500 million to transform its commercial van KD assembly plant in Charleston County, South Carolina, into a full-fledged truck factory. The German automaker reopened the renamed Mercedes Benz Vans North Charleston in September 2018 and launched serial production of Sprinter passenger and light commercial vans in January 2019. The 1,600-worker, 15,000-capacity facility produced 15,090 vehicles during that year (*Ward's* 1968–2020; Jacobs 2016; MBV 2021).

Lastly, although BMW among the German automakers remained the most dedicated to its US operations, it also expanded into Mexico in April 2019, when it inaugurated its 2,800-worker, 175,000-capacity San Luis Potosi Plant in Villa de Reyes. The facility produced 24,755 units of the 3-Series during that year. The combination of low wages and NAFTA's tariff-free exports to America and Canada were the two primary factors motivating BMW's decision. In the interim, the Bavarian firm enlarged capacity and output at its 11,000-worker Spartanburg global SUV export base to 450,000 and 411,620, respectively, in 2019. This included the introduction of a fifth crossover model, the flagship X7 SAV, which launched in South Carolina in December 2018 and helped turn the complex into BMW's largest production centre worldwide.

THE EMERGENCE OF KOREAN AUTOMAKERS UNDER NAFTA

The Korean automakers Hyundai and Kia operated three light vehicle plants in the NAFTA region in 2019, two in the US and one in Mexico (see table 2). In the last full year of NAFTA, these factories had a combined annual capacity of 1,150,000 units, built 896,000 light vehicles, and employed 8,414 people. A total of 750,000 of this capacity was in the US, where 620,000 vehicles were built and 6,075 workers were engaged in 2019. By comparison, 400,000 in capacity, 274,000 vehicles assembled, and 2,339 employees were situated in Mexico (*Ward's* 1968–2020; Kia 2020, 2021; HMMA 2021; Hyundai 2021).

As previously mentioned, with combined sales in North America falling to one-third their late 1980s peak, Hyundai Motors would shutter its failed plant in Bromont, Quebec, in March 1994. Thereafter, North American deliveries would remain flat through 1998. This situation would then improve, aided by Hyundai's takeover of its rival, Kia Motors, in December 1998. Kia, the nation's second largest automaker, and considered the manufacturer of Korea's best-built cars, had been forced into bankruptcy by the Asian fiscal crisis of 1997. Buoyed by Kia imports, Hyundai-Kia would register a record 330,568 in US and Canadian dealer sales in 1999 (Jacobs 2016).

In anticipation of continued growth, Hyundai began preparing for its second attempt to produce light vehicles in North America. The location of Montgomery, Alabama, was announced in April 2002, with the automaker commencing manufacture of Hyundai Sonata at its new 300,000-capacity plant there in April 2005. Hyundai Santa Fe SUVs followed in April 2006, a year in which Hyundai Montgomery produced 236,773 vehicles. Output then increased to 250,319 in 2007 before contracting during the global financial crisis to 195,561 in 2009. The downturn, however, would prove a mere blip in the group's NAFTA region growth trajectory (Jacobs 2016). In the meantime, with sales of Kia brand vehicles approaching 300,000 in the US and 100,000 in Canada, in March 2006 the Hyundai-Kia Group announced plans to erect a second 300,000-capacity plant, this time in West Point, Georgia. Five suppliers also agreed to locate at the site, situated seventy-five miles (120 kilometres) south-west of Atlanta and 95 miles (152 kilometres) north-east of Hyundai Montgomery. Kia received a then-record $409 million in state and local incentives for the 2,900-worker factory; Hyundai was gifted $253 million four years earlier by Alabama and local authorities. Even more amazingly, Kia officials stuck to their commitment to Georgia despite a last-minute offer of $983 million from Meridian/Lauderdale County, Mississippi. The latter package included $240 million in Hurricane Katrina-Gulf Opportunity Zone Act (GO Zone) related federal tax breaks and $515 million in state and local abatements (Jacobs 2012, 2016; Minchin 2021).

Kia West Point launched production of Kia Sorrento SUVs in November 2009 and built 15,500 vehicles in that year. With the shift of the Hyundai Santa Fe to the factory in September 2010 and the Kia Optima mid-size sedan in September 2011, output quickly ramped up at Kia Georgia to 358,199 in 2012 and then 368,510 in 2014. Concurrently, Hyundai Montgomery added a second engine plant, which helped push its vehicle assemblies to 300,500 in 2010, a still-record 399,495 in 2013, and 398,851 in 2014. Interestingly, these expansions occurred in the midst of two countervailing forces: (1) the US–Korea Free Trade Pact of 15 March 2012, which enabled the duty-free import of passenger vehicles from South Korea into the US; and (2) announced plans to build a Hyundai-Kia car factory in Mexico (Jacobs 2016).

Since 2012, news reports had regularly suggested that Hyundai-Kia was on the precipice of constructing a third US assembly plant, or perhaps a factory in Canada. These rumours were quieted, temporarily, when in June 2014 the group announced plans to construct a $1 billion, 300,000-capacity small car plant in Pesqueria, Nuevo Leon, Monterrey, Mexico. They were rekindled in 2016, based upon combined US-Canadian sales of more than 1.6 million and projected sales of new models, including from the group's Genesis luxury division (see *Ward's* 1968–2020; Jacobs 2016; Kia 2020, 2021; HMMA 2021; Hyundai 2021).

Nonetheless, capacity was instead enlarged at the now 3,000-worker, 390,000-capacity Hyundai Montgomery and 3,075-worker, 360,000-capacity Kia West Point. The former built 336,000 vehicles and the latter 274,000 in 2019. This included the February 2019 introduction of the Kia Telluride full-size CUV in Georgia. In contrast, Genesis luxury sedans and their new CUV siblings continued to be built at Hyundai Ulsan in South Korea, with output of small cars shifted from Korea to Kia Pesqueria since its opening in May 2016. The latter 2,339-worker, 400,000-capacity factory built 286,000 Kia Forte, Kia Rio, and Hyundai Accent in 2019. Expectations for further growth at the Mexican plant were high prior to the advent of COVID-19 in 2020 (see *Ward's* 1968–2020; Jacobs 2016; Kia 2020, 2021; HMMA 2021; Hyundai 2021).

OTHER FOREIGN BRAND PRODUCTION IN THE NAFTA REGION, 1994–2019

Whereas Japanese, German, and more recently Korean automakers have captured the headlines, five other foreign light vehicles brands were assembled in North America under NAFTA. Four of these brands – Volvo, Saab, Fiat, and Renault – had European origins, and the fifth was from China – Anhui Jianghuai Automobile Company (JAC). A sixth, BAIC of China, was in the process of opening a plant. All of these brands have had limited success in North America, with the most persistent among them being Fiat and Volvo.

After failing to make its mark in North America prior to 1993, Fiat made a forceful re-entry into the region in June 2009, when the Italian automaker secured a 20% stake in the bankrupt Chrysler Motors. After meeting three government-defined milestones, Fiat was granted management control over the American automaker in 2011 and complete ownership in 2014, upon which the company was renamed Fiat Chrysler Automobiles or FCA (Jacobs 2016).

In the interim, the automaker launched production of Fiat 500 minis at Chrysler Toluca Assembly in Mexico in December 2010, followed by Fiat Freemont SUVs in March 2011. The bulk of the plant's output at the time was the Freemont's donor vehicle, the Dodge Journey. A total of 457,061 Fiat brand vehicles, including 303,953 Fiat 500 and 153,108 Freemont were assembled at the 5,500 worker, 400,000-capacity FCA Toluca between 2010 and 2019. This included a peak of 71,321 units in 2014. Only 2,345 Fiat 500 were assembled in 2019, with production of the mini concluding that November. Output of the Freemont was discontinued in September 2015 (Jacobs 2016; Coppola 2019).

In addition to the automaker's Mexican production, a total of 9,413 Lancia Grand Voyager minivans were manufactured at Chrysler Windsor in Ontario between September 2011 and April 2013 (restamped Chrysler Town & Country/Dodge Grand Caravan and formerly the VW Routan); 7,028 Lancia Thema sedans were built at Chrysler Brampton in Ontario between September 2011 and May 2014 (rebadged Chrysler 300); and 2,473 Lancia Flavia convertibles were assembled at Chrysler Sterling Heights in Michigan between March 2012 and February 2014 (rebadged Chrysler 200). All of these vehicles wearing Fiat's luxury marques were exported to Europe, before poor sales led to the termination of this practice (see *Ward's* 1968–2020; Jacobs 2016).

On a smaller scale, Renault of France conducted similar activities with its partner Nissan Motors. Overall, 93,446 Renault brand light vehicles were produced at Nissan's Mexican plants between 2001 and 2019. The majority of these were Renault Clio II superminis for Latin American markets, of which 77,378 were built at Nissan Aguascalientes between December 2001 and October 2009. Clio II also were rebadged for Mexico as the Nissan Platina, with assemblies of both peaking in 2005 at 13,543 and 56,554 respectively. Meanwhile, Nissan Cuernavaca produced 6,588 Renault Scenic minivans between January 2001 and February 2004, and 9,480 Renault Alaskan pickups (rebadged Nissan Frontier) between October 2016 and December 2019 (see *Ward's* 1968–2020; Renault 2002–2010, 2020).

As for Volvo, in 1998, after thirty-five years of KD assembly in Nova Scotia, Canada, the Swedish automaker shuttered its plant in Halifax, that plant having built just 8,373 of its S70/V70 line of vehicles that year. Then, in March 1999, stockholders and the European Union approved the sale of Volvo's vehicle operations to Ford. From that point forward until Ford's own problems forced its sell-off of its Volvo business to Zhejiang Geely Holding Co., Ltd. (Geely) of China in March 2010, Volvo cars were imported into North America from either Belgium, Sweden, or the Netherlands (Jacobs 2016).

With Volvo sales moderately improving, and Geely determined to launch its Polestar or its namesake brand in the US market, rumours circulated that the automaker was scouting sites in the US or Mexico to build a car plant. This became a reality in May 2015, when Volvo's Swedish CEO announced plans to build a 150,000-capacity car plant in Berkeley County, South Carolina, near Ridgeville. Manufacture of the Volvo S60 executive sedan commenced in 2018 and the EX90 started in 2023 (Volvo 2023; South Carolina 2023).

Following its takeover by General Motors, Saab of Sweden also sporadically built cars in North America between 2005 and 2011.This included 21,077 Saab 9-7X mid-size SUVs built at GM Moraine in Ohio between April 2005 and January 2009. Another 700 units of its successor, the Saab 9-4X, were next assembled at GM Ramos Arizpe in the Mexican state of Coahuila between January and September 2011. In the interim, in December 2009, GM sold BAIC of China the GM2900 platform tooling and powertrain technology utilized in the first-generation Saab 9-5 and in certain versions of the Saab 9-3 car line. BAIC was not granted the rights to use the Saab brand name. Two months later, GM sold its Saab division to Dutch specialty carmaker Spyker Cars (Jacobs 2016).

Part of the Beijing Automotive Group, BAIC eventually began producing its own badged vehicles in China based on the Saab 9-3 and 9-5, the Senova D60 and D70 respectively. Later, in May 2017, BAIC was reported as having opened a 6,000-capacity KD facility in Puenta Nacional, Veracruz, Mexico, where it was said to be assembling its D20 compact and X25 crossover. Although the automaker registered combined Mexican sales for the two models of approximately 1,500 in 2018 and 2,000 in 2019, none of these vehicles were officially recorded as being assembled at the so-called AT Motors Veracruz plant. This was confirmed in December 2018, when BAIC announced that it would construct a 20,000-capacity factory in Yucatan state by 2022 (Cantera 2018; INEGI 2021).

Finally, BAIC's rival, JAC, opened its 300-worker, 6,000-capacity Giant Motors KD assembly plant in Sahagun, Mexico, in March 2017. The joint venture facility with Inbursa then completed its first JAC Sei 2 subcompact and Sei 3 compact CUVs that April, and finished 1,035 vehicles during that year. This total included 47 JAC J4 compact sedans, which launched in November 2017. After adding Sei 7 mid-size CUVs and Frison T6 pickups in September and December 2018, respectively, Giant Motors assembled 2,954 vehicles in 2018 and then 4,747 in 2019. In October of the latter year, the Sei 4 compact CUV was introduced, followed by the Nissan-derived JAC X200 light work trucks that December. In the process the firm, based in Hefei, Anhui province, became the first and only Chinese automaker to build its brand passenger cars in North America under NAFTA (see *Ward's* 1968–2020; INEGI 2021).

CONCLUSIONS, AND THE FUTURE OF NON-NORTH AMERICAN AUTO PLANTS IN THE NAFTA REGION

At the end of the NAFTA era, there were seventy-one plants assembling cars and light passenger trucks in North America: forty-three in the US, twenty in Mexico, and eight in Canada. Thirty-six of these were operated by the Detroit Three (Chrysler included), one by Tesla, and thirty-four by automakers headquartered outside of North America. The latter, of which eighteen were in the US, thirteen in Mexico, and three in Canada, had a combined capacity of 10,423,000 and produced 7,929,733 light vehicles wearing non-North American brand names in 2019. Overall, foreign brand models accounted for 48.96% of the 16,195,520 light vehicles assembled in the NAFTA region during that year. The percentage was even higher in Mexico, where 56.23% of the units, or 2,122,621 of 3,774,945, were stamped with non-North American marques. Similar to other trends in the region, this growth in production south of the border accelerated after 2009 (see tables 1 and 2).

By comparison to 2019, there were seventy-two light vehicle plants in North America at the end of 1993, numbering fifty-two in the US, twelve in Canada, and eight in Mexico. At that time, foreign-based automakers were the lead operators in sixteen of the plants: eight in the US, five in Canada, and three in Mexico. These sixteen factories had a combined capacity to produce 3,435,000 units wearing non-North American brands, and assembled 2,578,272 in 1993. This meant that foreign transplant output constituted 18.59% of the 13,867,984 light vehicles produced in the three nations in the year prior to NAFTA's promulgation. In other words, while adding a net eighteen assembly plants, new domestic automakers tripled their annual capacity and output during the NAFTA era. Notably, ten of these new plants were in Mexico, where the transplant capacity jumped from 550,000 at the end of 1993 to 3,228,500 in 2019, and final assemblies advanced five-fold, from just 423,759 in 1993.

As shown in tables 1–6, Toyota was the largest new domestic automaker in the NAFTA region in 2019, producing 1,855,915 Toyota and Lexus brand vehicles during that year. Its eight plants – four in the US and two each in Canada and Mexico – employed 31,732 people and had the capacity to build 2,246,000 vehicles at the end of 2019. The bulk of this was in the US, where Toyota assembled 1,194,961 vehicles, had a capacity of 1,380,000 units, and employed 19,638 people. Total employment rose to 31,463 in America and 43,714 in the NAFTA region when Toyota's components plants and headquarters were included. In contrast, Toyota's then three North American plants, two in the US and one in Canada, produced 634,707 Toyota and Geo brand vehicles in 1993, had a related capacity of 850,000, and employed 8,000 people. A total of 555,488 of this 1993 output and 780,000 in capacity was in the US, at Toyota Georgetown and its NUMMI joint venture with GM.

Toyota remains closely trailed by Honda, which assembled 1,817,223 Honda and Acura brand vehicles in the NAFTA region in 2019. Its seven assembly plants – four in America, two in Mexico, and one in Canada – employed 23,650 people and had the capacity to build 1,973,000 vehicles at the end of that year. Employment increased to 30,100 when powertrain and parts plants were included. Roughly two-thirds of this output, capacity, and workforce were in the US, where Honda assembled 1,205,044 light vehicles (beating Toyota), had 1,270,000 in capacity, and employed 14,500 people. Honda engaged another 4,650 at its American components plants. By comparison, Honda's three North American plants, two in the US and one in Canada, produced 504,396 Honda, had capacity to build 620,000 units, and employed 6,000 people in 1993. Of the later, 403,775 in output, 520,000 in capacity, and 5,000 workers were in the US.

Nissan was third, with its four North American factories and joint venture with Mercedes-Benz producing 1,417,570 Nissan and Infiniti brand vehicles in 2019. The Japanese automaker was followed by Hyundai-Kia of Korea at 896,600 and VW-Audi of Germany at 707,769. No automaker after that built as many as 500,000 vehicles in the NAFTA region in 2019. Interestingly, Nissan actually built more vehicles, 624,263, and had more capacity, 730,000, than Honda in North America in 1993. Its two US plants, however, produced just 54% of its total NAFTA output in 2019, as compared with 68% in 1993. Conversely, the VW Group assembled 85% of its North American–built vehicles in Mexico in 2019, as compared with 100%

and 239,077 at VW Puebla in 1993. The massive factory produced 443,414 vehicles in 2019. Meanwhile, after assembling only 14,585 KD kits at its failed Canadian plant in 1993, the Hyundai Group's two American plants built 610,000 Hyundai and Kia brand vehicles, or 70% of its NAFTA total in 2019.

According to a variety of sources, the thirty-four new domestic automaker assembly complexes employed 147,243 people in production, administration, and other on-site support activities: 82,363 in the US, 51,680 in Mexico, and 13,200 in Canada (see table 2). Bivens (2019) estimates that durable goods manufacturing multipliers for the US are 289.1 supplier jobs for every 100 direct jobs and 744.1 indirect jobs. Based on that, new domestic automakers helped create 425,680 off-site supplier jobs and almost 1.1 million indirect positions in the NAFTA region in 2019. If there were strict boundaries, this would have translated into the creation of 612,863 indirect jobs in the US, 384,551 in Mexico, and 98,221 in Canada. In other words, these factories contributed a combined 1.24 million jobs to the NAFTA economy in 2019. Of this, roughly 695,200 of these positions were in the US, 436,200 were in Mexico, and 111,400 were in Canada.

Thus, job growth has been substantial, especially considering the fact that the number of Detroit Three light vehicle plants shrunk by twenty between 1993 and 2019. More specifically, Mexico added two, Canada dropped two, and the US lost a net twenty assembly factories during the period. By comparison, the new domestics increased their plant total by a net eighteen under NAFTA, with US and Mexico gaining ten each and Canada losing two. In other words, both new plant construction and factory closings were very unevenly distributed across the region, with the combined number of assembly facilities contracting by ten in the US and by four in Canada during the NAFTA era, while increasing by twelve in Mexico.

On the surface, this suggested that the US should have lost approximately 30,000 direct production jobs and 223,000 jobs overall between 1993 and 2019. According to the US Census (2023), however, whereas employment in "Motor Vehicle Manufacturing" declined by 10,039 between 1993 and 2018, it increased in "Motor Vehicle Parts Manufacturing" by 179,063 during this time frame. The main reason for this was the massive expansions of new domestic automakers, which added 3,715,000 in vehicle capacity in the US and 6,983,500 overall in the region after 1993. These enlargements created approximately 102,460 new direct jobs in the region, including 56,360 in the US, 8,630 in Canada, and 37,470 in Mexican.

Nonetheless, as mentioned earlier, since the 2009 economic crisis, Japanese automakers have focused their NAFTA region production growth on Mexico. In fact, when it started production in 2021, the Mazda-Toyota factory in Huntsville, Alabama, was the first new Japanese assembly plant opened in the US in ten years. Meanwhile, a new plant has not been built in Canada since 2008. After first establishing themselves in the US, new domestic German and Korean automakers have followed a similar path since 2016. The exception has been VW, which operated exclusively in Mexico between 1989 and 2010. It further strengthened this base by opening an Audi plant south of the US border in 2016. Audi's luxury rivals Mercedes-Benz and BMW soon followed suit. For similar reasons, primarily much lower wages, Chinese automakers will almost assuredly enter the US market through Mexican production.

These trends invite several questions for future research. Will the shift to Mexico continue and accelerate under USMCA? What about Canada: does it have any real chance to attract a new major automaker plant under USMCA? Which companies will be the driving forces behind new plant construction in North America over the next ten years? Will growth in new capacity again be led by the Japanese, or will it be propelled by Chinese carmakers? JAC of China plans to increase output in Mexico to 40,000 per year within the next five years and begin exporting to America during that time frame. Its compatriots BAIC, Geely, SAIC, and Great Wall also plan to enter the US by 2030.

What about Stellantis, the polynational automaker recently created from an unwieldly amalgamation of PSA Peugeot-Citroen of France, GM Europe's Opel-Vauxhall, and Fiat Chrysler of the US and Italy? Will it open a plant for its French brands in the next five to ten years? What about the Indian automakers? Mahindra, which controls Ssangyong Motors, already builds four-wheel drive off-roaders in Michigan. Will it, or Tata Motors, which owns Jaguar Land Rover, launch light vehicle production in North America in the near future?

The answers to these questions will surely create interesting copy during the 2020s. Nevertheless, any such predictions or analysis will continue to require a thorough and comprehensive understanding of North American light vehicle production during the NAFTA era. A cursory knowledge of output during the earlier Canada-US Auto Pact period also would be beneficial.

REFERENCES

Anastakis, Dimitry. 2004. "Building a 'New Nova Scotia': State Intervention, the Auto Industry and the Case of Volvo in Halifax, 1963–1998." *Acadiensis: Journal of the History of the Atlantic Region* 34 (1): 3–30.

– 2005. *Auto Pact: Creating a Borderless North American Auto Industry,1960–1971*. Toronto: University of Toronto Press.

– 2013. *Autonomous State: The Struggle for a Canadian Car Industry from OPEC to Free Trade*. Toronto: University of Toronto Press.

Audi. 2020. *Audi 2019 Annual Report*. Ingolstadt, Germany: Audi AG.

Bivens, J. 2019. "Updated Employment Multipliers for the U.S. Economy." 23 January 2021. Washington, DC: Economic Policy Institute. https://www.epi.org/publication/updated-employment-multipliers-for-the-u-s-economy/.

BMW. 2021. "BMW Group Plants Worldwide." https://www.bmwgroup-werke.com/en.html.

Cantera, S. 2018. "Chinese Car Maker BAIC to Build Plant in Mexico." *El Universal*, 12 December 2018. https://www.eluniversal.com.mx/english/chinese-car-maker-baic-build-plant-mexico/.

Chung, M. 1998. "The Chance for a Peripheral Player: The Internationalization Strategies of the Korean Automobile Industry." In *One Best Way? Trajectories and Industrial Models of the World's Automobile Producers*, edited by M. Freyssenet, A. Mair, K. Shimizu, and G. Volpato, 185–208. New York: Oxford University Press.

Coppola, G. 2019. "Fiat Yanks 500, 500e from U.S. Market." *Automotive News*, 3 September 2019. https://www.autonews.com/sales/fiat-yanks-500-500e-us-market.

Daimler. 2021. "Daimler Global Media Site, Facts and Figures, Mercedes-Benz Ca and Vans Production Locations. https://media.mercedes-benz.com/content/company/locations/international.

HMMA. 2021. "Hyundai Motor Manufacturing Alabama." https://www.hmmausa.com/our-company/about-hmma/.

Honda. 2020. *2020 Honda Digital Factbook*. Updated 31 August. https://hondanews.com/en-US/honda-corporate/releases/release-554e3d8539c7f6db3b88b571930280ab-honda-2020-digital-factbook.

Hyun, Y., and J. Lee. 1989. "Can Hyundai Go It Alone?" *Long Range Planning* 22 (2): 63–9.

Hyundai. 2021. "History." Accessed 26 February 2021. https://www.hyundai.com/worldwide/en/footer/corporate/information/history/1967-2000.

INEGI (National Institute of Statistics and Geography). 2021. "Produccion de vehiculos ligeros por marca y modelo." https://www.inegi.org.mx/app/tabulados/interactivos/?px=RAIAVL_8_9&bd=RAIAVL.

Jacobs, A.J. 2012. "Collaborative Regionalism and FDI: The Case of the Southeast Automotive Core and the 'New Domestics.'" *Economic Development Quarterly* 26 (3): 199–219.

– 2016. *The "New Domestic" Automakers in the U.S. and Canada: History, Impacts, and Prospects*. Lanham, MD: Lexington Books.

– 2022. *The Korean Automotive Industry, Volume 1: Beginnings to 1996*. (New York: Palgrave Macmillan).

JAMA Canada. 2005. *A Short History of the Japanese Automotive Industry in Canada*. Toronto: Japan Automobile Manufacturers Association of Canada.

Karkaria, U. 2020. "Mercedes A-Class Production Heads to Germany, Affecting Canadian Supplier." *Automotive News Canada*, 18 July 2020. https://canada.autonews.com/suppliers/mercedes-class-production-heads-germany-affecting-canadian-suppliers.

Kia. 2020. *MOVE: Kia Motors Sustainability Magazine 2020*. [In Korean.] Seoul: Kia Motors.

– 2021. "Kia Motors Worldwide. https://www.scribd.com/document/511433272/2020-Sustainability-Magazine-Move.

Krampitz Jr, E. (2001). Volvo's US Car Assembly Plant. *Society of Automotive History Journal (June, 2001)*, 1-3.Mazda. 2020. *Company Profile 2020: Mazda in Brief.* Fuchu, Hiroshima: Mazda Motor Corporation.

MBUSI. 2021. "Mercedes-Benz U.S. International Facts and Figures." https://group.mercedes-benz.com/company/north-america/mercedes-benz-us-international.html.

MBV. 2021. "Mercedes-Benz Vans, Charleston." https://mbvcharleston.com.

McDermott, M. 1995. "The Development and Internationalization of the South Korean Motor Industry." *Asia Pacific Business Review* 2 (2): 23–47.

MexicoNow. 2017. "Infiniti Officially Starts Production of the QX50 in Aguascalientes." 30 November 2017. https://mexico-now.com/infiniti-officially-starts-production-of-the-qx50-in-Aguascalientes.

Minchin, T. 2021. *America's Other Automakers: A History of the Foreign-Owned Automotive Sector in the United States*. Athens: University of Georgia Press.

MMC (Mitsubishi Motors Corporation. 2019. "Mitsubishi Motors Facts & Figures." Accessed 7 March 2021. https://www.mitsubishi-motors.com/en/investors/library/fact.html.

Nissan Global. 2021. "Nissan Motor Corporation Heritage." Updated 20 December 2023. https://www/nissan-global.con/EN/HERITAGE/.

Renault. 2002–2010. *Renault Annual Reports* [from 2001 to 2009]. Boulogne-Billancourt, France: Renault.

– 2020. *Groupe Renault: Facts & Figures – March 2020 Edition*. Boulogne-Billancourt, France: Renault.

South Carolina. 2023. "Success Story: Volvo." https://www.sccommerce.com/industries/success-stories/volvo.

Subaru. 2021. "Subaru of Indiana Automotive History." https://www.subaru-sia.com/about#:~:text=In%20January%202003%2C%20SIA%20became,2007%2C%20under%20contract%20with%20Toyota.

Toyota. 2020. "2019 Toyota North American Operations." https:www.toyota.com/usa/operations/map.html.

US Census. 2023. U.S. County Business Patterns CBP Datasets (Washington, DC: US Department of Commerce). https://www.census.gov/programs-surveys/cbp/data.html.

Volvo. 2023. "From Sweden to South Carolina." https://www.volvocars.com/us/l/hometown/.

VW. 1968–2020. *Volkswagen Annual Report 1967–2019*. Wolfsburg, Germany: VW AG.

– 2020. "The Rich History of Volkswagen's Puebla Plant." Press release, 16 July 2020. https://www.media.vw.com/en-us/releases/1354.

Ward's Automotive Yearbook. 1968–2020. Detroit: Ward's Communications.

3

Mexico's Participation in the North American Automotive Manufacturing Industry

Clemente Ruiz Durán

The North American Free Trade Agreement (NAFTA) of 1994 provided the framework for the integration of the economies across its member nations, Mexico, the US, and Canada. The automotive sector provides the most evident example of that process. Since the NAFTA was implemented a series of competitive regional automotive manufacturing clusters have emerged. Those clusters have evolved – and in some cases arisen – throughout the NAFTA region, from central Mexico northward to Canada. The result of that process has been an overall strengthening of the North American automotive industry, particularly in Mexico. Despite that, tensions have occasionally arisen among and within the NAFTA's three member nations. Ultimately, those tensions helped create the conditions for modifications to the framework that binds the economies of its members. For the automotive industry, those modifications included adjustments to the rules of origin underpinning the agreement, and the promotion of higher regional content levels. Those changes are encapsulated in the US-Mexico-Canada Agreement (USMCA) of 2020.

The key automotive-related changes that arose from the USMCA occurred largely because of inconsistencies with respect to labour issues and workplace conditions across the NAFTA's three nations. By the late 2010s, regional (i.e., North American) automotive-based employment had reached approximately 2.3 million. However, that level reflected steady increases in Mexico but declines in the US and Canada. As that process unfolded, wages declined in Mexico yet increased in the US and Canada, further elevating intra-regional debate and anxiety. Through this, conditions were created for the amended provisions that manifest in the new USMCA. (The origins and outcomes of those tensions, at least as they have developed in Mexico, are also explored by Corvarrubias and Dufour-Poirier in chapter 13 of this collection.)

On top of regional concerns about wages and employment levels, North American automotive industry actors have also been increasingly seized by the challenges associated with the industry's transition away from the internal combustion engine (ICE), towards electrification (which Part 3 of this collection – "The Electrification of Mobility" – addresses more thoroughly). As that process takes hold, many regional automotive clusters within the USMCA are seeking to transform their production-based platforms into innovation hubs, a transformation that suggests a requirement for firms and policymakers to expand and reconsider their automotive-based strategies.

This chapter builds on other components of Part 1 of this compilation, "The Post-NAFTA Integration of the North America Auto Industry." It does so by detailing current conditions in the Mexican auto industry and the challenges that country can anticipate under a disrupted technological paradigm. An initial overview of the Mexican auto industry as it has evolved provides the basis for understanding how the new USMCA's requirements, in combination with emerging technological trends, will affect future trends governing automotive manufacturing there.

GLOBAL AUTOMOTIVE PRODUCTION

In chapter 1, Mordue and Sweeney described the post-2000 trifurcation of the global automotive industry as one that stratified the global industry into core, semi-periphery, and integrated periphery automotive manufacturing nations. Table 1 below provides further context for that trend, including important details of where growth (and decline) has subsequently occurred. Data from table 1 show that between 1999 and 2019 global vehicle production grew by more than 63%. (table 1 includes data from 2020, although pandemic and supply chain disruptions cause that year to be an anomaly.) Table 1 also shows that much of that growth occurred in China, where vehicle production grew from less than 2 million in 1999 to 25.7 million by 2019. Thus, more than two-thirds of the growth in the global automotive industry during the post-2000 period happened in China.

The fact that China's automotive industry constituted a large portion of global automotive production growth after 2000 should not suggest that other regions and countries experienced relative stability. In the NAFTA region, for example, table 1 shows that overall automotive production *was* relatively stagnant, dropping by less than 5% from 17.6 million in 1999 to 16.7 million in 2019. However, the table also shows that the period coincided with significant adjustments to each NAFTA member country's share. Production in Mexico, the region's low-cost "integrated periphery," jumped by 157%, from 1.5 million to almost 4 million.

Table 1. Worldwide Vehicle Production, 1999–2020

	Category	1999	2009	2019	2020
Worldwide	Cars	39,759,847	47,772,598	67,149,196	55,834,456
	Commercial vehicles	16,499,045	13,989,726	24,637,665	21,787,126
	World total production	56,258,892	61,762,324	91,786,861	77,621,582
NAFTA	Production	17,633,716	8,760,965	16,783,398	13,375,622
	Production out of total Production out of NAFTA (%)	31.3	14.2	18.3	17.2
Mexico	Production	1,549,925	1,561,052	3,986,794	3,176,600
	Production out of NAFTA (%)	8.8	17.8	23.8	23.7
	Production out of worldwide production (%)	2.8	2.5	4.3	4.1
China	Cars	565,366	10,383,831	21,360,193	19,994,081
	Commercial vehicles	1,264,587	3,407,163	4,360,472	5,231,161
	Total	1,829,953	13,790,994	25,720,665	25,225,242
	Percent of worldwide production	3.3	22.3	28.0	32.5

Source: OICA (2021).

MEXICAN AUTOMOTIVE TRADE

In 1989, Mexico introduced a national automotive decree marking a change in policy from import substitution to export-led development. Since then, and particularly under NAFTA (which came into force in 1994), about 80% of the country's automotive production has been directed to export markets. The overall effect has been that during the post-NAFTA period, the automotive industry has represented the foundation of the country's export-based industrialization strategy. (In chapter 13, Covarrubias V. and Dufour-Poirier list additional free trade agreements Mexico has subsequently negotiated.) Despite Mexico's increasingly outward orientation, as table 2 shows, the US has remained by far the most important market. That said, countries like Germany, Brazil, and China have assumed increasing importance, receiving 5.4% of Mexican automotive exports in 2019 (UN Comtrade 2021).

While the US has maintained its position as the Mexican automotive parts industry's most important market, table 2 shows Mexico has reduced its reliance on the US as a source of imported parts. Between 1995 and 2019, parts imported from China, Germany, Japan, Korea, and Canada increased significantly, mostly at the expense of the US. As subsequent sections of this chapter will reveal, one of the outcomes of that adjustment was elevated levels of tension among US automotive actors, tensions that ultimately manifest in a reconfiguration of local content provisions, from 62.5% regional (i.e., North American) content under the NAFTA to 75% under the USMCA.

Table 2. Mexico's Auto Parts Trade (US$ million)

		Exports							
		US$ millions				Percentage structure			
	Countries	1995	2007	2013	2019	1995	2007	2013	2019
	World	19,458.1	72,046.7	115,773.7	163,536.3	100	100	100	100
1	USA	16,839.6	60,431.7	96,119.6	137,985.8	86.5	83.9	83.0	84.4
2	Canada	1,374.9	2,108.0	4,278.4	8,614.2	7.1	2.9	3.7	5.3
3	Germany	92.5	2,948.5	2,454.5	4,918.2	0.5	4.1	2.1	3.0
4	Brazil	212.3	852.3	2,770.0	2,289.1	1.1	1.2	2.4	1.4
5	China	0.3	280.8	1,791.1	1,601.9	0.0	0.4	1.5	1.0
6	Colombia	54.6	1,001.8	1,127.5	893.1	0.3	1.4	1.0	0.5
7	Japan	5.8	381.1	349.0	807.1	0.0	0.5	0.3	0.5
8	Italy	4.2	42.3	331.2	756.2	0.0	0.1	0.3	0.5
9	Korea	1.6	34.9	284.3	497.8	0.0	0.0	0.2	0.3
10	Chile	176.0	366.1	465.5	426.8	0.9	0.5	0.4	0.3
11	Australia	1.3	306.1	305.6	425.5	0.0	0.4	0.3	0.3
12	Spain	75.5	80.9	144.0	374.7	0.4	0.1	0.1	0.2
13	Others	619.5	3,212.1	5,353.0	3,945.8	3.2	4.5	4.6	2.4

		Imports							
		US$ millions				Percentage structure			
	Countries	1995	2007	2013	2019	1995	2007	2013	2019
	World	8,480.4	35,861.2	59,438.5	71,730.0	100	100	100	100
1	USA	6,720.5	20,856.3	31,846.4	37,264.5	79.2	58.2	53.6	52.0
2	China	13.0	2,677.9	9,894.2	11,827.6	0.2	7.5	16.6	16.5
3	Germany	613.5	2,731.7	2,786.6	4,648.6	7.2	7.6	4.7	6.5
4	Japan	623.0	2,409.3	3,707.6	3,373.0	7.3	6.7	6.2	4.7
5	Korea	39.2	993.6	1,860.9	2,873.7	0.5	2.8	3.1	4.0
6	Canada	48.8	1,197.7	1,958.7	2,322.2	0.6	3.3	3.3	3.2
7	Italy	30.3	190.8	628.2	1,105.9	0.4	0.5	1.1	1.5
8	Vietnam	0.0	3.9	185.7	771.1	0.0	0.0	0.3	1.1
9	Brazil	69.1	1,076.6	1,150.9	743.7	0.8	3.0	1.9	1.0
10	Hungary	1.7	56.4	308.8	637.1	0.0	0.2	0.5	0.9
11	Other countries	321.32	3,667.04	5,110.51	6,162.63	3.79	10.23	8.60	8.59

Source: UN Comtrade (2021).

Table 3. Automotive Original Equipment Manufacturer Production Locations in Mexico

Region	Factories	Location	Production (thousands)	Share(%)
Bajío	General Motors	Silao	333.9	8.7
Bajío	General Motors	San Luis Potosí	283.0	7.4
Bajío	Renault/Nissan/Mitsubishi	Aguascalientes	346.1	9.1
Bajío	Renault/Nissan/Mitsubishi	Aguascalientes	176.5	4.6
Bajío	Honda	Celaya	168.3	4.4
Bajío	Honda	El Salto	36.1	0.9
Bajío	Toyota	Salamanca	24.7	0.6
Bajío	Toyota	Guanajuato	0.8	0.0
Bajío	Mazda	Salamanca	91.8	2.4
Bajío	Daimler	Aguascalientes	55.7	1.5
Bajío	BMW	San Luis Potosí	24.8	0.6
Bajíjo region (total)			**1541.7**	**40.4**
Central	Renault/Nissan/Mitsubishi	Cuernavaca	81.6	2.1
Central	Renault/Nissan/Mitsubishi	Cuernavaca	67.1	1.8
Central	VW	Puebla	443.4	11.6
Central	VW	San José Chiapa	156.7	4.1
Central	FCA	Toluca	267.6	7.0
Central	Ford	Cuautitlán	44.6	1.2
Central	Jianghuai	Ciudad Sahagún	4.7	0.1
Central region (total)			**1065.7**	**27.9**
North-east	General Motors	Ramos Arizpe	241.9	6.3
North-east	FCA	Saltillo	235.5	6.2
North-east	FCA	Saltillo	64.2	1.7
North-east	KIA	Monterrey	286.6	7.5
Northeast region (total)			**828.2**	**21.7**
North-west	Ford	Hermosillo	205.0	5.4
North-west	Toyota	Tijuana	177.5	4.6
Northwest region (total)			**382.5**	**10.0**
National total			**3818.1**	100.0

Source: Deloitte (2020).

AUTOMOBILE PRODUCTION IN MEXICO

As table 3 shows, automotive manufacturing in Mexico occurs in four geographic regions:

1 Central region (Mexico State and Puebla) with about 28% of national automotive production
2 Bajio region (Jalisco, Queretaro, Guanajuato, San Luis Potosi) with about 40% of automotive production
3 North-western region (Coahuila, Nuevo León, and Tamaulipas) with about 22% of automotive production
4 North-eastern region. (Baja California, Sonora, Chihuahua) with about 10% of national automotive production

Beyond production, each of those four regions has reached different stages in their development and specialization. For example, some regional clusters have received mandates for higher value-added activities; Ford and General Motors have developed facilities to conduct engineering research or design functions for Mexican-manufactured prototypes.

REGIONAL CLUSTERS OF NORTH AMERICAN AUTOMOTIVE MANUFACTURING

As Klier and Rubenstein document in chapter 4 of this collection, North America's automotive industry continues a process of rapid integration, facilitated by the movement of completed vehicles and parts across international borders in the so-called Auto Alley. As the map in figure 1 demonstrates, the Auto Alley displays a north-south orientation, with automotive manufacturing stretching from southern Ontario in Canada through the interior of the US between the Great Lakes and the Gulf of Mexico (Pavlakovich-Kochi 2017). In Mexico, as figure 1 shows, vehicle manufacturing occurs in the four regional clusters described in the previous section.

TENSIONS IN THE NORTH AMERICAN REGION: THE BASIS FOR ADJUSTING AUTOMOTIVE PROVISIONS IN THE USMCA

One of the main features of automotive industry trade in North America has been a growing pattern of disequilibrium among the three countries, which has contributed to increasing tension among actors and to the conditions for the USMCA. As table 4 shows, disequilibrium in intra-regional automotive trade resulted in Mexico earning a large trade surplus with both of its NAFTA partners. Table 4 shows that during the period NAFTA was in place (1994–2019),

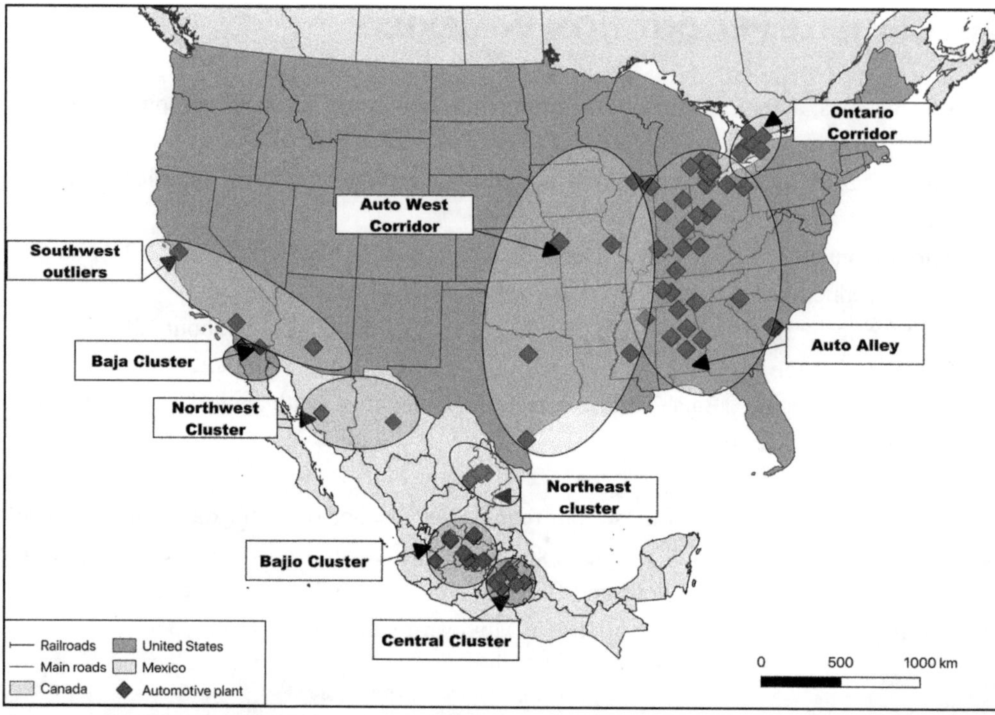

Figure 1. The Geographic Location of North America's Automotive Clusters (Auto Alley)
Source: Author's elaboration with data extracted from INEGI (2020) and Marklines (2020).

Mexico accumulated a surplus in automotive trade with the US and Canada of approximately US $87 billion and US $5 billion respectively. Canada experienced automotive trade deficits with both of its continental partners. Meanwhile the US experienced a substantial deficit with Mexico (US $71.6 billion) and a surplus with Canada ($14.4 billion).

Automotive trade patterns influencing the three NAFTA partners have also been affected by the growing prominence of suppliers from non-NAFTA countries. As table 5 shows, the US share of Mexican automotive imports dropped from 79.2% in 1995 to 52% in 2019. Concurrently, the shares occupied by non-NAFTA countries like China, Korea, and Italy climbed. Regardless of the import share any single country generated, all countries experienced significant growth in absolute dollars, a consequence of rapid assembly growth in Mexico. For example, even though US suppliers' *share* of imports to Mexico dropped by 34.3% between 1995 and 2019, in *dollar terms* US automotive suppliers' exports to Mexico climbed by 554% during that period.

Trade outcomes expressed in absolute dollars notwithstanding, the reconfiguration of automotive assembly – and the adjustments to parts-sourcing decisions emanating from that – contributed to significant discourse, particularly in the US. For example, during the US

Table 4. Matrix of North America Auto Industry Trade, 1994–2019 (US$ millions)

		Exports			
Country	**Mexico**	**USA**	**Canada**	**Total**	**Share (%)**
Mexico	-	120,153.7	7,220.9	127,374.6	60.2
USA	35,574.4	-	30,244.9	65,819.4	31.1
Canada	1,172.7	17,058.3	-	18,231.0	8.6
	36,747.1	**137,212.0**	**37,465.8**	**211,424.9**	**100.0**
		Imports			
Country	**Mexico**	**USA**	**Canada**	**Total**	**Share**
Mexico	-	33,074.7	2,283.1	35,357.8	17.16
USA	121,572.8	-	15,890.7	137,463.5	66.73
Canada	10,041.2	23,137.6	-	33,178.8	16.11
	131,614.1	**56,212.3**	**18,173.8**	**206,000.1**	**100.0**
		Balance			
Country	**Mexico**	**USA**	**Canada**	**Total**	
Mexico	-	87,079.0	4,937.8	95,079.1	
USA	−85,998.4	-	14,354.3	−71,644.2	
Canada	−8,868.5	−6,079.3	-	−14,947.8	

Source: UN Comtrade (2021).

Table 5. Mexican Automotive Parts Imports by Country

	US$ millions				Percentage structure			
Countries	1995	2007	2013	2019	1995	2007	2013	2019
World	8,480.4	35,861.2	59,438.5	71,730.0	100	100	100	100
1 USA	6,720.5	20,856.3	31,846.4	37,264.5	79.2	58.2	53.6	52.0
2 China	13.0	2,677.9	9,894.2	11,827.6	0.2	7.5	16.6	16.5
3 Germany	613.5	2,731.7	2,786.6	4,648.6	7.2	7.6	4.7	6.5
4 Japan	623.0	2,409.3	3,707.6	3,373.0	7.3	6.7	6.2	4.7
5 Korea	39.2	993.6	1,860.9	2,873.7	0.5	2.8	3.1	4.0
6 Canada	48.8	1,197.7	1,958.7	2,322.2	0.6	3.3	3.3	3.2
7 Italy	30.3	190.8	628.2	1,105.9	0.4	0.5	1.1	1.5
8 VietNam	0.0	3.9	185.7	771.1	0.0	0.0	0.3	1.1
9 Brazil	69.1	1,076.6	1,150.9	743.7	0.8	3.0	1.9	1.0
10 Hungary	1.7	56.4	308.8	637.1	0.0	0.2	0.5	0.9
Other countries	321.32	3,667.04	5,110.51	6,162.63	3.79	10.23	8.60	8.59

Source: UN Comtrade (2021).

presidential campaign of 2016, then Republican candidate Donald Trump argued that NAFTA was the worst trade deal ever made (see Wagner and Ries 2018). By 2020, Democrat senator Bernie Sanders was insisting that NAFTA and China trade cost thousands of US jobs (see Greenberg 2020). Both demanded changes to protect US workers. Their expectation was that changes to the NAFTA would enhance employment in the US and that new rules for regional content would reduce the US trade deficit (as captured in table 4).

The subsequent negotiation of the NAFTA's replacement, the USMCA, introduced a series of provisions governing North American regional value content (RVC) and labour value content (LVC) for passenger vehicles and light trucks. Key aspects of those provisions are captured in figure 2. They include RVC requirements for vehicles' core auto parts (including engines, transmissions, body and chassis, axle, suspension systems, steering systems, and advanced batteries), principal auto parts, (tires, rear view mirrors, fluid pumps, air-conditioning parts, bearings, bodies and bumpers, seats and seatbelts, and radiators and mufflers), and complementary auto parts (audio and remote-control equipment, belts, catalytic converters, steering wheels, lighting, locks, and wiring sets). Figure 2 shows that the USMCA also designated content requirements for purchases of steel and aluminium.

For passenger vehicles and light trucks, the USMCA's RVC requirement is 75% (versus 62.5% under the NAFTA). In addition, vehicles' core auto parts must also meet RVC of 75%. As well as setting higher regional content standards, the USMCA also expanded (and updated) the list of parts for inclusion in the RVC and LVC calculations. Additionally, to offset the effect of low-cost Mexican labour, the USMCA introduced a series of provisions specifying that significant portions of vehicle design and manufacturing processes be undertaken by "high-wage" workers. Specifically, the wage requirements stipulated that at least 40% of North American auto content be made by workers earning at least US $16 per hour, averaged by class, model, or plant, with credits for research and development and production (Congressional Research Service 2021).

It is anticipated that reversing investment and sourcing patterns established over the course of the NAFTA's twenty-five plus years of existence will be complex. While rules of origin are important, consistent with the message of Dziczek and Swiecki in chapter 6 of this work, Reinsch et al. (2019) argue that they do not by themselves determine how original equipment manufacturers (OEMs) construct supply chains. They suggest that the automotive industry's decision makers consider a range of factors when sourcing decisions or investment choices are made. For example, decisions about sourcing parts include considerations about supplier's quality, reliability, production capacity, and ability to manage risk. Investment decisions consider unused capacity, access to capital, availability of skilled labour, incentives offered, environmental and fuel efficiency regulations, availability and cost of purchasing inputs, regional/local supplier availability, labour costs, and the capacity of the location in question to support export abroad.

Ultimately, the result of elevated content and wage provisions of the USMCA may include some combination of higher wages in Mexico, increased content from higher-cost US or Canadian sources, or decreased content from countries outside the region, (e.g., China, Germany,

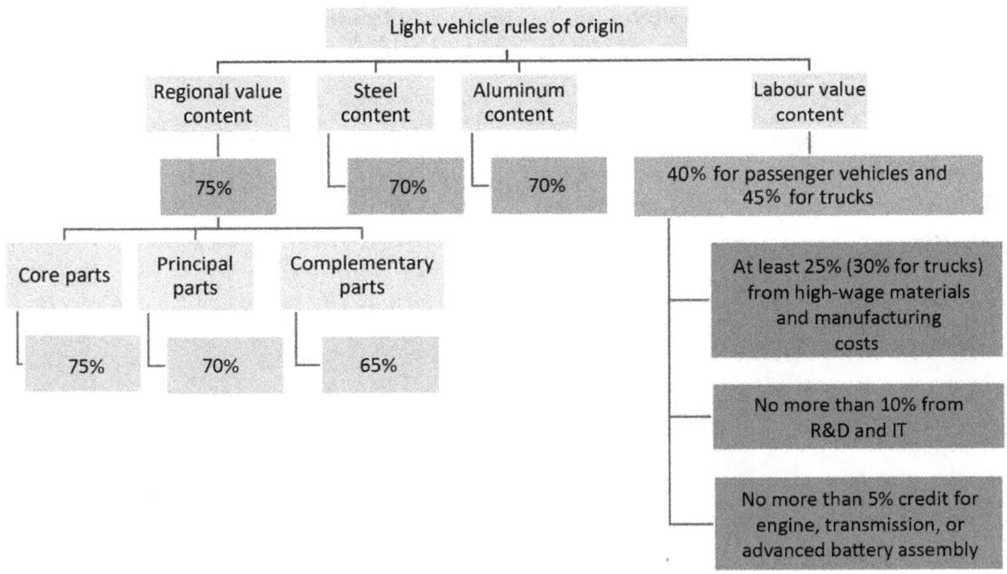

Figure 2. Rules of Origin of Light Vehicles According to USMCA Treaty
Source: US International Trade Commission (2019).
Note: High-wage material can be defined as the parts produced in an assembly plant where wages per hour are sixteen dollars or more on average. Expenses in R&D and IT follow a similar logic regarding high wages.

Japan, and Korea), which table 5 shows now provide more than one-third of imported inputs. Alternatively, it is possible that automotive OEMs will choose to forego tariff-inspired trade decisions altogether, determining that the preponderance of non-tariff sourcing-related factors inventoried by Reinsch et al (2019) and listed above provide sufficient counterbalance. Thus, firms may elect to simply absorb tariffs on completed vehicles, which are 2.5% for the US and 6.1% for Canada.

EMPLOYMENT

Asymmetries between supply chains in developed versus developing countries are common. In developing countries, we find low levels of capital accumulation and weak labour markets. These attributes push large parts of the workforces in such locations into informal segments of the labour market, which causes a negative effect on wages. In fact, Nikulin, Wolszczak-Derlacz, and Parteka (2021) confirm that sectors that experienced major increases in globally intertwined production between 2004 and 2014 underwent wage trends that were worse (i.e., lower) than in industries where no substantial change was registered.

Table 6. Auto Industry: Employment, Earnings, and Productivity

Region	2003	2008	2013	2018	Difference 2003–18
Employment (persons)					
Total	498,975	512,937	722,024	1,206,854	707,879
Northern region	336,851	293,329	431,554	660,833	323,982
Bajío region	55,075	85,975	127,822	298,635	243,560
Central region	63,080	84,101	105,809	151,639	88,559
Southern region	2,415	5,223	18,599	44,089	41,674
Average earnings (in US$)					
Total	8,866	10,205	8,982	7,210	−1,656
Northern region	7,553	8,989	7,868	6,471	−1,082
Bajío region	8,765	10,466	8,013	7,475	−1,290
Central region	10,484	10,458	12,444	8,932	−1,553
Southern region	2,525	659	5,083	5,464	2,940
Productivity (in US$)					
Total	29,981	37,317	39,436	41,288	11,307
Northern region	17,173	23,148	21,968	25,962	8,789
Bajío region	27,857	39,865	31,698	38,193	10,335
Central region	37,551	33,474	74,321	69,261	31,710
Southern region	7,902	13,494	10,663	6,372	−1,530

Source: INEGI (2004, 2009, 2014, 2019).

In the case of the auto industry in Mexico, we have established that employment growth was positive during the period 2003–2018: the largest of all manufacturing industries in Mexico, and only slightly lower than growth experienced by the country's service sector. In Mexico's auto industry employment increased from 498,975 jobs in 2003 to 1,206,854 in 2018. The country's northern region experienced the most dynamic growth with 660,833 total jobs, followed by the Bajío region with 298,635 and the central region with 151,639 (table 6).

As Nikulin, Wolszczak-Derlacz, and Parteka (2021) might have predicted, employment growth in Mexico was not paired with earnings growth during the period table 6 documents. That table shows that rapid employment growth was registered in all regions of Mexico except the southern region and that line growth occurred alongside losses in real wages. Paradoxically, it also shows that wage declines were accompanied by increasing productivity.

Figure 3 provides added context, comparing automotive employment levels across North America during the period 1994–2018. In Mexico, employment grew in a continuous manner with a particularly strong trend noted after 2008. In the US, there was decline for a ten-year period commencing in 1998 followed by modest recovery after 2008. The Canadian experience post-NAFTA implementation can be described as "stagnation."

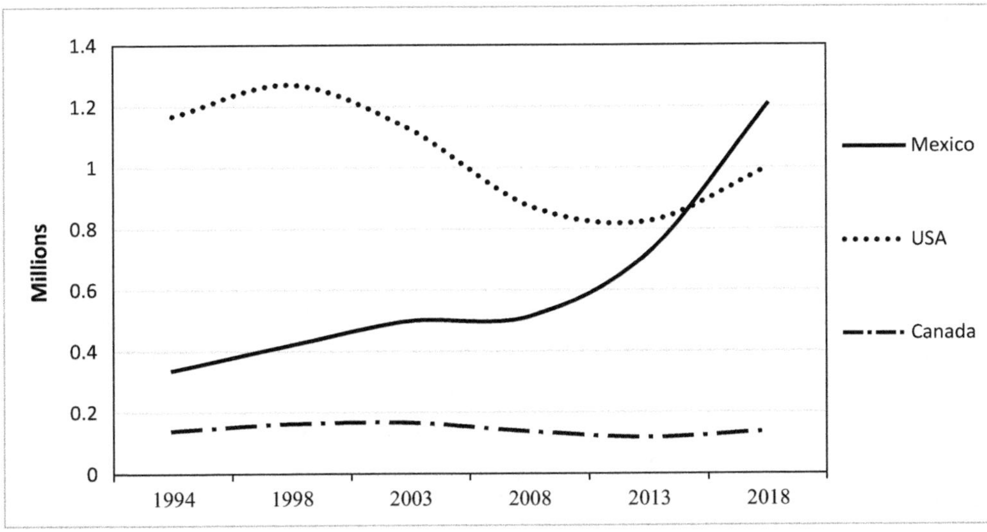

Figure 3. North American Automotive Industry Employment, 1994–2018
Source: Author's elaboration with data provided from US Bureau of Labor Statistics (2021), INEGI (1994, 1999, 2004, 2009, 2014, 2019), and Statistics Canada (2020).

The overall trend of declining automotive employment in the US provided context (and ammunition) for that country's agitation with trade in general and the NAFTA in particular (exemplified by the arguments advanced by Messrs. Trump and Sanders and described above.) As US politicians were expressing irritation, unions in the US were conveying similar forms of unease. However, when the results of the USMCA were revealed, US-based labour was placated, with American Federation of Labor and Congress of Industrial Organizations (AFL–CIO) president Richard Trumka declaring:

> Make no mistake, we demanded a trade deal that benefits workers, and fought every single day to negotiate that deal … Working people are responsible for a deal that is a vast improvement … For the first time, there truly will be enforceable labor standards – including a process that allows for the inspections of factories and facilities that are not living up to their obligations. (AFL-CIO 2019)

The shortcomings related to Mexico's workplaces – and suggested by the AFL-CIO's Trumka – include low labour standards, declining wages, limited worker rights, and weak or non-existent unions. The existence of so-called protection contracts is also prevalent, a situation where labour-management agreements are reached devoid of discussion or approval by the majority of workers. While such agreements give the impression that representation exists, "protection contracts" have the effect of suppressing wages and workers' rights (see Fischer-Daly 2022; Watts, 2019). (For a comprehensive discussion of these matters, including some of the trends influencing and affecting them, see chapter 13 by Covarrubias V. and Dufour-Poirier.)

To arrest some of these trends, Mexico introduced a new framework for labour standards in 2017 and reforms to its labour laws in 2019. Both initiatives are in line with commitments made by Mexico as part of the USMCA. The reforms encompassed modifications and enhancements to dispute mechanisms and included adjustments to increase access to labour courts at the federal and local levels. As well, responsibility for registration of unions and of collective bargaining agreements was assigned to an independent federal body.

Certainly, reforms to labour laws and enhancements to administrative mechanisms do represent progress and will affect workplaces throughout Mexico. Beyond that, additional measures contained in the USMCA will affect automotive workplaces uniquely. Key in that regard is the LVC requirements for automotive parts and vehicles contained in the USMCA, which, according to Uetz (2000), will drive higher wages across the USMCA zone, including Mexico. Thus, as Covarrubias V. and Dufour-Poirier explain in chapter 13, reform to Mexico's labour environment continues to move forward (although significant change will take time).

FUTURE CHALLENGES FOR AUTOMOTIVE MANUFACTURING IN MEXICO

Understanding the post-NAFTA evolution of the Mexican automotive manufacturing industry provides context for consideration of future avenues and options. Looking ahead, the Mexican industry can expect to be buffeted by multiple pressures, not least of which will be the transition necessitated by the profound disruptions that electrification of drivetrains will present. As Kazzaz, Greene, and Yates describe in chapter 9, nations, regions, and firms are announcing targets and making aggressive plans for that transition. Mexico's USMCA partner Canada, for example, has established a target that all new light-duty cars and passenger truck sales will be zero-emission by 2035, an acceleration of its previous goal of 100% sales by 2040 (Canada 2021). In the US, the federal administration has made electric vehicle development a priority, promising to install 500,000 charging stations across the US by 2030, providing incentives to boost purchases of EVs, as well as funding to retool factories to increase the domestic supply of batteries and EVs (Digges 2021). The urgency of managing the transition is captured in remarks by US president, Joe Biden:

> The future of the auto industry is electric. There's no turning back … the real question is whether we'll lead, or we'll fall behind in the race to the future … whether we'll build these vehicles and the batteries that go in them here in the United States or rely on other countries. (White House 2021)

At issue for Mexico is whether the evolving conditions (marked most prominently by the combination of the USMCA's new rules related to local content and wage and labour standards, and by the global trend to electrification) will curtail its post-NAFTA ascendancy as a major automotive manufacturing country. Beyond that, will the post-2000 rise of the automotive integrated periphery described by Mordue and Sweeney in chapter 1 – which has occurred on a global scale and given evidence on a North American basis via Mexico – endure? Will Mexico continue to gain mandates from the foreign-owned automotive OEMs that dominate its automotive industry? Will those investors transform traditional ICE plants into hybrid and electric vehicle operations? Even if they do, Mexico must acknowledge that the process needed to assemble an EV has fewer moving parts and a longer lifespan. In fact, the hours required to manufacture an EV drivetrain are barely half that required for an ICE (International Labour Organization 2020), potentially undermining the low-cost–high input labour model upon which the Mexican automotive manufacturing industry has been based.

Thus, since the 1994 implementation of the NAFTA, Mexico has accumulated a large and successful automotive manufacturing industry. That industry was built on a foundation of low-cost labour, significant investment by foreign-owned OEMs, and unimpeded access to a large and dynamic regional market (dominated by the US and, to a lesser degree, Canada). This chapter has described some of the conditions that gave rise to the NAFTA's replacement, the USMCA of 2020, capturing how some of the new pact's provision might affect the future trajectory of the automotive industry in Mexico. Those measures include the USMCA's requirement that minimum levels of vehicle content derive from higher cost (i.e., non-Mexico) labour. Additionally, measures have been taken to increase union transparency and workplace democracy. These measures, alongside the trend to electrification, have the potential to cause a shift in the trajectory and profile of automotive manufacturing in Mexico. Other chapters contained in this collection explore aspects of that transition. This chapter has provided a foundation for doing so.

ACKNOWLEDGMENTS

The author acknowledges the assistance and support of Jorge García, Rodrigo Chávez, and Rodrigo Arzate in preparing this chapter.

REFERENCES

AFL-CIO. 2019. "AFL-CIO Endorses USMCA after Successfully Negotiating Improvements." Press release, 10 December 2019. https://aflcio.org/press/releases/afl-cio-endorses-usmca-after-successfully-negotiating-improvements.

Canada. 2021. "Building a Green Economy: Government of Canada to Require 100% of Car and Passenger Truck Sales Be Zero-Emission by 2035 in Canada." https://www.canada.ca/en/transport-canada/news/2021/06/building-a-green-economy-government-of-canada-to-require-100-of-car-and-passenger-truck-sales-be-zero-emission-by-2035-in-canada.html.

Congressional Research Service. 2021. *USMC: Motor Vehicle Provision and Issues.* Updated 14 October 2021. https://crsreports.congress.gov/product/pdf/IF/IF11387.

Deloitte. 2020. *Perspectiva Industrial: Industria Automotriz.* https://www2.deloitte.com/content/dam/Deloitte/mx/Documents/finance/2020/Perspectiva-Industria-Automotriz-DEconosignal.pdf.

Digges, C. 2021. "Massive Biden Infrastructure Plan Gives Huge Boost to Electric Cars." 7 April 2021. Bellona Foundation. https://bellona.org/news/transport/2021-04-massive-biden-infrastructure-plan-gives-huge-boost-to-electric-cars.

Fischer-Daly, Matthew. 2022. "Structuring Workers' Bargaining Power in Mexico's StrawberryFields." *Global Labour Journal* 13, no. 1. https://doi.org/10.15173/glj.v13i1.4456.

Greenberg, Jon. 2020. "Sanders Is Correct: NAFTA, China Trade Cost Thousands of Jobs in Michigan." 10 March 2020. https://www.politifact.com/factchecks/2020/mar/10/bernie-sanders/sanders-correct-nafta-china-trade-cost-thousands-j/.

INEGI (National Institute of Statistics and Geography). 1994. "Censos Económicos 1994." https://www.inegi.org.mx/programas/ce/1994/.

– 1999. "Censos Económicos 1999." https://www.inegi.org.mx/programas/ce/1999/.

– 2004. "Censos Económicos 2004." https://www.inegi.org.mx/programas/ce/2004/.

– 2009. "Censos Económicos 2009." https://www.inegi.org.mx/programas/ce/2009/.

– 2014. "Censos Económicos 2014." https://www.inegi.org.mx/programas/ce/2014/.

– 2019. "Censos Económicos 2019." https://www.inegi.org.mx/programas/ce/2019/.

– 2020. "Directorio Estadístico Nacional de Unidades Económicas." https://www.inegi.org.mx/app/mapa/denue/.

International Labour Organization. 2020. *The Future of Work in the Automotive Industry: The Need to Invest in People's Capabilities and Decent and Sustainable Work.* 15 April 2020.ps://www.ilo.org/sector/Resources/publications/WCMS_741659/lang--ja/index.htm.

Marklines. n.d. *OEM Plants – U.S.A. and Canada.* https://www.marklines.com/en/global/usa.

Nikulin, D., J. Wolszczak-Derlacz, and A. Parteka. 2021, March. "Working Conditions in Global Value Chains: Evidence for European Employees." March 2021. https://journals.sagepub.com/doi/pdf/10.1177/0950017020986107.

OICA (International Organization of Motor Vehicle Manufacturers). 2021. "2021 Production Statistics." Accessed 12 May 2022. https://www.oica.net/category/production-statistics/2021-statistics/.

Pavlakovich-Kochi, V. 2017. "Arizona, Mexico, and North America's 'Auto Alley.'" 31 March 2017. https://www.azeconomy.org/2017/03/border-economy/arizona-mexico-and-north-americas-auto-alley/.

Reinsch, W., J. Caporal, M. Waddoups, and N. Tekarli. 2019. *The Impact of Rules of Origin on Supply Chains: USMCA's Auto Rules as a Case Study.* Washington, DC: Center for Strategic & International Studies. https://www.wita.org/wp-content/uploads/2019/04/190403_Scholl_RulesofOrigin_WEB_v3.pdf.

Statistics Canada. 2020. Table 14-10-0220-01: "Employment and Average Weekly Earnings (Including Overtime) for All Employees by Industry, Monthly, Seasonally Adjusted, Canada." Accessed 12 May 2021. https://www150.statcan.gc.ca/t1/tbl1/en/tv.action?pid=1410022001.

Uetz, A.M. 2020. "Calculation of Labor Value Content under the USMCA." *Manufacturing.net*, 27 August 2020. https://www.manufacturing.net/laws-regulations/article/21173049/calculation-of-labor-value-content-under-the-usmca.

UN Comtrade. 2021. "Trade Data." https://comtrade.un.org/data/.

United States International Trade Commission. 2019. *U.S-Mexico-Canada Trade Agreement: Likely Impact on the U.S. Economy and on Specific Industry Sectors.* Washington, DC: USITC. https://www.usitc.gov/publications/332/pub4889.pdf.

US Bureau of Labor Statistics. 2021. “Employment, Hours, and Earnings from the Current Employment Statistics Survey (National).” https://www.bls.gov/data/.

Wagner, M., and B. Ries. 2018. “Trump Gives Remarks on US-Mexico-Canada Deal.” 1 October 2018. https://edition.cnn.com/politics/live-news/trump-us-mexico-canada-remarks-oct-18/h_2c0a8c6bad4dc7a2f98acda7c57ea454.

Watts, Rebecca. 2019. “NAFTA in the Time of AMLO.” In *North American Congress Latin America Report on the Americas* vol. 51(1): 9–12. https://doi.org/10.1080/10714839.2019.1593681.

White House. 2021. “Remarks by President Biden on a Future Made in America.” 18 May 2021. https://www.whitehouse.gov/briefing-room/speeches-remarks/2021/05/18/remarks-by-president-biden-on-a-future-made-in-america/.

4

Spatial Integration of the North American Auto Industry under NAFTA

Thomas H. Klier and James M. Rubenstein

Motor vehicle manufacturing is regarded as an example of a globalized industry. Carmakers that once confined their production and sales to only a few locations now operate around the world. The thousands of parts that go into assembling vehicles may be sourced from dozens of countries. Today's motor vehicle industry, while global in nature, is also highly integrated within specific regions, including North America (Klier and Rubenstein 2015; Pavlínek 2019). While the leading carmakers have global footprints, their cross-border initiatives are principally at the regional scale (Dziczek et. al. 2018, 1).

The extent of regional integration of an industry can be measured through either a macro or a micro approach. Several studies have attempted to measure the level of spatial integration of the North American auto industry at an aggregated level by using the World Input-Output Database. The database, released in 2016, covered forty-three countries and fifty-six industrial sectors for the period 2000–2014 (Dietzenbacher et al. 2014; Timmer et al. 2015; Timmer et al. 2016). For example, De Gortari (2019) uses a macro approach by combining the input-output tables of individual countries to get a better handle on the source of value added by industry. He reports that in 2014, US-produced vehicle parts accounted for 38% of the value added in light vehicles assembled in Mexico and exported from there to the US market.

Klier and Rubenstein (2007) utilized data publicly available through the American Automobile Labeling Act (AALA) to learn about regional integration of the North American auto industry at a micro scale. However, the information available from the AALA is not reported comprehensively for the industry. In contrast, this chapter utilizes comprehensive data on sourcing, albeit on only two vehicle components. We find that while most vehicles assembled in North America source engines and transmissions from within the same region, sourcing is regionally integrated and became more so during NAFTA.

INTEGRATION OF PRODUCTION IN THE AUTO INDUSTRY

Motor vehicles are put together at final assembly plants using thousands of parts made at factories located for the most part in other locations. Early in the twentieth century, Ford and General Motors dominated worldwide production and sales of motor vehicles in part through integration strategies. Ford was the leader in vertical integration, that is, setting up plants to produce parts as well as assemble vehicles (Nevins 1954). William C. Durant initially built GM through acquisitions of a large number of independent parts suppliers as well as independent car makers (Cray 1980).

Menk, Chen, and Cregger (2012) at the Center for Automotive Research (CAR Group) estimated the share of the value of a vehicle associated with the principal elements of production. For a typical vehicle assembled in North America, final assembly accounts for 29% of the value and parts for 71%. Within the parts share, they estimate that an engine accounts for 14% of the vehicle's value, a transmission 7%, body parts 6.5%, interior parts 9%, chassis parts 6.5%, and other parts including electronics 28% (Menk, Chen, and Cregger 2012, 5).

Carmakers continue to produce some of the key parts of a vehicle, including most engines and transmissions. For vehicles assembled in North America, only 5% of engines and 12% of transmissions are outsourced to independent suppliers. Many stampings, such as body panels, are also still done mostly in-house. However, carmakers now acquire most other parts from independent suppliers. In the section that follows, we highlight the role of spatial integration as well as of economies of scale in vehicle production and powertrain sourcing.

AGGLOMERATION ECONOMICS

Enduring economic geography principles, notably agglomeration economics, underlie the pattern of assembling most vehicles in the same region as they are sold (Klier and Rubenstein 2015, 2017). "Agglomeration is the association of productive activities in proximity to one another" (Smith 2009, 14). According to Ellison, Glaeser, and Kerr (2010, 1195), "the benefits of agglomeration ultimately reflect gains that occur when proximity reduces transport costs." They summarize three types of reduced transport costs that encourage agglomeration (1195), as identified by Alfred Marshall in his *Principles of Economics* (1936, 271–3): the costs of moving goods, of moving people, and of moving ideas.

Motor vehicle production typically is highly agglomerated, as it represents what Weber and Friedrich (1929) defined as a bulk-gaining industry (Brincks et al. 2018). Bulk-gaining industries are characterized by a fabricated product that is heavier and occupies a greater volume than its inputs (Rubenstein 1992, 11). To minimize the aggregate costs of bringing in raw materials and shipping out finished products, final assembly in a bulk-gaining industry, such as motor vehicles, tends to locate near consumers (Klier and Rubenstein 2015, 104).

Conversely, a bulk-reducing industry – in which the inputs are heavier or more voluminous than the product – is more likely to be located near the source of the inputs. For example, mills that concentrate, smelt, and refine copper are bulk-reducing industries that locate production facilities near copper mines, their source of inputs.

ECONOMIES OF SCALE

The geography of motor vehicle production and powertrain sourcing is also influenced by underlying variations in economies of scale between final assembly and powertrain production. Economies of scale influence how many plants are needed for assembly operations and for powertrain production (Klier and Rubenstein 2015, 104; Lung 2004; Truett and Truett 1996, 2001, 2003; Wynn-Williams 2009). Importantly, economies of scale in powertrain production are substantially larger than those in vehicle assembly. For example, Husan (1997, 40) cites studies conducted in the 1970s that identified annual economies of scale ranging from 400,000 to 2 million for pressing body panels, from 250,000 to 1 million for powertrain fabrication, and from 200,000 to 300,000 for final assembly. According to Rhys (1977, 316), "motor industry sources put the car assembly optimum output in the range of 200,000 to 300,000 units per year on a two-shift basis, with that for powertrain manufacture being 500,000 identical units."

As a result, carmakers can manufacture in powertrain plants more blocks, heads, gears, and other parts to go into engines and transmissions than they can assemble finished vehicles in a given time period. A single line in a final assembly plant can turn out approximately one vehicle per minute. However, the scale at which a powertrain plant operates is significantly larger. According to Rhys (2005, 264), the optimum scale of engine casting is 1 million units per year, nearly twice as large as that of engine machining and assembly (approximately 600,000 units). Thus, one casting operation can support several engine machining and assembly lines.

A feature related to the differences in economies of scale in vehicle and powertrain production is that engines and transmissions are typically not unique to individual vehicle models but are shared across a range of models. This approach is common to all large-volume vehicle producers, as engines and transmissions not only exhibit larger economies of scale than vehicle production but also different, typically much longer, development and production cycles (Center for Automotive Research 2017).

Our data support findings from the earlier literature about different magnitudes in economies of scale between vehicle assembly and powertrain production. In North America, we calculate mean output in 2016 of 281,000 vehicles at final assembly plants, 421,000 at engine plants, and 526,000 at transmissions plants (table 1). To illustrate the differences in size, figure 1 displays the cumulative distribution of North American assembly, engine, and transmission plants in 2016.

Table 1. Number and Output of Final Assembly and Powertrain Plants in North America, 2016

	Assembly	Engine	Transmission
Number of included plants	63	37	27
Est. mean plant production (000 units)	281	421	526

Source: Authors' calculations based on data from IHS Markit as of October 2017.
Note: Unless otherwise stated, all data exclude vehicle assembly plants that produced less than 50,000 units in 2016, as well as assembly plants performing contract work for carmakers. The estimated mean includes production at engine and transmission plants known to be shipped to assembly plants in North America and an estimate of units shipped to the rest of the world.

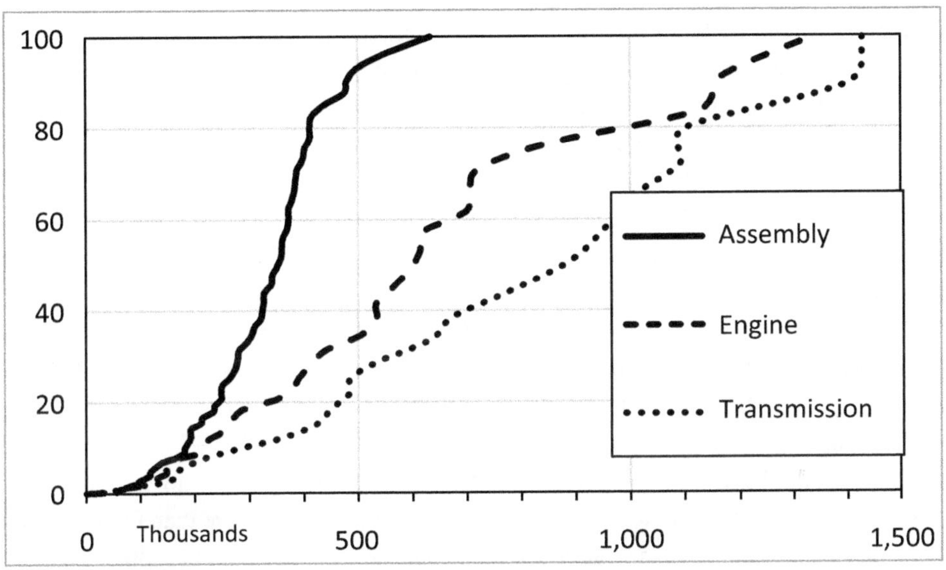

Figure 1. Cumulative Share of Assembly, Engine, and Transmission Plant Output in North America, 2016
Source: Authors' calculations based on data from IHS Markit as of October 2017.

NORTH AMERICA'S EVOLVING TRADE POLICIES

For most of the twentieth century, US-owned carmakers dominated production and sales of vehicles in Canada and Mexico. However, because of high tariffs, stringent rules of content, and other trade barriers, few vehicles produced in one North American country were sold in either of the other two countries.

Prior to the early 1960s, Canada's motor vehicle industry was organized separately from that of the United States (Reisman 1978, 1–25; Rubenstein 1992, 223). Canada's two principal surviving carmakers were outgrowths of its two leading nineteenth-century carriage makers: Gordon McGregor's Walkerville Wagon Works and father and son Robert and Sam McLaughlin's McLaughlin Carriage Company. In 1904, McGregor gave the Ford Motor Company 51% of the stock in his company in exchange for exclusive rights to make and sell Ford cars in Canada and to use the name Ford Motor Company of Canada (Anastakis 2004, 219–20). Ford of Canada retained considerable legal and organizational autonomy until 1948, when Ford-US restructured the Canadian company into a subsidiary (Anastakis 2004, 232).

McLaughlin began to build cars in 1907 by obtaining drivetrains from the Buick Motor Company's plant in Flint, Michigan. Buick and McLaughlin each held a substantial amount of stock in the other company (Pound 1934, 236). When Buick owner William C. Durant formed General Motors in 1908, Sam McLaughlin became vice-president; when Durant lost control of GM in 1910 and bought Chevrolet in 1912, McLaughlin was a major investor and president of Chevrolet Canada; and when Durant regained control of GM in 1916, McLaughlin again was vice-President. General Motors of Canada was incorporated in 1918 and bought McLaughlin and Chevrolet Canada. Sam McLaughlin served as chair of the board of General Motors of Canada until 1967, five years before his death at age one hundred.

Through the 1920s, Canada ranked second in the world in vehicle production and registrations, behind only the United States (Flink 1988, 192; Reisman 1978, 3–4), and third in production and registrations into the 1950s (*Automotive News* 1989, 3; US Department of Commerce, Bureau of the Census 1955, 964). Production was encouraged by a 17.5% tariff on imported vehicles, as well as a 60% Commonwealth content requirement (Lyndon B. Johnson School of Public Affairs 1985, 1). Canadian production benefited from the fact that vehicles could be imported into British Commonwealth countries at a much lower tariff rate from Canada than from the United States (Dykes and Anastakis 2013). In 1929, for example, Canada exported 101,700 vehicles, amounting to 42% of production, with more than two-thirds of the exports headed to other British Commonwealth countries (Flink 1988, 129–30).

According to Dykes and Anastakis (2013), "Ford and GM prospered in Canada through the 1920s because American firms ... took advantage of the British preferential system to export from Canada to other countries at a lower tariff rate, since the goods they built were made in Canada." Thus, prior to the Second World War, Canada's auto industry "had been essentially the export branch of the American industry" (Flink 1988, 252).

However, after the Second World War, "with the expansion overseas of Ford and GM, and the emergence of a European-owned industry producing for a mass market, the relative position of the Canadian industry deteriorated" (Flink 1988, 251). By the end of the 1950s, the Canadian car industry "had lost all its export markets" (Anastakis 2004, 238).

The Canadian government in 1960 appointed the Royal Commission on the Automotive Industry, headed by Vincent Bladen, to investigate the Canadian industry's competitive position. In 1961, the Bladen Commission reported that the fundamental problem was the limited size of the country's domestic market (Reisman 1978, 16–17). Canadian assembly plants and suppliers incurred high costs because they had to produce small batches of a wide variety of models (Rubenstein 1992, 223). Productivity in Canadian plants was "about 60–65 per cent of U.S. levels" (Crane 2006).

In response to the Bladen Commission, the Canadian government adopted the Drury Plan – named for the minister of industry, C.M. Drury – which began a process of dismantling tariffs. Eliminating trade barriers was designed to encourage Canadian parts makers to expand into the much larger US market (Lyndon B. Johnson School of Public Affairs 1985, 2). Ultimately, the United States and Canada negotiated the Automotive Products Trade Agreement of 1965, eliminating all tariffs on vehicles and parts passing between the two countries (Reisman 1978, 26–30). Of more significance, US-owned carmakers provided several letters of understanding guaranteeing a level of production in Canada exceeding the level of sales (Rubenstein 1992, 223; Lyndon B. Johnson School of Public Affairs 1985, 3). The 1965 agreement marked the beginning of the integration of the motor vehicle industries in the United States and Canada. Subsequently, the Detroit-based producers rationalized their operations in Canada and fully integrated them with their US operations. In the process, Canada became a net exporter of vehicles to the United States, exceeding the production-sales ratios agreed upon in the trade pact (see Kumar and Holmes 1998).

Mexico, like Canada, had a long history of motor vehicle production dominated by US companies. As Canada and the United States were dismantling trade barriers during the 1960s, Mexico was reinforcing protection of its auto industry. A 1962 automotive decree required that 60% of the parts in vehicles sold in Mexico be produced in Mexico, and that the respective parts suppliers had to have at least 60% Mexican ownership (Brincks et al. 2018, 5). In response to the 1962 decree, five carmakers constructed or expanded assembly operations in Mexico during the 1960s: Chrysler, Ford, GM, Nissan, and VW. (For more details on Mexico's history of auto industry trade barriers, see Klier and Rubenstein 2015.)

Mexico began to liberalize its trade policies during the 1980s. An 1989 automotive decree reduced the local content requirement to 36% and permitted carmakers with assembly operations in Mexico to sell some imported vehicles (Klier and Rubenstein 2017; Moreno Brid 1996; Womack, Jones, and Roos 1990, 266). The 1990 Programa de Importación Temporal para Producir Artículos de Exportación (PITEX), as well as expanded use of the 1965 Border Industrialization Program (which authorized maquiladora plants), facilitated the duty-free import of parts for use in Mexican final assembly plants (De La Cruz et al. 2011, 4; Klier and Rubenstein 2017; Rice 1998, 380).

The North American Free Trade Agreement (NAFTA) was ratified in 1993 and came into force in January 1994. Efforts to bring Mexico into the North American free trade area had started after Canada and the United States reached a free trade agreement covering the two countries. Its implementation reaffirmed the free movement of parts and vehicles between Canada and the United States and – following a transition period – removed the remaining trade barriers between Mexico and the other two countries. For the first ten years of the agreement, the only carmakers that could take full advantage of the removal of trade barriers were the five that had invested in Mexico during the 1960s (see Klier and Rubenstein 2017 for details of the transitional provisions).

DATA

This chapter relies primarily on data obtained from IHS Markit, which is now called S&P Global Mobility as a result of the merger of S&P Global and IHS Markit in February 2022. The data provide the source of engines and transmissions for every light vehicle produced in North America between 2000 and 2016. Note that the data are compiled from the perspective of vehicle assembly in North America. Because each vehicle with an internal combustion engine features an engine and a transmission, the data show a 1:1 correspondence among assembled vehicles, engines, and transmissions. We focus exclusively on vehicles that feature internal combustion engines and exclude electric vehicles assembled in North America.

Data obtained from IHS Markit enable us to document the location of engine and transmission sourcing in relation to vehicle assembly, thus providing a detailed understanding of the extent of the spatial properties of the supply chain for the two largest (by value) vehicle components. The data do not tell us where the various engine and transmission parts originate. While information on vehicle final assembly is available only for North America, information on the source of engines and transmissions has a worldwide scope. Note that the data do not necessarily account for 100% of engines and transmissions produced at powertrain plants in North America, as some of their output may be exported to assembly plants outside of North America.

CHANGING PRODUCTION FOOTPRINT

We describe the changing geography of vehicle production during the three decades of NAFTA by means of two patterns: changes in the distribution of production facilities among Canada, Mexico, and the United States, and changes in the movement of powertrains and vehicles across the borders of the three countries. This section focuses on the location of final assembly and powertrain plants among the three countries. The next section discusses cross-border movement among the three countries with a focus on the linkages between final assembly operations and powertrains.

Final Assembly Plants

North America had sixty-six final assembly plants that produced at least 50,000 vehicles in 2020. (In 2020, eight assembly plants, representing less than 1% of North America's total vehicle production, produced fewer than 50,000 vehicles.) The sixty-six plants comprised seven in Canada, nineteen in Mexico, and forty in the United States. These plants produced 13.3 million vehicles, including 1.4 million in Canada, 3.0 million in Mexico, and 8.8 million in the United States. Canada thus assembled 11% of the vehicles, Mexico 23%, and the United States 66% (table 2).

Table 2. Assembly Plants and Output, 1990 and 2020

	1990			2020		
	# Plants	Output*	Share	# Plants	Output*	Share
Canada	11	1.9	15.1	7	1.4	10.9
Mexico	8	0.8	6.5	19	3.0	22.8
US	57	9.8	78.4	40	8.8	66.4
Total	76	12.6	100	66	13.3	100

* Million vehicles
Source: Automotive News Data Center.

Table 3. Assembly Plant Openings and Closures by Decade, 1990-2020

		1990-2000		2000-10		2010-20		
	Open in 1990	Closed	Opened	Closed	Opened	Closed	Opened	Open in 2020
Canada	11	1	0	4	1	0	0	7
Mexico	8	2	3	0	2	0	8	19
US	57	7	3	21	11	5	2	40
Total	76	10	6	25	14	5	10	66

Source: Automotive News Data Center.

Table 4. Light Vehicle Production by Country and Decade, 1990-2020

	Volume (million vehicles)				Share of regional production (%)			
	1990	2000	2010	2020	1990	2000	2010	2020
Canada	1.9	2.9	2.1	1.4	15.1	16.9	17.1	10.9
Mexico	0.8	1.9	2.3	3.0	6.5	10.9	19.0	22.8
US	9.8	12.5	7.8	8.8	78.4	72.2	63.9	66.4
Total	12.6	17.3	12.2	13.3	100.0	100.0	100.0	100.0

Source: Automotive News Data Center.

We next document changes in the distribution and output of assembly plants between 1990 and 2020. Breaking down the assembly plant count and production volume for each of the three decades reveals distinctive patterns of change for each of the three countries.

In 1990, before the implementation of NAFTA, the region was home to seventy-six final assembly plants: eleven in Canada, eight in Mexico, and fifty-seven in the United States (table 3). During the three decades of NAFTA, one final assembly plant was opened and five plants were closed in Canada, thirteen were opened and two were closed in Mexico, and sixteen were opened and thirty-three were closed in the United States.

Production in 1990 totalled 1.9 million vehicles in Canada (15% of regional output), 800,000 in Mexico (7% of regional output), and 9.8 million vehicles in the United States (78% of regional output). Production in Canada declined from 1.9 million vehicles in 1990 to 1.4 million in 2020, increased from 800,000 to 3.0 million in Mexico, and decreased from 9.8 million to 8.8 million in the United States (table 4). Between 1990 and 2020, the share of the NAFTA region's assembly output declined from 15% to 11% in Canada, increased from 7% to 23% in Mexico, and declined from 78% to 66% in the United States.

Assembly Changes by Decade

The total number of assembly plants in North America declined by about 13% between 1990 and 2020. The change in assembly plant counts varied by decade: during the 1990s the plant count declined slightly, and between 2000 and 2010 it fell quite noticeably, only to increase somewhat during the 2010s. Meanwhile, total light vehicle production in North America increased substantially during the 1990s, decreased sharply between 2000 and 2010, and increased modestly during the 2010s. Note that overall regional vehicle production was roughly equivalent in 1990, 2010, and 2020.

1990–2000. In the first years after NAFTA, production in Mexico more than doubled, from 800,000 in 1990 to 1.9 million in 2000. However, the assembly plant count changed modestly, increasing on net by only one. Mexico featured eight assembly plants in 1990, two each by Chrysler, Ford, and General Motors and one each by Nissan and Volkswagen. Chrysler and GM each had one plant dating back to the 1930s; both of these plants were replaced during the 1990s. Thanks to these replacements, production increased between 1990 and 2000 from 74,000 to 445,000 at GM's two Mexican plants and from 108,000 to 405,000 at Chrysler's two Mexican plants. By opening a second plant in Mexico in what would later become a massive production centre at Aguascalientes in 1992, Nissan more than tripled its Mexican production during the 1990s from 98,000 to 313,000.

Similarly, Canada and the United States both experienced increasing production during the 1990s while the number of assembly plants in both countries slightly declined. In Canada, mean production increased at Detroit Three plants from 260,000 in 1990 to 300,000 in 2000 and at Honda and Toyota plants from 86,000 in 1990 to 255,000 in 2000. Most of the closures were old GM plants, whereas the newcomers were Japanese-owned plants. By closing six plants during the 1990s, GM increased its mean plant production from 144,000 in 1990 to 211,000 in 2000. Overall in North America, average output per assembly plant increased from 170,000 in 1990 to 240,000 in 2000. The substantial increase in mean production was largely attributable to the diffusion of Japanese-inspired lean production processes into North America's assembly plants during the decade, including at many older plants that the Detroit Three carmakers modernized (Womack, Jones, and Roos 1990).

2000–2010. The first decade of the twenty-first century saw a substantial decline in production in North America, from 17.3 million to 12.2 million vehicles, as the severe recession of 2008–9 was still affecting the industry in 2010. The United States experienced the sharpest decline in production, from 12.5 million vehicles in 2000 to 7.8 million in 2010, a 38% decline. During the decade, twenty-one assembly plants closed, most of them plants by the Detroit Three carmakers. That was partially offset by eleven assembly plant openings, primarily by Asian and German carmakers. The decline of light vehicle production in Canada was not quite as severe: 28%. Production and plant count increased during the decade in Mexico, but only modestly.

2010–2020. The most significant feature of North America's assembly operations during the 2010s was the substantial investment in new assembly plants in Mexico. Eight new final assembly plants were opened in Mexico, mostly by carmakers with minimal if any prior operations in the country, including Audi, BMW, Honda, Hyundai, Mazda, Mercedes-Benz (jointly with Nissan), and Toyota. Nissan also added a second assembly plant in Aguascalientes. The delay in the observed growth in vehicle assembly capacity in Mexico in relation to when NAFTA became effective in 1994 is related to one of the agreement's features. It specified a ten-year period subsequent to the implementation of NAFTA during which newcomers were precluded from taking advantage of duty-free movement between Mexico and the United States. To be able to sell their output in Mexico, auto firms not producing there when NAFTA began had to have around 30% of their vehicles' parts originate in that country; however, this onerous requirement for new entrants was phased out by 2003 (Womack 1994). Even though production had not yet ramped up to full capacity at all new assembly plants by 2020, Mexico had increased its overall vehicle production from 2.3 million to 3.0 million units in the most recent decade, increasing the country's share of the regional total from 19.0 to 22.8%.

Canada saw no change in its assembly plant count. However, its plants suffered a steep decline in production during the 2010s, from 2.1 million to 1.4 million vehicles, representing a drop from 17.1 to 10.9% of the regional total. In the United States, six new assembly plants opened and three existing ones closed during the decade. Light vehicle production increased during the 2010s, in both absolute and relative terms. The bump from 63.9% to 66.4% of the regional total represented the first increase in the country's share since the 1970s.

In summary, between 1990 and 2020 vehicle production increased modestly in North America as a whole yet was rebalanced across the three countries. Production increased substantially in Mexico and decreased in Canada and in the United States. Similarly, during the thirty-year period, the number of assembly plants decreased in Canada and the United States and increased in Mexico. Changes were most pronounced in the United States during the first decade of the twenty-first century and in Canada and Mexico during the 2010s. With the inclusion of Mexico in the North American free trade zone we observed a rebalancing of production within North America. That process played out over several decades and involved both the Detroit-based as well as foreign-headquartered vehicle producers. By 2020, foreign-headquartered producers accounted for the majority of light vehicle production in Mexico (figure 2).

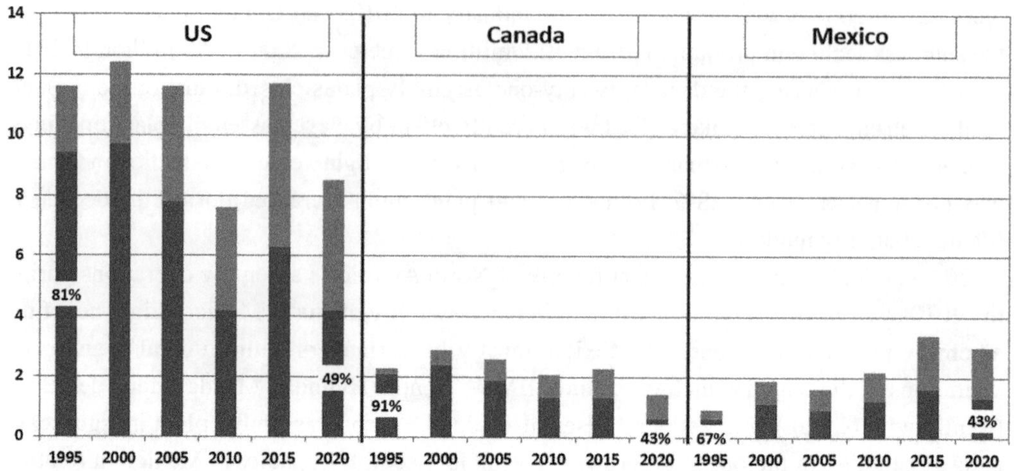

Figure 2. Light Vehicle Production by Original Equipment Manufacturer Type and Country (Million Units)
Source: Authors' calculations based on Ward's Intelligence (https://wardsintelligence.informa.com/datacenter).
Note: The darker portions of the bars represent the share of production by Detroit Three carmakers, and the lighter portions represent foreigh-headquartered carmakers.

Powertrain Plants

In 2020 North America was home to thirty-eight engine plants that produced at least 50,000 units: four in Canada, eleven in Mexico, and twenty-three in the United States (table 5). The region featured twenty-three transmission plants, one in Canada, seven in Mexico, and fifteen in the United States.

Overall change 1990–2020. The distribution of powertrain plants changed between 1990 and 2020 in the following way. During the three decades of NAFTA, the region gained a net of twelve engine plants and six transmission plants. Twenty-two engine plants started production and ten stopped. Note the terms "start" and "stop," rather than "open" and "close." Many of the facilities that stopped manufacturing powertrains remained open for other activities, such as final assembly. Eighteen transmission plants started production and twelve stopped.

Between 1990 and 2020, engine production started at two plants in Canada, six plants in Mexico, and fourteen plants in the United States. Engine production stopped at one plant each in Canada and Mexico and eight in the United States. Transmission production started at one plant in Canada, six in Mexico, and eleven in the United States; it stopped at one plant in Canada, none in Mexico, and eleven in the United States. Thus, Mexico gained a net of five engine plants and six transmission plants, thereby substantially increasing the country's powertrain production footprint. The United States gained six engine plants, not quite maintaining its

Table 5. Powertrain Plant Changes by Decade, 1990–2020

		1990–2000		2000–10		2010–20		
	Open in 1990	Closed	Opened	Closed	Opened	Closed	Opened	Open in 2020
Engine plants								
Canada	3	0	1	1	1	0	0	4
Mexico	6	0	1	1	1	0	4	11
US	17	1	5	3	7	4	2	23
Total	26	1	7	5	9	4	6	38
Transmission plants								
Canada	1	0	0	0	0	1	1	1
Mexico	1	0	1	0	3	0	2	7
US	15	2	5	4	3	5	3	15
Total	17	2	6	4	6	6	6	23

Source: Authors' calculations based on data from IHS Markit as of October 2017 and from Automotive News Data Center.

regional share, with no change in the number of transmission plants, and Canada had virtually no change in either.

The changing role of each of the three North American countries as a source for powertrains utilized in North American vehicle production between 2000 and 2016 is shown in table 6. Between 2000 and 2016, Mexico gained a substantial share: for vehicles assembled in North America the share of engines sourced from Mexico increased from 10 to 23% and the share of transmissions from 2 to 19%. The United States and Canada both experienced declines in their shares of engine and transmission sourcing. Canada's share of engine sourcing for North American assembly fell from 12 to 5%, and its share of transmission sourcing from 5 to 1%. The US share of engine sourcing decreased from 66 to 58% and for transmission sourcing from 68 to 56%.

Imports from outside North America accounted for around one-eighth of engines and one-fourth of transmissions shipped to the region's final assembly plants in 2016. The share of imports changed only modestly between 2000 and 2016, from 12 to 14% for engines and from 25 to 24% for transmissions.

Engines and transmissions are shipped from plants elsewhere in the world for two principal reasons. One reason for importing powertrains is the varying economies of scale between final assembly plants and powertrain plants. Given that a powertrain plant operates most efficiently at a higher volume of output than a final assembly plant, a carmaker entering or expanding in the North American market needs to build up its assembly operations to a volume that justifies investment in powertrain plants.

Table 6. Powertrain Sourcing by Country, 2000 and 2016 (%)

	Engine		Transmission	
Source country	2000	2016	2000	2016
Canada	12.4	5.1	5.4	1.1
Mexico	9.8	23.0	1.6	19.0
US	66.2	57.8	67.9	56.4
Other regions	11.6	14.1	25.1	23.5
Number (million vehicles)	**17.1**	**17.6**	**17.1**	**17.6**

Source: Authors' calculations based on data from IHS Markit as of October 2017.

Another reason for maintaining imported powertrains is that demand in North America for a particular type of engine or transmission may be low enough in that region so that it is more efficient to ship it from a plant elsewhere in the world where demand is higher. Examples include small-litre engines and manual transmissions.

Changes by decade. The total number of both engine and transmission plants in North America increased in all three decades, growing by 46 and 35%, respectively. This consistent increase in powertrain plants deviates from the pattern for final assembly operations, which declined by 13% between 1990 and 2020.

The United States accounted for most of the change in powertrain plants during the 1990s. During the first decade of the twenty-first century, the United States accounted for the NAFTA region's increase in engine plants but experienced a decline in transmission plants. During the 2010s, the US plant count declined for both engines and transmissions. Meanwhile, during the 2010s only Mexico experienced a net increase in powertrain plants.

What accounts for the discrepancy between changes in assembly plants and changes in powertrain plants? Due to the larger scale of powertrain plants compared to vehicle assembly plants, there is typically a time lag of several years between when car companies open assembly plants and when they open powertrain plants. As a rule of thumb, it takes at least two assembly plants to generate enough demand to site one engine plant or one transmission plant in the same region. In the aggregate, that can explain the pattern described above. For example, as discussed in the next section, Honda opened its first assembly plant in Mexico a decade before starting to produce powertrains in Mexico. Honda commenced powertrain production in Mexico the same year as it opened its second assembly plant there.

CROSS-BORDER SUPPLY CHAIN LINKAGES

The extent of cross-border linkages within North America can be displayed especially well through patterns of assembly plant sourcing of engines and transmissions. This study is able to

Table 7. Number of Powertrain and Assembly Plants by Country, 2020

	Final assembly		Engine		Transmission	
Location	Number	Share (%)	Number	Share (%)	Number	Share (%)
Canada	7	10.6	4	10.5	1	4.2
Mexico	19	28.8	11	28.9	7	23.0
US	40	60.6	23	60.5	15	65.2
Total	66	100.0	38	100.0	23	100.0

Source: Authors' calculations based on data from IHS Markit as of October 2017 and from Automotive News Data Center.

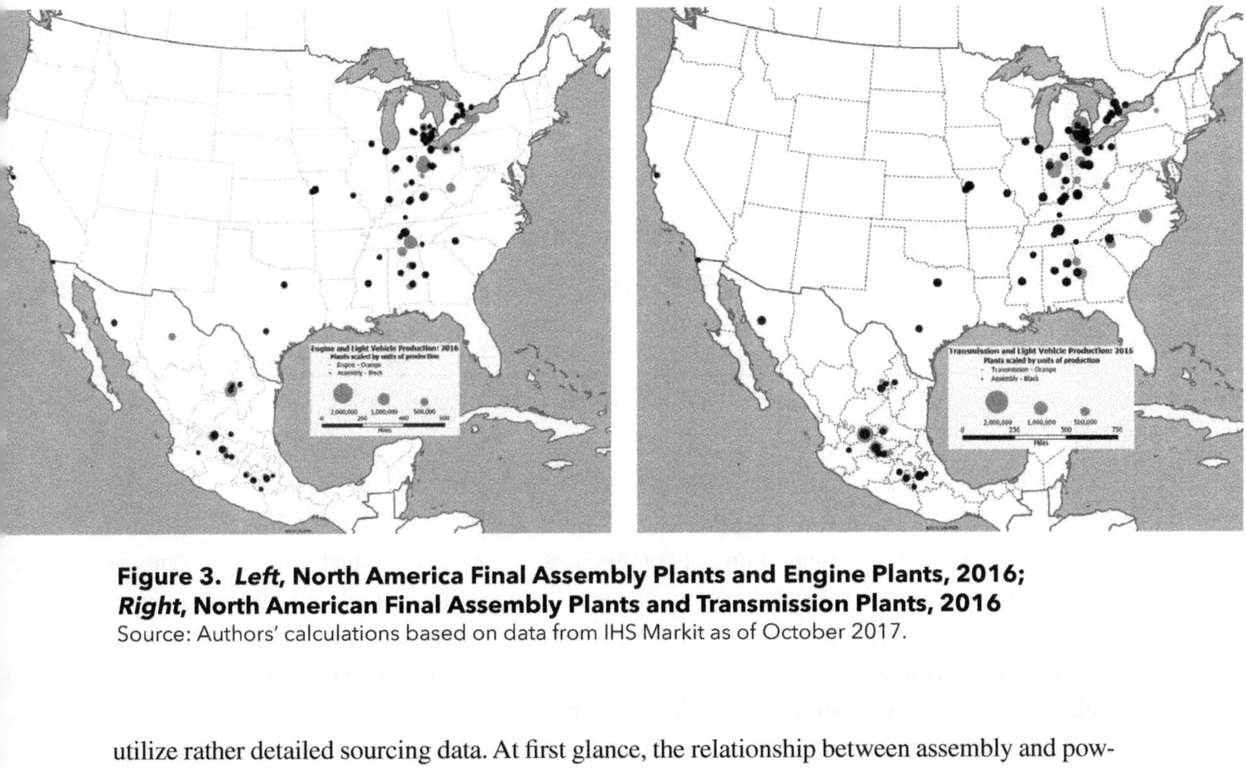

Figure 3. *Left,* North America Final Assembly Plants and Engine Plants, 2016; *Right,* North American Final Assembly Plants and Transmission Plants, 2016
Source: Authors' calculations based on data from IHS Markit as of October 2017.

utilize rather detailed sourcing data. At first glance, the relationship between assembly and powertrain operations within North America would appear to be straightforward, as the share of final assembly plants and engine plants hosted by each of the three countries is nearly identical. The United States has around 60% of final assembly and engine plants, Mexico around 30% of each, and Canada around 10% of each (table 7). The share of transmission plants is slightly lower in Canada and Mexico and slightly higher in the United States. The similarities might suggest that there is little need for cross-border shipments of powertrains within the region.

Figure 3 illustrates the close spatial relationship between the locations of powertrain and vehicle assembly plants.

Table 8. Powertrain Sourcing Compared with Vehicle Assembly Operations (%)

	Engine		Transmission	
	2000	2016	2000	2016
Same country as final assembly	57.7	54.9	49.4	48.8
Different country in NAFTA	30.7	30.9	25.5	27.8
Elsewhere	11.6	14.1	25.1	23.3

Source: Authors' calculations based on data from IHS Markit as of October 2017.

Table 9. Origin and Destination of Powertrains Used in North American Assembly (%)

	From Canada		From Mexico		From US		From elsewhere	
	2000	2016	2000	2016	2000	2016	2000	2016
From engine plant to assembly plant								
To Canada	18.2	6.7	1.0	9.2	75.2	82.5	5.6	1.6
To Mexico	8.6	3.2	44.8	54.0	33.9	16.5	12.8	26.2
To US	11.6	5.3	6.7	16.7	68.9	64.9	12.8	13.1
From transmission plant to assembly plant								
To Canada	0.0	7.5	0.4	11.9	90.2	58.2	9.4	22.4
To Mexico	2.3	0.0	7.3	30.1	37.0	34.3	53.4	35.6
To US	7.1	0.1	1.0	17.2	67.3	62.6	53.4	24.6

Source: Authors' calculations based on data from IHS Markit as of October 2017.

However, table 7 and figure 3 do not communicate the extent to which assembly plants in one country source their powertrains from plants in another country. Overall, only around one-half of engines and around one-half of transmissions are sourced from the same country that is home to the vehicle assembly plant (table 8). The other one-half is sourced elsewhere, from either other countries in North America or other regions of the world.

For North America as a whole, sourcing patterns did not change significantly between 2000 and 2016 for either engines or transmissions. At this level of aggregation, NAFTA appears to have had little impact on cross-border powertrain sourcing.

However, when the sourcing of powertrains is disaggregated among the three countries, more nuanced patterns emerge. US vehicle assembly plants source about two-thirds of their engines and transmissions from US powertrain plants, though in both engines and transmissions that share declined between 2000 and 2016 (table 9). During the same time period US assembly plants increased sourcing from Mexico from 7% in 2000 to 17% in 2016 for engines

Table 10. Share of Powertrain Sourced in Same Country as Assembly Plant by Component, 2016

Canada total share of North American production	13.4
Both engine & transmission	0.0
Engine only	0.9
Transmission only	1.0
Neither engine nor transmission	11.5
Mexico total share of North American production	19.5
Both engine & transmission	3.9
Engine only	6.6
Transmission only	1.9
Neither engine nor transmission	7.1
US total share of North American production	67.0
Both engine & transmission	27.0
Engine only	16.3
Transmission only	14.8
Neither engine nor transmission	8.9
All 3 countries total share of North American production	100.0
Both engine & transmission	30.9
Engine only	23.8
Transmission only	17.7
Neither engine nor transmission	27.5

Source: Authors' calculations based on data from IHS Markit as of October 2017.

and from 1% to 17% for transmissions. Sourcing of powertrains from Canada declined for both engines and transmissions.

With limited domestic facilities, Canadian assembly plants get very few powertrains from domestic sources, only around 7% in 2016 for both engines and transmissions. The share of engines sourced from the United States increased from 75% in 2000 to 83% in 2016, whereas the share of transmissions from the United States declined sharply from 90% to 58%, offset by increases from Mexico and imports from outside North America.

Light vehicle assembly plants located in Mexico increased domestic powertrain sourcing between 2000 and 2016, modestly in the case of engines and sharply in the case of transmissions. For engines, Mexican assembly plants reduced sourcing from the United States and increased sourcing from outside North America. For transmissions, sourcing from domestic plants largely replaced imports from abroad.

When we compare the geography of vehicle assembly, as well as engine and transmission sourcing, for North America as a whole, the importance of cross-border linkages becomes more visible. Only 31% of vehicles produced in North America in 2016 were assembled in the same country from which the engine and transmission were sourced (table 10). Four per

Table 11. Same-Country Sourcing of Powertrains (%)

	Percent sourced in same country as assembly plant				
Assembly plant location	Both engine & transmission	Engine only	Transmission only	Neither engine nor transmission	2016 assembly output (million vehicles)
Canada	0.0	6.7	7.5	85.8	2.4
Mexico	20.1	33.8	9.9	36.2	3.5
US	40.3	24.4	22.1	13.2	11.9
Overall	**30.9**	**23.8**	**17.8**	**27.5**	**17.7**

Source: Authors' calculations based on data from IHS Markit as of October 2017.

cent of vehicles produced in North America had final vehicle assembly, as well as engine and transmission production in Mexican plants, and 27% had all three activities take place in US plants. No vehicles were assembled in Canada with both Canadian engines and Canadian transmissions. Another 24% of all vehicles assembled in North America had the engine sourced from the same country as the final assembly plant, and 18% of vehicles had transmissions sourced from the same country as the final assembly plant. Importantly, nearly 28% of vehicles assembled in North America in 2016 sourced both engine and transmission from a different country.

Alternatively, one can break down the geography of powertrain sourcing by vehicle assembly country. The three countries display differences in same-country sourcing, understandably given the widely varying magnitude of production. In 2016, 40% of vehicles assembled in the United States sourced both engines and transmissions from US powertrain plants (table 11). The remaining 60% included 24% with a US-sourced engine but not transmission, 22% with a US-sourced transmission but not engine, and 13% with neither engine nor transmission sourced from US plants.

Only 20% of the vehicles produced in Mexico's assembly plants had both engines and transmissions sourced from Mexican powertrain plants, although 34% had a Mexican engine. As already noted in table 11, not a single vehicle assembled in Canada in 2016 had both an engine and a transmission sourced from Canadian plants; 86% of the country's vehicle output sourced both engine and transmission from plants in other countries, for the most part the United States.

Median distance between powertrain and final assembly plants. Although powertrain plants and final assembly plants are typically clustered in relative proximity to each other, the distances that engines and transmissions travel from production to vehicle assembly can be relatively large. The reason is that assembly plants do not get all of their engines and transmissions from the nearest powertrain plants.

Table 12. Median Distance (km) from Powertrain Plants to Assembly Plants, 2016

Median distance (km) to final assembly plant	From engine plant	From transmission plant
Canada	689	744
Mexico	676	3,381
US	552	808
Auto alley	*480*	*616*
Other	*1,624*	*1,574*
Total	**605**	**1,167**

Source: Authors' calculations based on data from IHS Markit as of October 2017.

Table 13. Share of Powertrains Shipped Less than 725 km (One-Day Delivery)

Percent shipped less than 725 km	Engines	Transmissions
US	63.4	46.3
Auto alley	*70.4*	52.4
Other	*9.9*	*0.0*
Canada	76.2	*45.6*
Mexico	54.0	28.8
Total	**63.3**	**42.8**

Source: Authors' calculations based on data from IHS Markit as of October 2017.

We utilize the median to measure distances between powertrain production and final assembly operations. For our analysis, this measure provides a meaningful metric, as a relatively small number of engines and transmissions are shipped from other regions of the world, corresponding to long shipping distances. That would inflate the mean much more than the median.

In 2016, the overall median distance to final assembly plants was 605 kilometres from engine plants and 1,167 kilometres from transmission plants (table 12). For engines, the median shipping distance to final assembly plants is nearly identical for the three countries. The only outliers are assembly plants in the United States outside of auto alley. For transmission plants, median distance is nearly identical for assembly plants in Canada and the United States, in both cases that metric is a bit higher than for engines. The exception is Mexico, whose assembly plants are receiving many of the transmissions from relatively distant plants in Europe and Asia.

One-day delivery. In principle, carmakers seek to minimize transportation between powertrain and assembly plants. Given the limitation on the amount of time that a truck can be driven before the driver needs to stop for an extended rest period, locating plants to maximize same-day delivery is an important factor. Specific one-day driving distances can vary, depending on prevailing road and driving conditions. Consistent with the literature, we use a distance of 725 kilometres (450 miles) as a rule of thumb for daily delivery distance (Klier and Rubenstein 2017).

In 2016, final assembly plants received 63% of their engines from production facilities located within 725 kilometres (table 13). The share of one-day delivery of engines was comparable in all three countries. We find transmissions less likely to be shipped than engines from plants within one-day delivery range. Mexico exhibits a noticeably lower level of transmission sourcing from within the 725 km distance, as a relatively large share of transmissions used for vehicle assembly in Mexico are sourced from Europe and Asia.

CASE STUDY: HONDA NORTH AMERICA

Once the production footprint of a carmaker in a production region is large enough to support several powertrain plants, the location decisions get rather complex, as in all likelihood the company has settled on several different locations for vehicle assembly, based on the underlying industry geography. We illustrate that point in more detail with the specific example of Honda's North American locations.

In 2016 Honda operated seven vehicle assembly plants and six powertrain plants in North America. Those plants can be grouped in four clusters: Midwest, South, Canada, and Mexico (figure 4). Note that that three of the four clusters of Honda's footprint feature comparable volumes of final assembly, engine production, and transmission production. The exception is Alliston, which did not have a transmission plant in 2016 (table 14).

In reality, large numbers of Honda's engines and transmissions are shipped across the four clusters. Table 15 displays in the left column Honda's range of engines and the plants in which they were produced. Each column shows the company's North American assembly plants, indicating the plant from which vehicle engines were sourced. The shaded areas indicate the extent of engine sourcing within the same production cluster.

Overall, only 32% of transmissions were sourced from within the same cluster, along with 68% of engines (table 16). The Midwest and South clusters receive nearly all of their engines from the same cluster, though less than half their transmissions. The Canada and Mexico clusters received most of their engines and transmissions from other clusters.

Figure 5 depicts the increasing complexity in the movement of engines and transmissions within North America, as Honda opened more assembly and powertrain plants. As part of that process the number of border crossings between Canada, Mexico, and the United States increased. We chose Honda for figure 5 because its North American powertrain logistics are more straightforward than those of the other major carmakers. Attempts to portray the other major carmakers in the same format used for figure 5 would result in a tangle of lines that could not be viewed clearly.

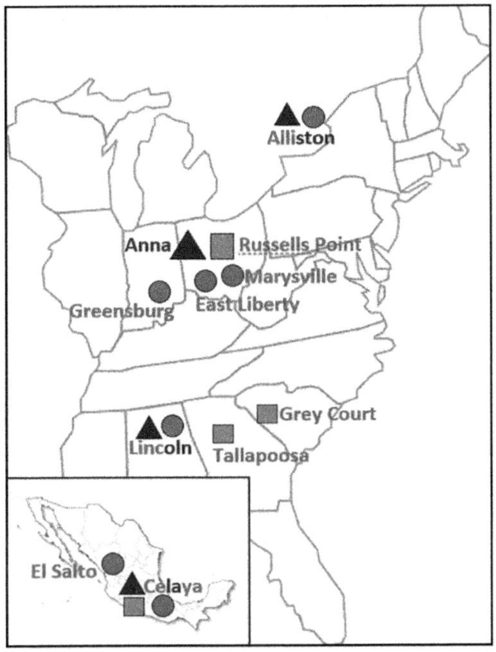

Figure 4. Honda's North American Production Clusters, 2016
Source: Authors' calculations based on data from IHS Markit as of October 2017.
Note: Assembly plants are represented by circles, engine plants by triangles, and transmission plants by squares.

Table 14. Honda Production Clusters (2016 Production Capacity, in Thousands)

Assembly			Engine			Transmission		
Location	Start	Capacity	Location	Start	Capacity	Location	Start	Capacity
Midwest cluster								
Marysville1	1982	220	Anna	1985	1,180	Russells Pt	1997	1,000
Marysville2	1985	220						
East Liberty	1989	240						
Greensburg	2009	250						
Canada cluster								
Alliston 1	1986	195	Alliston	2008	200			
Alliston 2	1998	195						
South cluster								
Lincoln 1	2001	170	Lincoln	2001	340	Tallapoosa	2006	375
Lincoln 2	2004	170						
Mexico cluster								
Celaya	2014	200	Celaya	2014	200	Celaya	2015	350
El Salto	1995	60						

Source: Authors' calculations based on data from IHS Markit as of October 2017.

Table 15. Honda Shipments from Engine Plants to Assembly Plants, 2016 (Units)

Engine plant & engine size, by cluster	Final assembly plants, by cluster							Total engine Sourcing
	Midwest			South	Canada	Mexico		
	East Liberty	Greenville	Marysville	Lincoln	Alliston	Celaya	El Salto	
Anna 1.8						127,632		127,632
Anna 2.0		174,176			144,035		5,928	324,139
Anna 2.4	154,368		297,439		198,954		53,380	704,141
Anna 3.0	1,348			1,689				3,037
Anna 3.5	66,124		113,516					179,640
Lincoln 3.5			26,603	367,857				394,460
Alliston 1.5	12,258	74,644			68,115			155,017
Alliston 2.0					58			58
Celaya 1.5						40,617		40,617
Swindon (U.K.) 1.6						25,528		25,528
Total vehicle production	234,098	248,820	437,558	369,546	411,162	193,777	59,308	1,954,269

Source: Authors' calculations based on data from IHS Markit as of October 2017.

Table 16. Honda Cross-Shipments: Share of Powertrains Received from Same Cluster as Assembly Plant

Cluster	Assembly total production	% Sourced in same cluster as final assembly	
		Engines	Transmissions
Midwest	920,476	87.7	44.6
South	411,162	99.5	44.7*
Canada	369,546	16.6	n/a
Mexico	253,085	16.0	13.6
Total	1,954,269	67.5	32.2

* 99.5% if ZF Group's Grey Court plant is included.
Source: Authors' calculations based on data from IHS Markit as of October 2017.

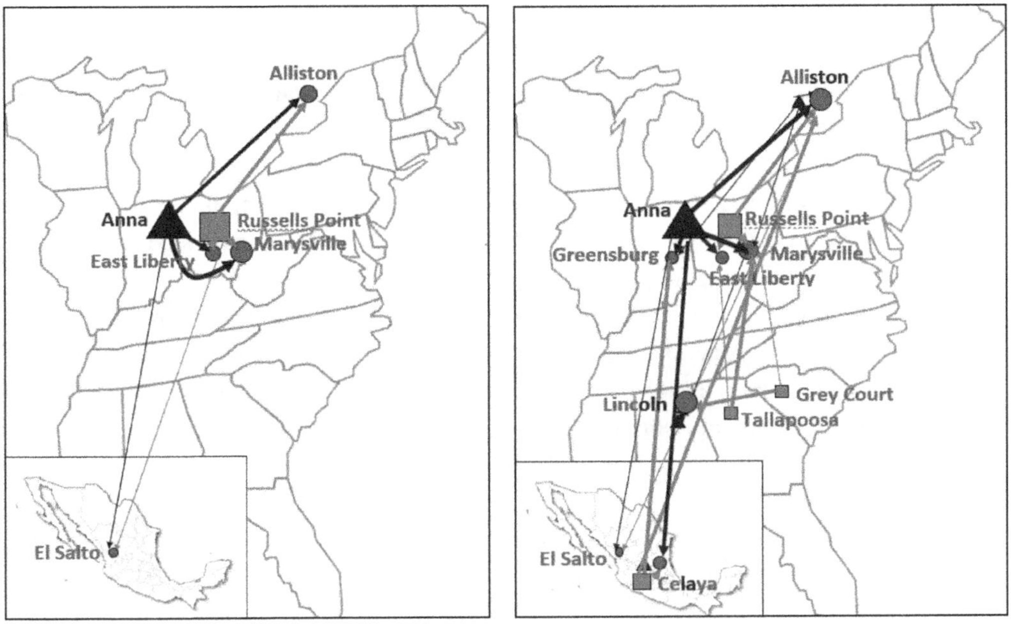

Figure 5. Honda's Connections between Final Assembly and Powertrain Plants, (*left*) 2000 and (*right*) 2016

Source: Authors' calculations based on data from IHS Markit as of October 2017.

Note: Assembly plants are represented by circles, engine plants by triangles, and transmission plants by squares.

DISCUSSION

The auto industries of Canada, Mexico, and the United States are highly integrated with each other. Utilizing detailed data on powertrain sourcing we have shown that the degree of integration in the industry increased subsequent to the implementation of NAFTA.

This chapter highlights two enduring principles underlying this pattern. First, motor vehicle production is highly agglomerated. The clustering occurs because as an overall principle, it is most efficient to produce vehicles as close as possible to their markets. Second, complex relationships arise among the principal elements of vehicle production, notably powertrain and final assembly, because of differing economies of scale. Under the influence of these two principles, less than one-third of the vehicles assembled in North America have engine production, transmission production, and final assembly all located in the same country.

The findings in this chapter offer insights into possible impacts of replacing the NAFTA with the United States-Mexico-Canada Agreement (USMCA). The new agreement for North American trade does not change the geographic scope of the previous regional trade agreement, but it does introduce new rules to trade. Those can affect location decisions within the region. All of North America must consider revised rules of origin for vehicle and parts production, including higher requirements for regional content (Congressional Research Service 2019). USMCA requires that at least 75% of parts defined as "core" (essentially engine and transmission) originate in North America (Dziczek et al. 2018, 4; "United States-Mexico-Canada Agreement" 2018). In addition, the new agreement introduces wage provisions to trade in the North American auto industry, the first time such provisions have been incorporated.

Overall, the new trade agreement may well result in more sourcing of powertrains from plants located in North America, thereby further strengthening regional integration. According to the *Financial Times*, the takeover proposed in March 2021 by Canadian Pacific Railway of the Kansas City Southern Railroad is "a bet on smooth commerce between the three North American countries" (Meyer and Fontanella-Khan 2021).

REFERENCES

Anastakis, Dimitry. 2004. "From Independence to Integration: The Corporate Evolution of the Ford Motor Company of Canada, 1904–2004." *Business History Review* 78 (2), 213–53.

Automotive News. 1989. "Automotive News Market Data Book."

Brincks, Corey, Bolesław Domański, Thomas Klier, and James Rubenstein. 2018. "Integrated Peripheral Markets in the Auto Industries of Europe and North America." *International Journal of Automotive Technology and Management* 18 (1): 1–28.

Center for Automotive Research. 2017. "Automotive Product Development Cycles and the Need for Balance with the Regulatory Environment." 20 September 2017. https://www.cargroup.org/automotive-product-development-cycles-and-the-need-for-balance-with-the-regulatory-environment/.

Congressional Research Service. 2019. "USMCA: Motor Vehicle Provisions and Issues." Updated 14 October 2021. https://crsreports.congress.gov/product/pdf/IF/IF11387.

Crane, David. 2006. "Canada-US Auto Pact," *The Canadian Encyclopedia*. Updated 12 June 2017. https://www.thecanadianencyclopedia.ca/en/article/canada-us-automotive-products-agreement.

Cray, Ed. 1980. *Chrome Colossus: General Motors and Its Times*. New York: McGraw-Hill.

de Gortari, Alonso. 2019. "Disentangling Global Value Chains." Working Paper no. 25868, National Bureau of Economic Research. https://www.nber.org/system/files/working_papers/w25868/w25868.pdf.

De La Cruz, Justino, Robert B. Koopman, Zhi Wang, and Shang-Jin Wei. 2011. "Estimating Foreign Value-Added in Mexico's Manufacturing Exports." US International Trade Commission, Office of Economics, Working Paper no. 2011-04A, April 2011. https://www.usitc.gov/publications/332/EC201104A.pdf.

Dietzenbacher, Erik, Bart Los, Robert Stehrer, and Gaaitzen J. de Vries. 2014. "The Construction of World Input-Output Tables in the WIOD Project." *Economic Systems Research* 25 (1): 71–98. https://www.researchgate.net/publication/263231850_The_Construction_of_World_Input-Output_Tables_in_the_WIOD_Project.

Dykes, James G., and Dimitry Anastakis. 2013. "Automotive Industry." *The Canadian Encyclopedia*. Updated 21 May 2021. www.thecanadianencyclopedia.ca/en/article/automotive-industry.

Dziczek, Kristin, Michael Schultz, Yen Chen, and Bernard Swiecki. 2018. *NAFTA Briefing: Review of Current NAFTA Proposals and Potential Impacts on the North American Automotive Industry*. Ann Arbor, MI: Center for Automotive Research.

Ellison, Glenn, Edward L. Glaeser, and William R. Kerr. 2010. "What Causes Industry Agglomeration? Evidence from Coagglomeration Patterns." *American Economic Review* 100 (3): 1195–1213. https://www.jstor.org/stable/27871244.

Flink, James J. 1988. *The Automobile Age*. Cambridge, MA: MIT Press.

Husan, R. (1997). "The Continuing Importance of Economies of Scale in the Automotive Industry." *European Business Review* 97 (1): 38–42.

Klier, T.H., and J.M. Rubenstein. 2007. "Whose Part Is It? – Measuring Domestic Content of Vehicles." *Chicago Fed Letter*, no. 243, October 2007. https://www.chicagofed.org/publications/chicago-fed-letter/2007/october-243.

– 2015. "Auto Production Footprints: Comparing Europe and North America." *Economic Perspectives* 39 (4). https://www.chicagofed.org/publications/economic-perspectives/2015/4q-klier-rubenstein.

– 2017. "Mexico's Growing Role in the Auto Industry under NAFTA: Who Makes What and What Goes Where." *Economic Perspectives* 41 (6): 1–29. https://www.chicagofed.org/publications/economic-perspectives/2017/6.

Kumar, Pradeep, and John Holmes. 1998. "The Impact of NAFTA on the Auto Industry in Canada." In *The North American Auto Industry under NAFTA*, edited by Sidney Weintraub and Christopher Sands, 92–183. Washington, DC: Center for Strategic and International Studies

Lung, Y. (2004). The Hanging Geography of the European Automobile System. *International Journal of Automotive Technology and Management* 3(2–3): 137–65.

Lyndon B. Johnson School of Public Affairs. 1985. *The U.S.-Canadian Automotive Products Agreement of 1965: An Evaluation for Its Twentieth Year*. Policy Research Project report no. 68. Austin: University of Texas at Austin.

Marshall, Alfred. 1936. *Principles of Economics*. 8th ed. London: Macmillan.

Menk, Debbie Maranger, Yen Chen, and Joshua Cregger. 2012. *Methodology for Creating a Matrix to Assess the Domestic Content of a Vehicle by Make and Model*. Ann Arbor, MI: Center for Automotive Research. https://www.cargroup.org/wp-content/uploads/2017/02/AAPC-Domestic-Content-Final.pdf.

Meyer, Gregory, and James Fontanella-Khan. 2021. "Rail Deal Is $29 Bet on Trade Pact between Canada, US and Mexico." *Financial Times*, 22 March 2021. https://www.ft.com/content/13d92e28-eac1-4139-b36f-823c40e6cd44.

Moreno Brid, Juan Carlos. 1996. "Mexico's Auto Industry after NAFTA: A Successful Experience in Restructuring?" University of Notre Dame, Helen Kellogg Institute for International Studies, Working Paper no. 232, 19 August.

Nevins, Allan. 1954. *Ford: The Times, the Man, the Company*. New York: Charles Scribner's Sons.

Pavlínek, Petr. 2019. "Restructuring and Internationalization of the European Automotive Industry." *Journal of Economic Geography* 19 (2): 1–33. https://academic.oup.com/joeg/article/20/2/509/5303643.

Pound, Arthur. 1934. *The Turning Wheel*. Garden City, NY: Doubleday, Doran.

Reisman, Simon. 1978. *The Canadian Automotive Industry: Performance and Proposals for Progress*. Ottawa: Minister of Supply and Services Canada.

Rhys, D.G. 1977. "European Mass-Producing Car Makers and Minimum Efficient Scale: A Note." *Journal of Industrial Economics* 313–20. https://www.jstor.org/stable/2098178.

– 2005. Competition in the Auto Sector: The Impact of the Interface between Supply and Demand. *International Journal of Automotive Technology and Management* 5 (3): 261–83. https://www.researchgate.net/publication/240295737_Competition_in_the_auto_sector_The_impact_of_the_interface_between_supply_and_demand.

Rice, Justin Gazer. 1998. "PITEX and Maquiladora Import Programs: A Working Guide and Comparative Evaluation." *Texas International Law Journal* 33 (2): 365–80. https://heinonline.org/HOL/LandingPage?handle=hein.journals/tilj33&div=26&id=&page=.

Rubenstein, James M. 1992. *The Changing U.S. Auto Industry*. London: Routledge.

Smith, Derek. 2009. "Agglomeration." In *Dictionary of Human Geography*, 5th ed., edited by Derek Gregory, Ron Johnston, Geraldine Pratt, Michael J. Watts, and Sarah Whatmore, 14. Chichester, UK: Wiley-Blackwell.

Timmer, Marcel P., Erik Dietzenbacher, Bart Los, and Gaaitzen J. de Vries. 2015. "An Illustrated User Guide to the World Input-Output Database: The Case of Global Automotive Production." *Review of International Economics* 23: 575–605. https://ideas.repec.org/a/bla/reviec/v23y2015i3p575-605.html.

Timmer, Marcel P., Bart Los, Robert Stehrer, and Gaaitzen J. de Vries. 2016. "An Anatomy of the Global Trade Slowdown Based on the WIOD 2016 Release." GGDC Research Memorandum no. 162, University of Groningen, Netherlands.

Truett, L.J., and D.B. Truett. 1996. "Economies of Scale in the Mexican Automotive Sector." *Journal of Product Analysis* 7: 429–46. https://doi.org/10.1007/BF00162051.

Truett, L.J., and D.B. Truett. 2001. "The Spanish Automotive Industry: Scale Economies and Input Relationships." *Applied Economics* 33 (12): 1503–13. https://doi.org/10.1080/00036840012960.

Truett, L.J., and D.B. Truett. 2003. "The Italian Automotive Industry and Economies of Scale." *Contemporary Economic Policy* 21 (3): 329–37.

US Department of Commerce, Bureau of the Census. 1955. *Statistical Abstract of the United States*. Washington, DC: Government Printing Office.

"United States-Mexico-Canada Agreement." 2018. "Chapter 4: Rules of Origin." https://usmca.com/rules-of-origin-usmca/. Accessed 12 February 2023.

Weber, A., and C.J. Friedrich. 1929. *Alfred Weber's Theory of the Location of Industries*. Chicago: University of Chicago Press.

Weintraub, Sidney, and Christopher Sands, eds. 1998. *The North American Auto Industry under NAFTA*. Washington, DC: Center for Strategic and International Studies,

Womack, James P., Daniel T. Jones, and Daniel Roos. 1991. *The Machine That Changed the World: The Story of Lean Production*. New York: Harper Perennial.

Womack, James P. 1994. "The North American Auto Industry under NAFTA: Making the Positive Sum Solution Happen." *North American Outlook* 5 (November): 3–19.

Wynn-Williams, M.S. 2009. Economies of Scale in the Automobile Industry. In *Surfing the Global Tide: Automotive Giants and How to Survive Them* (41–71). London: Palgrave Macmillan.

PART 2

Automotive Investment and Trade

5

Reorganization and Restructuring in the North American Automotive Industry

Mike Smitka

At the turn of the previous century the business of making cars was a quintessential high-tech industry. Articles about technical developments associated with the automobile frequented the pages of *Scientific American*. New firms raised funds from networks of wealthy individuals. Indeed, the contemporary equivalent of a venture capitalist, Billy Durant, created General Motors (GM), assembling a mix of "automotive" firms to tap a frenzied stock market. Investors paid little heed to the poor profit potential of the resultant hodgepodge of firms. Ultimately, Durant was fired by his board. (Eventually, he took GM over again, and was fired again!) When he died, he did so in genteel poverty. Similarly, Henry Ford ran through two sets of investors before achieving success on his third attempt.

The frenzy in the industry at the start of the 2020s would look familiar to that first generation of entrepreneurs. New technologies that promise electric cars, autonomous driving, and online retailing are generating a similar rush in the stock market with multi-billion-dollar valuations of firms with no revenue, no business model, and no prospect of near-term profits. However, the difference between now and the early 1900s is that the industry is now global in scale with a capacity to turn out 100 million vehicles a year. Supply and distribution channels are equally complex. The industry has also become global from a manufacturing and brand perspective with massive cross-border trade of components and finished vehicles.

It is useful to step back and look at how all of this developed. Doing so helps place the impact of the evolving North American trade regime in perspective. I do so by considering the North American auto industry in the context of structural changes, focusing primarily on the last fifty years. The data used are specific to the United States; other chapters add nuance on how the experience of the Canadian and Mexican industries differed.

In the broadest of terms, the key transformations that have emerged over the past one-hundred-plus years include the end of the hegemony of the Detroit Three; the decline of original equipment operators' (OEMs) vertical integration into parts production; the concomitant rise of globally oriented, technology-intensive Tier 1 suppliers; and the rise of labour productivity. In fact, the final item renders autos a declining industry in terms of aggregate employment. It also raises a key observation that most jobs in the industry – functions downstream from manufacturing in sales, finance, insurance, and services – have, to date, been little affected by the cross-border integration of the production side of the industry. These wider trends have also undergirded a shift in the location of where cars and components are made, and hence the geography of employment (items that the chapters comprising Section 4 of this work discuss in detail).

NEW ENTRIES AND THE END OF OLIGOPOLIES

The 1920s saw the rise of the "Detroit Three" oligopoly, with GM surpassing Ford and Chrysler entering the market. GM became the dominant firm, controlling half the market. The structure that emerged set the stage for a form of tacit collusion, with GM setting prices and the others following. The cartel that emerged lasted for the next fifty years and proved remarkably robust, breaking into a price war only once, in 1955. It also proved highly profitable. Throughout the late 1950s and 1960s GM was the world's most profitable firm, with a 20% return on investment and a 40% return on equity (see Smitka and Warrian 2017)

During these halcyon years, high pricing encouraged new entrants to explore the North American market, but those firms never really caught fire. For example, the first wave of external, non–Detroit Three competition came from imported European subcompacts, in 1958. That wave soon subsided. The next wave arose in the late 1960s, this time by Japanese subcompacts. However, unlike the European-based wave of the late 1950s, Japanese-owned firms' market share stabilized. Then, a decade later – over the period 1979–82 – a third wave of imported subcompacts hit North American shores, led again by the Japanese. This time, they expanded the base of operations established a decade or so earlier.

The wave of the late 1970s–early 1980 had a lasting effect. Coming amidst a steep recession, imports led the new Reagan Administration to negotiate a "voluntary" export restraint (VER) agreement with Japan, which took hold in May 1981, capping the number of vehicles Japanese automakers could export to the US. Prior to the VER, Japanese vehicle makers competed fiercely with one another. With the VER, that ended, and retail prices promptly rose by 25%. One side effect, a typical response to the binding numerical – not dollar-based – VER quota system, was that it encouraged the Japanese to move upmarket from subcompact to compact and, later, mid-sized cars. As that occurred, the VER gave them the funds to develop new, more profitable models. All of this proved very fortunate for the Japanese. By the mid-1980s, the subcompact market had shrunk from 30% to 7% of the US market. The result was that, on the backs of the VERs, Japanese firms were able to move upmarket. VERs also encouraged Japanese car companies to build "transplant" factories in North America, effectively circumventing VER strictures altogether. All of this meant that by the end of the 1980s, domestic (i.e., North American) production by Japanese firms had become well established, even as imports from Japan continued to capture over 20% of the market. The effect: the Detroit Three cartel collapsed.

As for the rest of North America – Canada and Mexico – slightly different factors were at play. With respect to Canada, its automotive industry commenced a formal process of integration with the US following the 1965 Canada-US Auto Pact. (For an overview of the policy measures that bound the Canadian automotive industry with the US see the introduction to this book.) Then, in the 1980s, three Japanese automakers (Honda, Toyota and Suzuki) – replicating the pattern some of those firms were establishing in the US – established "transplant" factories in the Province of Ontario.

The trajectory of the industry in Mexico proved quite different. As is typical of countries adhering to an import substitution industrialization (ISI) policy, Mexico had an excess of producers focused on its still small domestic market. With sales of cars and trucks never surpassing 500,000 per year prior to the 1980s, Mexico's automobile factories were small and inefficient, surviving based on tariff barriers that helped keep margins high. As traced in other chapters in this collection focused on Mexico (see, for example, chapters 10 and 13), the North American Free Trade Agreement (NAFTA) of 1994 represented a repudiation of Mexico's ISI policies, instilling new competition from imports from the US and Canada. It also turned Mexico's auto industry into a major platform for export.

Over the long term, the collapse of the US oligopoly had many implications. One was the negative impact it had on its members' shareholders and employees. The collapse also coincided with new entrants establishing operations south of the old core for automotive manufacturing locations in the upper mid-west and Ontario. Meanwhile, the collapse of its market share caused the Detroit Three to close assembly plants. When that happened, the plants of the Detroit Three that were located outside the automotive core proved to be most vulnerable. Eventually, all of the Detroit Three's plants on the east and west coasts were shuttered. Through all of this, the United Auto Workers tried – but failed – to unionize the new entrants' plants. The only exceptions to the UAW's string of setbacks were the joint ventures the new entrants established with the Detroit Three. While wages in the new ventures of the 1980s–2000s were comparable to those at unionized plants, the new employers no longer provided guaranteed pensions or health care for retirees. That difference was significant. Benefits for retirees cost GM $109 billion in the decade leading up to their Chapter 11 bankruptcy in 2009. Finally, the end of the oligopoly contributed to a transformation of parts manufacturing, the topic of the next section.

THE DECLINE IN VERTICAL INTEGRATION AND THE RISE OF GLOBAL "TIER 1" SUPPLIERS

A turning point in the oligopoly mindset – recognition that its dominance had passed – accelerated in the late 1980s. The challenges facing the US industry were captured most vividly in the 1989 publication of key findings of the second round of the MIT International Vehicle

Program's widely read *The Machine That Changed the World.* The research upon which the publication was based demonstrated wide disparity across the global industry, with the US behind in productivity and quality. The Detroit Three's pattern of vertical integration was also shown to be idiosyncratic. This included, for example, disparate activities like glass and steel production by Ford in its Rouge assembly complex in Dearborn, Michigan, and semiconductor fabrication by the GM Delphi division in Kokomo, Indiana, an operation that briefly made it the world's fourth largest chip maker.

The 1990s ushered in a period of change. One impetus for that was government policy. More stringent safety, fuel efficiency and emissions regulations forced the industry to reach outside for catalytic converters, anti-skid brake (ABS) systems, fuel injectors, sensors, and microprocessors. A second spur came from the need to raise efficiency and quality. However, investment in automation strained investment budgets across the Detroit Three as falling profits dried up available resources. That was most evident at GM, where bringing its paint shops into compliance with volatile organic compound emissions regulations cost the company more than $20 billion (Kachman 2015; Keller 1989). Turning to outside suppliers helped. A third change emanated from the example of the Japanese car companies. They had always been far less vertically integrated, reflecting endemic capital scarcity during the Japanese industry's formative years in the 1950s and 1960s. (For similar reasons, European makers also had low levels of vertical integration.) While the transplant factories initially relied upon imported parts to feed their new North American assembly plants, their supply bases quickly adapted. By 1990, Japanese and European parts companies each had built or acquired three hundred plants in the US to address new business opportunities there.

At the close of the 1990s, amidst continued poor profitability, GM and Ford spun off their internal parts operations as Delphi (1999) and Visteon (2000). GM and Ford were now free to purchase components from the new "Tier 1" universe of direct automotive suppliers. Of course, Delphi and Visteon were also freed to pursue new business from across the industry. The transformation was stormy, including bankruptcies at Delphi and Visteon, the reacquisition or subsidization by GM and Ford of portions of the firms to keep essential factories in operation, and multiple spin-offs. The Korean supplier Halla Climate Control, for example, ended up with Ford's old HVAC business (now called Hanon); GM's Saginaw Steering and Delco Chassis operations are now owned by Chinese firms; Delphi spun off its electronics operations; and BorgWarner acquired the remainder of Delphi in 2021. Meanwhile, other previously smaller independents also grew. For instance, the 1990s witnessed the transformation of the Canadian firm Magna from a modest-sized diversified industrial firm into the fourth-largest global automotive supplier. By 2020, its annual sales approached US $40 billion.

Similar restructurings occurred within the supplier sector. One example is a pioneer of airbag manufacturer, Breed Technologies, which bought the automotive safety systems business of Allied Signal. That did not go well, and after a bankruptcy reorganization, it was acquired by a private equity firm and later spun off as Key Safety Systems. KSS, in turn, bought the remaining operations of the Japanese supplier Takata, where a recall of more than one hundred million defective airbag inflators led to its bankruptcy. KSS was subsequently acquired by a large Chinese supplier of seatbelts and airbags and is now known as Joyson Safety Systems. Even though ownership had changed, supply contracts persisted, so individual plants and engineering centre were not immediately affected. Similarly, over the course of two decades one piston engineer interviewed for this project worked at six different suppliers – all without changing his desk – before finally moving in 2020 to a newly built engineering centre ten miles away. Of course, some mergers were of overlapping businesses, aimed at consolidating small plants.

Regulatory mandates leading to new suppliers, entry by firms following their customers to North America, and changing adherence to the notion of vertical integration were not the only forces shaping the industry. By the end of the 1990s the global industry had shifted to a "platform" model of new vehicle development. The most expensive part of bringing a new model to market had long been associated with engineering of the chassis, steering/suspension, and drivetrain. However, by the late 1990s, car companies learned to perform those functions as a "platform" on which multiple "top hats" could be placed. This had the effect of lowering the overall costs of developing a new model. In addition to multiple models sharing a common platform, those models could also be made on the same assembly line. This helped elevate plant utilization rates to more profitable levels.

The shift to multi-vehicle platforms also led to further consolidation of suppliers (i.e., a limited number of platforms underpinning several models that, in turn, promoted the award of large contracts for single suppliers of similar or complementary parts). Interdependencies among parts of a platform meant that changes would cascade across multiple systems around the world. Hence, a platform supplier needed to be a global supplier, able to deliver effectively identical components, made with the same materials and using the same production processes in each major market. That also meant that they would have to undergo the validation process – the system to ensure a supplier is able to produce quality parts that meet common dimensional and performance specifications – only once.

It is also relevant to note that as this process unfolded – as suppliers were awarded bigger contracts with global reach – they were also expected to provide more comprehensive sales engineering to operations in multiple markets. In the early days of the migration to platform management, few suppliers had the capacity to offer or perform the breadth or depth of functions that ultimately became expected. In the mid-1990s, for example, only about thirty firms had sales over US $1 billion. However, by 2019 the top twenty-eight Tier 1 suppliers had global sales of more than $10 billion. Even the smallest of the top one hundred had over $3 billion in revenue (Automotive News Top Supplier Rankings 1995, 2005, 2019).

As with new entry by car companies, new suppliers set up their factories outside of the previous manufacturing core: in rural areas, in the US south, and in Mexico. As with the new assembly plants, they proved outside the reach of organized labour, with compensation matching the prevailing rate in the local market rather than the higher levels automotive manufacturing workers earned in the upper midwest.

One new phenomenon – examined at a more abstract level in the next section on productivity – is that the Tier 1 and Tier 2 suppliers became much more adept at the development, design, and process engineering associated with new technologies. While there remains a fringe of suppliers making parts to blueprints using standard manufacturing methods (Helper and Kuan 2018), a key part of the transformation that has taken hold since the late 1990s – facilitated, in part, by the transition to platform management – is the transformation of the components industry to the role of "solutions provider." Today, it is suppliers that undertake advanced product development and present roadmaps of potential technologies to their upper-tier and OEM customers (Smitka and Warrian 2017, chap. 7). All of this engenders elevated levels of integration. For example, greater torque and peak rotation speed of an electric drive motor requires gearing that operates at limits outside those of internal combustion engines. Higher currents demand new types of wiring and connectors. The overall system may be limited by the switching speed of parts of the power controls. In short, in the 1980s new suppliers arose to meet novel requirements coming out of regulatory needs. Today, the much larger supply industry relies on the systematic improvement of seemingly mundane parts to reduce costs, improve functionality, and avoid being rendered a low-profit source of commoditized parts.

INCREASING PRODUCTIVITY: IS AUTOMOTIVE A DECLINING INDUSTRY?

The reorganization of supply chains and the expanded role of a consolidated roster of (ever) larger suppliers represents an important transition that the automotive industry has experienced over the previous three decades. A potentially bigger force of change over that time has come from prolonged and steady increases in labour productivity. Some of that improvement has occurred via trade. For example, even before the NAFTA, labour-intensive processes such as wire harness assemblies were migrating to Mexico's maquiladora region, a pattern that has caused the productivity of remaining US automotive operations to be seen as rising. On top of that, the greater scale of the industry following the Auto Pact and then NAFTA allowed greater specialization at the plant level, both for finished vehicle manufacturing and parts and components. Hence, the valve for a gasoline engine may be cast in Indiana, machined in northern Mexico, put into an engine in Canada, and then assembled into a finished vehicle in the US. The overall results of these processes are explained by Klier and Rubenstein in chapter 4 in their discussion of the spatial integration of the industry in North America taken as a whole. These outcomes are in line with the well-established trade theories of comparative advantage as well as the newer trade theories of horizontal specialization based upon economies of scale.

Improvements in productivity also reflect greater efficiency within manufacturing processes, better management at the factory level, and improved coordination along the supply chain. Over time, the industry has employed new materials and processes, replacing slow and expensive machining, for example, with moulding and stamping. Automation has also eliminated many of the physically demanding and repetitive tasks. Robots do all the painting and most welding. Loading and unloading has been automated. Robots now apply glue and install front windows in assembly plants. The design of production lines benefits from ergonomics simulation, with the accumulation of many small improvements. Today, factories are laid out differently and more efficiently. Items like seats are made at a supplier in the sequence they will be used in the assembly plant process, going directly from the delivery truck to the line. Just-in-time controls in other areas have eliminated the need to stock and then retrieve parts in process, up and down the value chain. Quality control methodologies lower scrap and eliminate the waste of labour that bad parts entail. Through all of this, even though there is greater complexity in today's vehicles, employment has fallen.

The engineering process has also benefited. The platform approach has allowed more models to be made with similar inputs. Digital engineering tools allow a vehicle to be designed virtually, including the performance of virtual crash tests and the simulation of friction and noise in mechanical parts. All of this can be managed in real time, between suppliers, and between suppliers and OEMs. Rooms full of draftsmen and the smell of blueprints are things of the past. The process is cumulative: a new algorithm for checking heat flow in a motor, for example, is thereafter available to engineers with a similar need. 3-D printing is shortening the turnaround time for functional testing and validation of software models.

It is anticipated that automotive industry productivity will continue to climb. In many ways, productivity increases are a mixed blessing. On one hand, higher productivity supports higher incomes. However, it also implies fewer total manufacturing jobs across the region. As with most manufactured goods, demand is inelastic, with the share in expenditures falling as incomes rise. Combined with the increase in labour productivity, this means that total employment in the industry will continue to fall. In short, not only is manufacturing, in the aggregate, a declining industry, so too is its automotive component. The data bear these trends out. As figure 1 shows, after US manufacturing employment peaked at 19.5 million in 1979, it hovered between 17 million and 18 million for the next twenty years. After 2000 it fell sharply, and now rests at 12.3 million. Figure 1 shows that as a share of the overall labour force, manufacturing employment peaked even earlier – in 1953 – at just under one-third of the labour force. From there, it declined monotonically to 2009. However, after 2010 the decline moderated, and in July 2021 manufacturing represented 8.4% of total employment. For context, health care alone now employs more than all of manufacturing.

The combination of data contained in figures 1, 2, and 3 provides a more thorough indication of the factors affecting the industry. As explained, the overall trajectory of manufacturing employment is down (figure 1). Significantly, real output in the auto industry has *not* fallen. Meanwhile, as figure 2 shows, the auto industry's share of US manufacturing employment has been relatively stable (post 2008–9 financial crisis fallout notwithstanding). Therefore, the

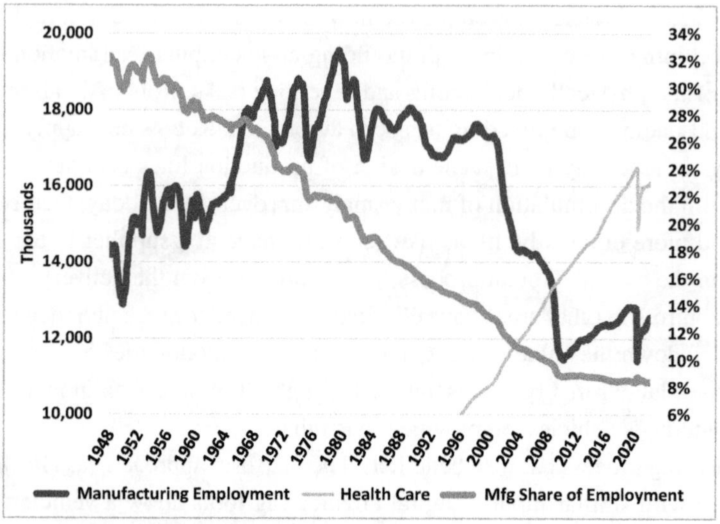

Figure 1. Decline of Manufacturing Employment (Thousands)
Source: Bureau of Labour Statistics CES0000000001 (https://data.bls.gov/timeseries/CES0000000001); CES3000000001 (https://data.bls.gov/timeseries/CES3000000001); Federal Reserve Bank of St. Louis (https://fred.stlouisfed.org/series/CES6562000101).
Note: Though this figure does not show it, over the past two decades the share of the industry in manufacturing has risen, from 6% to 7.5%. At the same time, absolute employment declined from 1.3 million in 2000 to 0.9 million in July 2021.

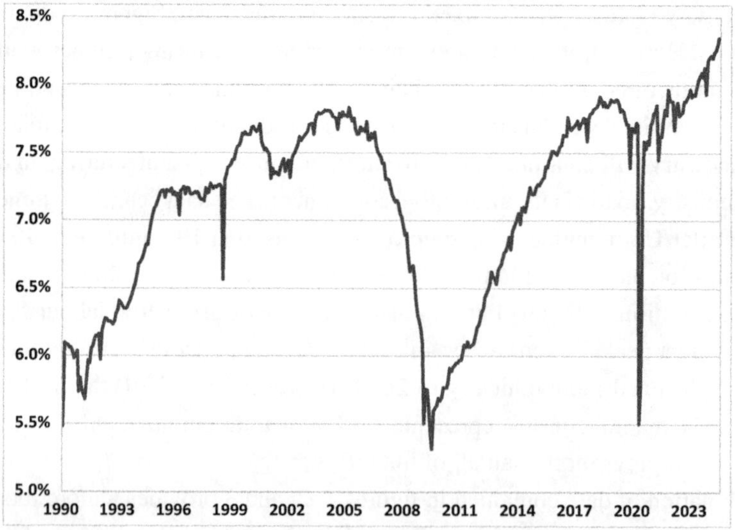

Figure 2. Auto Share of US Manufacturing Employment
Source: Bureau of Labour Statistics CES0000000001 (https://data.bls.gov/timeseries/CES0000000001); CES3000000001 (https://data.bls.gov/timeseries/CES3000000001); Federal Reserve Bank of St. Louis (https://fred.stlouisfed.org/series/CES6562000101).
Note: For the auto industry, data limits the analysis to the period from 1990.

Figure 3. Automotive GDP (US$ billions)
Source: Federal Reserve Bank of St. Louis (https://fred.stlouisfed.org/graph/?graph_id=931270 series A953RX1Q020SBEA).

combination of figures 1 and 2 indicates a downward trend in US automotive employment. As described earlier, what *has* changed is productivity: the number of workers needed to produce a dollar of output (or a unit of finished vehicles). Again, notwithstanding interruptions associated with the 2008–9 financial crisis, figure 3 shows that real GDP generated by the US auto industry has remained stable: this, despite declining levels of employment. The use of just-in-time management in the supply chain, improved sensors for monitoring quality and reducing scrap, better production equipment and tooling, design improvements using digital engineering, and automation of material handling have all contributed to a need for fewer workers on the factory floor.

Productivity improvements achieved by the US automotive industry over the past thirty-plus years are captured in figure 4, which validates the combined messages contained in figures 1, 2, and 3. Specifically, even though automotive industry manufacturing employment has experienced a multidecade period of decline, output continues to climb. Therefore – as the data upon which figure 4 is based demonstrate – US automotive industry labour productivity has grown by a substantial margin: almost 2.4 times.

The advent of battery electric vehicles (BEVs) will cause further adjustments, because the labour content of an electric battery pack and drivetrain is lower than that of internal combustion engines (ICEs) plus associated fueling system and transmissions. However, the provisions of the 2022 Inflation Reduction Act will lead to the relocation of the battery supply chain from China to the USMCA, mitigating the aggregate impact within North America even if it does not help workers displaced by individual engine and transmission plant closures. The shift away from the internal combustion engine will be gradual, but it will contribute to continuing increases in productivity and accompanying reductions in employment.

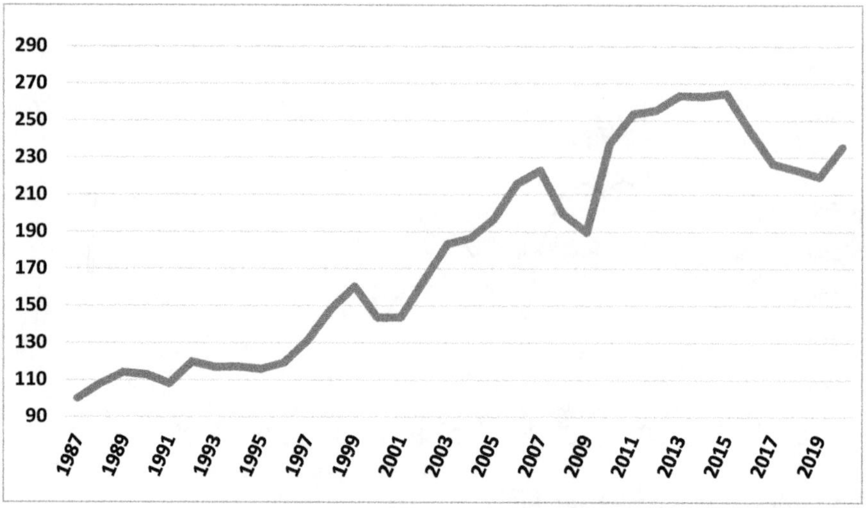

Figure 4. Automotive Labour Productivity (1987 = 100)
Source: Federal Reserve Bank of St. Louis (https://fred.stlouisfed.org/series/IPUEN3361W001000000).

AUTOMOTIVE: A QUINTESSENTIAL NON-TRADED SERVICE INDUSTRY

The fulcrum and focus of this collection is the evolving trade regime and its effect on the structure and direction of the automotive industry. While the focus has been on automotive manufacturing, the reality is that for every job making cars and their components, there are four jobs in retailing and service. The effect of trade agreements on such processes, functions, and services is modest, but that fact does not make them less important. Employment there is a function of aggregate vehicle demand and the number of vehicles in use.

Some context: in 2022, 14 million new light vehicles were sold (US Bureau of Transportation Statistics 2024). In addition, 36.3 million used vehicles changed hands (Cox Automotive 2023), or 2.6 used for every new vehicle. The process of vehicle sales requires sales staff, title transfers, registrations, financing, and insurance. Often, the vehicles traded in for new cars are wholesaled among dealers, as are vehicles that come off lease or that are "defleeted" from rental car companies. Each function requires additional personnel. Enterprise Car Rental, the largest in the industry, purchased and eventually resold roughly one million vehicles in 2019. Most of those vehicles required truck transport from the seller, typically with an intermediate stop at an auction run by a company like KAR Adesa, Cox Manheim, or one of their many smaller rivals, before reaching a retail lot. Additionally, there are approximately 280 million registered cars, light trucks, and heavy trucks in the US, travelling 3.26 trillion miles per year.

Along with the need to undertake regular service of these vehicles – the average light vehicle is twelve years old – there were also 6.7 million reported vehicular accidents in 2019: those vehicles needed to be repaired or salvaged. Supporting that process are insurance claims adjusters, collision repair shops, and specialized auctions (Insurance Auto Auctions and CoPart) that sell "totalled" vehicles from insurance companies to salvage yards and scrap dealers. On top of that, vehicles get dirty. Even something as mundane as car washing employed an estimated 185,000 workers in the US in 2021.

Meanwhile, data on many auto-related sectors are simply unavailable. That is because the portions of the finance, insurance, and legal systems devoted to supporting the motor vehicle industry are not carved out. Similarly, infrastructure, road construction and maintenance, and taxi and truck operators are overlooked. Perspective is provided when one considers the fact that vehicle repair and servicing is larger than all "upstream" automotive manufacturing combined. In the end, only about 20% of automotive industry jobs are in manufacturing. While those jobs are important, in the USMCA region the service sector dominates. That means that even though, as the introduction to this collection reminds us, the automotive industry remains "iconic," changes in the details of international trade arrangements – as momentous as they might be for OEMs, suppliers, labour, and policymakers – matter little for most of the people whose livelihood revolves around automobiles.

CONCLUSIONS

Over the past several decades the effect of "distance" on automotive manufacturing has dissipated. As this volume has inferred, a key factor influencing the declining effect of distance has been an evolving series of trade policy mechanisms. The process unfolded starting with the Canada-US Auto Pact and Mexico's maquiladora export-processing system in the mid-1960s and then adjusted and expanded via a cycle of additional instruments including the Canada-US Free Trade Agreement of 1988, the NAFTA of 1994, and most recently the USMCA.

In addition to the formal trade policy instruments listed above, the effect of distance has also been discounted via a range of additional factors, factors that have contributed to further integration of the North American industry. It should be noted, however, that even though individual instruments are important, only rarely do they solely inspire automotive investment decisions. In chapter 6, for example, Dziczek and Swiecki are careful to remind us that local content provisions contained in trade agreements do not independently affect automotive investment decisions. Similarly, trade agreements alone do not inspire continental integration.

Over the past few decades, the effect of distance has also been lessened – and the pattern of integration amplified – by shipping costs that have fallen dramatically, an outcome of deregulation of railroads and trucking in the US, the development of electronic documentation and logistics software, the use of containers for parts transport, and roll-on/roll-off ships for water transport. Even air freight has become available to overcome distance, supporting the movement of high-value parts or as a countermeasure for short-term supply chain interruptions.

As regional integration has accelerated (see, for example, the preceding chapter), the effects and opportunities of globalization have also taken hold. Emblematic of that is BMW's South Carolina plant, the only source of most BMW X-Series and the largest automotive exporter in the US. Similarly, the Audi plant outside Puebla, Mexico, makes the Q5 and SQ5 for global markets, complemented by production of the Q5L in China. Several assembly plants in Mexico export to markets throughout South America.

Many of the trends observed within the North American auto industry and discussed in this chapter have also taken shape in regions outside of North America. For example, trade liberalization has contributed to the decline of automotive oligopolies elsewhere. This includes the old national champions of eastern and Mediterranean Europe as well as those in Asia. Toyota has long been the dominant producer in Japan, but now faces vigorous competition from VW, BMW, and Mercedes in the luxury segment there. In fact, Toyota's luxury brand Lexus is a response to that. In China, one-time national champions like First Automotive Works and Second Automotive Works (now Dongfeng) have relinquished their dominant position, a consequence of foreign investment by VW, GM, and others. As of 2022, China's long-standing requirement that foreign automotive OEMs manufacturing cars there (to sidestep steep import tariffs) form a fifty-fifty joint venture with a local firm was eliminated, a measure that is sure to affect the structure of the Chinese industry.

In the end, it does seem possible that William Durant or Henry Ford, whom we discussed at this chapter's outset, *would* recognize aspects of the automotive industry as it has subsequently developed: its continuing high-tech orientation, the passion of its leadership, its capacity to evolve. However, Ford and Durant might also be intrigued by additional developments this chapter has revealed and explored. For example, they might be taken aback by the fact that the oligopolistic industry in which they operated had largely evaporated by the 1990s. By contrast, it is possible they would be intrigued by the policy measures that gave rise to a more regionally (i.e., North American) integrated automotive industry that started to unfold in the mid-1960s, perhaps judging that development as a means by which to extend the hegemony of the firms they founded and led. How would they react to the expansion of the geographic footprint of automotive manufacturing in North America to places like the southern US and Mexico? How would their investment decisions be affected by local content rules embedded in the NAFTA and USMCA? It is the last question that Dziczek and Swiecki explore in the next chapter: just one example of the myriad challenges buffeting the industry and its actors.

REFERENCES

Automotive News. 1995. "Top Supplier Rankings (North America, Europe, Global)." Detroit: Crain.

– 2005. "Top Supplier Rankings (North America, Europe, Global)." Detroit: Crain.

– 2015. "Top Supplier Rankings (North America, Europe, Global)." Detroit: Crain.

– 2019. "Top Supplier Rankings (North America, Europe, Global)." Detroit: Crain.

Cox. 2023. "Used-Vehicle Sales Lose Ground in 2022." https://www.coxautoinc.com/market-insights/used-vehicle-sales-lose-ground-in-2022/.

Helper, Susan, and Jennifer Kuan. 2018. "What Goes On under the Hood? How Engineers Innovate in the Automotive Supply Chain." In *U.S. Engineering in a Global Economy*, edited by Richard B. Freeman and Hal Salzman, 193–214. National Bureau of Economic Research. Chicago: University of Chicago Press. http://www.nber.org/chapters/c12690.pdf.

Kachman, Nicholas. 2015. *GM: Paint It Red*. Buena Vista, VA: Mariner.

Keller, Maryann. 1989. *Rude Awakening: The Rise, Fall and Struggle for Recovery of General Motors*. New York: William Morrow.

Smitka, Michael, and Peter Warrian. 2017. *A Profile of the Global Auto Industry: Innovation and Dynamics*. New York: Business Expert Press.

US Bureau of Transportation Statistics. 2024. "New Passenger Car and Light Truck Sales and Leases." https://www.bts.gov/content/new-and-used-passenger-car-sales-and-leases-thousands-vehicles.

6

NAFTA vs. USMCA Content Rules Comparison with Evidence from Automakers' Investment Strategies

Kristin M. Dziczek and Bernard Swiecki

The United States-Mexico-Canada Agreement (USMCA) officially replaced the North American Free Trade Agreement (NAFTA) on 1 July 2020. The USMCA requires substantially higher North American content for light vehicles and parts to trade within the region without incurring tariffs. These higher-content thresholds and novel concepts, such as a steel and aluminium origination rule and a rule that ties free trade preferences to the average wages earned by production and trades workers, were meant to draw increased investment and jobs to North America. In signing the USMCA, then US president Donald J. Trump proclaimed it "a truly fair and reciprocal trade deal that will keep jobs, wealth and growth right here in America" (Swanson and Cochrane 2020). The United States International Trade Commission's (2019) assessment of the deal projected that the USMCA would create 28,000 new auto and parts jobs and 80,000 new jobs tied to the auto industry, and would increase investment in the sector by US $30 billion. This chapter examines automakers' investment announcements in the early days of the USMCA.

The USMCA and NAFTA before it did not create the North American automotive footprint. Automakers have manufactured vehicles in all three North American countries since the earliest days of the twentieth century. However, as the laws in Canada, Mexico, and the United States changed and trade agreements developed, the North American automotive manufacturing industry evolved and grew (Cooper 1994; Garber 1994; Anastakis 2005; Klier and Rubenstein 2008).

Automakers began manufacturing vehicles in each country to serve the local market and sometimes markets beyond. Canadian automotive exports, for example, were enabled by Canada's favourable trading relationships with the Commonwealth countries (Graham 2017). In the beginning, the Detroit automakers organized their manufacturing as a network of branch plants that each produced a range of models for each market (Hurley 1959). With the advent of global vehicle architectures and modular assembly (Simpson 2005), the North American auto industry is now a fully integrated manufacturing system. Global automakers – no longer just the Detroit Three – currently manufacture a full range of parts, components, and vehicles in the North American region, with trade among the three countries enabled by NAFTA and now USMCA (Klier and Rubenstein 2017). The North American region is the third-largest producer of light-and medium-duty vehicles and the second-largest producer of automotive parts in the world (Ward's Intelligence 2021).

Canada and Mexico supply the United States with nearly half of its US motor vehicle parts imports. Similarly, Canada and the United States supply Mexico with over 63% of its motor vehicle parts imports, and Mexico and the United States account for nearly 62% of all motor vehicle parts imports to Canada (Statistics Canada 2019; Observatory for Economic Complexity 2019; US Bureau of the Census 2021). As Canada's minister of Innovation, Science, and Industry, François-Philippe Champagne, observed in 2017, "We don't just sell to each other – this is kind of a unique relationship in the world … we make things together" (Morrow 2017).

North American supply chains are in flux as producers seek to comply with the USMCA that took effect in July 2020. However, USMCA is not the only factor shifting motor vehicle supply chains; the trade disruption in the wake of the COVID-19 pandemic and the rapid introduction of battery electric vehicles (BEVs), hybrid electric vehicles (HEVs), and all forms of driving automation are driving manufacturing location decisions – especially for new vehicle content that does not yet have a fully robust supply chain in North America.

The concept of "making things together" is changing as the industry and its supply chain evolve. In the 1990s and 2000s, suppliers located in Mexico mainly to take advantage of the significantly lower wages available in that country, a tendency that was explained by Shaiken (1994) and updated and expanded by Vallejo et al. in chapter 10 of this collection. Automakers and suppliers could then export parts back to their plants in Canada and the United States without tariffs and use these inputs to produce vehicles in Mexico. The United States was the destination market for 68% of all light vehicles produced in Mexico in 2020 (IHS Markit 2020). After the 2008–9 recession, a flood of new investment flowed to Mexico, but this time it was for new automotive assembly plants and companies that supply them. These nine new assembly operations benefit from lower wages in Mexico and a favourable free trade environment that allows producers to reach over half of the global market for new vehicles without tariffs (OICA 2021; Swiecki and Menk 2016). As figure 1 shows, even with the expanded reach of Mexico's free trade agreements (FTAs), the share of Mexico's production that automakers exported beyond North America shrank between 2002 and 2019 as a growing share of light vehicles produced in Mexico were again sold in the US market. In addition, the proportion of Mexican light vehicle production that stays in Mexico to serve its market has been falling since 2002 (IHS Markit 2020).

Even though Mexico's exports beyond North America as a share of production have been shrinking, one cannot discount the importance of the market reach of a country's comprehensive

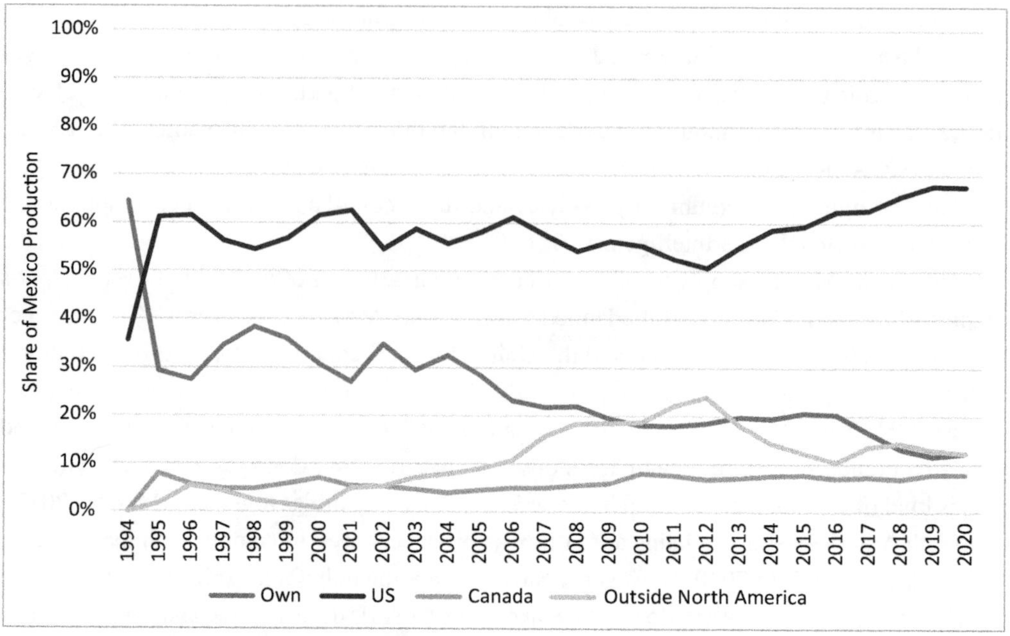

Figure 1. Mexican Light Vehicle Exports by Region, 1994–2020
Source: IHS Markit (2020); Harvard University (n.d.); Ward's Intelligence (2021); Statistics Canada (2019); US International Trade Administration (n.d.); authors' estimates.

set of trade agreements. The significance of market reach is made clear in a 2016 analysis performed by the Center for Automotive Research (CAR). For an average sedan exported to Europe, CAR found that the producing automaker could save US $2,500 in avoided tariffs if the vehicle were produced in Mexico and not the United States (Swiecki and Menk 2016). Because Canada enjoys an even more comprehensive range of free trade agreements than Mexico, it likewise has this advantage over the United States. For those automakers seeking investment in vehicle capacity with the intention of exports beyond North America, relative global free trade market reach could prove to be a decisive factor.

As in Mexico, figure 2 shows most of the light vehicles produced in Canada were exported to the United States between 1994 and 2020 (IHS Markit 2020). Also, like Mexico, the Canadian government has pursued expanded free trade access to global markets. Vehicle exporters can reach over 54% of the worldwide market for new light vehicles from their Canadian plants (OICA 2021). However, Canada has not benefited as much as Mexico from investment in new light vehicle assembly plants in this period. Instead, Canada has lost plants and has captured only a fraction of all North American automaker investments (CAR 2009–2020).

The United States, by comparison, can only reach 28% of the global market for new light vehicles without tariffs. Figure 3 shows that the US market itself represents 19% of the global light vehicle market, so just 9% of the US free trade reach is beyond its shores (OICA 2021).

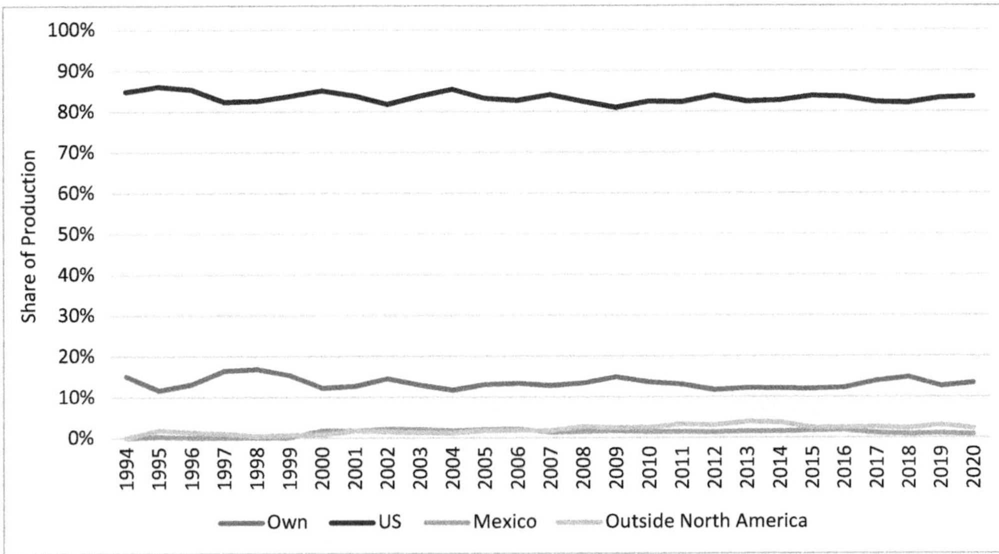

Figure 2. Canadian Light Vehicle Exports by Region, 1994–2020
Source: IHS Markit (2020); Harvard University (n.d.); Ward's Intelligence (2021); Statistics Canada (2019); US International Trade Administration (n.d.); authors' estimates.

It is worth noting that the nexus of decision making has shifted since 1994. In fact, automakers that produced light vehicles in Canada, Mexico, and the United States were nearly all US-based transnational firms – American Motors, Chrysler, Ford, and General Motors until 1978. In that year, Volkswagen established the first German auto assembly plant in Westmoreland, Pennsylvania, and four years later, in 1982, Honda built the first Japanese automaker operations in North America (Swiecki et al. 2021; Bennett and Sharpe 1985; Holmes 1992). The pace of foreign direct investment (FDI) has increased since these first plants. In 2020, nearly 60% of the United States' light vehicle productive capacity was foreign owned, while 100% of Canadian and Mexican auto capacity was foreign owned (Ward's Intelligence 2021). Foreign ownership means that nearly all of the significant decisions regarding investments, products, and supply chain locations in Canada and Mexico are made in other countries, as are a majority of these decisions about US operations.

Of the top one hundred North American automotive suppliers, just thirty-two have their global headquarters in the region – twenty-six are US based, five are based in Canada, and just one is headquartered in Mexico. The top decision makers at two-thirds of the largest Tier 1 suppliers in North America are located in headquarters elsewhere – with Japan (twenty) and Germany (eighteen) comprising the largest share of ownership of top suppliers in the region (*Automotive News* 2021).

All North American automakers and nearly all top automotive suppliers are transnational companies with production and sales operations located throughout the world. The USMCA

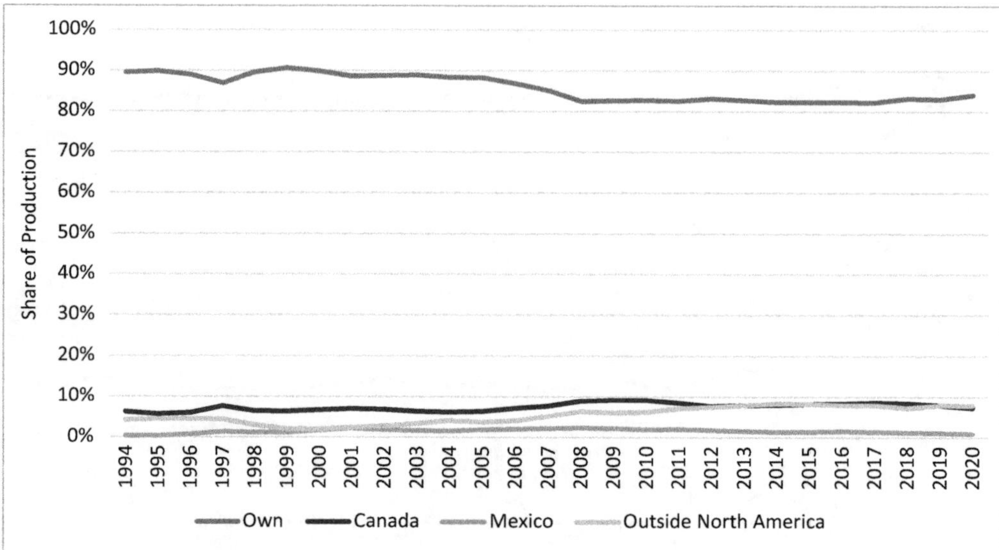

Figure 3. US Light Vehicle Exports by Region, 1994–2020
Source: IHS Markit (2020); Harvard University (n.d.); Ward's Intelligence (2021); Statistics Canada (2019); US International Trade Administration (n.d.); authors' estimates.

requirements may influence North American investments, but these firms have many options for where to invest to satisfy the global market for their products.

COMPARISON OF NAFTA VS. USMCA CONTENT RULES

The USMCA, which went into force on 1 July 2020, represents a complete rewriting of the rules of origin (ROO) for tariff-free treatment of light vehicles and motor vehicle parts. On 1 January 1994, NAFTA eliminated "7,000 tariffs, duties, and non-tariff barriers" among the three North American trading partners (Cooper 1994). The agreement created the world's largest free trade area at that time, representing 30.5% of the global gross domestic product (GDP).

The USMCA trading bloc currently makes up 30% of global GDP (Brodzicki 2021). Even though the region's share of GDP hasn't changed much, North America is no longer the largest free trade area in the world. At US $24.2 trillion in GDP, USMCA is slightly smaller in terms of market size than the US $26.2 trillion in GDP represented by the Regional Comprehensive Economic Partnership (RCEP; https://rcepsec.org/) signed in November 2020. RCEP brings together the ten countries that were in the Association of Southeast Asian Nations (ASEAN) – Brunei, Cambodia, Indonesia, Laos, Malaysia, Myanmar, the Philippines, Singapore, Thailand, and Vietnam – with Australia, China, Japan, New Zealand, and South Korea. The population of the RCEP trading bloc dwarfs that of the USMCA, however – with 2.3 billion people to the USMCA region's 493 million population (World Bank 2019).

The North American region remains significant for automotive production. The three partner countries have 21 million units of light vehicle production capacity and represent the third-largest production region in the world after China and the EU (OICA 2021).

> Changes to modernize the NAFTA ROO were long overdue. NAFTA required light vehicles to have 62.5 per cent North American–originating Regional Value Content (RVC) for parts on a tracing list to qualif for free trade preference. Many of the parts on the tracing list, however, were no longer in modern cars – such as distributor caps and 8-track tape players – and many current and emerging automotive parts were not on the list – such as advanced lithium-ion batteries and lidar pucks (NAFTA, chap. 4, 1994).

When it was enacted, the NAFTA RVC was the highest regional value content requirement of any US FTA. The USMCA, however, raises the RVC rule to 75% of light vehicle parts having to be "originating" to qualify for trade preference within the three countries – which now represents the highest RVC in any US trade agreement.

There are several differences between NAFTA and USMCA ROO for motor vehicles and parts. These include:

- NAFTA addressed only light vehicles; USMCA set ROO for both light- and medium-duty vehicles.
- NAFTA only considered the content of parts on the tracing list – a list that quickly became out of date; USMCA is broadly encompassing of all content in a vehicle.
- Motor vehicle parts that were not included on the NAFTA tracing list were "deemed originating" – a concept that allowed automakers to roll up the value of parts not on the tracing list to the value of the component or system into which they were assembled. The USMCA eliminated the "deemed originating" concept in favour of counting essentially all of a light vehicles' parts content towards the RVC.
- NAFTA had only one category for motor vehicle parts; USMCA distinguishes between parts that are considered "core" that must be originating and must meet a 75% threshold, "principal" parts that must meet a 70% threshold, and "complementary" parts that must meet a 65% threshold. Core parts are those that make a car a car – the engine, transmission, advanced battery, body, chassis, axles, suspension, and steering systems. Principal parts include gears, clutches, bearings, seat belts, and the like. "Complementary" parts include tubes, valves, light bulbs, switches, and small electrical parts (USMCA 2018) (see table 1 for more details).

The USMCA introduced several novel concepts to the North American trading system, including (see table 1):

Table 1. USMCA Regional Value and Labour Value Content Requirements

	Category	Required content	Description of category and phase-in period
Regional Value Content	Light vehicles	75%	3-year transition, but automakers can appeal for a 2-year extension for a limited amount of production (~10%) if they have a "credible plan" to meet the new ROO
	Core parts	75%	Includes engine, transmission, body & chassis, axle, suspension, steering (all 3-year transition), and advanced batteries (5-year transition). Must be originating for the vehicle to be originating
	Principal parts	70%	Includes tires, glass, pumps & compressors, A/C, bearings & bearing housings, electric motors used as the primary source of propulsion, electric motors for electrical variable transmission, electromagnets, starter motors & generators, bumpers, safety belts, brakes, road wheels, radiators, mufflers, clutches, airbags, seats, and parts of seats
	Complementary parts	65%	Includes dies, locks, catalytic converters, valves, taps & cocks, electric motors & universal AC/DC motors not exceeding 37.5W, DC motors & generators not exceeding 750W, other batteries, distributors & ignition coils, electrical lighting, windshield wipers/defrosters, sound recording/reproducing apparatus, switches, insulating wiring sets, headlamps, electronic instruments & measurement equipment.
	Steel & aluminium	70%	Day 1 rule, no transition
Labour Value Content	Overall		Hourly wage (production/trades/temps) above US $16/hour Can average within one country across vehicle class, model, or plant Up to 10% credit for R&D and IT content Up to 5% credit for assembly in a high-wage region
	Passenger cars	40%	At least 25% from materials & manufacturing content
	Pickup trucks & cargo vehicles	45%	At least 30% from materials & manufacturing content

Source: Center for Automotive Research (https://www.cargroup.org/meet-the-new-nafta/).

- A requirement that 70% of steel and aluminium used in light vehicle manufacturing must originate from North American sources. This rule went into effect on 1 July 2020.
- A labour value content (LVC) rule that 40% of the value of passenger cars and 45% of the value of light trucks must be made by workers who earn an average wage of US $16 per hour or more. Automakers can meet the LVC by using research and development (R&D) and information technology (IT) expenditures to satisfy ten percentage points of the requirement and high-wage assembly to meet five percentage points of the requirement. This rule is subject to a three- to five-year grow-in schedule – depending on whether or not the automaker has an approved alternative staging regime (ASR).
- A method for automakers to petition for an ASR, whereby the manufacturers would have five years to comply with the USMCA rules vs. the standard three years in the text. To get the additional two years to comply, the automaker must demonstrate a credible plan for reaching the new thresholds at the end of the five years. All three countries accepted ASR requests, and all companies that submitted ASR petitions had them approved. The list of approved ASR requests is published in Canada, Mexico, and the United States. Most major automotive original equipment manufacturers received ASRs in the early USMCA period.

The consequence of not meeting the USMCA ROO is that non-compliant manufacturers would incur most favoured nation (MFN) tariffs on goods traded with the United States. These tariffs would be 2.5% on cars and most auto parts and 25% on pickup trucks and cargo vehicles imported into the United States. US exports to Canada would incur a 6.1% tariff on cars and trucks and 6.0% on motor vehicle parts, and US exports to Mexico would incur a 15% tariff on cars and trucks and up to 50% on motor vehicle parts (World Bank n.d.). Canada and Mexico would also pay MFN rates on trade between the two countries that does not comply with USMCA and also does not comply with the Comprehensive and Progressive Trans-Pacific Partnership (CPTPP). The CPTPP ROO set a lower RVC threshold of 45% for light vehicles and 35–45% for motor vehicle parts (Global Affairs Canada 2018).

An FTA with a stringent ROO runs the risk of having the rules become non-binding, which would result in a surge of imports from outside the FTA region. A profit-maximizing firm will choose the lowest-cost option to serve the US, Canadian, and Mexican markets – and that lowest-cost option could be to pay tariffs instead of complying with the requirements to achieve free trade status (Celik, Karabay, and McLaren 2018). Once an importer is paying MFN tariffs, the company could import the same goods from any member of the World Trade Organization (WTO) – potentially at lower landed cost – and face the same tariff barriers.

Importers may not claim a trade preference for two reasons: (1) the traded good does not comply with the ROO to trade without tariff, or (2) the importer chooses to pay the tariff instead of incurring the cost of documenting trade agreement compliance. In 2019, the last full year of NA'TA, US trade data indicate that complying with the agreement's requirements

Table 2. Percentage of Motor Vehicle Parts Imports Claiming NAFTA or USMCA Preference, 2019–20

Date		2019	January–June 2020	July–December 2020
Canada	Motor vehicles	96.5	98.1	97.2
Canada	Motor vehicle bodies & trailers	88.0	48.4	50.2
Canada	Motor vehicle parts	88.6	79.0	72.8
Canada	**Canada total**	95.0	91.8	90.0
Mexico	Motor vehicles	97.1	99.5	96.0
Mexico	Motor vehicle bodies & trailers	16.9	10.6	6.6
Mexico	Motor vehicle parts	80.5	70.9	66.7
Mexico	**Mexico total**	92.7	85.9	82.4
	Canada/Mexico total	93.5	87.7	84.6

Source: US Bureau of the Census (2021).

for tariff-free access to the US market was likely no longer the lowest-cost path for a large portion of the traded goods. Table 2 shows that in 2019, while just 3.5% of vehicles entered the United States from Canada without claiming the NAFTA preference, 12% of bodies and trailers and 11.4% of motor vehicle parts were imported to the United States from Canada without claiming NAFTA preference. In addition, just 2.9% of vehicles entered the United States from Mexico without claiming the NAFTA preference, and even fewer bodies, trailers, and parts imported from Mexico to the United States qualified for NAFTA preferences – with 83.1% of bodies and trailers and 19.5% of motor vehicle parts not claiming the NAFTA free trade preference (US Bureau of the Census 2021).

In the final six months of the NAFTA agreement (January–June 2020), while more fully assembled light vehicles claimed the NAFTA preference, manufacturers imported even fewer parts from Canada and Mexico to the United States without paying tariffs. Nearly 52% of body and trailer imports from Canada eschewed the trade preference, as did 21% of motor vehicle parts imports – a substantial increase from the import shares that did not claim NAFTA preferences in 2019. Similarly, 89.4% of body and trailer imports and 29.1% of parts imports from Mexico to the United States did not claim preference in the first half of 2020, again a marked increase from the import shares subject to the MFN tariff rates in 2019 (US Bureau of the Census 2021).

During the first six months after the USMCA enter-into-force date of 1 July 2020 (July–December 2020), even fewer motor vehicle, body, trailer, and parts imports from Canada and Mexico to the United States claimed the USMCA preference. Specifically, 2.8% of motor vehicles, 49.8% of bodies and trailers, and 27.2% of parts from Canada did not claim preference, and 4% of motor vehicles, 93.4% of bodies and trailers, and 33.3% of parts from Mexico did not (US Bureau of the Census 2021). It appears that the higher regional content rules have not yet resulted in a larger share of imports that meet the thresholds.

Of course, 2020 was an unusual year for the motor vehicle industry due to the COVID-19 pandemic and the forced production stoppages in all three North American countries from March to May. Overall North American light vehicle production fell 20% in 2020 due to the shutdown and subsequent supply chain disruptions. Still, the fact that a smaller share of traded motor vehicles, bodies, trailers, and parts took advantage of the trade preference indicates that it is becoming increasingly difficult for manufacturers to comply with the trade rules in North America. Higher shares of imported parts that do not claim the USMCA trade preference weaken the incentive to locate more of the automotive supply chain in the North American region.

Average production wages are another incentive (or disincentive) for investment in a region. The USMCA's US $16/hour average wage under the LVC rule was intended to draw new investment, production, and jobs to higher-wage countries (Canada and the United States) and put upward pressure on Mexican production wages. When the USMCA was negotiated, it may have seemed implausible that auto suppliers in Mexico would pay three times the average industry wage to meet the LVC rule. However, there are media reports that several suppliers did just that – proving it was cheaper for employers to pay substantially higher wages in Mexico than to uproot the production facility to move it to the United States or Canada (Nakayama and Asayama 2020).

WHY SUPPLY CHAINS SHIFT

Where automakers and suppliers invest and locate their supply chains involves a complicated set of decisions. In interviews with automakers, suppliers, and site selection consultants, CAR researchers have found that trade agreements are not the primary drivers of location decisions. The existence of FTAs and relative MFN tariffs are essential cost considerations. However, these issues only come into play if there is a strong business case to invest in a particular country or location. Automakers and suppliers weigh the fully landed costs of imports relative to localizing production in a region.

Automakers and suppliers often re-evaluate their suppliers and supply chain locations to assess the potential for lower-cost or lower-risk supply arrangements. A new model launch or complete model refresh provides firms with an opportunity to examine and re-optimize their supplier relationships and footprint decisions. Natural disasters – such as tsunamis, floods, fires, and earthquakes – also prompt companies to reassess the risks inherent in their supply chains.

The COVID-19 pandemic has also spurred supply chain realignment, with companies both moving more production "on-shore" within North America and distributing risk by distributing their suppliers in more global markets. The pandemic has been uniquely disruptive to products such as semiconductors that have both long lead times and long supply chains. In addition, COVID has disrupted international shipping due to increased health and safety measures at the ports, higher costs for shipping containers, and worker shortages.

In addition to dealing with new vehicle launches, natural disasters, and the aftermath of the COVID-19 pandemic, the auto industry is in the midst of one of the most significant technological transformations in history as vehicles become more electrified and automated. Both electrification and automation require new parts and components, new suppliers, new competitors, new processes, and new investment in the automotive ecosystem. Some parts and components that enable these technological shifts – such as advanced batteries and lidar pucks – are not produced anywhere in the world in sufficient quantities to support the move to mass production. The industry needs to develop wholly new supply chains to support the shift to EVs and automated driving. These trends are driving a surge in investment in North America that may be completely unrelated to the USMCA entry into force.

Looking forward, automakers and public-traded auto suppliers are becoming increasingly concerned about decarbonizing not just their vehicles and factories but also the carbon emitted by the entire supply chain (CAR 2021). Wall Street investors are rewarding firms that are disrupting the industry and addressing climate change with their products and processes. A host of measurements and indices now exist to evaluate manufacturers' sustainability efforts, including the Dow Jones Sustainability Index, S&P ESG Indices, MSCI, Carbon Disclosure Project, FTSE4Good, and the Environmental Sustainability Index. While these indices measure environmental, social, and governance sustainability, reducing carbon for environmental sustainability and combat climate change is significant. Compact, localized supply chains with logistics that run on low- or no-carbon fuels are a growing trend in the industry that may confound attributing any changes in North A'erican investments to the USMCA entry into force.

AUTOMAKERS' INVESTMENT STRATEGIES

Many factors come into play when automakers and suppliers choose a location for a new facility. Some factors, such as investment incentives, tax rates, infrastructure enhancements, and utility access, are controlled by local and state governments. Others, such as the proximity of key suppliers and distance from critical transportation infrastructure, such as ports, cannot be influenced by officials in a given community to make their site more attractive to a potential investor (Yates and Lewchuk 2017). Compensating for these factors is an essential function of investment incentives, including grants and tax abatements.

Because automotive manufacturing typically provides well-paying jobs and the likelihood of additional follow-on investment from suppliers, competition to secure these investments is intense. Local and state governments collaborate to maximize the perceived value of the factors under their control to secure these investments. Successful collaboration between community, county, and state officials is critical. In Canada and Mexico, in particular, federal-level officials may be involved. Federal involvement is particularly important in Mexico, which has created the ProMexico organization to provide a single source of contact for potential investors (Piecyk, Mordue, and Yates 2016). Failure to include the Mexican federal government in investment negotiations can present issues in Mexico, as demonstrated by the negotiations regarding Kia Motors' new assembly plant in the state of Nuevo Leon. The Kia Motors deal had to be renegotiated in 2016 when a newly elected state governor refused to honour the deal struck with his predecessor. The facility was nearly complete when the new terms were finalized. Intervention from South Korea's president Park Geun-hye during a summit with Mexican president Enrique Peña Nieto was necessary to resolve the deadlock (Reuters 2016).

Investment incentives, such as financial grants, tax abatements, and low-cost or free land, have come to play a critical role in investment attraction, though they have also brought controversy (Yates and Lewchuk 2017). To secure automotive investments, communities often spend funds and forego tax revenue. Critics of these deals argue that they don't earn a net positive return for the community and that intense competition has driven the cost of securing critical automotive investments to unreasonable levels. The greater a bidding war a given incentive creates, the greater the benefit to the investing company, but the greater the chance that the cost of the incentive will exceed its benefits.

The costs associated with compliance with applicable trade agreements are one factor companies consider when making investment decisions. The cost of trade agreement compliance constitutes another variable outside the control of local governments vying for a potential investment. Investment sites with less favourable trade conditions require larger incentives to be competitive.

CAR analysed the decision factors influencing automotive manufacturing investment decisions in 2016 (see table 3). While this analysis chiefly addressed dynamics between the United States and Mexico, the advantages and disadvantages attributed to the United States also consistently apply to Canada.

As a result of its low-cost labour force, Mexico is the preferred destination for manufacturing operations with significant non-skilled labour content. Manufacturing operations that require a more specialized workforce are better suited to locations in the United States and Canada. Those operations are also more likely to make use of sophisticated tooling and newer processes. Therefore, the United States and Canada are a better fit, as both countries have more developed tooling and robotics industries and a more comprehensive supply base of service providers with the capability to supply these operations.

For manufacturing operations whose output will be exported outside North America, Mexico holds a substantial advantage over the United States that may negate some of its disadvantages in other categories. Canada features tariff-free export reach even broader than

Table 3. Facility Location Decision Factors National Comparison

Factor	High	Low	Why?
Labour content	Mexico	US	Labour is undeniably less expensive in Mexico than in the United States and Canada. Cost savings can be achieved in Mexico for processes with high labour content, but production that requires low labour content is more likely to stay or locate in the United States.
Automation & tooling transport	US	Mexico	Mexico does not have as robust a base of tooling expertise to support, maintain, and replace tooling as that found in the automotive clusters of the United States and Canada. Particularly for smaller firms, who have less developed internal tooling support capability, production that is highly dependent on automated processes is more likely to stay or locate in the United States and Canada.
Advanced materials	US	Mexico	Advanced materials, such as specific grades of high-strength steel, high-grade aluminium, carbon fibre, etc., are generally more readily available in the United States and Canada. Because materials sourced from the United States and Canada are less expensive if they are used near where they were produced, supplier manufacturing operations that are highly dependent on these materials are less likely to locate in Mexico.
Process-intensive	US	Mexico	Secondary processing providers (e.g., heat-treating and powder-coating) are more difficult to find in Mexico. US locations with access to these processes are more likely to retain or attract production for businesses requiring these processes. Manufacturers that do not need these processes are more likely to produce in Mexico.
Utility cost	US	Mexico	Utility costs are higher in Mexico, so energy-intensive production may not realize savings in Mexico. Therefore, processes that require high utility usage are more likely to remain or locate in the United States.
Non-NAFTA exports	Mexico	US	Due to Mexico's numerous free trade agreements, a Mexican vehicle or component exported outside of the NAFTA region may avoid the tariffs that US exports face. For this reason, manufacturers shipping outside of North America may choose to move to or locate in Mexico.
Specialized workforce	US	Mexico	Mexican workers, in general, have less specialized training in automotive production. Manufacturing that requires a great deal of specialized labour is often done in the United States, while production requiring little or no specialization may move to or locate in Mexico.

Source: Swiecki and Menk (2016).

Table 4. North American Investment Announcements, 2009–20 (US$)

	US	Canada	Mexico
2009	3,348,700,000	85,100,000	410,000,000
2010	11,237,905,862	927,200,000	3,088,000,000
2011	13,917,200,000	750,300,000	3,340,000,000
2012	3,759,700,000	183,000,000	4,236,000,000
2013	6,298,700,000	946,850,000	1,500,000,000
2014	10,506,700,000	750,000,000	7,011,000,000
2015	29,854,710,000	1,475,515,745	3,013,000,000
2016	653,400,000	1,219,696,000	300,000,000
2017	9,842,910,000	779,265,063	150,000,000
2018	2,755,500,000	1,076,658,500	0
2019	23,273,550,000	476,000,000	0
2020	3,478,250,000	3,866,490,000	170,000,000

Source: CAR (2009–20).

that offered by Mexico, but it doesn't share Mexico's low labour cost advantage. However, export-intensive operations locating in Mexico may be challenged by the country's constrained seaport system (DHL Global Forwarding 2021). This issue may particularly come into play for automotive manufacturing operations dependent on inputs imported from overseas.

Automakers announced a total of US $154.7 billion of automotive investments in North America from 2009 through 2020 (see table 4). Over this period, the United States accounted for 76.9% of these investments, with Canada garnering 8.1% and Mexico 15% (CAR 2009–2020).

Automaker investment activity in Mexico recently peaked in 2014, when automakers announced over US $7 billion of investments in the country, accounting for over 38% of all automaker investment in North America. While this peak was followed by a strong US $3 billion of investment in 2015, subsequent years saw a significant decline in automaker investment commitments in Mexico, with a total of only US $0.6 billion announced from 2016 through 2020 combined.

The transition from NAFTA to the USMCA can only partially explain the decline noted in automaker investment in Mexico. The decline began in 2016, while the expectation of a revision of NAFTA didn't become a factor until mid-2017. Meanwhile, US light vehicle sales reached a record level of 17.5 million units in 2016 and have not returned to those levels since, bottoming out at 14.4 million units in 2020 (Ward's Intelligence 2021). Automotive industry stakeholders had widely expected this downward trend in the automotive sales cycle. With nearly US $23 billion invested in Mexico between 2009 and 2015, it is likely the industry had already established the Mexican capacity it anticipated needing for the near-term future and saw little need for additional investment there. While automakers announced nearly US $70 billion in investments in the United States between 2015 and 2020, it is essential to note that a majority of those investments (76%) occurred in 2015 and 2019, when the Detroit Three renegotiated their agreements with the United Auto Workers (UAW) union. One hundred per cent of the investment announced due to these contract renegotiation agreements was dedicated to updating and expanding existing facilities, as was most of the remaining investments made by other automakers (CAR 2009 –2020). This reinvestment represents a contrast with Mexico, where most investments were to construct new assembly and powertrain plants.

Between September 2020 and January 2021, Canada secured more automaker investment than it had in any of the previous ten years, over US $4.7 billion, importantly to retool three of its eleven assembly lines – FCA-Windsor, Ontario; Ford-Oakville, Ontario; and GM-CAMI in Ingersoll, Ontario – to produce BEVs (CAR 2009–2020; Unifor 2020a, 2020b, 2020c, 2021). The Canadian and Ontario governments' role in securing these investments cannot be discounted (McIntyre and Hemmadi 2020).

NORTH AMERICAN VEHICLE PRODUCTION TRENDS

Vehicle production in North America is cyclical, changing in lockstep with automakers' anticipated sales volume and inventory replenishment needs. Data from table 5 show that production volumes recovered quickly following the Great Recession, peaked at 18.1 million units in 2016 (Ward's Intelligence 2021), and had begun a widely expected dip in 2017 when the anticipation of a new NAFTA agreement – the USMCA – began.

Vehicle production in Mexico followed a slightly different pattern than for North America as a whole since there is a delay from the time new factory announcements peaked in 2014 to when those new facilities begin high-volume production. Data from figure 4 show that vehicle production in Mexico peaked at a level of 4.1 million units in 2018, two years later than for North America as a whole and two years before the USMCA entered into force (US Department of Transportation 2021).

The US share of North American vehicle production has held steady since 2009, standing at 65% in 2009 and 66% in 2020. Canada and Mexico, however, have seen significant change during that period. In 2009, the two countries' share of North American production was nearly identical, at 17% for Canada and 18% for Mexico. As the announced vehicle production capacity came online in Mexico, however, the two countries' production share began to travel in opposite directions. By 2020, Canada's share of North American production had fallen to 10% while Mexico's had increased to 24%. It is important to note that the last new vehicle assembly plant in Mexico was announced in 2015, with no new capacity announcements since. Partially as a result, the growth in Mexico's share of North American production began to taper off in 2017, growing only by 0.4% from then until 2020 (US Department of Transportation 2021, OICA 2021).

Table 5. North American Vehicle Production by Country, 2009–20 (Thousands)

	2009	2010	2011	2012	2013	2014	2015	2016	2017	2018	2019	2020
Canada	1,490	2,068	2,135	2,463	2,380	2,394	2,283	2,371	2,194	2,026	1,917	1,376
Mexico	1,561	2,342	2,681	3,002	3,051	3,368	3,565	3,600	4,070	4,101	3,989	3,176
United States	5,709	7,743	8,655	10,333	11,066	11,661	12,105	12,178	11,190	11,298	10,874	8,822
TOTAL	8,760	12,153	13,471	15,798	16,497	17,423	17,954	18,149	17,454	17,424	16,779	13,374

Source: US Department of Transportation (2021), OICA (2021)

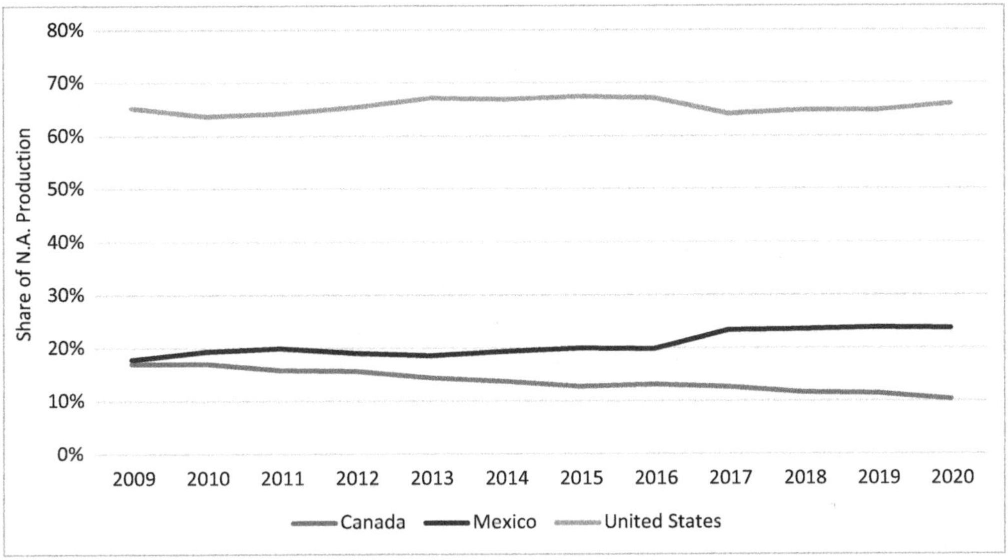

Figure 4. North American Vehicle Production Share by Country, 2009–20
Source: US Department of Transportation (2021); OICA (2021).

CONCLUSION

Trade agreements can play a significant role in automotive manufacturing investment decisions. However, their degree of importance can vary greatly based on whether production will rely on imported inputs, whether the product produced will be exported beyond the North American region, and other factors unrelated to trade. The North American automotive industry has been distributed across the region partly due to these factors, functioning as an integrated and highly productive symbiotic system.

Intra-regional trade is not the only trade-related factor driving investment location decisions in the North American automotive industry. Both Canada and Mexico feature a wider breadth of free trade deals than the United States, resulting in those countries being better suited to attract manufacturing investment that is either reliant on inputs imported from outside the region or focused on making products that will be exported beyond North America.

As the automotive industry continues to globalize, the proportion of automakers and suppliers with manufacturing locations in North America but headquartered in Asia or Europe has grown. Increasingly, this means that decisions regarding North American investments are made overseas.

Overall automaker investment growth in North American has accelerated since the three countries' leaders signed the USMCA – and the investments are growing mainly in the United States and Canada. In 2019 and 2020, US automaker investments were US $8.3 billion higher than the average of the two-year periods between 2009 and 2018. This increase represents roughly 28% of the US $30 billion in total automotive sector investment growth that the US International Trade Commission (2019) predicted the USMCA would incentivize.

The USMCA is more than merely an update of NAFTA. It brings with it content requirements that have already begun to affect automotive supply chains' location and cost performance. USMCA also entails new requirements for regional steel and aluminium sourcing and new labour value content requirements.

The transition from NAFTA to the USMCA arrived at a time coincident with the largest global pandemic in a century and seismic shifts in the automotive industry resulting from the approaching conversion to electrified and automated vehicles. These dynamics continue to affect the automotive industry, and their massive impact will be a critical driver of investment decisions that will transform the North American and global automotive industry. The USMCA will be an important, but not necessarily determinative, part of the context in which those investment decisions will be made.

REFERENCES

Anastakis, Dimitry. 2005. *Auto Pact: Creating a Borderless North American Auto Industry, 1960–1971.* Toronto: University of Toronto Press.

Automotive News. 2021. "Top Suppliers – North America, Europe and the World." 28 June 2021. https://shorturl.at/qzGQ7.

Bennett, Douglas C., and Kenneth E. Sharpe. 1985. *Transnational Corporations Versus the State: The Political Economy of the Mexican Auto Industry.* Princeton: Princeton University Press.

Brodzicki, Tomasz. 2021. "USMCA – An Enhanced Framework for Trade within North America" (blog). IHS Markit, 28 April 2021. https://www.spglobal.com/marketintelligence/en/mi/research-analysis/usmca-an-enhanced-framework-for-trade-within-north-america.html.

Center for Automotive Research. 2009–2020. *Book of Deals Investment Database.* Ann Arbor: CAR.

– 2021. *Sustainability Database.* Ann Arbor: CAR.

Celik, Levent, Bilgehan Karabay, and John McLaren. 2018. "Fast-Track Authority: A Hold-Up Interpretation." Working Paper no. 24427, March 2018, National Bureau of Economic Research. http://www.nber.org/papers/w24427.

Cooper, Jonathan M. 1994. "NAFTA'S Rule of Origin and Its Effect on the North American Automotive Industry." *Northwestern Journal of International Law & Business* 14 (2): 442–70. https://scholarlycommons.law.northwestern.edu/cgi/viewcontent.cgi?article=1387&context=njilb.

DHL Global Forwarding. 2021. "Ocean Freight Market Update." July 2021. https://globalmaritimehub.com/wp-content/uploads/2021/07/glo-dgf-ocean-market-update.pdf.

Garber, Peter M., ed. 1994. *Mexico-U.S. Free Trade Agreement.* Cambridge, MA: MIT Press.

Global Affairs Canada. 2018. *What Does the CPTPP Mean for the Automotive Sector?* Modified 7 February 2018. https://www.international.gc.ca/trade-commerce/trade-agreements-accords-commerciaux/agr-acc/cptpp-ptpgp/sectors-secteurs/auto.aspx?lang=eng.

Graham, Jeff. 2017. "Canada's Automotive Industry: A History in Exporting" (blog). Export Development Canada, 28 June 2017. https://www.edc.ca/en/blog/canadas-automotive-industry-exporting-history.html.

Harvard University. n.d. *The Atlas of Economic Complexity.* Accessed 14 July 2021. https://atlas.cid.harvard.edu/explore/geo?year=1995&country=39&productClass=HS&product=185&target=Product&partner=undefined&startYear=1995.

Holmes, J. 1992. "The Continental Integration of the North American Automobile Industry: From the Auto Pact to the FTA and Beyond." *Environment and Planning A: Economy and Space* 24 (1): 95–119. https://doi.org/10.1068/a240095.

Hurley, Neil P. 1959. "The Automotive Industry: A Study in Industrial Location." *Land Economics*, 35 (1): 1–14. https://www.jstor.org/stable/3144703.

IHS Markit. 2020.

Klier, Thomas, and James M. Rubenstein. 2008. *Who Really Made Your Car? Restructuring and Geographic Change in the Auto Industry.* Kalamazoo, MI: W.E. Upjohn Institute for Employment Research. https://research.upjohn.org/up_press/3/.

– 2017. "Mexico's Growing Role in the Auto Industry under NAFTA: Who Makes What and What Goes Where." *Economic Perspectives* 41 (6): 1–29. https://www.chicagofed.org/publications/economic-perspectives/2017/6.

McIntyre, Catherine, and Murad Hemmadi. 2020. "Canada's Electric Dream: Are Government Incentives and Smart R&D Enough to Build a Domestic EV Industry?" *The Logic*, 16 October 2020. https://thelogic.co/news/the-big-read/canadas-electric-dream-are-government-incentives-and-smart-rd-enough-to-build-a-domestic-ev-industry/.

Morrow, Adrian. 2017. "U.S. Withdrawal from NAFTA Is Back on Table: Wilbur Ross." *Globe and Mail*, 9 May 2017. https://www.theglobeandmail.com/news/world/us-withdrawl-from-nafta-is-back-on-table-wilbur-ross/article34934318/#c-image-0.

NAFTA. 1994. "Chapter 4: Rules of Origin. Annex 403.1: List of Tariff Provisions for Article 403(1)." https://www.international.gc.ca/trade-commerce/trade-agreements-accords-commerciaux/agr-acc/nafta-alena/fta-ale/04.aspx?lang=eng.

Nakayama, Shuji, and Ryo Asayama. 2020. "Japan Auto Companies Triple Mexican Pay Rather Than Move to US." *Nikkei Asia*, 28 June 2020. https://asia.nikkei.com/Business/Automobiles/Japan-auto-companies-triple-Mexican-pay-rather-than-move-to-US.

Observatory for Economic Complexity. 2019. *Mexico.* https://oec.world/en/profile/country/mex.

OICA (International Organization of Motor Vehicle Manufacturers). 2021. "2021 Production Statistics." https:/"www.oica.net/category/production-statistics/2021-statistics/.

Piecyk, Aleksander, Greig Mordue, and Charlotte Yates. 2016. *One-Stop Shopping Investment Attraction: Does the ProMexico Model Work for Canada?* Toronto: Automotive Policy Research Centre.

Reuters. 2016. "Mexico State Govt Reaches Deal with Kia to Cut Tax Breaks." 8 June 2016. https://www.reuters.com/article/mexico-kia-idCNE1N18K00G.

Shaiken, Harley. 1994. "Advanced Manufacturing and Mexico: A New International Division of Labor?" *Latin American Research Review* 29 (2): 39–71. https://www.jstor.org/stable/2503593.

Simpson, Timothy W. 2005. "Product Platform Design and Customization: Status and Promise." *Artificial Intelligence for Engineering Design, Analysis, and Manufacturing* 18 (1): 3–20. https://doi.org/10.1017/S0890060404040028.

Statistics Canada. 2019. "Table 12-10-0140-01." https://www150.statcan.gc.ca/t1/tbl1/en/tv.action?pid=1210014001.

Swanson, Ana, and Emily Cochrane. 2020. "Trump Signs Trade Deal with Canada and Mexico." *New York Times*, 29 January 2020. https://www.nytimes.com/2020/01/29/business/economy/usmca-trump.html.

Swiecki, Bernard, and Debbie Maranger Menk. 2016. *The Growing Role of Mexico in the North American Automotive Industry: Trends, Drivers, and Forecasts.* Center for Automotive Research. https://www.cargroup.org/wp-content/uploads/2017/02/The-Growing-Role-of-Mexico-in-the-North-American-Automotive-Industry-Trends-Drivers-and-Forecasts.pdf.

Swiecki, Bernard, Michael Schultz, Terni Fiorelli, Edgar Faler, and Yen Chen. 2021. *An Assessment of Japanese Automakers' Impact and Activity in the United States.* Center for Automotive Research. https://www.cargroup.org/wp-content/uploads/2020/07/JAMA-Publication.pdf.

Unifor. 2020a. "Unifor Fiat Chrysler Bargaining Report." https://www.unifor.org/sites/default/files/legacy/documents/document/local_1285_bargaining_report.pdf.

– 2020b. "Unifor-Ford of Canada Bargaining Report." https://uniforlocal707.org/wp-content/uploads/2020/09/ford_master_bargaining_brochure-final.pdf.

– 2020c. "Unifor General Motors Bargaining Report." https://www.unifor.org/sites/default/files/legacy/documents/document/gm_master_bargaining_report-final_0.pdf.

2021. "Unifor Local 88 General Motors Bargaining Report." https://www.unifor.org/sites/default/files/legacy/documents/document/gm_local_88_bargaining_report-final.pdf.

US Bureau of the Census. 2021. *USA Trade Online.* https://usatrade.census.gov/.

US Department of Transportation, Bureau of Transportation Statistics. 2021. https://www.bts.gov/content/world-motor-vehicle-production-selected-countries.

US International Trade Commission. 2019. *United States-Mexico-Canada Agreement: Likely Impact on the U.S. Economy and On Specific Industry Sectors*. Washington, DC: ITA. https://www.usitc.gov/publications/332/pub4889.pdf.

– n.d. "Trade Data and Analysis." Accessed 14 July 2021. https://www.trade.gov/trade-data-analysis.

USMCA (*United States-Mexico-Canada Agreement*). 2018. "Appendix to Annex 4-B of Chapter 4." 30 November 2018. https://ustr.gov/sites/default/files/files/agreements/FTA/USMCA/Text/04-Rules-of-Origin.pdf.

Ward's Intelligence. 2021. https://wardsintelligence.informa.com/datacenter.

World Bank. 2019. *Population Estimates and Projections.* https://datacatalog.worldbank.org/dataset/population-estimates-and-projections.

– n.d. "World Integrated Trade Solution." Accessed 14 July 2021. http://wits.worldbank.org/WITS/.

Yates, Charlotte, and Wayne Lewchuk. 2017. "What Shapes Automotive Investment Decisions in a Contemporary Global Economy?" *Canadian Public Policy* 43 (S1): S16–S29. https://doi.org/10.3138/cpp.2016-043.

7

From Automotive to Mobility Value Chains: Variety of Embeddedness and Regional Value Capture in Baden-Wurttemberg, Michigan, and Ontario

Elena Goracinova

The automotive industry is undergoing a technological transformation with automakers rebranding themselves as enablers of "transportation, mobility, and movement" rather than vehicle manufacturers exclusively (Koenig 2018). The transition away from mere "makers of cars" to "movers of people" presents new opportunities for firms, regions and communities. An important part of this metamorphosis entails automakers – and the vehicles they make – becoming a mere component of a more extensive system, not the central feature. As that process occurs, both automakers *and* tech companies must be engaged.

As automakers become transportation providers and rethink their position in an emergent mobility industry, so too should regions – where employment has historically depended on the manufacture and sales of vehicles – reconsider their strategies. Services – dealing with systems and data, fleet management, mobility operation, and mobility aggregation – rather than products are likely to represent an increasing portion of value in the emergent "mobility" space (Möller et al. 2019). New opportunities (and challenges) will emanate from the shift (Mögele and Rau 2020). In fact, studies have already shown that the way regions adjust to the opportunities digitization presents depends largely on their pre-existing conditions (Trippl et al. 2021).

For regions, the transition to a digitalized future (e.g., one where fewer cars are made and more "miles" are sold), autonomy, connectivity, electrification, and shared mobility may be prohibitively expensive (see Möller et al. 2019). Consequently, regions may seek to position themselves in the emerging mobility space via partnerships with target groups, including technology companies *and* traditional automotive players.

Here, I examine the capacity of regions with strong or emerging information, communications, and technology (ICT) sectors to combine those strengths with capabilities they already hold in the traditional automotive sector. I suggest that doing so may enable such regions and communities to extend long-held capabilities in vehicle manufacturing and propel them to a new "mobility-based" future. I also consider opportunities through that process for new, often small or medium-sized entrants, to emerge. That said, I also recognize that dynamics can differ between automotive jurisdictions.

This chapter examines traditional automotive regions' positions in global production networks (GPNs) and their ability to respond to the ongoing transition. I do so through case studies of Baden-Wurttenberg (B-W), Michigan, and Ontario. Each have strong automotive and ICT sectors. Two belong to the automotive "core" (B-W and Michigan) and one (Ontario) is a member of the automotive "semi-periphery." (For a brief explanation of automotive core and semi-periphery see chapter 1 of this collection.) Using quantitative and qualitative data from ninety-one stakeholders, the chapter delves into how the relationship between the auto and ICT sectors is affecting each region's trajectory – and if cross-sectoral linkages differ between core and semi-periphery regions.

The research finds that in core automotive regions – such as Baden-Wurttemberg and Michigan – automotive incumbents steer regional-level cooperation. I also find that the process of innovation is primarily performed by large incumbents or large new entrants, with local networks of small and medium-sized technology and service companies engaged in incremental improvements only. The latter struggle to keep up with the expectations of their (often larger) buyers or competition from their (often international) tech counterparts. Thus, in automotive core locations, significant segments of the regional economy do not benefit from the transition, and risk being left behind as original equipment manufacturers (OEMs) draw on ICT expertise and innovation from abroad. Because local tech firms remain captive to lead companies, such regions are also more vulnerable when automakers lose their dominant position in the new and broader "mobility" space.

On the other hand, I show that it has also been challenging to encourage weakly embedded automotive OEM and Tier 1 firms to innovate in Ontario, an automotive semi-periphery. The OEM–Tier-1 vacuum leaves more room for entrepreneurship. In Ontario, ICT multinational enterprises (MNEs) and a vibrant landscape of small and medium-sized enterprises (SME) tech firms are mobilizing a more significant share of available capital and labour resources to innovate in the emerging mobility space. This may enable a broader set of new entrants – and the region as a whole – to capture more high-value functions in global mobility value chains. This includes intelligent infrastructure and insurance solutions (aspects of the mobility space that traditional automakers are less likely to enter). Companies from outside the traditional automotive ecosystem are unlikely to start manufacturing vehicles themselves. Instead, they use their competencies in data management and software to sell platforms to established automotive firms and other actors (e.g., cities), which are becoming increasingly important actors in mobility ecosystems. Thus, this chapter argues that regions in the semi-periphery of automotive GPNs (e.g., Ontario) are not necessarily disadvantaged compared to core jurisdictions (B-W and Michigan) when it comes to reaping the benefits from digital mobility ecosystems.

As well, this chapter provides an overview of political science and economic geography literature to examine how regions' position in global value chains affects cross-sectoral dynamics, and how path dependence in these arrangements shapes industry transitions. The literature review helps to form hypotheses about how a region's pre-existing linkages with incumbents may lead to different outcomes across automotive jurisdictions. From there, I test hypotheses and discuss the findings.

DISRUPTION IN INCUMBENT INDUSTRIES: REGIONAL EMBEDDEDNESS AND VALUE CAPTURE IN NEW MOBILITY ECOSYSTEMS

Software, large computing power, and advanced sensors increasingly enable innovations in the mobility space, including advances associated with efficiency, connectivity, autonomous driving, and electrification. Software is also being integrated into roads and infrastructure. A growing ecosystem of connected devices exists along roadsides, including cameras to monitor traffic situations and sensors to gauge temperature and driving conditions (Heineke et al. 2019). All these devices must communicate … with cars as well as with central intelligent traffic management systems. New mobility services will be based on the data generated from vehicles, infrastructure, and passengers' mobile devices. In line with this, value creation will be based on new revenue streams, cost reduction, and increased safety. Therefore, automotive regions are obliged to position themselves not just as vehicle producers, but as partners in the development of the next generation of mobility systems, services, and products (see figure 1).

To achieve this, automotive regions will be expected to support a unique combination of capabilities. Certainly, automakers are expected to remain at the centre of the transformation, supporting core products, including the development, production, and sale of vehicles. At this stage, however, it is not yet clear who will dominate connectivity-oriented ecosystems. For example, automakers have been hesitant to develop new offerings such as insurance solutions or invest in the public infrastructure necessary to facilitate automation and autonomy (Möller et al. 2019). Studies also predict that mobility service ecosystems – which provide transportation options that go beyond traditional car ownership – may be dominated by companies new to the mobility sector (Heineke et al. 2019; Marletto 2019; Möller et al. 2019). Thus, hesitancy and ambiguity in such areas leave gaps in the system, creating a combination of opportunities and challenges for regions and firms.

The way automotive jurisdictions respond to this opportunity, or the extent to which indigenous companies – whether automotive or ICT – can extract value from these new mobility niches often differs. Depending on a region's historically inherited arrangements, the transition can have varied effects on its economic structure and ability to support next-generation mobility systems (Marletto 2019), aspects the next section of this chapter explores.

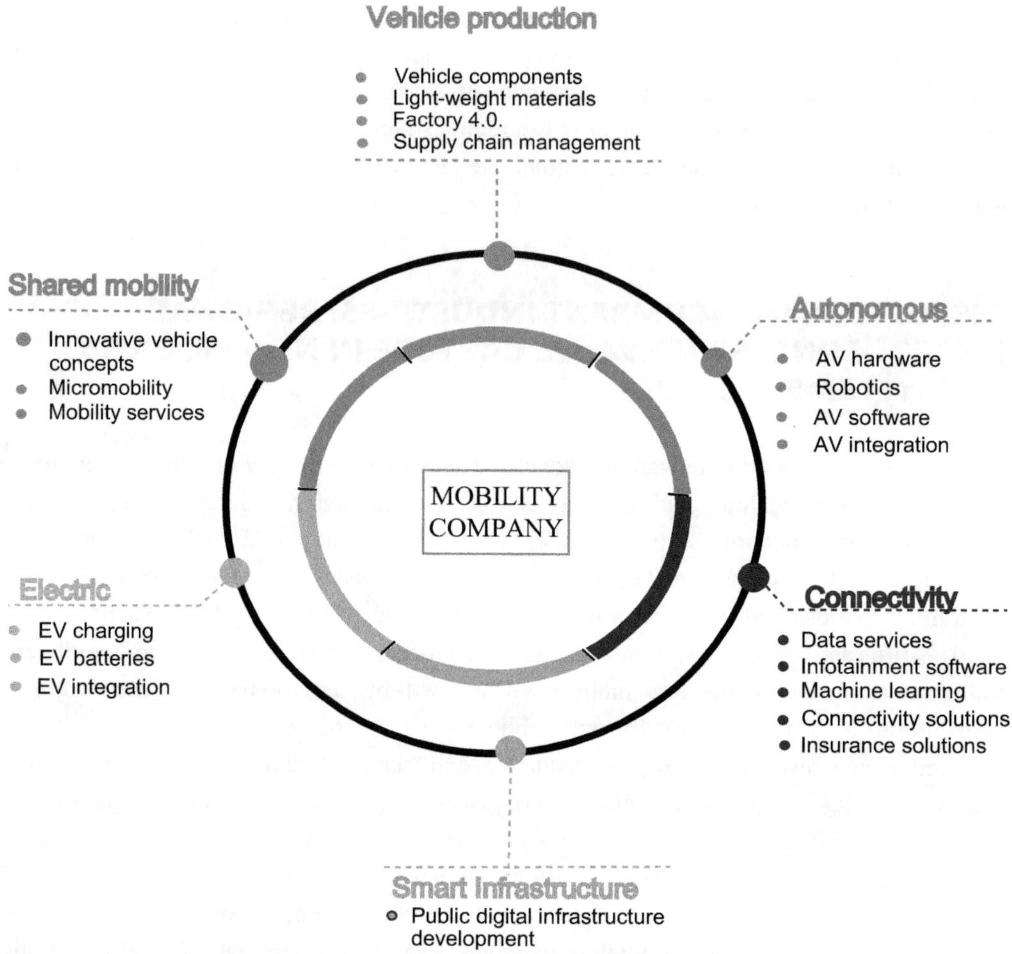

Figure 1. Emergent Mobility Ecosystems
Source: Heineke et al. (2019); author's research.

VARIETIES OF EMBEDDEDNESS AND VALUE CAPTURE

Automotive jurisdictions have unique positions in global value chains. For example, Canada is part of the global automotive industry's semi-periphery (Pavlínek 2018; Mordue and Karmally 2020). It has high levels of foreign ownership, lacks domestic OEMs, and has relatively high production costs. Meanwhile, B-W and Michigan are core automotive regions host to OEM headquarters. It is in core automotive regions where most automotive R&D occurs, not just by the OEMs but also by and with networks of suppliers and other technology-oriented firms.

In addition to jurisdictions' position in global value chains, one must also consider their systems of governance structures and intra-regional relationships. For example, automotive lead firms have different degrees of power, dependent on the region (in this case, core or semi-periphery) in question. Automakers in automotive core regions – like B-W and Michigan – are at the centre of the regional hub (Boja 2011; Portugal Ferreira et al., 2012). There, innovation is tailored to the hub's needs and, to some extent, driven by the primary hub firm (i.e., the automaker) itself. This includes innovation from the ICT sector, where firms have evolved to meet the automotive incumbent's needs, a pattern that contributes to further economic specialization in the region. Scholars view lead firms as the sparks that encourage cross-industry collaboration and technological change (Portugal Ferreira et al. 2012; Mayer 2013). Subcontracting in the anchor's local ecosystem fosters complex supplier networks, including the growth of small niche service SMEs, in related – in this case, automotive – industries (Nakano and White 2006).

Economic geographers and political economists propose that regions with embedded multinationals (MNEs) derive significant benefits (see Coe et al. 2004; Baglieri et al. 2010; Driffield, Lancheros, and Temouri 2015; Guimón et al. 2018; Yeung and Coe 2015). They promote knowledge spillovers and, by doing so, increase new firm formation rates; they generate externalities for existing local firms; and they help attract new investments from outside the local area. Therefore local actors, including policymakers, are encouraged to cultivate relationships with anchors, a process referred to as strategic coupling (see Yeung and Coe 2015; MacKinnon 2012) focused on the attraction of high value-added automotive investment (often R&D operations) and embedding MNEs in the local community (Coe et al. 2004; Driffield, Lancheros, and Temouri 2015; Guimón et al. 2018; Yeung and Coe 2015).

Positive attributes of such hub-and-spoke arrangements notwithstanding, the dominance of a lead firm also presents vulnerabilities. These become most evident when the core industry – and the lead firm – undergoes transformation. As well, in hub-and-spoke (i.e., lead-firm dominated) ecosystems, the firms constituting the spoke often show an intense rivalry, an outcome of their competing for contracts from the hub firm and which limits knowledge flows within the ecosystem. Information in such regions also risks becoming concentrated in a few key actors, effectively limiting entrepreneurship and the innovative capabilities of the region overall (Meyer et al. 2011). Additionally, overdependence on anchor firms can prove problematic in circumstances when the anchor, seeking new knowledge, distances itself from the region it dominates (Parrilli 2019).

In the end, hub-and-spoke structures can give rise to distinctive hierarchies of power and governance (Nakano and White 2006). As a counterbalance, institutions and firms within the region sometimes evolve to drive the creation of dynamic local enterprises capable of interacting on an equal basis with the large and powerful hub firm(s), potentially opening new market channels within and outside the sector. That said, such policies are often opposed by established interests within the region (for a discussion of this dynamic, see Christopherson and Clark 2007).

Hypothesis 1: In automotive regions where the automotive MNEs are firmly embedded and have longstanding inter-path linkages with the ICT sector, there is unlikely to be broad participation of domestic enterprises in mobility innovation. Consequently, innovation will be focused within the core product ecosystem.

The cluster model differs between automotive regions. Even in some core regions, like Bavaria in Germany, the home of BMW, automakers have less influence on the regional economy (Goracinova 2021). Automakers also have a less central position in semi-peripheral regions, where they are almost entirely externally oriented (Portugal Ferreira et al. 2012). These firms have limited intra-cluster exchanges. Instead, they favour stronger ties to the parent headquarters and sister subsidiaries elsewhere. For example, Canada is part of the global automotive industry's semi-periphery, where automakers are less embedded in the local knowledge economy (Pavlínek 2018; Mordue and Sweeney 2020). The challenges experienced in semi-peripheries are compounded in less developed, lower-wage countries like Mexico (members of the automotive "integrated periphery"), a situation that Vallejo et al. explain in chapter 10 of this collection.

Due to a transition of automobile production to lower-labour-cost nations, semi-peripheral automotive locations have recorded both an absolute *and* relative decline in vehicle production since 2000. As a result, they are now seeking to redefine or even re-establish their competitive advantages that neither stem from the power of core locations (such as the US or Germany) nor the cost competitiveness of the integrated periphery (like Mexico or countries in eastern Europe) (Mordue and Sweeney 2020). At the same time, incumbent and new actors in neighbouring regimes (e.g., software, urban planners, technical bureaucracy) may be more active innovators. Automotive regions with weakly embedded automakers and robust ICT trans-local actors, or at least ones that have evolved separately from the region's automotive industry, may be more open to experimenting with new mobility solutions (Turnheim and Geels 2019). Studies have shown that unlike automotive incumbents, which are primarily involved in core products, ICT companies are active across value chains from end to end (Manders and Klaassen 2019). They have offerings for connectivity, such as software or data services, whereas traditional OEMs do not. While they collaborate with non-automotive players to develop new offerings, such as insurance solutions or public infrastructure, traditional OEMs are unlikely to enter such areas.

Opportunities also exist for smaller firms and new entrants, a function of the fact that the sector's modularity lowers barriers to entry. Unlike the automotive industry, aside from a few global companies the software industry presents a highly fragmented structure (Hajela and Akbar 2013), with many start-ups and innovative SMEs. Studies have found evidence of the positive effect of co-location with incumbent ICT firms, including knowledge spillovers (Hannigan, Cano-Kollmann, and Mudambi 2015). From this, we derive a second hypothesis:

Hypothesis 2: In automotive regions where mature entrants from the ICT industry (or other neighbouring sectors) are more embedded and independent from the automotive industry, there is more scope for innovation outside the core product ecosystem led by new entrants.

Table 1. Case Study Interviews by Type

Organizations		Ontario	B-W	Michigan
Firms	Automotive	5 (OF:1-OF:5)	6 (BF:1-BF:6)	4 (MF:1-MF:4)
	ICT (including primarily automotive suppliers)	21 (OF:6-OF:26)	14 (BF:7-BF:20)	2 (MF:5-MF:6)
Intermediaries	Technology consortia, clusters, chambers of commerce	6 (OI:1-OI:6)	5 (BI:1-BI:5)	2 (MI:1-MI:2)
	Research org.	2 (OI:7-OI:8)	5 (BI:6-BI:10)	1 (MI:3)
Policymakers		10 (OP:1-OP:10)	7 (BP:1-BP:7)	1 (MP:1)

In satellite platform clusters, studies have also documented efforts to embed MNEs and improve endogenous innovation capacities. In such locations, the effectiveness of policy measures tends to be limited by other factors, including home country effects, locally specific context, and FDI-host relationships (Rutherford et al. 2018). Even so, institutional actors in branch-plant economies may serve to avoid capture by large corporates if MNEs are less embedded in the political system. Therefore, to gain understanding about the process of path formation in automotive jurisdictions, we must consider MNE embeddedness and the effects of local institutional actors.

METHODS

To test the hypotheses, outcomes are compared via case studies in core and semi-peripheral automotive regions. The jurisdictions selected have robust automotive and ICT sectors. They have taken different routes and adopted different strategies in response to the transformations. The analysis presented here relies on intensive interviewing to gather observations on policy processes, social attributes, and interactions (in both the public and private sphere). Those interviews were conducted between 2016 and 2020. As per table 1, a total of ninety-one interviews were completed in Ontario (ON), B-W, and Michigan with a broad range of actors. While the identity of interviewees is not provided, the geographic location and the type of organization from which they were recruited is indicated. Those aspects are delineated in table 1 below. Recruitment was accomplished with the snowball method. Interviewees included (1) innovation intermediaries (eight in ON, ten in B-W, three in Michigan); (2) automotive incumbents and Tier 1 suppliers (five in ON, six in B-W, and four in Michigan); (3) traditional and digital tech SMEs and start-ups (twenty-one in ON, fourteen in B-W, and two in Michigan); and (4) policymakers (ten in ON, seven in B-W, one in Michigan).

The results from Michigan are also based on extensive secondary work done on the region's automotive sector transformation (Hannigan, Cano-Kollmann, and Mudambi 2015; Sturgeon, Biesebroeck, and Gereffi 2009; Pavlínek 2012; Harpel 2011; Klepper 2010; Jacobs 2009; Brogan 2018).

BADEN-WURTTEMBERG AND MICHIGAN: CONTRASTING CASES OR SIMILAR TRAJECTORIES?

The automotive industry has been central to both B-W's and Michigan's economies. Scholars argue that B-W and Michigan are contrasting cases of development in the automotive industry (see Strambach and Klement 2012). Whereas the latter provides a textbook example of industrial decline and all its devastating impacts on urban and socio-economic developments, the former has been a model for how to master several crises.

The two regions exhibit similarities in their position in GPNs. Specialization of the automotive industry in both regions has been fuelled by economies of scale in inputs and access to labour pools (Hannigan, Cano-Kollmann, and Mudambi 2015). In both, lead firm concentration rose and supplier networks tightened, resulting in a hub-and-spoke configuration (see Klepper 2010; MacDuffie 2013; Markusen 1996; Digaetano and Lawless 1999). In both cases, there has been an ongoing transition from production to innovation, albeit the change has happened at different paces, with Michigan shedding manufacturing jobs more quickly. However, even in B-W, automakers have started to offshore a substantial portion of manufacturing (see Cody 2015).

In both cases, the profiles of the automotive industry have undergone significant transformation. For example, service jobs related to the automotive sector now outpace the growth of manufacturing ones (see Dispan et al. 2017; Pittelko, Bommersbach, and Erickcek 2016; Harpel 2011). The profile of the automotive industries in both locations is also adjusting due to the increasing importance and influence of the ICT sector. Additionally, the proportion of engineers in the labour force in both regions is above the national average, and their professional scientific and technical services industries have thrived (Pittelko, Bommersbach, and Erickcek 2016; Piazza et al. 2012). In both regions innovation, as measured by the output of patents, is increasing. It is also becoming increasingly concentrated in the automotive sector. In Detroit, for example, more than 40% of patents belong to the Big Three and its suppliers (Hannigan et al. 2015; Simons 2019). In the case of B-W, four large companies (Bosch, Daimler, ZF Friedrichshafen, and Porsche) filed approximately 50% of all patents in 2014 (Koch et al. 2018).

Throughout their history, these two regions have taken differing but on the whole non-interventionist approaches to economic development. In Michigan, the state government has never had a comprehensive, long-term development policy, despite calls to do so and some efforts to diversify the economy (Jacobs 2009). Unlike Michigan, in Germany there is ample support for vocational education/training and a technology transfer system (Cody

2015), its institutions evolving to focus on larger enterprises with limited attention on SMEs (Goracinova 2021). In fact, SMEs report limited access to institutions like the Fraunhofer Institute (Schröder 2013; Sternberg 2002; Fuchs and Shapira 2005).

INSTITUTIONAL AND FIRM EVOLUTION DURING TECHNOLOGICAL TRANSITION

The ongoing transition to "mobility" based framework has required that private-sector actors assume roles of prominence (Brogan, 2018; Bartik, 2017, 2019; Glynn, Shen, and Goetz 2020). In Michigan, the process is driven by a network of economic development interests, bridging public and private sectors. The influence of the Big Three and other automotive stakeholders is notable (Glynn, Shen, and Goetz 2020). For example, through the Michigan Department of Transportation and the Michigan Economic Development Corporation, the state supports and partially funds cross-sectoral projects focused on its transportation infrastructure. Additionally, Mcity is a major public-private R&D initiative between the University of Michigan and a group of companies, including auto manufacturers, suppliers, insurance companies, and telecommunications and data management firms. By 2024, it had conducted $28 million in reseach projects and had 150 researchers engaged (University of Michigan 2024). At Mcity, companies test their connected and automated vehicle technologies products and services in the world's first controlled test environment (University of Michigan 2024). However, only two of the founding companies are SMEs, an indication that domestic, standalone ventures are often crowded out from cluster activities by the presence of large domestic and multinational firms (interview MF:5, also see Mack, Credit, and Suandi 2018).

Meanwhile, in Michigan, mobility-oriented start-ups do have access to grants up to $1 million via the state's PlanetM program. The program seeks to support or attract start-up enterprises, locally or internationally (interviews with MF:5–6). To date, there is little evidence to suggest the Big Three are interested in spawning new entrepreneurial companies in the Detroit region; interviewees suggesting automotive OEMs often have adversarial relationships with start-ups (interviews with MF:5 and MF:3; also see Mudambi et al. 2017). Consistent with that, a study of 265 autonomous vehicle (AV) firms across the world shows that few are located in Michigan (Bezruchonak 2018). Instead, the region remains dependent on automotive lead firms for technological upgrading.

In Michigan, large incumbents also tend to spearhead initiatives to encourage partnerships between mobility companies and cities to address the latter's transportation challenges. For example, in 2018 the Detroit Mobility Innovation Initiative was formed, bringing together ten public, private, and philanthropic partners into six twelve-month transportation-oriented pilot projects, each costing between $200,000 and $600,000 and funded by the partners. Key private-sector partners included large automakers and Tier 1 automotive suppliers.

Similarly, large incumbents also tend to drive change in Baden-Württemberg. There, large MNEs like Daimler, Porsche, and Bosch are implementing projects to transform aspects of their businesses to introduce new technology and address emerging "mobility" needs. The B-W government has financially supported research centres like the Automotive Simulation Centre and the incubator ARENA2036, which brings together automakers with large-scale suppliers, ICT companies, and university researchers. Interviews with the two intermediaries and five of the companies involved suggest these activities have been dominated by large enterprises.

Several public and private connected and autonomous vehicle (C/AV) testbeds also operate in the B-W region. Private testbeds are dominated by (large) OEMs and Tier 1s. Public testbeds tend to be facilitated by grants to academic and research institutions. Few SMEs are engaged. Beyond that, other publicly supported initiatives in B-W include cluster-affiliated accelerators to support start-ups. Interviews with intermediaries suggest that their primary goal is to connect start-ups or established ICT businesses with traditional automotive businesses, the main objective being revitalization of the latter rather than the growth or success of the former.

In B-W, when OEMs see value in local technology, interviewees suggest their main method of accessing it is via acquisition (interview BF:16–20). B-W automotive OEM and supplier interviewees also indicated they do not consider undertaking measures to support the creation of an entrepreneurial ecosystem in B-W as an objective. Rather, they are comfortable with accessing global and extra-regional pipelines to access new technologies. These findings are in line with the conclusion by scholars such as Stahlecker and Zenker (2017), who claim that technological change in B-W tends to occur within the context of the established automotive industry, either regionally or globally. Development of relationships with actors outside the established automotive sector are rare (also see Späth et al. 2016).

On the whole, the initiatives captured in table 2 do help automakers connect with ICT companies. However, less than 20% of the ICT companies engaged in these "mobility innovation initiatives" are domestic or indigenous to the region. Interviews in B-W help explain this phenomenon. There, more than 50% of SME ICT companies reported their focus as being on incremental innovations aimed at meeting automaker expectations (rather than R&D or development of new mobility verticals, such as mobility as a service). Meanwhile, the more R&D-intensive start-ups do *not* view working with OEMs as aligned with their interests. In fact, their tendency is to view potential OEMs' or Tier 1s' interest in their technology as something to be removed from market, away from competitors.

Therefore, much of the local ICT sector, and especially SMEs, remains captive to incumbent automotive firms. This gap in innovation capabilities can further increase asymmetries between firms, with some increasingly more competitive than others. Small firms' failure to diversify along with their over-reliance on automakers also contributes to faltering financial performance, especially if their main clients lose their dominant position in mobility value chains. This phenomenon can lead to a hollowing out of the core domestic industrial base and a decline in international competitiveness (Cowling and Tomlinson 2003).

Table 2. Overview of B-W and Michigan C/AV Initiatives by Type

	B-W	Michigan
Coordination between industry-academia-government to develop/test technology	Automotive Simulation Centre ARENA2036	MTC Mcity Project Kinetic
Inclusion of start-ups/SMEs in cluster- and sector-spanning activities	Start-up Autobahn No direct funding Cluster networks across the land try to support start-ups/SMEs in the space	Tech Stars Planet M testing grants

ONTARIO: OPPORTUNITY IN THE SEMI-PERIPHERY?

Ontario has historically been an important North American automotive production location, a consequence of several specific, yet related, structural conditions: (1) early investments by American MNEs in the province, (2) the existence of several Canadian-owned Tier 1 suppliers headquartered there (e.g., Magna International, Linamar, Wescast, ABC Technologies, and Martinrea), and (3) a borderless North American environment created and nurtured by a series of continental trade and production zones, including the Canada-US Auto Pact in 1965, the Canada-US Free Trade Agreement (FTA) of 1988, and the North American Free Trade Agreement (NAFTA) of 1993. In the latter part of the previous century, Ontario's foreign-owned OEM presence expanded to include two Japanese MNEs, Toyota and Honda. Since 2000, however, Canadian (i.e., Ontario) vehicle production has contracted, the result of US MNEs closing plants and shifting production to lower-cost areas in the North American region. (For a comprehensive discussion of North American–wide patterns affecting automotive assembly plant openings and closures, including the public policy measures supporting those decisions see chapter 2 of this collection.)

Unlike the cases of Michigan and B-W, Ontario's share of automotive R&D has not increased, an indication of OEMs' weak embeddedness in Ontario and the dearth of lead firms in general (Mordue and Karmally 2020). Despite its strengths in ICT, Ontario is a *relevant* R&D centre, just not a *strategic* one. Even Canadian-headquartered Tier 1 suppliers are reluctant to invest in R&D in the area, making most of their investments abroad (these include Magna, Martinrea, and Linamar) (Carey and Mordue 2022; Mordue and Sweeney 2020). In the absence of large, indigenous anchor firms – which are more likely than SMEs to use patents to protect their innovations – the region is not a leader in automotive patenting (Hughes and Mina 2010; Athreye and Fassio 2018). Subsidiaries remain tightly controlled by their parent companies and are not granted the mandates or resources necessary to pursue ambitious innovation projects. It is also challenging for subsidiaries to form long-term relationships with university researchers who prioritize other goals, such as training highly qualified personnel and advancing their own research agendas (Goracinova 2019).

More evident in semi-peripheral automotive regions like Ontario are horizontal power-sharing networks. Indigenous ICT SMEs and start-ups have grown outside of the captive relationships that dominate the automotive industry. Unlike the automotive industry, ICT clusters emerged by exploiting the local knowledge base to commercialize new products and services (Lucas et al. 2009). Since the early 1960s, Ontario has been home to several dynamic and growing ICT clusters formed around foreign and domestic flagship MNEs and research institutions. Over time, Ontario's ICT clusters have experienced successive waves of entrepreneurial start-ups (Spigel 2017; Denney, Southin, and Wolfe 2020; Haley, Creutzberg, and Julie 2017). ICT subsidiaries have also been attracted by regional capabilities, causing them to invest in high-value-added R&D.

Ontario's R&D-related ICT sector is spatially concentrated in three cities (Trippl et al. 2021). First, Ottawa offers access to hardware skills and experience, allowing companies to develop reliable networking technologies for the Internet of Things. Ottawa also hosts R&D and production activities by established foreign firms (Alcatel-Lucent, Cisco Systems Canada, Huawei Technologies Canada, CIENA Corporation, and Mitel Networks) as well as several newcomers (Corsa Technologies and CENX) and domestic leaders like QNX, a subsidiary of Blackberry (Haley, Creutzberg, and Julie 2017). Second, Toronto is a leading hub for artificial intelligence, with Google, Nvidia, LG, and Samsung operating artificial intelligence (AI) labs there (Denney, Southin, and Wolfe 2020). Third, Kitchener-Waterloo has strengths in various ICT industries (communications equipment manufacturing, software, etc.) and hosts the headquarters of large domestic technology companies like Blackberry and Open Text. Nonetheless, other than QNX, few domestic software companies interviewed have a significant presence in the automotive industry (interviews OF:6–21).

In Ontario, the provincial and federal govenments have sought to attract high-value-added FDI across a range of sectors, including both automotive and ICT. In fact, Canada offers one of the highest rates of government support for university-industry research collaboration in the world (Croteau 2017). Both the federal and Ontario governments have invested heavily in ICT and automotive R&D via fundng support to universities, Centres of Excellence, and public research facilities. Together, both governments have taken a decidedly more activist approach than in Michigan or B-W, spending aggressively in support of indigenous tech companies (Schienstock 2007; Constantelos 2014). Because of this, a broader range of economic interests are represented in the region's economic development efforts. For instance, Vinodrai's (2016) work on Waterloo and Haley, Creutzberg, and Julie's research on Ottawa (2017) suggest that there is (relatively) broad-based participation of economic actors in regional strategic management.

An essential part of both the federal and Ontario governments' funding for innovation has been grants to centres/intermediaries to encourage both individual firm, inter-firm, and university-industry collaboration (Haddow 2015, 184; Haley, Creutzberg, and Julie 2017). Generally co-funded by industry, many intermediaries are led by regional non-state actors with knowledge of the unique dynamics affecting the technology and digital sectors (Croteau 2017). Such measures have persisted since the 1960s, helping the provincial government support regional economic growth (Bradford and Wolfe 2013).

In recent years, as the transition to a mobility-focused framework took hold, some actors in Ontario started to suggest that the province's growing and successful ICT sector offered potential to help position the province as a leader in mobility technologies (interviews OI:5–6; OF:6-15). However, unlike in the cases of B-W and Michigan, our investigation has not found evidence of formalized OEM-led cross-sectoral and cross-industry initiatives – between automakers, telcos, vendors, and universities. Instead, in contrast to B-W and Michigan, automotive actors in that space in Ontario have tended to perform R&D independent of other actors.

Research that does occur in Ontario OEM facilities is generally focused on niche activities, entailing limited interaction with indigenous tech firms (interviews OF:6–10). Mobility-oriented SMEs interviewed for this project suggested OEM research facilities compete with what *they* are doing. The remainder said little overlap exists between OEM research and their own. Consistent among all SME and start-up interviewee responses is their observation that research by and with OEM subsidiaries is curtailed by OEMs' limited authority: "For any purchase decisions, we have to go to the HQ. It doesn't really matter to us that Company A has R&D offices here" (interview OF:20).

In light of these limitations, we note growing will at every level of government to invest in C/AV testbed infrastructure and aid in the development and strategic coupling of local resources into global networks (interviews OP:1–6). Starting in the early 2010s, Ontario's dynamic infrastructure of intermediaries helped facilitate a range of stand-alone temporary initiatives supporting a new bottom-up sociotechnical path for Ontario. The initiative superseded a previous focus on car manufacturing to include a broader interpretation of the Ontario mobility ecosystem – all goods and people that move. Through this, an increasingly multisector approach has been adopted, including the provision of funding for vehicle-related technology projects.

Actors involved in the initiatives have described the goal as being centred on growing domestic ICT enterprises in the new mobility verticals, the focus an outcome of traditional automotive actors having limited interest in using the region as a platform for development of new in-vehicle technologies (even though initiatives were initially marketed as interventions to strengthen the automotive sector exclusively). "Public officials affiliate themselves with a broad vision of 'smart mobility' and look at it from the perspective of cities, environment" the customer journey and not just from the automotive perspective" (interview OI:4).

Starting in 2014, we note the emergence of a modest CDN $3 million connected vehicles/autonomous vehicles public funding program (CVAV). CVAV was a pilot partnership involving the Ontario Ministry of Transportation and the Ontario Ministry of Economic Development, Job Creation and Trade. It was the first step towards development of a coordinated approach in Ontario for connected, autonomous, and shared mobility. In it, the Ontario Centres of Excellence (OCE) was charged with setting priorities in the C/AV space, serving as an interface between various actors and institutions involved. Initially, the CVAV program was meant to focus on the automotive industry. However, subsequent engagement with network actors showed that the initiative needed to take a more holistic approach to transportation (interviews OI:8, OP:1–3). They discovered that ICT companies were also anxious to become involved, adding autonomy and connectivity to vehicles (from personal cars to public transit, including rail and non-passenger vehicles) and developing the architecture upon which C/AVs would be based.

In 2017, the provincial government moved to support resource formation and enhance organizational coherence between local government/public-private efforts. The initial $3 million CVAV program was expanded to a five-year, $80 million autonomous vehicle innovation network (AVIN). Like the 2014 CVAV pilot, AVIN aligned the OCE team with the Ministry of Transportation and the Ministry of Economic Development, Job Creation and Trade to manage day-to-day operations. An industry advisory group was also established consisting of companies of various sizes and stages in their development.

AVIN had two main goals. The first was to help de-risk the development of new technologies and create the organizational preconditions (e.g., networking opportunities) to help network members access global markets (interviews OP:1–6). The second was to help cities and other local authorities to develop the capacity to adopt new mobility technologies across Ontario through pilot projects (see table 3). Additionally, AVIN coordinated a competition for six regional technology development sites. It also incentivized local organizations – including cities, regional economic development agencies, regional innovation centres, and universities – to form alliances to help individual regions transition to C/AV mobility.

In line with Ontario's historically decentralized approach, the goals of local actors in so far as the mobility-oriented framework is concerned are not uniform. Each is motivated by local knowledge of how their region functions and the capabilities and interests of its firms (many of which are SMEs) (interviews OI:1–8). The intention is that they identify and deploy the research infrastructure and equipment to experiment and develop in the area(s)/research streams they have identified (e.g., using test tracks, incubators/accelerator programs, etc.). The objective is that the six sites established through AVIN help create a more effective research and commercialization environment upon which companies can draw for support and expertise. Moreover, setting targeted mandates for each region is expected to allow "fewer redundancies/overlaps" (interviews OF:16–19)."For instance, if a company wants to test their product, they would come to us [Ottawa L5 Demonstration Track], but if they need help with software, we will send them to Waterloo. We also collaborate with MaRS for data purposes" (interview OI:4).

Table 3. Regional Technology Development Centres Funded by AVIN in Ontario

Region/type of partner	Durham region	Hamilton region	Ottawa region	Toronto region	Waterloo region	Windsor-Essex
Regional innovation centre	Spark Centre	Innovation Factory	Invest Ottawa	MarS	Communitech	We Tech Alliance
University	Ontario Tech University	McMaster	Carleton University of Ottawa	University of Toronto Ryerson York	University of Waterloo	University of Windsor
College	Durham College	Mohawk	Algonquin			St. Clair College
Regional Municipality/ city/regional economic development agency	Region of Durham	City of Hamilton	City of Ottawa		Waterloo Region Economic Development Corporation	Windsor Essex Economic Development Corporation/ City of Windsor

The province renewed the program in the 2021 budget with an additional CDN $56.4 million for four years under the new name Ontario Vehicle Innovation Network (OVIN). Regional sites anticipate that they will continue to form an important component of the new OVIN. It is also expected that, in addition to the C/AV space, OVIN will expand emphasis to encompass electric and shared mobility, a strategy consistent with the view espoused in the expert panel report *Choosing Canada's Automotive Future* (Council of Canadian Academies 2021).

Meanwhile, the OCE is also coordinating Ontario's efforts to advance C/AV and 5G technology, making it easier for SMEs to access 5G testbeds by connecting AVIN sites with resources from ENCQOR. (ENCQOR is a public-private network that, as part of its mandate, is exploring transportation products and services in a 5G environment in collaboration with local SMEs and universities. Its membership includes the governments of Ontario, Quebec, and Canada.) ENCQOR and OVIN demonstrate the public sector's prominent role in incentivizing foreign investment and leveraging it for the domestic ICT sector's benefit.

A series of federal initiatives are also at play, providing further evidence of the elevated (relative to Michigan and B-W) role of the public sector. For example, the federal Industrial Research Assistance Program (IRAP) joined with an Ottawa-based accelerator (L-Spark) in 2018. It subsequently approached QNX with an offer to help recruit tech firms to build connected car technologies and secure Internet of Things solutions on its platform. As well, the federal government's Next Generation Manufacturing (NGen) Supercluster initiative has afforded smaller technology firms like Clearpath Robotics and Myant opportunities to co-create mobility solutions with domestic Tier 1 automotive suppliers. Another federal-level program that complements provincial efforts is the Advance Connectivity and Automation in the Transportation System (ACATS) program led by Transport Canada. ACATS has funded a standards association, an innovation consortium, and cities, supporting mobility-oriented research projects and pilots. It has also helped Ontario's Ministry for Transportation enhance automated and connected vehicle implementation pilot programs in Ontario cities.

Overall, institutional actors in Ontario have sought to not just attract or retain automotive FDI but also capture and facilitate benefits for technology firms. Interviews suggest that the initiatives have drawn the most active participation from local tech-SMEs and academics, including increased activity along several mobility verticals. This includes smart infrastructure, mobility as a service platform, and data services. Unlike in B-W and Michigan, the focus in Ontario has been less on helping automakers modernize by connecting that industry with ICT but rather on growing tech firms in emerging verticals. This path has the potential to alter the geography of the automotive sector, a consequence of places like Ottawa and Waterloo adopting increasing profiles in the emerging mobility-oriented space.

Ontario-based initiatives have also drawn the attention of domestic and foreign multinationals (interviews OF:1–5, 16–18). Interviewees note more interest from large tech companies (e.g., software, telecom, networking), both foreign and domestic, than automakers. It is suggested that this is an outcome of the ICT industry providing more channels for the entry of SMEs into global value networks. This occurs partly because of the ICT industry's global governance structure. It is also an outcome of ICT actors being more strongly embedded in the region. This pattern heralds a disruption in the existing industry structure. In other words, a mobility-oriented framework is causing power and attention to tilt to new actors, not the near-exclusive interest of large foreign automotive OEMs.

Representatives from AVIN/OVIN and the regional centres it supports are seeking relations with technology-based OEM partners like Ericsson or QNX, as doing so allows more SMEs to be involved. For instance, Invest Ottawa staff were eager to be involved in the ENCQOR initiative because doing so meant Ericsson, Ciena, and other large tech partners would provide the 5G infrastructure for the L5 test track project. Similar behaviour is evident in federally funded projects. After SMEs and start-ups were chosen for the L-Spark-QNX program (described above), they received technical support and advice from QNX engineers. SMEs have learned that they can use an association with technology-based MNEs and OEMs to pursue various operational, commercial, technological, or reputational benefits that may be difficult or impossible to attain via transactional relationships (interview OF:21). For large technology companies looking to establish a profile in the automotive/mobility space, initiatives like AVIN and ENCQOR are helpful. Those firms understand that they are able to help them discover mobility-related applications for their underlying technologies or platforms (QNX platform, 5G technology). It also helps ICT MNE subsidiaries connect with Canadian tech MNEs like Blackberry QNX (Saba 2019; interviews OF:16–18).

While Ontario-located technology firms have gained some traction in the emerging mobility space, they have been less successful in seeking to engage with automotive OEMs. That said, Canadian companies do have occasion to present their technology to Tier 1 automotive suppliers. For example, the Automotive Parts Manufacturers Association (APMA), which runs a test zone in Stratford, Ontario, has put out a call for proposals for companies to integrate their technologies in twenty vehicles (sedans, CUVs, SUVs, transit buses, and utility trucks). However, it has been discovered that subsidiaries of automotive OEMs have limited mandates to source new suppliers or new technology. Their interests are confined to specific types of partnerships (either with start-ups or universities) dictated by headquarters (interviews OF:1–5). The hurdles experienced by SMEs in Ontario are in line with other research underlining the difficulties SMEs face working with automotive OEMs (Dodourova and Bevis 2014).

DISCUSSION AND CONCLUSION

This chapter shows that mobility transitions occur because of intricate interaction patterns between a range of actors with different strategies, interests, and motivations. The continued success of Ontario in the transformation of the mobility system will depend not only on firm-side asset modification but also on a wide range of system-level actors, including all three levels of government, post-secondary education organizations, intermediaries, and industry associations. The degree of structural transformation is often shaped by these interactions, which have an emergent character grounded in pre-existing regional characteristics.

The chapter draws on recent conceptual advances from evolutionary economic geography to develop an analytical framework that casts light on how regional preconditions underpin different routes of transformation. The framework is applied to a qualitative comparative analysis of industrial path development in three automotive regions: Ontario, Baden-Wurttemberg (B-W), and Michigan. It finds that it is not just a region's position in global production networks that shapes its trajectory. We discover that in automotive jurisdictions, we must also examine how lead firms interact with local firms and'non-firm actor' to affect innovation in and across enterprises.

B-W's and Michigan's embeddedness in GPNs has contributed to industrial structure continuity, while Ontario's branch plant dynamics have made room for more innovation among new and often smaller entrants. In B-W and Michigan, the dominance of incumbent automakers, coupled with laissez-faire policies, has opened few opportunities for new entrants to disrupt the existing industry structure. Traditional automotive OEMs and Tier 1 suppliers are innovating in the electric and autonomous vehicle space. There, SMEs serve a supporting function where necessary. Overall, regional assets are dedicated to retaining and attracting new MNEs, while local SMEs remain captive.

In Ontario, it has been challenging to encourage weakly embedded OEM and Tier 1 firms to perform more R&D in the region, and there has been limited growth of engineering and design capabilities among suppliers. This has translated into automotive incumbents having more limited power than in B-W and Michigan. That said, policy has historically been more activist. In this context, the technology sector, encompassing a multitude of technology-based SMEs and global technology lead firms, has evolved independently from automotive needs. However, more strongly embedded ICT MNEs *have* supported innovation in the space, often in policy-driven partnerships with local technology-oriented SMEs. Moreover, innovation activities in Ontario, unlike in Michigan and B-W, are focused on areas such as smart infrastructure and a range of data services. These are areas in which automakers are less likely to heavily invest.

These findings support the chapter's hypotheses and challenge and qualify extant research by economic geographers and political economists, which proposes that regions must seek to embed MNEs within the local ecosystem (Coe et al. 2004; Yeung and Coe 2015; Driffield, Lancheros, and Temouri 2015; Guimón et al. 2018). There may be a trade-off between a more flexible but poorly supported branch plant economy on the one hand versus a more embedded but fragile ecosystem on the other. Because of this, a careful balance between the described advantages, challenges, and risks of MNE regional embedding is necessary.

REFERENCES

Athreye, S., and C. Fassio. 2018. "When Do Firms Not Use Patents and Trademarks to Protect Valuable Innovations? Evidence from the SIPU 2015 Survey." Newport: Intellectual Property Office. https://lucris.lub.lu.se/ws/portalfiles/portal/53835815/Athreye_Fassio_SIPU_WP_version.pdf.

Baglieri, D., G. Dagnino, F. Rosario, and F. Garaffo. 2010. "Dropping the Anchor in Regional Innovation and Development: A Bibliometric Analysis, Conceptual Extension and Research Agenda. https://lucris.lub.lu.se/ws/portalfiles/portal/53835815/Athreye_Fassio_SIPU_WP_version.pdf.

Balsillie, Jim. 2019. "Opinion: Canada Is Pushing Its Tech Sector into a Race to the Bottom." *Globe and Mail*, 21 September 2019. www.theglobeandmail.com/opinion/article-canada-is-pushing-its-tech-sector-into-a-race-to-the-bottom/.

Bartik, Timothy J. 2017. A New Business Incentives Database: Implications for Michigan. https://research.upjohn.org/cgi/viewcontent.cgi?article=1023&context=testimonies.

Bartik, T.J. (2019). *Making Sense of Incentives: Taming Business Incentives to Promote Prosperity*. Kalamazoo, MI: W.E. Upjohn Institute for Employment Research. https://research.upjohn.org/cgi/viewcontent.cgi?article=1277&context=up_press.

Bezruchonak, A. 2018. "Driverless Mobility and the Geographic Analysis of Contemporary Autonomous Vehicles Start-Up Ecosystem." *Prace Komisji Geografii Komunikacji PTG* 21 (4): 7–13. https://doi.org/10.4467/2543859XPKG.18.019.10777.

Boja, C. 2011. "IT Clusters as a Special Type of Industrial Clusters." *Informatica Economica* 15 (2): 184–93. https://www.researchgate.net/publication/227363826_IT_Clusters_as_a_Special_Type_of_Industrial_Clusters.

Bradford, N., and D.A. Wolfe. 2013. "Governing Regional Economic Development: Innovation Challenges and Policy Learning in Canada." *Cambridge Journal of Regions, Economy and Society* 6 (2): 331–47. https://doi.org/10.1093/cjres/rst006.

Brogan, P. 2018. *Autonomous Vehicle Development in Michigan.* CLOSUP Student Working Paper Series no. 42. Ann Arbor: University of Michigan. https://closup.umich.edu/sites/closup/files/uploads/student-working-papers/closup-swp-42-Autonomous-Vehicle-Development-in-Michigan.pdf.

Carey, J., and G. Mordue. 2022. "Why Industry 4.0 Is Not Enhancing National and Regional Resiliency in the Global Automotive Industry." *International Journal of Automotive Technology and Management* 22 (1): 52–81.

Christopherson, Susan, and Jennifer Clark. 2007. *Remaking Regional Economies: Power, Labor, and Firm Strategies in the Knowledge Economy*. London: Routledge.

Cody, John. 2015. "How Labor Manages Productivity Advances and Crisis Response: A Comparative Study of Automotive Manufacturing in Germany and the US." Global Labour University Working Paper no. 32. Geneva: International Labour Office. https://www.econstor.eu/bitstream/10419/110663/1/817621997.pdf.

Coe, N.M., M. Hess, H. Wai-chung Yeung, J. Henderson, and P. Dicken. 2004. "'Globalizing' Regional Development: A Global Production Networks Perspective." *Transactions of the Institute of British Geographers* 29 (4): 468–84. https://www.jstor.org/stable/3804369.

Constantelos, J. 2014. "Vetoes and Venues: Economic Crisis and the Roads to Recovery in Michigan and Ontario." *Canadian Journal of Political Science* 47 (4): 827–53. https://doi.org/10.1017/S0008423914001073.

Council of Canadian Academies. 2021. *Choosing Canada's Automotive Future*. The Expert Panel on Connected and Autonomous Vehicles and Shared Mobility. Ottawa: Council of Canadian Academies. https://www.cca-reports.ca/reports/connected-and-autonomous-vehicles-and-shared-mobility/.

Cowling, K., and P.R. Tomlinson. 2003. "The Problem of Regional "Hollowing Out" in Japan: Lessons for Regional Industrial Policy." In *Urban and Regional Prosperity in a Globalised New Economy*, edited by R. Sugden, R. Hartung Cheng, and G. Meadows. Cheltenham, UK: Edward Elgar, 33–58. https://doi.org/10.4337/9781781951217.00014.

Croteau, M.J.P. 2017. "Characteristics of Successful Commercialization from University Research Collaboration in Ontario, Canada." DBA thesis, Henley Business School, University of Reading. https://centaur.reading.ac.uk/84591/1/18900231_Croteau_Thesis.pdf.

Denney, S., T. Southin, and D.A. Wolfe. 2020. "Entrepreneurs and Cluster Evolution: The Transformation of Toronto's ICT Cluster. *Regional Studies* 55 (2): 196–207. https://doi.org/10.1080/00343404.2020.1762854.

Digaetano, A., and P. Lawless. 1999. "Urban Governance and Industrial Decline: Governing Structures and Policy Agendas in Birmingham and Sheffield, England, and Detroit, Michigan, 1980–1997." *Urban Affairs Review* 34 (4): 546–77. https://doi.org/10.1177/10780879922184077.

Dispan, J., A. Koch, P. Luitjens, and B. Seibold. 2017. *Strukturbericht Region Stuttgart 2017: Entwicklung von Wirtschaft und Beschäftigung; Schwerpunkt: Digitaler Wandel.* Stuttgart: Verband Region Stuttgart/Industrie- und Handelskammer Region Stuttgart/IG Metall Region Stuttgart/Handwerkskammer Region Stuttgart. https://www.ssoar.info/ssoar/bitstream/handle/document/54704/ssoar-2017-dispan_et_al-Strukturbericht_Region_Stuttgart_2017_Entwicklung.pdf?sequence=3.

Dodourova, M., and K. Bevis. 2014. "Networking Innovation in the European Car Industry: Does the Open Innovation Model Fit?" *Transportation Research Part A: Policy and Practice* 69: 252–71. https://doi.org/10.1016/j.tra.2014.08.021.

Driffield, N., S. Lancheros, and Y. Temouri. 2015. "Refining Inward Investment Policy." In *New Perspectives on Industrial Policy for a Modern Britain*, edited by D. Bailey, K. Cowling, and P. Tomlinson, 327–342. Oxford: Oxford University Press. https://doi.org/10.1093/acprof:oso/9780198706205.003.0017.

Fuchs, G., P. Shapira, eds. 2005. *Rethinking Regional Innovation and Change: Path Dependency or Regional Breakthrough*. New York: Springer.

Glynn, R., K.X. Shen, and M. Goetz. 2020. *Avenues of Institutional Change: Technology and Urban Mobility in Southeast Michigan*. MIT Work of the Future Working Paper no. 8–2020. https://workofthefuture-taskforce.mit.edu/research-post/avenues-of-institutional-change-technology-and-urban-mobility-in-southeast-michigan/.

Goracinova, E. 2019. "The Role of University-Industry Research Centers in Embedding Foreign Subsidiaries: Insights from Automotive Research and Development in Ontario." *Geography Compass* 13 (6). https://doi.org/10.1111/gec3.12442.

– 2021. "Varieties of Embeddedness: Essays on Technological Transition in Automotive Regions." PhD diss., University of Toronto. https://tspace.library.utoronto.ca/bitstream/1807/126955/1/Goracinova_Elena_202103_PhD_thesis.pdf.

Guimón, J., C. Chaminade, C. Maggio, and J.C. Salazar-Elena. 2018. "Policies to Attract R&D Related Investments to Small Emerging Countries: The Experience of Chile." *Journal of International Management* 24 (2): 165–78.

Haley, B., T. Creutzberg, and T. Julie. 2017. "Capturing Value from GPNs: Locally Led Strategic Coupling in Ottawa's Digital Sector." Paper presented to the Creating Digital Opportunity Conference, Montreal, 3 May.

Haddow, R.S. 2015. *Comparing Quebec and Ontario: Political Economy and Public Policy at the Turn of the Millennium*. Toronto: University of Toronto Press.

Hajela, A., and M. Akbar. 2013. "Internationalisation of Small and Medium Software Firms from India." *International Journal of Technological Learning, Innovation and Development* 6 (1/2): 88. https://doi.org/10.1504/IJTLID.2013.051699.

Hannigan, T.J., M. Cano-Kollmann, and R. Mudambi. 2015. "Thriving Innovation amidst Manufacturing Decline: The Detroit Auto Cluster and the Resilience of Local Knowledge Production." *Industrial and Corporate Change* 24 (3): 613–34. https://doi.org/10.1093/icc/dtv014.

Harpel, E.D. 2011. "Services in the Detroit Regional Economy: Implications for a City in Transition." *Service Industries Journal* 31 (4): 597–612. https://doi.org/10.1080/02642069.2010.504825.

Heineke, K., A. Ménard, F. Södergren, and M. Wrulich. 2019. "Development in the Mobility Technology Ecosystem – How Can 5G Help?" McKinsey & Company, 27 June 2019. https://www.mckinsey.com/industries/automotive-and-assembly/our-insights/development-in-the-mobility-technology-ecosystem-how-can-5g-help.

Hughes, A., and A. Mina. 2010. "The Impact of the Patent System on SMEs." Working Paper no. 411. Centre for Business Research, University of Cambridge. https://citeseerx.ist.psu.edu/document?repid=rep1&type=pdf&doi=3df7a3dc143dd8803a19c09c4485a8b8e5cacc6e.

Jacobs, A.J. 2009. "The Impacts of Variations in Development Context on Employment Growth: A Comparison of Central Cities in Michigan and Ontario, 1980–2006." *Economic Development Quarterly* 23 (4): 351–71. https://doi.org/10.1177/0891242409343304.

Klepper, S. 2010. "The Origin and Growth of Industry Clusters: The Making of Silicon Valley and Detroit." *Journal of Urban Economics* 67 (1): 15–32. https://doi.org/10.1016/j.jue.2009.09.004.

Koch, T., J. Egeln, J. Diekhof, J. Kinne, F. Koll, J.P. Kramer, M. Neumann, et al. 2018. *Moderations- und Explorationsstudie: Regionale Innovationssysteme in Baden-Württemberg-Bestandsaufnahme und Schlussfolgerungen*. Mannheim, Germany: ZEW-Gutachten und Forschungsberichte.

Koenig, B. 2018. "Ford, Declaring Itself a Mobility Company, Revisits an Old Strategy." SME Media. https://www.sme.org/technologies/articles/2018/november/ford-declaring-itself-a-mobility-company-revisits-an-old-strategy/.

Lucas, M., A. Sands, and D.A. Wolfe. 2009. "Regional Clusters in a Global Industry: ICT Clusters in Canada." *European Planning Studies* 17 (2): 189–209. https://doi.org/10.1080/09654310802553415.

MacDuffie, J.P. 2013. "Modularity-as-Property, Modularization-as-Process, and 'Modularity'-as-Frame: Lessons from Product Architecture Initiatives in the Global Automotive Industry." *Global Strategy Journal* 3 (1): 8–40. https://doi.org/10.1111/j.2042-5805.2012.01048.x>

Mack, E.A., K. Credit, and M. Suandi. 2018. "A Comparative Analysis of Firm Co-location Behaviour in the Detroit Metropolitan Area." *Industry and Innovation* 25 (3): 264–81. https://doi.org/10.1080/13662716.2017.1334539.

MacKinnon, D. 2012. "Beyond Strategic Coupling: Reassessing the Firm-Region Nexus in Global Production Networks. *Journal of Economic Geography* 12 (1): 227–45. https://doi.org/10.1093/jeg/lbr009.

MacKinnon, D., S. Dawley, A. Pike, and A. Cumbers. 2019. "Rethinking Path Creation: A Geographical Political Economy Approach." *Economic Geography* 95 (2): 113–35. https://doi.org/10.1080/00130095.2018.1498294.

Manders, T., and E. Klaassen. 2019. "Unpacking the Smart Mobility Concept in the Dutch Context Based on a Text Mining Approach." *Sustainability* 11 (23): 6583. https://doi.org/10.3390/su11236583.

Markusen, A. 1996. "Sticky Places in Slippery Space: A Typology of Industrial Districts." *Economic Geography* 72 (3): 293–313. https://doi.org/10.2307/144402.

Marletto, G. 2019. "Who Will Drive the Transition to Self-Driving? A Socio-technical Analysis of the Future Impact of Automated Vehicles." *Technological Forecasting and Social Change* 139: 221–34. https://doi.org/10.1016/j.techfore.2018.10.023.

Mayer, H. 2013. "Entrepreneurship in a Hub-and-Spoke Industrial District: Firm Survey Evidence from Seattle's Technology Industry." *Regional Studies* 47 (10): 1715–33. https://doi.org/10.1080/00343404.2013.806792.

Meyer, A.D., K. Aten, A.J. Krause, and M.L. Metzger. 2011. "Creating a University Technology Commercialisation Programme: Confronting Conflicts between Learning, Discovery, and Commercialisation Goals." *International Journal of Entrepreneurship and Innovation Management* 13 (2): 179–98. https://papers.ssrn.com/sol3/papers.cfm?abstract_id=1604589.

Mögele, M., and H. Rau. 2020. "Cultivating the 'Car State': A Culturally Sensitive Analysis of Car-centric Discourses and Mobility Cultures in Southern Germany." *Sustainability: Science, Practice and Policy* 16 (1): 15–28. https://doi.org/10.1080/15487733.2020.1756188.

Möller, T., A. Padhi, D. Pinner, and A. Tschiesner. 2019. "The Future of Mobility Is at Our Doorstep." McKinsey & Company. mckinsey.com/industries/automotive-and-assembly/our-insights/the-future-of-mobility-is-at-our-doorstep.

Mordue, G., and D. Karmally. 2020. "Frontier Technologies in Non-core Automotive Regions: Autonomous Vehicle R&D in Canada." *Canadian Public Policy* 46 (1): 73–93. https://doi.org/10.3138/cpp.2019-015.

Mordue, G., and B.A. Sweeney. 2020. "Neither Core nor Periphery: The Search for Competitive Advantage in the Automotive Semi-Periphery." *Growth and Change* 51 (5): 34–57. https://www.researchgate.net/publication/338254995_Neither_core_nor_periphery_The_search_for_competitive_advantage_in_the_automotive_semi-periphery.

Mudambi, R., S.M. Mudambi, D. Mukherjee, and V.G. Scalera. 2017. "Global Connectivity and the Evolution of Industrial Clusters: From Tires to Polymers in Northeast Ohio." *Industrial Marketing Management* 61: 20–9. https://doi.org/10.1016/j.indmarman.2016.07.007.

Nakano, T., and D.R. White. 2006. "The Large-Scale Network of a Tokyo Industrial District: Small-World, Scale-Free, or Depth Hierarchy?" Working Paper, Center on Organisational Innovation, Columbia University, New York. https://citeseerx.ist.psu.edu/document?repid=rep1&type=pdf&doi=7506fb7c611d6b9e332e3e77f05bff8b48c9da0c.

Parrilli, M.D. 2019. "Clusters and Internationalization: The Role of Lead Firms' Commitment and RIS Proactivity in Tackling the Risk of Internal Fractures." *European Planning Studies* 27 (10): 2015–33. https://doi.org/10.1080/09654313.2019.1635087.

Pavlínek, P. 2012. "The Internationalization of Corporate R&D and the Automotive Industry R&D of East-Central Europe." *Economic Geography* 88 (3): 279–310. https://doi.org/10.1111/j.1944-8287.2012.01155.x.

Pavlínek, P. (2018). "Global Production Networks, Foreign Direct Investment, and Supplier Linkages in the Integrated Peripheries of the Automotive Industry." *Economic Geography* 94 (2): 141–65.

Piazza, Merissa, Joan Chase, Chang-Shik Song, Elorm Tsegah, and Ziona Austrian. 2012. Detroit *Regional Analysis: Demographics, Economy, Entrepreneurship and Innovation*. Report. EngagedScholarship @ Cleveland State University. https://engagedscholarship.csuohio.edu/urban_facpub/110.

Pittelko, Brian, Bryan Bommersbach, and George Erickcek. 2016. *The Employment Impact on the New Economy Initiative (NEI) of the Detroit Region and the State of Michigan*. Kalamazoo, MI: W.E. Upjohn Institute for Employment Research. https://neweconomyinitiative.org/wp-content/uploads/2018/09/2016-8-July-NEI-Employment-Impact-Final.pdf.

Portugal Ferreira, M., F. Ribeiro Serra, B. Kramer Costa, E.A. Maccari, and H. Ritor Couto. 2012. "Impact of the Types of Clusters on the Innovation Output and the Appropriation of Rents from Innovation." *Journal of Technology Management & Innovation* 7 (4): 70–80. https://doi.org/10.4067/S0718-27242012000400006.

Rutherford, T.D., G. Murray, P. Almond, and M. Pelard. 2018. "State Accumulation Projects and Inward Investment Regimes Strategies." *Regional Studies* 52 (4): 572–84. https://doi.org/10.1080/00343404.2017.1346368.

Saba, R. 2019. "Start Your Engines: Ottawa's Private AV Test Track Opening Soon." *Ottawa Business Journal*, 4 February 2019. https://obj.ca/start-your-engines-ottawas-private-av-test-track-opening-soon/

Schienstock, G. 2007. "From Path Dependency to Path Creation? Baden-Württemberg and the Future of the German Model." In *Social Innovations, Institutional Change, and Economic Performance: Making Sense of Structural Adjustment Processes in Industrial Sectors, Regions, and Societies*, edited by T.J. Hämäläinen, R. Heiskala, and SITRA, the Finnish Innovation Fund, 159–213. Northampton, MA: Edward Elgar. http://ndl.ethernet.edu.et/bitstream/123456789/13555/1/66%20.%20Timo_J._Hamalainen%2C.pdf#page=182.

Schröder, C. 2013. "New Insights on the ICT Sector in Germany: Empirical Studies on ICT Firm Growth and Knowledge Spillover, ICT Cooperation Networks, and Early Stage Venture Capital

Investments." PhD diss., Universitäts Wuppertal. https://elekpub.bib.uni-wuppertal.de/ubwhsmig/content/zoom/3962167.

Simons, G. 2019. "Innovation in West Michigan." *Seidman Business Review* 25 (1). https://scholarworks.gvsu.edu/sbr/vol25/iss1/7.

Späth, P., H. Rohracher, and A. von Radecki. 2016. "Incumbent Actors as Niche Agents: The Germa" Car Industry and the Taming of the 'Stuttgart E-Mobility Region.'" *Sustainability* 8 (3): 252. https://doi.org/10.3390/su8030252.

Spigel, B. 2017. "The Relational Organization of Entrepreneurial Ecosystems." *Entrepreneurship Theory and Practice* 41 (1): 49–72. https://doi.org/10.1111/etap.12167.

Stahlecker, T., and A. Zenker. 2017. "Das baden-württembergische Innovationssystem im Wandel: Akteure vor neuen Herausforderungen." *Standort* 41 (3): 180–85. https://doi.org/10.1007/s00548-017-0491-z.

Sternberg, R. 2002. "The Regional Impact of Innovation Networks." In *Technological Change and Regional Development in Europe*, edited by L. Schätzl and J.R. Diez, 135–55. Physica: Heidelberg. https://doi.org/10.1007/978-3-642-57467-2_9.

Strambach, S., and B. Klement. 2012. "Cumulative and Combinatorial Micro-dynamics of Knowledge: The Role of Space and Place in Knowledge Integration." *European Planning Studies* 20 (11): 1843–66. https://doi.org/10.1080/09654313.2012.723424.

Sturgeon, T. J., Biesebroeck, J. V., & Gereffi, G. 2009. "The North American Automotive Value Chain: Canada's Role and Prospects." *International Journal of Technological Learning, Innovation and Development* 2 (1/2): 25–52. https://doi.org/10.1504/IJTLID.2009.021955.

Trippl, M., S. Baumgartinger-Seiringer, E. Goracinova, and D.A. Wolfe. 2021. "Automotive Regions in Transition: Preparing for Connected and Automated Vehicles." *Environment and Planning A: Economy and Space* 53 (5). https://doi.org/10.1177/0308518X20987233.

Turnheim, B., and F.W. Geels. 2019. "Incumbent Actors, Guided Search Paths, and Landmark Projects in Infra-System Transitions: Re-thinking Strategic Niche Management with a Case Study of French Tramway Diffusion (1971–2016)." *Research Policy* 48 (6): 1412–28. https://doi.org/10.1016/j.respol.2019.02.002.

University of Michigan. 2024. "MCity: Who We Are." https://mcity.umich.edu/who-we-are/.

Vinodrai, T. 2016. "A City of Two Tales: Innovation, Talent Attraction and Governance in Canada's Technology Triangle." In *Growing Urban Economies: Innovation, Creativity, and Governance in Canadian City-Regions*, edited by M.S. Gertler and D.A. Wolfe, 211–38. Toronto: University of Toronto Press.

Yeung, H.W., and N.M. Coe. 2015. "Toward a Dynamic Theory of Global Production Networks: GPN Theory." *Economic Geography* 91 (1): 29–58. https://doi.org/10.1111/ecge.12063.

PART 3

The Electrification of Mobility

8

The Political Economy of Energy Transitions in Canada: Implications for the Auto Industry

David A. Wolfe and Nathan Lemphers

This chapter explores the broader implications of the current energy transition from a carbon-based energy paradigm to one based on decarbonized energy sources for the automotive and broader transportation sector. This transition carries existential questions for two of Canada's leading economic sectors, automotive and oil and gas – two of the sectors that will be most directly affected by the prospective transition. The chapter focuses on the two provinces most directly affected by this transition, Ontario and Alberta, but also explores the implications for Quebec. Ontario's automotive sector is on the cusp of a major restructuring that will determine whether it continues to enjoy the status of a semi-peripheral automotive region it has held since the mid-1960s under the Auto Pact and the successor North American trade agreements, or whether it follows the steady path of decline that it has been on since the early 2000s (Mordue and Sweeney 2017, 2020; Anastakis 2013). While this restructuring most directly implicates Ontario's manufacturing sector, the energy shift creates broader implications for the political economy of the Canadian federation through its impact on the provincial economies of Alberta and Quebec, given that energy products and motor vehicles combined accounted for 37% of Canada's total exports in 2022. The Ontario and Alberta economies, based as they are on manufacturing and resources, have long been viewed as representing antithetical interests, particularly since the OPEC price revolution of the 1970s (Simeon and Robinson 1990, 236–49). In contrast, we argue that, since the late 1940s, the two provinces have been equally locked into the "carbon trap" in terms of the mutual dependence of their primary economic sectors on the production and consumption of carbon-based energy (Haley 2011). Consequently, they face similar challenges in restructuring their economic base in the coming transition to decarbonized energy sources and electrified transportation.

The future of the global automotive industry itself is being reconfigured by the shift in the sociotechnical regime from the carbon-based technology of internal combustion engine vehicles (ICEVs) to the emerging battery electric vehicle (BEV) paradigm (Dijk 2016). Sociotechnical transformations, in turn, are driven by the complex interaction of institutions, networks, and firms that comprise the prevailing paradigm (Weber and Rohracher 2012; Markard, Raven, and Truffer 2012). As Matthews (2013, 11) has observed, carbon lock-in was a dominant feature of the fourth techno-economic paradigm that emerged in the 1940s: "The breaking of carbon lock-in via creative destruction [is] the key challenge for the emergence of a new era based on renewable energies" (see also Freeman and Louçã 2001). While the pace of this transition remains open, the latest data indicate that BEVs are progressing from a small niche in the automotive market to an ever-larger share of automotive sales. Global electric vehicle sales are experiencing exponential growth with 10 million units sold in 2022, representing 14% of all vehicle sales. Between 2017 and 2022, EV sales increased from 100,000 units to 10 million, driven largely by sales in China and Europe (International Energy Agency 2023a, 14). This shift towards electromobility forms one part of a larger disruption in the automotive sector that includes the introduction of connected and autonomous vehicles (C/AVs), and new forms of shared mobility (Covarrubias V. 2018; Council of Canadian Academies 2021). The pressure on traditional automotive regions and conventional automotive producers is intensified by the challenge from new technology competitors from outside the traditional industry (Proff 2020, 341), and the growing presence of Chinese producers backed by strong state support (Jetin 2020). Governments in the US and Europe have also dramatically expanded their support for the shift to BEVs (Goracinova, Galvin, and Wolfe 2022).

The complex mix of technology systems that comprise automobiles today compounds the challenge of restructuring. Current technologies include new applications based on sophisticated embedded electronics that provide new functionality for automobiles. Key among these changes is the move towards electric mobility, with the extent of the disruption given evidence in the integration of electric components, advanced materials, and battery packs and associated battery materials. These challenges are explored by Kazzaz, Greene, and Yates in chapter 9.

As the transition to electrification unfolds, manufacturers will confront a range of challenges, including the introduction of new producers from a cross-section of industries into the automotive sector's value chain. Meanwhile, intensified competition for a dwindling supply of natural resources will accelerate the pressure for product and manufacturing energy and resource efficiency. That process will highlight issues surrounding the organization of regional supply chains. At the core of these developments rests the difficulty of separating R&D/design and manufacturing processes because of complementary relationships between product and process innovation (Breznitz and Cowhey 2011; Pisano and Shih 2009, 2012). This issue goes to the heart of Ontario's challenge in managing the transition to BEV production based on different components and manufacturing processes than the ones in which it has traditionally excelled. Likewise, the accelerating shift to decarbonized energy sources for power generation and transportation and the concomitant decline in fossil fuel demand underlines the vulnerability of Alberta's economy, as witnessed during the COVID-19 pandemic. While no other sector offers wealth generation on the same scale as fossil fuels, Alberta can encourage economic activity in sectors, technologies, and services that will expand as the world moves away from its fossil fuel dependence. As this chapter demonstrates, lessons can be learned from Alberta's previous efforts at economic diversification and emerging initiatives to improve the province's competitiveness in a rapidly decarbonizing global economy. If applied well, these lessons could diminish the growing threat of populist reaction from Alberta. The big winner in this transition may prove to be Quebec, whose hydroelectric-based energy source, cross-sectoral innovation policy, and well-established development coalitions afford it an early head start in the emerging sociotechnical energy system.

THEORETICAL PERSPECTIVES

The chapter draws upon two distinct bodies of literature to analyse the implications of the current energy transition for Canada's broader political economy and the future role of the automotive sector within it. First is the work in economic geography on new path creation and asset modification in terms of how the emergence of new technologies and new industries affects the trajectory of development in regional economies. Neither sociotechnical systems nor institutional settings exist in abstract space, but rather in real geographic places that constitute their respective national and regional innovation systems, with distinct power relations, governance arrangements, and firm and network dynamics. Economic geographers have long observed that complex systems of technology, production processes, industrial organization, and their supporting infrastructures of social and political institutions exhibit distinctive spatial characteristics. Periods of transition from one set of technologies, and its associated production paradigm, to another tend to coincide with a reorganization of the spatial distribution of production. The term "territorialization" describes the range of economic activity that depends on resources that are territorially specific. The types of resources involved can include assets that reside only in a certain place or, more critically, assets whose real value emerges from geographically proximate inter-organizational or firm-market relations. The more rooted the economic activities of a region are in the assets of that region, the more fully territorialized are those activities (Storper 1997).

The way the pattern of production is reorganized within a given region in the context of a major paradigm shift alters its developmental path. The concept of new path development is used to analyse the ways in which existing sectors change or new ones emerge in a regional economy (Hassink, Isaksen, and Trippl 2019). Trippl et al. (2020) advance a typology of four path development processes relevant to a green economy: path renewal, diversification, importation, and creation. Path renewal refers to intra-path changes within established sectors.

These changes could include new technologies, organizational innovations, or business models that improve environmental performance. Path diversification describes the "process through which knowledge and other assets from existing green industries or brown sectors are transferred to emerging green industries that might be either related or unrelated to the established economic structures" (3). This intentional transfer manifests as the branching of firms, spin-offs, and the mobility of entrepreneurs and qualified labour. Path importation means the establishment of new green regional industries through the inflows and anchoring of non-local assets, which could include firms, talent, or knowledge. Path creation represents the rise of new green industries and often emerges from academic spin-offs and the development of new green firms.

Frameworks for analysing new path development identify several key elements that constitute a comprehensive basis for analysis (Hassink, Isaksen, and Trippl 2019; Mackinnon et al. 2019). They suggest the need for a multi-actor perspective that accords attention to the role played by different economic and institutional agents. Ideational factors, such as actor expectations about future technology trends and opportunities, also play an important role in shaping the current strategies towards the realization of future opportunities (Grillitsch and Sotarauta 2020). However, a set of interrelated factors operating across multiple geographic scales also shape the process of new path development. Multinational enterprises (MNEs) pursue actor-level strategies in their global operations that may intersect with those adopted by agents at the regional level and impact regional path development through the process of strategic coupling (Mackinnon 2012; Cantwell 2017; Yeung 2020). This underlines the need to recognize the linkages between local innovation-related assets (technological capabilities, firms, and institutional supports) and the interests, needs, and strategies of translocal actors, particularly MNEs (Coenen, Benneworth, and Truffer 2012). The challenge is to reconcile the explanatory factors that influence the evolution of existing industrial structures and institutional capabilities of a region with the disruptive changes occurring in technology systems and global innovation networks at broader geographic scales (Mackinnon et al. 2019; Binz and Truffer 2017).

The second body of work this chapter draws upon from political science and political economy concerns how underlying changes in the economic structure of regions and nations affect the alignment of social and political forces in support of alternative directions of economic development to form new development blocs/development coalitions. For political scientists, dynamics among established institutions embed and coalesce the existing power relations among groups in society. Institutional change reflects deeper realignment of societal power relations. The application of path dependence to institutional trajectories is echoed in the work of John Zysman (1994, 1996), who argues that distinctive institutional structures across nations are the product of historically conditioned political and industrial development, which defines the choices available to firms or actors as they respond to new economic or technological trends. For Zysman, historically conditioned and nationally specific institutional structures create distinctive patterns of constraints and incentives that frame the choices of individuals and structure the terms on which agency problems are confronted. Contemporary political economies operate within an institutional framework that originated in the political process of state building, which accompanied and facilitated the emergence of modern industrial economies. The critical factor in determining national and regional institutional trajectories was how political coalitions formed around choices framed in response to the crises associated with the emergence and development of industrial economies. (See also Gourevitch 1986.) The key question for this chapter is how regional economies directly tied to the carbon economy will respond to economic crises transmitted by exogenous economic and technological changes and how domestic coalitions will align to allocate the distributive implications of the transition.

We link this analysis to recent work by Bernstein and Hoffmann (2018), who attempt to explain the politics behind experimental initiatives and how these interventions can catalyse broader decarbonization. Through normalization, capacity building, and coalition building, they argue, discrete governance interventions can propagate wider system effects of scaling and entrenchment, potentially leading to a trajectory of transformative emission reductions. This approach stresses the similarity of climate governance experiments by tracking three political causal mechanisms within mutually reinforcing subsystems across multiple scales. Incumbent economic actors and institutions largely shape the degree of contestation and cooperation exhibited in policy experiments focused on decarbonization. The transformative mechanism of capacity building works through changing the material, institutional, and cognitive capacities of actors (Bernstein and Cashore 2012). Norm change alters expected appropriate behaviour. Mediated by local politics and institutions, norms represent a key driver of public policy change and actor interests (Finnemore and Sikkink 1998). Coalition building identifies and links winners and can neutralize losers. It works through empowering certain actors, building constituencies, and using market forces.

The key issue to be explored is how the potential distributive consequences of the technology transition from carbon-based energy and automotive systems to decarbonized ones – creating winners and losers throughout — will affect the political and policy responses in the regions affected. How are the processes of new path development playing out in the regions highly dependent on traditional carbon-based energy systems, such as Ontario and Alberta? As Zysman (1994, 1996) argues, this will depend on trajectories of policy development and the role played by coalitions of regional interests in allocating the gains and losses arising from the transition to the new paradigm. The fundamental questions are how coalitions are forged in the respective regions and whether coalitions are used to build the winning conditions for the emerging paradigm. Bernstein and Hoffmann (2018) build on Zysman's insights on coalition building to consider the role of norms and capacity building. How do regional actors come together in coalitions, reallocate resources, to normalize and realize a post-carbon energy system? Coalitions without capacity or even well-resourced coalitions shouting from the margins of society are not necessarily powerful. But if you pull them all together that can help shift a region's trajectory.

THE ENERGY TRANSITION IN THE POLITICAL ECONOMY OF THE CANADIAN FEDERATION

Canadian federalism complicates the transition to a more sustainable energy paradigm. This shift will play out in a constantly evolving national political economy with changing interprovincial relations. Two outstanding features of Canadian political economy have fundamentally structured regional development: a highly decentralized federal system of government and an equally regionalized economy. Indeed, the country's immense physical geography concentrates diverse resources in specific regions, each with distinct economic structures, industrial cultures, and policy challenges (OECD 2002). Far from being static, the political economy of the Canadian federation has evolved over the past century and a half. The complex interaction between the underlying organization of the economy across its diverse regions and the coalitions of social actors rooted in the productive sectors of those regions – mediated by ethnic and regional identities – has driven this evolution. According to Simeon and Robinson (1990, 9–16), understanding the dynamics of the federal system in Canada requires a blend of a society-centred and state-centred perspective. To this we would add that the dissolution and reconstitution of coalitions of economic and social actors in response to the sociotechnical transitions discussed above exerts a strong influence on the framing of societal interests.

The structural break between the dominant, carbon-based Fordist paradigm of the post-war period and the emerging paradigm of the post-carbon economy has direct bearing on how these social, political, and economic relations will be reconstituted. Typically, the interests of Central Canada – Ontario and Quebec – are pitted against Alberta and Saskatchewan as manufacturing regions versus resource and energy-producing regions. This facile categorization overlooks subtle differences and similarities that carry significant implications as the country undergoes the transition from a carbon-based to a decarbonized energy paradigm. Throughout the post-war period, both the Alberta and Ontario economies were inextricably tied to the carbon energy paradigm. One region emerged as the key producer of carbon-based energy and the other became home to the automotive manufacturing sector – a key consumer of carbon-based energy through the dominant design of the internal combustion engine (ICE). Similarly, regional interests in Canada are frequently positioned as conflicting with those of the federal government. A rapidly decarbonizing global economy cares not about these distinctions, as declining fossil fuel demand will exert pressures on both orders of government. Instead, this demand destruction of the world's primary energy source will re-order social, political, and economic relations throughout Canada, regardless of the party in power.

In the late 1940s, several factors crystallized to form the basis for a new accumulation model that underlay the long wave of post-war economic expansion. The core technologies of low-cost oil, petrochemicals, and synthetic materials sustained this accumulation model. Together with consumer durables and motor vehicles, these materials powered a carbon-based, energy-intensive, mass production paradigm of economic growth. Petroleum was embedded at the heart of this paradigm. The widespread adoption of new refining techniques in the 1940s dramatically transformed oil production and, along with advances in electricity generation, helped to lower its relative cost curve (Freeman and Louça 2001, 271–82; Perez 1983). The carrier branches of the new technological style consisted of the automotive and petrochemical industries, whose products created intensive demand for the resource. The collaborative R&D effort by most of the leading oil companies between 1938 and 1942 was especially consequential. It led to the development of the fluid catalytic cracking process that ensured a steady supply of fuel to meet both civilian and military demand. By the end of the war, the interrelated technologies were positioned to power the dynamism of the new growth model into the post-war era. Not surprisingly, the technologically intensive industries associated with the new style, including crude and refined oil, natural gas, motor vehicles, chemical products, electrical equipment, rubber, and plastics, were among the fastest-growing sectors in the post-war period across the leading industrial economies (Freeman and Louçã 2001, 284–5).

The discovery of oil at Leduc in 1947 quickly transformed Canada from an energy-importing economy into an energy-producing and -exporting economy. But it also dramatically transformed the balance of power within the federal system between the federal government and the provinces, as the beneficial impact of the petroleum-based economy was not restricted to Western Canada. Rather, its economic benefits extended into the central Canadian heartland, as Ontario benefited from the dramatic expansion of the Sarnia petrochemical complex developed during the Second World War, the continuing expansion of its automotive sector, and the widespread use of coal and later natural gas to expand the province's electricity-generating capacity. Petroleum's growing importance transformed the balance of power between levels of government within the federation and among different regions.

As Garth Stevenson (1977, 78) has noted, the rise of new regional centres of power in the Canadian federation during the post-war period, particularly Toronto, Vancouver, and Calgary, was closely tied to the shift in the locus of economic activity to new resource-based economic activities, largely under provincial jurisdiction and closely tied to the strong inflows of foreign direct investment from the US. The economic prosperity of both Ontario and Alberta was tied to the dramatic expansion of the carbon-based energy system. In turn, that system was linked to new petroleum-refining techniques and the diffusion of standardized techniques of mass production that originated in the automotive assembly sector of the economy. Beginning in the 1960s and 1970s, several observers commented on the emerging regional dynamics at the provincial level, most clearly reflected in the "prairie capitalism" of the western provinces (Richards and Pratt 1979). Despite the growing tension from the 1970s between energy consumers in the manufacturing heartland and energy producers in the resource-based hinterland, we suggest that the post-war rise of these regional centres shares more in common than they differ regarding their mutual dependence on the production and consumption of carbon-based forms of energy.

THE EVOLUTION OF ONTARIO'S AUTO SECTOR

Ontario rode the long wave of post-war economic expansion in both the manufacturing and resources sectors to replace Quebec as the economic heartland of the economy as Canada's trading patterns shifted from an east-west to a north-south basis and the inward flow of US branch plants to the southern Ontario economy. Historically, much of Ontario's resource economy supplied the US need for industrial materials, particularly minerals and pulp and paper. Today, the province retains its dominant export orientation. In the earliest phases of industrialization, British firms comprised the principal sources of investment capital in Central Canada, though American interests usurped their dominant position by late in the nineteenth century and the trend has continued to the present. Most of Ontario's manufacturing industry grew up behind the sheltering walls of the protective tariff. As the industrial heartland of the national economy, Ontario benefited disproportionately from federal tariffs and other policies that promoted import substitution industrialization. The result was a truncated manufacturing sector, relying excessively on the presence of foreign branch plants, with production geared to supplying the domestic economy. This trend was reinforced by the signing of the Canada-US Auto Pact in 1965 (Anastakis 2005; Wolfe 1978).

Ontario, as the industrial heartland of the national economy, experienced many of the same trends that affected the country. In the expansionary atmosphere of the "golden age" after the Second World War, provincial governments in Ontario relied upon federal management of the economy and Canada's improved trade relations to create the appropriate context for provincial economic development. Throughout the period of its economic ascendency, Ontario's economic and political elites were largely the same as national elites and viewed their interests as strongly aligned; "until the early 1970s Ontario basked in the economic and political glow of its position within the federation" (Courchene and Telmer 1998, 15). To the extent they pursued a consistent set of economic development policies, provincial governments focused on the provision of infrastructure investment in highways, electric-power-generating capacity, support for municipalities in building water and sewage systems, and, in the decade of the 1960s, a dramatic expansion of the post-secondary educational system. The Automotive Products Agreement negotiated by the Canadian federal government with the US in 1965 represented the most significant piece of industrial policy for Ontario in this period (Rea 1985; Anastakis 2005).

The long period of growth and prosperity began to fade in the 1970s as the pressure of trade liberalization produced by the successive rounds of GATT negotiations exposed the structure of the domestic economy to more intensive international competition. This occurred in tandem with slowing economic growth, declining productivity levels, and rising unemployment resulting from the exhaustion of the growth potential in the post-war paradigm of standardized mass production (Glyn et al. 1990, 72–98). The dual energy crises in 1973–4 and 1979–80 hit Ontario hard, but the province was spared the worst effects of the energy price shocks by the federal government's two-price energy policy – especially in comparison to the US where the manufacturing sector immediately absorbed the full impact of the price hikes. For the most part, Ontario was spared the major job losses, downsizing, and restructuring that occurred in the US Midwest during the recession of the early 1980s (Anastakis 2013; Courchene and Telmer 1998).

The province's economic outlook changed dramatically in 1990. Although Ontario became gradually more integrated into the North American economy over the post-war period, the introduction of the Free Trade Agreement with the US in 1989 accelerated the restructuring of the manufacturing sector. While the notion of province-building in Ontario as the industrial heartland did not originate in the 1980s and 1990s (Nelles 1974), Ontario's determination to focus on the development of its regional system of innovation represented a dramatic break with the role it has played in the federation since 1945. The Liberal government in power from 1985 to 1990 voiced significant opposition to the federal government's negotiation of the Free Trade Agreement with the US, which it feared would undermine the protected position of its manufacturing sector. The more activist role adopted by the province was symptomatic of the growing divergence between Ontario's perception of its need for a regionally based development strategy and the federal government's reliance on a trade-led adjustment strategy (Cameron 1994, 114–17).

Within Ontario's manufacturing sector, the automotive industry holds a dominant place as the site of a significant proportion of North America's auto assembly by US OEMs and, since the 1980s, by Japanese OEMs. This was reflected in the oft-repeated phrase that "one in six" jobs in the province were linked to auto assembly (Anastakis 2013, 335–7). During this period of rapid expansion in auto production, close alignment arose between the federal and provincial governments, provincial economic elites, and the union representing autoworkers, now Unifor, in securing production at existing and new automotive assembly plants. Beginning with three major investments by Japanese transplants in the 1980s – Honda, Toyota, and GM-Suzuki – virtually every new investment by an OEM was subsidized by one or both governments, including the bailout of GM and FCA after the 2008–9 financial crisis (Anastakis 2013; Mordue 2020; Gertler and Wolfe 2004). Besides the five OEMs currently assembling vehicles in the province, the region is also home to over seven hundred parts producers in the supply chain plus five hundred tool, die, and mould makers, with 85% of the product exported (Government of Ontario 2019). Ontario also boasts several domestic Tier 1 suppliers who have expanded under the continental trade and production agreements to become large global industrial entities, including Magna International, ranked sixth in the world, Linamar, Multimatic, Wescast, Woodbridge Foam, AGS Automotive, and Martinrea (Sweeney 2020; Council of Canadian Academies 2021, 39). However, a series of disruptions in the North American automotive industry since the early 2000s, including the increased commoditization of auto manufacturing, changes in consumer demand for the product mix allocated to Ontario plants, and the impact of the 2008–9 financial crisis, has resulted in a shift of production to the American south and Mexico (Klier and Rubenstein 2013; Mordue and Sweeney 2017; Yates and Holmes 2019). As a result, the value of automotive production has fallen from a peak of $18.9 billion in 2005 to $15.4 billion in 2019 and employment in assembly and parts manufacturing declined from its peak of 175,000 in the late 1990s to 133,000 in 2019 (Sweeney 2020; Clean Energy Canada 2020).

Ontario's position as a semi-peripheral automotive region is captured by Mordue and Sweeney in chapter 1 of this collection. Key attributes of such locations include growing global competition arising from a steady and increasing process of commoditization of automobile production as well as a relative lack of R&D. Canada's automotive industry ranks among its least R&D-intensive industries, with the level of investment at about 12% of the OECD average. The reliance on foreign technology in the largest manufacturing sector has been identified as a key factor explaining Canada's weak innovation performance, consistent with its status as a semi-peripheral automotive region (Council of Canadian Academies 2009, 2018). Landmark agreements such as the Canada-US Auto Pact and NAFTA, which prioritized production over innovation-related activities, reinforced this reliance (Anastakis 2005, 2013). Recent studies maintain that manufacturing R&D in the automotive sector continues to gravitate towards those jurisdictions in which MNEs headquarters are based, suggesting a relatively bleak future for the region (Mordue and Sweeney 2020). However, automotive R&D spending increased from $213 million in 2014 to $329 million in 2019, reflecting the recent expansion of software R&D facilities by GM and Ford, among others (Sweeney 2020, 12).

The enduring semi-peripheral status of the Ontario automotive sector and the relative lack of automotive R&D jeopardize its future as the foreign OEMs have accelerated their transition to BEVs and plug-in hybrid electric vehicles (PHEVs) over the past half decade. While Ontario is home to the assembly of two conventional hybrid models by Toyota and one PHEV model by Stellantis, prior to the round of labour negotiations in the fall of 2020, it risked being left behind without substantially larger EV production mandates, as both American and Japanese assemblers shifted their production to non-ICE technologies. The closure of GM's last assembly plant in Oshawa in December 2019 sounded a premonitory warning for the sector and entering the round of collective bargaining in the fall of 2020, seasoned observers believed that the future of other assembly plants could be at risk as well.

THE OIL AND GAS ERA IN ALBERTA

Like Ontario, we view Alberta as a region state: an area with shared economic interests, of sufficient size to maintain the digital and physical infrastructure and supporting professional services required to support a regional concentration of firms that can compete in the global economy (Ohmae 1995). Many scholars have pointed out the inherent tension between greater globalization and the increasing importance of regionally concentrated firms and industries. In the current era, the twin crises of the COVID-19 pandemic and the climate emergency underscore the need for increased resilience in global supply chains and regional economies. Materially, this can mean both regionalizing supply chains to protect against distant disruptions or diversifying the regional supply base. Past economic and political crises faced by Alberta and the ongoing challenge of diversifying its economy offer some insights into how Alberta can navigate its future in a post-carbon world.

While Ontario has long enjoyed its position at the centre of political and economic power in Canada, since its creation in 1905 Alberta has sought to wrest economic control from Central Canada (Janigan 2012), more specifically from federal legislators in Ottawa and industrialists and financiers in Toronto. Unlike British Columbia, which secured control over natural resources when it joined confederation in 1871, it took until 1930 for Alberta to gain jurisdiction over the development of its vast natural resources. Despite this clarified division of powers – enshrined in the 1982 Constitution Act – and the diversification of capital sources for Alberta away from Central Canada, interprovincial political animosities have remained. This conflict was epitomized in the struggle over oil prices in the late 1970s between Alberta premier Peter Lougheed and Prime Minister Pierre Trudeau and the ill-fated National Energy Program of the early 1980s. In the early 2010s, this regional friction resurfaced as Alberta's booming oil exports to the United States drove the value of the Canadian dollar higher, eroding a key competitive advantage for Ontario's export-oriented auto-manufacturing sector.

Notwithstanding these sometimes fractious political and economic dynamics, Alberta and Ontario remained firmly entangled in carbon-based industrial development. In Alberta, oil and gas extraction became a major industry following the 1947 discovery of oil in Leduc, just south of Edmonton. As family farms disappeared with the increasing productivity of agriculture, many rural communities depopulated and faced economic hardship. In this context, the ascendent oil and gas industry assumed even greater importance for Alberta's prosperity and provided an economic lifeline for those communities. The Alberta Treasury and the balance sheets of municipalities and households grew more dependent on oil and gas production as a fount of prosperity. This reliance on significant oil and gas-related revenue allowed the province to keep taxes much lower than other Canadian provinces; however, it also bound the province's fiscal fortune to the fluctuations of a highly volatile commodity (figure 1).

Like Ontario, Alberta's economic development relied on foreign direct investment to fund its economic growth through the post-war period. The rapid influx of foreign oil companies in the 1950s and 1960s brought many political, economic, and social changes to the province. During the 1950s and 1960s, local capitalists were unable to compete with large, integrated US oil majors and, with a few exceptions, played a marginal role in the development of the industry, often relegated to ownership of oilfield services companies. During this period, concerns were expressed about the rising influence of foreign, particularly American, firms in

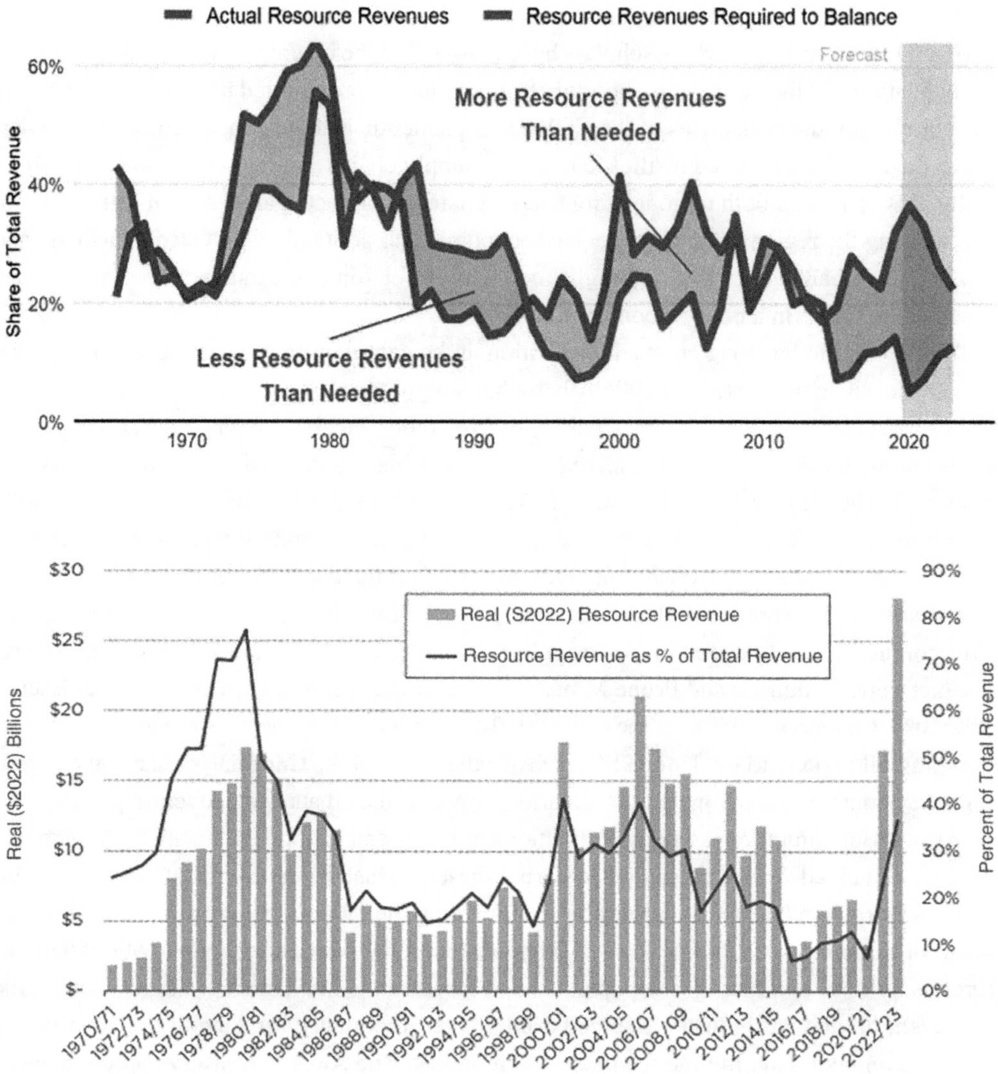

Figure 1. Government of Alberta Resource Revenues as a Percentage of Total Government Revenue

Source: Emes and Hill (2023; Kneebone and Wilkins (2016); Alberta Budget (2021).

Note: All values in top graph are presented on a "Fiscal Plan" basis. The top graph was created by Trevor R. Tombe.

Canada, a concern that extended both to Alberta's oil and gas industry and to Ontario's auto sector (Government of Canada 1972). Amidst calls for more assertive federal government action to Canadianize industries, provinces like Alberta also wrestled for control. At that time, American oil firms held 70% of mineral leases, 80% of proven oil reserves, and most major oil pipelines and refineries (Richards and Pratt 1979). Richards and Pratt (1979) argued that local elites did not play a "comprador" function, selling out natural resources to foreign capital; rather, that role was played by Central Canadian finance capital and their local branches.

Efforts by Alberta-based elites to assert more control over the industry succeeded, and by the early 1970s Canadian ownership eclipsed that of non-residents. Attracted by oil and the jobs it created, masses of people moved to Alberta; the province's population doubled between 1946 and 1976 (Stevenson 2009). By the 1970s, a regional economic elite emerged in Alberta. Richards and Pratt (1979) defined this incipient regional elite as including the owners and managers of Alberta-based companies, urban upper-income white-collar professionals who seek regional economic growth, senior provincial Conservative politicians, and government bureaucrats. This nascent class, buoyed by their growing wealth, harnessed the provincial state to capture additional resource rents, create and deepen industrial linkages, and compete with foreign companies to execute large private industrial projects. Alongside Albertan efforts to assert more control over this highly profitable industry, the federal government also sought to Canadianize the oil industry, through the creation of Petro-Canada in 1975 and the National Energy Program in the 1980s (Doern and Toner 1985).

Once established, this regional elite sought to accumulate wealth through additional oil and gas production and related diversification. The massive bituminous oil sands were developed. The Alberta Research Council created steam-assisted gravity drainage (SAGD) technology to access deep and abundant bitumen deposits without the need for a costly open-pit mine. Industry and political leaders pushed for domestic upgrading and refining and helped establish a provincial petrochemicals industry. Peter Lougheed was the most prolific province-building premier. During the 1970s and early 1980s, the Lougheed government transformed a quasi-state energy company, the Alberta Energy Company, mandating it with commercializing SAGD technology, and created a joint venture, Syncrude, to develop the oil sands. Using a host of financial and tax incentives, the government attracted international chemical companies like Dow and Celanese, who used local oil and gas as feedstocks for their products. These actions enabled Alberta to compete against the Ontario refining and petrochemical complex in Sarnia – which first began refining oil in 1862 and expanded rapidly during the Second World War to become the centre of Canada's petrochemical industry (Egan 2015).

Layered upon these tensions, the global oil crises of the 1970s and the federal government's heavy-handed response to Canadianize the industry enabled Alberta to adopt a stronger entrepreneurial approach to economic development and bolster its capacity as a regional state. Subsequent Alberta governments re-enacted this script, which, along with low corporate taxes and royalties, was used to entice foreign investment in the oil sands. Furthermore, these conditions convinced Royal Dutch Shell and Exxon-controlled Imperial Oil to relocate their Canadian head offices from Toronto to Calgary in 1984 and 2004, respectively. These moves, in part, signalled the arrival of Calgary as a globally important city for the fossil fuel industry.

With the rapid adoption of a neo-liberal policy framework in the 1990s, Alberta sold off many of its provincial assets in the energy industry, halted its attempts to diversify the provincial economy, and proceeded with a single-minded fixation to rapidly expand oil sands production. It was not until 2010, after the Global Financial Crisis, that the Stelmach government (2006–11) secured investment in another upgrader – a facility that enables bitumen to be converted into a higher-value synthetic crude oil – in the province through a public-private partnership and subsidized the first carbon capture and storage (CCS) project in Alberta. The Notley government (2015–19) subsequently provided $3.6 billion in subsidies for additional partial upgrading, petrochemical plants, and natural gas infrastructure (Varcoe 2019). While these investments created jobs, enabled Alberta to grow regional demand for fossil fuels, and captured more value from raw natural resources, they were not of the scale or direction needed for Alberta to weather the impending economic dislocation created by the decline in demand for oil and gas sparked by the pandemic and the growing global trends towards electrifying transportation.

IMPLICATIONS OF THE CURRENT TRANSITION FOR ONTARIO AND ALBERTA

As the preceding section makes clear, Ontario and Alberta were equally unprepared for the gradual decline in demand for carbon-based energy and ICEVs produced by the leading sectors of their respective provincial economies. Alberta strove to expand production of relatively heavy and sour oil sands crude, which is more expensive to extract and refine than light, sweet crude produced throughout the United States. Meanwhile, hydraulic fracturing and horizontal drilling technologies made it possible to dramatically increase US light oil production in the 2010s, which eroded the demand for Alberta bitumen (Yergin 2020). In Ontario's case, changes in consumer demand for the product mix allocated to Ontario plants and the growing commoditization of the industry placed growing pressure on the long-term viability of the province's auto sector (Mordue and Sweeney 2017). Although the recent developments documented below provide some positive signs for both regions, it is also clear that the legacies of their past development paths are positioning their respective economies in a different place for the transition to a post-carbon energy regime.

THE ELECTRIC REVOLUTION COMES TO ONTARIO

While the long slow decline over the past two decades rang a warning bell for the long-term future of Ontario's auto sector (Yates and Holmes 2019), General Motors' unprecedented

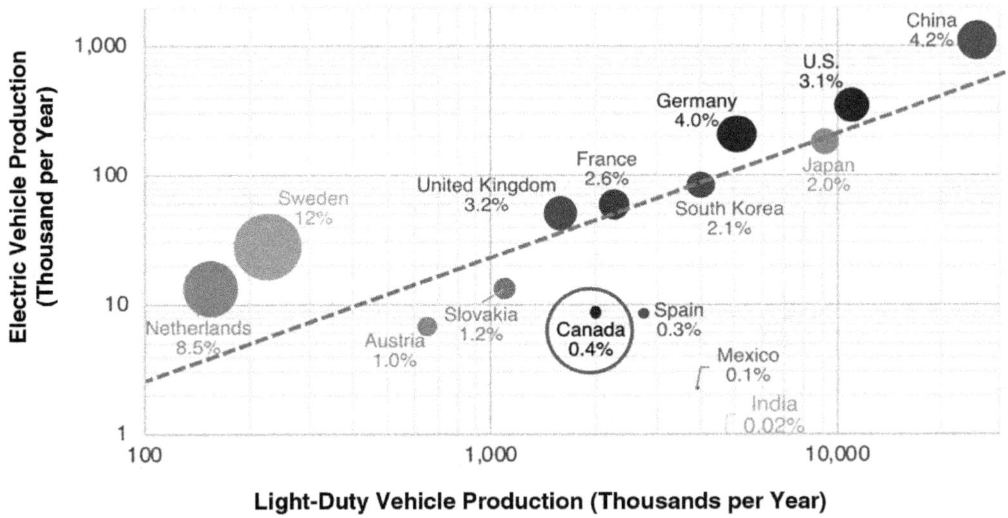

Figure 2. Proliferation of Electric Vehicles in Major Market
Source: Sharpe et al. 2020.

announcement of the closing of the last of its Oshawa assembly plants in December 2019 drove home the precarity of the entire sector. While some analysts saw potential resilience in the growing investment by automakers in advanced R&D sectors (Trippl et al. 2021), others remain more sceptical of the industry's ability to overcome the legacy of its semi-peripheral status (Mordue and Karmally 2020; Mordue and Sweeney 2020). RBC Economics (2021) estimates that *without* a pivot to battery cell and power electronics production and other EV-specific parts, Ontario's auto part sector could lose up to four thousand jobs. Unifor, the union representing autoworkers, was aware of the fragility of the sector and the uncertain future for its members. In an editorial, Unifor's president pointed to the global competition for investment in BEVs that was ramping up and argued that without a national strategy and active government involvement, the prospects for the Canadian industry looked dim (Dias 2020).

In the fall of 2020, as the three US-based OEMs entered negotiations with the autoworkers' union, Unifor, external observers warned that the outcome of the negotiations could precipitate the closure of another major assembly plant, which had not yet been assigned a new product mandate (confidential interview). Overall, Ontario appeared weakly positioned for the transition to the manufacture and assembly of BEV light trucks and passenger vehicles given the very limited presence of battery manufacturers in the province and the lack of product mandates for BEVs from the OEMs. While Canada ranked twelfth globally in vehicle production, a report in April 2020 noted that the country accounted for just 0.4% of global electric vehicle production (Sharpe et al. 2020, 5). By the time negotiations began, only Toyota, which assembled two conventional hybrid models in Cambridge, and FCA (now Stellantis), which assembled the Chrysler Pacifica PHEV in Windsor, were shifting from their reliance on ICEVs (Austen 2021).

Thus, the outcome of the fall 2020 round of collective bargaining between the OEMs and Unifor was critical for the future of the auto sector in Ontario. The results came as a major surprise to many observers with the announcement of major new BEV mandates assigned to the Ford assembly plant in Oakville and the FCA (Stellantis) assembly plant in Windsor, as well as the conversion of a GM plant in Ingersoll to the production of the new BrightDrop EV delivery van. Out of the first round of its negotiations with Ford, Unifor emerged with a commitment by the company to invest $2 billion. Most of that spending was slated for Ford's assembly plant in Oakville, Ontario, in support of plans to launch five new BEV models between 2025 and 2028. However, upgrades were also planned for two engine assembly plants in Windsor, Ontario. Ford's commitment was underpinned with commitments of $295 million each from the federal government and Ontario to subsidize the total cost of converting the plant to assemble BEVs. The successful conclusion of labour negotiations was followed up within a week by Stellantis's announcement that it would invest $1.5 billion to retool its Windsor plant to assemble both a PHEV and BEV by 2023 with an additional model added by 2025. The retooling will give the plant two platforms – one for the Pacifica and Voyager minivans and the second for the new PHEV or BEV model. While there was no concurrent announcement of government subsidies, the union said Stellantis was in talks with both levels of government for financial support (Jarratt 2020; Woynillowicz 2020; Austen 2021). However, there is little disagreement that the conclusion of the 2020 round of union negotiations has given Ontario's auto sector a new lease on life and underlined the accelerating transition from ICEVs to BEVs (Anastakis 2021; Clean Energy Canada 2020).

The final piece of relatively good news from the fall negotiations was the conclusion of a deal between General Motors and Unifor that the company would invest a total of $1.2 billion to reopen the Oshawa assembly plant to produce GMC trucks that were in high demand and convert its plant in Ingersoll to produce a new EV. In early 2021 the company announced that the retooling was proceeding ahead of schedule and the plant would recommence production before the end of the year. While GM made no commitment as to how long it would maintain truck production in Oshawa, the reopening was widely viewed as another bright sign for the future of the industry in Ontario. However, the most significant development came in early January 2021 with the successful conclusion of a deal between GM and Unifor that would transform the CAMI plant in Ingersoll (site of the original GM-Suzuki joint venture) into a centre to produce GM's new line of commercial electric vehicles, dubbed the BrightDrop Zevo 600s, with an estimated range of 250 miles, that had just been announced at the virtual Consumer Electronics Show the same week. The plant opened ahead of schedule in December 2022 as the first BrightDrop vehicles rolled off the assembly line (Office of the Premier 2022). The new line of commercial electric vehicles also incorporates a suite of software tools that GM has developed to provide an EV ecosystem for its commercial customers, commencing with an initial deal with FedEx. The cloud-based software platform, accessible via the web or a mobile app, provides users with information that can be used to optimize delivery routes and other aspects of fleet management. According to Scott Bell, president of GM Canada, "GM Canada engineers were instrumental in the early stages of ideation and testing of this solution for the delivery industry" (Legatos 2021). The indication of a clear link between the expanded GM R&D operations at its Oshawa and Markham Technical Centres afforded the first indication that the fruits of the enhanced R&D efforts being undertaken by the OEMs in Ontario would create regional linkages to enhanced auto assembly in the province (Balakrishnan 2022).

The Ontario government has been quick to claim credit for the turn to electric vehicles in the province and the dramatic revival of the auto sector's prospects. Economic development minister Victor Fedeli claimed that a host of measures adopted by the province, besides the direct subsidy to Ford and possibly Stellantis, had laid the basis for the new automotive investments. The minister touted the province's reduction in Workplace Safety and Insurance Board premiums, the introduction of acceleration capital cost depreciation measures to provide additional tax benefits for new investments, lower electricity rates in the province, and reduced business education taxes as having lowered business costs by $7 billion a year in the province since 2018. He also pointed to efforts by Hydro One and Ontario Power Generation, the two arms of the provincial electrical utility, to add 160 fast-charging stations to the 1,500 already in the province as an additional inducement for EV production and adoption (Thompson 2021). In the provincial budget for 2021, the province targeted additional spending at enhancing its support for the manufacture of BEVs. It committed $56.4 million to transform the existing automated vehicle innovation network (AVIN) into the Ontario Vehicle Innovation Network (OVIN) with a mandate to facilitate partnerships between universities, startups, the auto industry, and the battery sector to build on existing capabilities. This measure was in addition to the existing automotive modernization program (O-AMP) introduced in 2019 to assist auto parts manufacturers in making the investments needed to stay globally competitive. Ontario's support for the transition to EVs was provided as Phase 2 of its automotive strategy, outlined in *Driving Prosperity* (Government of Ontario 2021).

The momentum gained with the new product mandates for the US-based OEMs accelerated through 2022–23 with the further announcement of investments in major new battery plants in Windsor, Oakville, Ingersoll, and St. Thomas by four of the largest global OEMs. The first announcement out of the gate was a $5.1 billion investment by NextStar Energy, a joint venture of Stellantis and L.G. Energy Solutions, to construct a 4.5-million-square-feet facility in Windsor (Jarratt 2021). The plant will employ up to 2,500 workers and produce sufficient batteries to power 400,000 vehicles, commencing in 2025. In addition, Stellantis is investing $200 million to expand and modernize its automotive research and development centre in Windsor to support the company's electrification targets. In April 2023, Ford announced that it would add a new 407,000-square-feet battery assembly plant adjacent to its new EV assembly line in Oakville. Shortly after, GM announced that it would also build a battery pack assembly plant adjacent to its BrightDrop factory in Ingersoll (Bank 2023) and Umicore announced it would build a $2.1-billion cathode active material factory in Loyalist, Ontario (Jarrett 2023b). But the blockbuster development came a few weeks later, with the announcement that Volkswagen would invest $7 billion to construct its first overseas battery manufacturing plant in St. Thomas, representing the largest electric vehicle investment in Canadian history. Both the federal and provincial governments have provided Volkswagen with production support to match that available under the Inflation Reduction Act in the US, estimated to be worth between $8 and $13 billion. However, the governments maintained that the full cost of the subsidy would be recovered within the first five years of the plant's life, although this timeline was subsequently disputed by the Parliamentary Budget Office (Office of the Premier 2023; PBO 2023).

Some small indigenous battery manufacturers are also present in Ontario, such as Electrovaya, which produces batteries for buses and commercial vehicles, and Lion Electric (2021) has recently announced it will produce batteries in Quebec. Another leading parts supplier, Martinrea, has formed a joint venture with Montreal graphene producer NanoXplore to launch a demonstration facility in a Montreal suburb, with plans for a 10GWh battery cell plant potentially employing two thousand people to follow (Buchanan 2021).

Thus, over the past three years, the bleak future of the province's auto sector has changed substantially. However, the one murky spot in the automotive innovation system remains the parts sector of the industry. Magna, the largest domestically controlled automotive parts company, and sixth largest in the world, has increasingly been locating key parts of its R&D activities outside Ontario, in Michigan and Austria to a great extent (Trippl et al. 2021; Mordue and Karmally 2020). It has announced several strategic alliances with auto manufacturers to produce electric vehicles in China and in Europe. In October 2020 it announced an agreement with Fisker Automotive to build the Fisker Ocean SUV, which will use a modified version of a Magna-developed EV platform to power Fisker's FM29 platform. The Ocean SUV will be built exclusively by Magna in Europe. In January 2021, the two companies announced a new collaboration to develop an advanced driver assistance system (ADAS) for the Ocean SUV that draws on Magna's unique capabilities in automated driving systems (Clean Energy Canada 2020, 10). However, in a move to join the EV bandwagon, Magna announced a $471 million investment in the EV supply chain in February 2023, including a new battery enclosure plant in Brampton to support Ford's F-150 Lightening program (Jarratt 2023a). Linamar, the second-largest Ontario-based auto parts manufacturer, announced its first-quarter sales results for 2021, which were up 15% versus 2020, with more than one-third of new business wins in the quarter accounted for by electrified vehicles (Linamar 2021). Thus, while some domestic parts manufacturers in Ontario on the scale of Magna and Linamar are expanding their production capabilities in both BEVs and CA/Vs, the degree to which this will extend to the rest of the parts sector remains unclear.

Another initiative that warrants attention is Project Arrow, launched by the Automotive Parts Manufacturers' Association (APMA) at the 2020 Consumer Electronics Show. The APMA conceived the Arrow project as an all-Canadian effort to design and build a world-class vehicle incorporating the best Canadian technology in the realm of electric, C/AV, and lightweight materials. The design phase of the competition was won by a team from Carleton University's School of Design and the Vehicle Build team is led by Ontario Technical University in Oshawa working with the Virtual Build team in the Windsor Essex Economic Development Commission's virtual reality CAVE. Project Arrow was completed on time and assembled a prototype vehicle integrating the capabilities of fifty-eight Canadian industry partners. The first preview of the vehicle occurred at the APMA's seventieth annual meeting in Windsor in October 2022, and the global reveal took place at the CES trade show in Las Vegas in early 2023 (see APMA 2022).

The other segment of the transportation equipment industry that has not traditionally been considered with the conventional automotive sector is the bus industry. In contrast to the light-duty vehicle section of the industry, which is mostly located in Ontario, the heavy-duty vehicle (HDV) section – which includes school buses, urban transit, and intercity buses – is concentrated primarily in Manitoba and Quebec. According to Clean Energy Canada, currently six electric bus manufacturers operate in Canada – New Flyer Industries, Nova Bus, the Lion Electric Company, the GreenPower Motor Company, Vicinity Motor Corp, and BYD – three of which are domestically owned. Although starting from a relatively low base, sales of electric HDVs in Canada have grown significantly over the past three years, largely the result of increased procurement of electric buses by municipal transit agencies, with support from the federal $180 billion Investing in Canada Plan. CN is also participating in a pilot project using eight Class 8 electric trucks built by Lion Electric to be deployed in Vancouver, Toronto, and Montreal. Canada is currently one of a relatively small number of countries with multiple OEMs making electric heavy-duty vehicles. It appears likely that with the coming shift to connected, automated, and shared electric (CASE) vehicles, the public transit sector will constitute a key driver for sales of this segment of the industry (Clean Energy Canada 2020; Sharpe et al. 2020, 15–17; Council of Canadian Academies 2021).

A critical question for the Ontario industry in the coming shift to BEV is the extent to which the newly announced battery plants will supply the needs for domestic production or whether foreign battery manufacturers will remain critical to the supply chain. Battery costs currently comprise more than 40% of electric vehicle production costs but are projected to fall to between 26 and 31% by 2025, with the electric drivetrain components constituting another 13% of the cost (Sharpe et al. 2020). At present, the major suppliers of batteries for passenger EV produced in North America are all Asian companies: Panasonic, AESC, BYD, and LG Chem. Where Ontario does enjoy some notable strengths is in battery research – with Tesla's battery R&D lab in Waterloo and McMaster's Automotive Resource Centre (MARC), that conducts research in transportation electrification and smart mobility solutions using advanced electric motors, power electronics, energy management systems, and controls to electrified powertrains, electric vehicles, and autonomous systems. Given the significant portion of BEV production accounted for by the batteries and related electronic components, there have been considerable efforts made to attract new battery manufacturing investments to both Ontario and Quebec (Sharpe et al. 2020, 9–11; Clean Energy Canada 2020, 10).

This leads to the final area where Ontario is viewed as enjoying a competitive advantage to produce BEVs – as a source of the critical minerals needed for battery manufacturing. Canada, and Ontario, contain significant reserves of many of the critical minerals essential for battery production, particularly cobalt, nickel, copper, graphite, and most recently lithium. Canada also boasts a relatively abundant source of low-carbon, low-cost electricity, which is viewed as a key asset for securing its place in the battery supply chain (Clean Energy Canada 2020, 10; Sharpe et al. 2020, 11). These facts have been noted by the federal and provincial governments. The Government of Ontario announced a $5 million investment in First Cobalt's smelter in December 2020, and Minister Fedeli has underlined the strategic importance for the province of graphite mining in Hearst and lithium mining near Red Lake. For his part, former federal innovation minister Navdeep Bains was an early promoter of this perspective, coining the phrase "mines to mobility" to signify that Canada's comparative advantage in the race to electrification involved more than just the building of cars and trucks, but also included its strategic positioning to develop the next generation of battery supply chains needed to be a leader in all forms of electric mobility (Bains 2020).

The prospects for the future of Ontario's automotive sector, and indeed the entire electrified battery supply chain, certainly look more promising than they did in mid-2020. While the critical implications of recent negotiated settlements around BEV mandates, the sourcing of battery production, and how much Ontario and Canada's critical mineral resources are integrated into BEVs domestically remain to be seen, the prospects for the future of the semi-peripheral auto industry look brighter than they did. These recent developments also reveal that Ontario may succeed in avoiding the worst distributional consequences arising from the decarbonization of its auto sector through the shift to BEV assembly, although there will certainly be job losses entailed in the process. What is also clear is that the past trajectories of industrial development in the province, combined with the presence of strong system-wide assets, will continue to provide the region with the basis for diversifying into the emerging field of EV assembly and production (Gertler and Wolfe 2004; Hassink, Isaksen, and Trippl 2019). Both the speed and effectiveness of the transition reflect the fact that the traditional development coalition that has underpinned the success of the provincial automotive sector since the combined threat posed by Japanese transplants and the deindustrialization of the US Midwest in the 1980s (Anastakis 2013) – including the leading multinational OEMs, domestic auto suppliers, their respective industry associations, the sector union, and the federal and provincial governments – all mobilized to support the automotive sector as it begins to transition to the new energy paradigm. Undoubtedly many challenges remain, and new distributional issues will emerge. The ability of the development coalition to hold will be a critical factor in determining how those challenges are met.

IMPLICATIONS OF THE CURRENT TRANSITION FOR ALBERTA

As the world rapidly decarbonizes, it remains uncertain if Alberta can smoothly transition. The fiscal reliance on expanding fossil fuel production and the wealth this industry has brought to the province makes a move from hydrocarbons extremely fraught. By design, past efforts to diversify Alberta's economy (e.g., petrochemicals, plastics, refining and upgrading) deepened linkages with fossil fuels and stimulated *additional* demand for oil and gas production rather than develop new industries or strengthen existing industries not directly linked to fossil fuels. A powerful regional development coalition of political and economic elites emerged that ensured dependence on this resource increased and endured changes in government.

For the past two decades, efforts have been made to reduce the carbon intensity of the sector by pursuing more efficient extraction processes. For instance, most oil sands mines no longer burn petroleum coke – which has a higher carbon content than coal – to produce electricity and heat. Instead, these facilities now use natural gas co-generation units. However important such measures are in attempting to reduce total emissions, increased extraction rates have erased any incremental intensity improvements. These rising total emissions – which increasingly concern investors, the federal government, and the Canadian public – further entangle fossil fuels within the fate of the province. What was once an asset has become a liability.

As the federal government attempted to implement more ambitious climate policy, Alberta's regional development coalition has actively resisted most of these attempts. From ratifying the Kyoto Protocol to emission reduction target-setting, early efforts to price carbon, enhanced environmental assessment legislation, clean electricity standards, clean fuel regulations, and a cap on upstream oil and gas industry emissions, Alberta has sought to slow and weaken federal efforts to address the carbon liabilities of its principal industry.

Moreover, the province's oil and gas industry is acutely vulnerable because of its monopsonic relationship with the US – its only export market. Even if Alberta or Canada were to stimulate more domestic demand, this would have little impact compared to shifts in demand and supply of fossil fuels from the United States. In 2019, 88% of Alberta's oil production was exported to the United States (Canada Energy Regulator 2020). Alberta has no ability to shift American consumer demands, and little if any capacity to influence ambitious private- and public-sector offerings (e.g., electric vehicles and high-speed intercity rail) and net-zero aligned policies (e.g., renewable fuel and electricity standards) implemented south of the border. In many respects, Alberta remains a price and policy taker. The International

Energy Agency's business-as-usual scenario sees global oil demand peak in the late 2020s and reach net-zero by 2050 (International Energy Agency 2023b). Selling additional petroleum to Asian or European markets enables some hedging of risk, but these regions are also pursuing ambitious decarbonization programs. Moreover, Alberta's carbon-intensive oil sands remain far more costly to extract than conventional crude oil (McKenzie et al. 2023). Alberta cannot escape its geology, its geography, or its location in the global economy. For resource extraction, the petroleum-laden province remains at the end of the supply chain, distant from major markets. Importantly, this remoteness matters less for digital innovation and export-oriented services.

Considering the dependence of Alberta on the oil and gas industry, a global shift of this magnitude would carry severe economic and social hardship, if policymakers remain unprepared. TD Bank estimates that 50 to 75% or 312,000 to 450,000 workers directly or indirectly employed in the oil and gas sector could be displaced in a clean energy transition (Caranci and Fong 2021). Proportionally, the lion's share of these workers would be in Alberta. Of course, Ontario will still feel an impact from job losses at Ontario-based refineries and refuelling stations. As discussed above, Ontario's auto sector will also be affected by the transition.

To minimize this economic and social suffering in Alberta, insights can be drawn from Trippl et al.'s (2020) scholarship on green industrial path development and from Bernstein and Hoffmann's (2018) political analysis of policy pathways to decarbonization. Alberta is not a *tabula rasa*. Existing political, economic, and geographic conditions enable and constrain future development. Its existing industrial structure is strongly oriented towards supporting the oil and gas industry. Hundreds of billions of dollars of physical assets linked to fossil fuel extraction, processing, and transportation exist in the province. While Alberta's economy is far less diversified than Ontario's, other industries do exist, such as agriculture and tourism. The province's renewable energy industry is booming with 118 proposed projects worth over $33 billion (Wang and Noel 2023). Alberta also has a rapidly growing technology sector, which has increased 233% since 2012 (Alberta Enterprise 2021). Of the over three thousand companies in this sector, only 15% serve the oil and gas industry. However, these industries do not generate the same historic revenues as the fossil fuel industry. A complex organizational support structure has evolved to support the oil and gas industry (e.g., finance, universities, provincial and federal innovation agencies, and non-profit or private-sector-led consortia). In a world where the transportation sector rapidly decarbonizes, these organizations would need to retool and change their missions to support Alberta-based businesses in other sectors. Some of this work is already underway as many of Alberta's post-secondary institutions create and expand renewable energy programs and local economic development corporations pursue diversification goals. Many existing provincial and relevant federal laws, regulations, and public-sector funding in Alberta facilitate increased fossil fuel extraction (e.g., reclamation liability management regime, royalty framework, subsurface mineral rights, program funding for decarbonization projects, public ownership of refineries and pipelines). These institutions will need to shift to promote more efficient extraction of existing projects while stimulating economic diversification, particularly in regions acutely dependent on the oil and gas industry. Political and economic actors in Alberta can build upon the province's abundant natural assets beyond its hydrocarbon endowment: forestry, agriculture, wilderness areas, solar and wind resources. Recalibrating these extant industrial structures, organizational supports, institutions, and natural assets will not replace the economic wealth generated by business-as-usual oil and gas development. Rather, they hold the potential to grow green industrial development in Alberta and better manage the risks associated with the decline of the province's oil and gas sector.

For Alberta to thrive in a world with a decarbonized transportation system, new coalitions need to be built and strengthened and powerful existing coalitions reoriented or neutralized. To accomplish this, reformers can use the fear of sanction – a key precondition for experimental governance (Sabel and Victor 2015) – towards productive ends. Besides the risk of reduced demand for oil, the dismal prospect of Ottawa raising more tax revenue from the province – as upheld in the Supreme Court of Canada (2021) reference case on the constitutionality of carbon pricing – offers the stick to bring Alberta-based stakeholders to the table and collaborate on provincial measures to reduce greenhouse gas emissions and keep the tax revenue in the province.

This regional coalition could include many members of the business elite that developed in the 1970s as Alberta sought to gain control over its oil and gas industry from American companies and guard against encroachment by the federal government. This province-building elite, as Richards and Pratt (1979) call them, can be used to strengthen the regional state as global energy markets decarbonize. Indeed, some institutions active during the Lougheed government, such as Alberta Innovates (formerly the Alberta Research Council), are partnering with oil sands companies and petroleum engineering firms to investigate non-combustive end uses of bitumen (e.g., asphalt, carbon fibre, carbon nanotubes), which could offset the potential decline in transportation fuel demand and accommodate continued oil sands expansion (Alberta Innovates 2021). While these end uses do not address significant extraction-related greenhouse gas emissions – approximately 20% of life cycle emissions – nor do they address the other environmental impacts of oil sands extraction (e.g., seepage from toxic tailings ponds, other airborne pollutants, water extraction from the Athabasca River), the province and industry have long hoped that widespread application of CCS technology could enable net-zero greenhouse gas emissions from extraction.

Crisis also creates new opportunities and new influential actors. Moments of international economic shocks open "systems of relationships, making politics and policy more fluid" (Gourevitch 1986, 22). The Energy Futures Lab, an initiative that began in 2013 by the environmental organization the Natural Step Canada, has emerged a key convener to advance what they call "future-fit hydrocarbons." This program includes a partnership with Alberta Innovates and oil companies and explores the potential of aviation biofuels, hydrogen use for transportation and industry, and carbon capture utilization and storage in Alberta. Other programs from the Energy Futures Lab investigate how to leverage existing skills from the oil and gas industry to extract lithium, generate geothermal power, or find new uses for inactive wells. More recently, the Transition Accelerator, another non-governmental organization, has brought together a range of public- and private-sector stakeholders to pilot hydrogen fuel cell technology in a fleet of Alberta-based transport trucks.

Electrifying transportation holds the potential to strengthen coalitions beyond Alberta and deepen economic links across the Canadian federation. Alberta could become a supplier of materials (e.g., lithium, carbon fibre) or fuels (e.g., hydrogen, renewable gas) for zero-emission vehicles made in Ontario or Quebec. In turn, British Columbia could supply Alberta with low-carbon hydroelectric power. As Garth Stevenson (2009, xii) has noted, NAFTA caused a decline in Ontario's traditional interdependence with the rest of Canada and resulted in more "self-centred" relations with other provinces. The CUSMA, with its heightened North American sourcing requirement for auto parts, may create opportunities for deepened interprovincial trade in Canada centred on the decarbonizing transportation, in addition to protecting existing north-south trade.

Coalition building is closely tied to capacity building. Indeed, initiatives like the Energy Futures Lab and the Transition Accelerator accomplish both. The Government of Alberta can also initiate further province-led diversification. In the second half of the twentieth century, the Alberta Energy Company and the Alberta Gas Trunk Line were implicitly used to train managers and capitalists who could then "provincialize" Alberta's economy after the international oil companies had left (Richards and Pratt 1979). Richards and Pratt (1979) noted the parallel with the role of another provincial state enterprise, Hydro-Québec, in advancing regional economic development and the interests of Quebec's francophone middle class. Perhaps now is the time for an Alberta Energy Company 2.0? This new entity could, at a scale befitting the challenge, support technological innovation and economic development in rural regions acutely dependent on oil and gas production.

Compared to Alberta's leaders from the 1970s, twenty-first-century province builders can leverage the material, institutional, and cognitive capacity accumulated from decades of significant oil and gas revenues: strong research universities, high-quality health care system, new infrastructure, and a young and educated workforce. Drawing on these varied capacities will also attract new, influential coalition members that can support economic diversification.

Alongside coalition and capacity building is the ideational work of norms. Reformers can harness pre-existing norms of entrepreneurialism, independence, and resilience to convince Albertans that change is underway, and opportunities exist for them in a decarbonized world. Unlike the long-standing norm of grievance that many Alberta premiers have invoked to advance Alberta's interests and stoke animosity with the federal government, Ontario, or the environmental community, these other norms need not alienate important strategic partners.

In turn, new interventions can spawn additional norms that help make a decarbonized transportation system seem common sense.

What modest initiatives that do exist in Alberta to help the province cope with a global decline in transportation fuel demand and position itself to compete in a decarbonized economy have yet to scale or entrench themselves in any meaningful way. Thus far, the provincial government and the private sector have not expanded any of these economic diversification or decarbonization projects to the scale seen during the concerted push to rapidly expand oil sands production in the mid-1990s (cf. Alberta Chamber of Resources 1995).

Bernstein and Hoffmann (2018) remind us of the importance of understanding governance experiments in light of expected reductions of greenhouse gas emissions. Not all "green" industrial pathways will lead to transformative decarbonization. It remains to be seen if the CCS and hydrogen technologies being advanced in Alberta will further entrench fossil fuel extraction. In Alberta, hydrogen is produced using natural gas via steam methane reforming, as opposed to electrolysis using clean electricity. Natural gas-sourced hydrogen would still produce significant emissions even if CCS were employed due to unmitigated production and transportation-related emissions. Moreover, in certain industrial applications carbon capture and storage can still result in additional emissions. For instance, enhanced oil recovery reinjects carbon dioxide to repressurize depleted reservoirs to extract residual oil, further increasing emissions and extending regional reliance on fossil fuel extraction.

With the end goal of net-zero emissions in mind, several insights from Trippl et al. (2020) are germane to this analysis. (1) Many pathways exist to green industrial development. Beyond renewal of existing industries – as with CCS for the oil and gas industry – reformers can pursue simultaneous pathways. Policymakers can help orient Alberta's economy to compete in a world with electrified transportation by diversifying oil and gas industry into hydrogen production for long-distance trucking, importing renewable energy technologies (e.g., wind and solar) for regional deployment, or creating a new industry to recover valuable metals and minerals from oil and gas industry waste streams for use in EV batteries. (2) Transition policies can leverage existing local assets. Rather than creating a new industry unlinked from existing assets, policymakers can build on existing institutions, organizations, industrial structures, and natural assets to reduce the transition risks faced by incumbent economic actors and local communities (e.g., promoting geothermal energy). (3) Strategic asset destruction may be necessary for green path development. To introduce new technologies or stimulate new green industries, Alberta's existing institutional structure, which facilitates expansion of the oil and gas industry, may need to be modified (e.g., by providing new policy direction to the Alberta Energy Regulator). By intentionally destabilizing business as usual while providing necessary social and economic guardrails, policymakers can exercise system-level agency and guide the regional economy towards a more competitive position in a net-zero economy.

Regardless of what is or is not happening in Alberta, the rest of Canada will suffer if Alberta suffers. As the global transformation of the auto sector advances and historic projections of ever-increasing growth in fossil fuel demand seem increasingly outdated, Alberta could be increasingly marginalized – economically and politically – in the Canadian federation. In those places with a dim future, Rodríguez-Pose (2018, 189) warns of a populist-driven "revenge of the places that don't matter." A populist turn in Alberta is already underway. The rightward shift in conservative politics and renewed calls for secession speak to the mounting discontent (Mintz, Morton, and Flanagan 2020). Even if separation from Canada remains remote, the invocation of this "nuclear option" by Albertans suggests a perceived lack of paths forward.

In this context, place-sensitive development policies are necessary (Rodríguez-Pose 2018) – policies that make use of local assets and reduce the likelihood of populist reactions. However, as Alberta's economy becomes increasingly stressed, a stronger federal presence in Alberta is likely required. This was seen during the COVID-19 pandemic, when federal support in the form of wage subsidies, loans, bailouts, and reclamation funding were directed to the province's struggling oil and gas sector. To help Alberta manage the transition to a net-zero emission economy, a place-sensitive federal government will need to "take provinces and province-building seriously" (Richards and Pratt 1979, 7).

CONCLUSION

The substantive question for this chapter remains: how will the existing governing blocs and development coalitions, which have guided the trajectory of development in the two regions and been its major beneficiaries, respond to the challenge posed by the transition to a post-carbon era? As the preceding analysis suggests, both regional economies have been more closely tied to the carbon-intensive techno-economic paradigm than popular narratives suggest. Thus, while they face similar challenges in transitioning off their carbon dependence, their underlying systems of technology, existing production processes, industrial organization, and supporting infrastructures of social and political institutions afford them different regional assets. Alberta-based policy entrepreneurs have initiated important experiments to generate economic development outside the oil and gas industry and to reduce the greenhouse gas emission intensity from oil and gas production. However, the developmental pathway to successful asset modification remains long and challenging. Ontario, in contrast, has demonstrated a capacity to adapt its existing asset base to a new BEV production paradigm more quickly than was expected. Major challenges remain for Ontario's innovation system to ensure that (a) all product mandates announced are launched into development and production, (b) the complex auto supply chain transitions to EV production without major dislocation, and (c) battery production (involving more than just the supply of critical materials) continues to expand in the province.

At this point, the critical difference between the two regions appears to be the facility with which regional economic and political elites have shifted to support a post-carbon path trajectory. In Alberta, large portions of the oil and gas sector remain wedded to the current production paradigm, albeit with the hope that new techniques can incrementally reduce the carbon footprint of their production and make better use of CCS technology. The relatively small-scale experiments underway need considerably more support to expand to the point where they can have a broader economic or environmental impact. What is striking in Ontario, however, is the speed with which the provincial government has moved off its anti-EV stance to not only support the shift to electromobility but even take credit for it. Equally notable is the degree of consensus between OEMs, the parts association, and the union on the need for a shift to the new paradigm. While cracks will undoubtedly appear in the current coalition, there seems to be strong agreement that pulling together is essential for securing the future of the provincial auto sector.

If the two regions continue to develop along divergent pathways, this risks creating uneven distributional consequences for parts of the federation that will pose greater threats to its governance. While the prospect of moving to a post-carbon energy paradigm holds some initial promise that Ontario and Alberta's interests may become more aligned, the uneven pace of the developmental trajectories suggests that the country may be in danger of revisiting the energy wars of the 1980s. The federal government's position remains more tenuous. It has pursued an ambivalent strategy with respect to reducing oil and gas supply in Western Canada, both purchasing pipelines and introducing carbon taxes, that has left its overall strategy confusing. Regarding Ontario's automotive sector, the provincial government has been supportive of the recent developments but is clearly playing catch-up to the initiatives of the domestic subsidiaries, the union, the APMA, and an emerging sector of renewable energy providers. Absent at this point is a clear national strategy that maps a trajectory for shifting the developmental pathways of both the energy-producing and energy-consuming sectors of the national economy. Failure to provide one could result in increased regional tensions, and a populist response from those regions of the country that appear to suffer the greatest economic dislocation – with the potential for a "revenge of the places that don't matter" that has been identified as a clear source of populist reaction in both Europe and the US (Rodríguez-Pose 2018).

The internal contradictions between Central and Western Canada may be exacerbated to a greater degree by the unique position occupied by Quebec in the coming energy transition. While realization of the radical transformation underway in global auto manufacturing has been slow in Ontario and especially Alberta, decades ago prescient Quebec policymakers and private-sector leaders foresaw the economic opportunities associated with electrifying transportation (Haley 2015). Since then, a broad and effective coalition of existing actors has formed across the electromobility supply chain, from mining companies and electric utilities to manufacturers of recreational vehicles and medium and heavy-duty vehicles (Lemphers et al. 2021). These actors rallied around the widely held norms of electricity-driven, Quebec-led economic development and environmental stewardship. Historically, Quebec has been an EV policy setter in Canada, although many of these policies were pioneered in other jurisdictions, notably California. Beyond participating in the same cap-and-trade market for GHG emissions as California, Quebec mimicked California's ZEV mandate and GHG emission standard and adopted the same date for the banishment of new passenger ICEV sales. Further, Quebec-based companies with EV-related business lines also sell their products and services to a rapidly growing EV market in California. Unlike Alberta and Ontario, in Quebec cross-party consensus has long existed on the economic opportunities associated with transportation electrification. This agreement produced a more stable and predictable public policy environment for the private sector. Beyond these existing players, many new companies are emerging in Quebec that assemble and recycle EV batteries and install and manage charging network infrastructure; also emerging is a growing ecosystem of policies to make EV ownership easier. All told, this broad, diverse, and expanding coalition, grounded in regionally specific norms and capacities, advances a more compelling vision of the future of transportation than has existed in Ontario and certainly Alberta. Failure by the federal government to formulate a national strategy that builds upon existing regional assets and supports the integrated transition to a post-carbon economy across the country risks exacerbating the underlying regional tensions to the detriment of future national prosperity.

REFERENCES

Alberta Chamber of Resources. 1995. *The Oil Sands: A New Energy Vision for Canada*. Edmonton: Alberta Chamber of Resources. https://inis.iaea.org/search/search.aspx?orig_q=RN:27020356.

Alberta Enterprise. 2021. *2021 Alberta Technology Deal Flow Study*. Edmonton: Government of Alberta. https://www.alberta-enterprise.ca/wp-content/uploads/2021/04/AEC-Deal-Flow-Report-2021-April-21.pdf.

Alberta Innovates. 2021. "Advanced Hydrocarbons – Bitumen Beyond Combustion." Government of Alberta. Accessed 15 March 2021. https://albertainnovates.ca/strategic-initiatives/bitumen-beyond-combustion-bbc/.

Anastakis, Dimitry. 2005. *Auto Pact: Creating a Borderless North American Auto Industry, 1960–1971*. Toronto: University of Toronto Press.

– 2013. *Autonomous State: The Struggle for a Canadian Car Industry from OPEC to Free Trade*. Toronto: University of Toronto Press.

– 2021. "Reinvestment in Automotive Sector Will Change Ontario's Future." *Toronto Star*, 3 January 2021. https://www.thestar.com/business/reinvestment-in-automotive-sector-will-change-ontario-s-future/article_9b60a88b-f56f-5652-bf6b-c7b5a1926689.html.

APMA (Automotive Parts Manufacturers' Association). 2022. "Project Arrow." https://apma.ca/project-arrow/.

Austen, Ian. 2021. "Canada Catches Up in the Race to Produce Zero-Emission Vehicles." *New York Times*, 26 February 2021. https://www.nytimes.com/2021/02/26/world/'anada/canada-zero-emission-vehicles.html.

Bains, Navdeep. 2020. "Mining Gives Canada a Competitive Advantage in Electric Vehicle Market." *Policy Options*, 17 September 2020. https://policyoptions.irpp.org/magazines/september-2020/mining-gives-canada-a-competitive-advantage-in-electric-vehicle-market/.

Balakrishnan, Anita. 2022. “General Motors Once Sold More than Half the Cars in the U.S.” *The Logic*, 20 October 2022.

Banks, Brian. 2022. “GM Building Battery Pack Assembly Unit at Ontario BrightDrop Plant.” *Electric Autonomy*, 20 April 2023. https://electricautonomy.ca/2023/04/20/gm-battery-pack-assembly-brightdrop/.

Bernstein, Steven, and Benjamin Cashore. 2012. “Complex Global Governance and Domestic Policies: Four Pathways of Influence.” *International Affairs* 88 (3): 585–604.

Bernstein, Steven, and Matthew Hoffmann. 2018. “The Politics of Decarbonization and the Catalytic Impact of Subnational Climate Experiments.” *Policy Sciences* 51 (2): 189–211.

Binz, Christian, and Bernhard Truffer. 2017. “Global Innovation Systems – A Conceptual Framework for Innovation Dynamics in Transnational Contexts.” *Research Policy* 46 (7): 1284–9.

Breznitz, Dan, and Peter Cowhey. 2011. *America’s Two Systems of Innovation: Recommendations for Policy Changes to Support Innovation, Production and Job Creation*. San Diego: Connect Innovation Institute, University of California San Diego. https://shorturl.at/cgH03.

Buchanan, Emma. 2021. “Auto Parts Maker Martinrea Spearheading New EV Battery-Making Venture near Montreal.” *Electric Autonomy*, 12 May 2021. https://electricautonomy.ca/2021/05/12/voltaxplore-battery-factory/.

Cameron, David R. 1994. “Post-Modern Ontario and the Laurentian Thesis.” In *Canada: The State of the Federation 1994*, edited by Douglas M. Brown and Janet Hiebert, 109–32. Kingston: Institute of Intergovernmental Relations, Queen’s University.

Canada Energy Regulator. 2020. “Crude Oil Annual Export Summary – 2019.” Accessed 24 September 2020. https://www.cer-rec.gc.ca/nrg/sttstc/crdlndptrlmprdct/stt/crdlsmmr/crdlsmmr-eng.html.

Cantwell, John. 2017. “Innovation and International Business.” *Industry and Innovation* 24 (1): 41–60.

Caranci, Beata, and Francis Fong. 2021. “Don’t Let History Repeat: Canada’s Energy Sector Transition and the Potential Impact on Workers.” TD Bank. https://economics.td.com/esg-energy-sector.

Clean Energy Canada. 2020. *Taking the Wheel: How Canada Can Cut Carbon Pollution and Revitalize Its Auto Sector*. Vancouver BC: Clean Energy Canada. https://cleanenergycanada.org/wp-content/uploads/2020/12/Report_Taking_the_Wheel_December2020.pdf.

Coenen, Lars, Paul Benneworth, and Bernhard Truffer. 2012. “Toward a Spatial Perspective on Sustainability Transitions.” *Research Policy* 41 (6 July): 968–79.

Council of Canadian Academies. 2009. *Innovation and Business Strategy: Why Canada Falls Short*. Report of the Expert Panel on Business Innovation in Canada. Ottawa: Council of Canadian Academies. https://cca-reports.ca/reports/innovation-and-business-strategy-why-canada-falls-short/.

– 2018. *Competing in a Global Innovation Economy: The Current State of R&D in Canada*. Report of the Expert Panel on the State of Science and Technology and Industrial Research and Development in Canada. Ottawa: Council of Canadian Academies. https://cca-reports.ca/reports/competing-in-a-global-innovation-economy/.

– 2021. *Choosing Canada’s Automotive Future*. Report of the Expert Panel on Connected and Autonomous Vehicles and Shared Mobility. Ottawa: Council of Canadian Academies. https://www.cca-reports.ca/reports/connected-and-autonomous-vehicles-and-shared-mobility/.

Courchene, Thomas J., and Colin J. Telmer. 1998. *From Heartland to North American Region State: The Social, Fiscal and Federal Evolution of Ontario*. Monograph Series on Public Policy, Centre for Public Management. Toronto: Faculty of Management, University of Toronto.

Covarrubias V, Alex. 2018. “When Disruptors Converge: The Last Automobile Revolution.” *International Journal of Automotive Technology and Management* 18 (2): 81–104.

Dias, Jerry. 2020. "The Auto Industry Is Suffering but with a Helping Hand from Government It Can Flourish Once More." *Globe and Mail*, 12 August. https://www.theglobeandmail.com/business/commentary/article-the-auto-industry-is-suffering-but-with-a-helping-hand-from-the/.

Dijk, Marc. 2016. "Electric Revenge after 100 Years? Comparing Car Market Patterns around 1900 and 2000." *International Journal of Automotive Technology and Management* 16 (2): 147–67.

Doern, G. Bruce, and Glen B. Toner. 1985. *The Politics of Energy: The Development and Implementation of the NEP*. New York: Methuen.

Egan, Phil. 2015. *Sarnia's First Refinery*. Sarnia: Sarnia Historical Society. https://www.sarniahistoricalsociety.com/story/sarnias-first-refinery/#:~:text=(2015)%20In%20his%201961%20book,%E2%80%9Cfirst%20of%20Sarnia's%20refineries.%E2%80%9D

Emes, Joel, and Tegan Hill. 2023. "Alberta's Windfall – An Opportunity to Stabilize Provincial Finances," in *Don't Spend Away the Windfall: Better Options for Albera's Unexpected Revenues*, edited by Tegan Hill, 11–19. Vancouver: Fraser Institute. https://www.fraserinstitute.org/sites/default/files/dont-spend-away-the-windfall-better-options-for-alberta-revenues.pdf.

Finnemore, Martha, and Kathryn Sikkink. 1998. "International Norm Dynamics and Political Change." *International Organization* 52: 887–917.

Freeman, Christopher, and Francisco Louçã. 2001. *As Time Goes By: From the Industrial Revolutions to the Information Revolution*. Oxford: Oxford University Press.

Gertler, Meric S., and David A. Wolfe. 2004. "Ontario's Regional Innovation System: The Evolution of Knowledge-Based Institutional Assets." In *Regional Innovation Systems,* 2nd ed., edited by Philip Cooke, Hans-Joachim Braczyk, and Martin Heidenreich, 91–124. London: Taylor and Francis.

Glyn, Andrew, Alan Hughes, Alain Lipietz, and Ajit Singh. 1990. "The Rise and Fall of the Golden Age." In *The Golden Age of Capitalism: Reinterpreting the Postwar Experience*, edited by Stephen A. Marglin and Juliet B. Schor, 39–125. Oxford: Clarendon Press.

Goracinova, Elena, Patrick Galvin, and David A. Wolfe. 2022. "Emerging Models of Networked Industrial Policy: Comparative Trends in Automotive Policy in the US and Germany." *International Journal of Automotive Technology and Management* 22 (1): 29–51. http://dx.doi.org/10.1504/IJATM.2022.122096.

Gourevitch, Peter. 1986. *Politics in Hard Times: Comparative Responses to International Economic Crisis*. Ithaca: Cornell University Press.

Government of Canada. 1972. *Foreign Direct Investment in Canada*. Ottawa: Information Canada.

Government of Ontario. 2021. *Driving Prosperity: Ontario's Automotive Plan, Phase 2*. Toronto: Ministry of Economic Development, Trade and Job Creation. https://files.ontario.ca/medjct-driving-prosperity-ontario-automotive-plan-phase-2-en-2021-11-23.pdf.

Grillitsch, Markus, and Markku Sotarauta. 2020. "Trinity of Change Agency, Regional Development Paths and Opportunity Spaces." *Progress in Human Geography* 44 (4): 704–23.

Haley, Brendan. 2011. "From Staples Trap to Carbon Trap: Canada's Peculiar Form of Carbon Lock-In." *Studies in Political Economy* 88 (Autumn): 97–132.

– 2015. "Low-Carbon Innovation from a Hydroelectric Base: The Case of Electric Vehicles in Québec." *Environmental Innovation and Societal Transitions* 14: 5–25.

Hassink, Robert, Arne Isaksen, and Michaela Trippl. 2019. "Towards a Comprehensive Understanding of Regional Industrial Path Development." *Regional Studies* 53 (11): 1636–45.

International Energy Agency. 2021. *Global EV Outlook 2021*. Paris: IEA.

– 2023a. *Global EV Outlook 2023*. Paris: IEA.

– 2023b. *World Energy Outlook*. Paris: IEA.

Janigan, Mary. 2012. *Let the Eastern Bastards Freeze in the Dark: The West Versus the Rest since Confederation*. Toronto: Knopf Canada.

Jarratt, Emma. 2020. "Fiat Chrysler and Unifor Announce $1.5 Billion Investment to Build EVs in Windsor." *Electric Autonomy*, 15 October 2020. https://electricautonomy.ca/2020/10/15/fiat-chrysler-unifor-build-evs-windsor/.

– 2021. "Vying for Canada's Flagship Battery Manufacturing Facility." *Electric Autonomy*, 5 March 2021. https://electricautonomy.ca/2021/03/05/canada-battery-manufacturing-facilities/.

– 2023a. "Magna Pouring $471 Million into EV Supply Chain in Ontario." *Electric Autonomy*, 15 February 2023. https://electricautonomy.ca/2023/02/15/magna-ontario-ev-supply-chain/.

– 2023b. "Umicore Finalizes $2.1B Cathode Factory Deal with Ontario, Federal Government." *Electric Autonomy,* 16 October 2023. https://electricautonomy.ca/2023/10/16/umicore-finalizes-cathode-factory-ontario/.

Jetin, Bruno. 2020. "Who Will Control the Electric Vehicle Market?" *International Journal of Automotive Technology and Management* 20 (2): 156–77.

Klier, Thomas, and James Rubenstein. 2013. "Restructuring of the U.S. Auto Industry in the 2008–2009 Recession." *Economic Development Quarterly* 27 (2): 144–59.

Legatos, Jasmin. 2021. "GM's New Electric Delivery Vans Will Be Made in Canada." *Electric Autonomy*, 18 January 2021. https://electricautonomy.ca/2021/01/18/gm-electric-delivery-van-made-in-ontario/.

Lemphers, Nathan, David A. Wolfe, Matthew Hoffmann, and Steven Bernstein. 2021. "Electromobility as an Innovation and Decarbonization Catalyst in California, Norway, and Québec." *Energy Research & Social Science* 87 (May 2022): 102462.

Linamar. 2021. "Linamar First Quarter Earnings More than Double Q1 2020 on Strong Markets & Market Share Gains." 6 May 2021. https://linamar.com/de/sites/default/files/press/Q1%202021%20Press%20Release.pdf.

Lion Electric. 2021. "Lion Electric Announces the Construction of Its Battery Manufacturing Plant and Innovation Center in Quebec." 15 March 2021. https://shorturl.at/nrJY3.

Mackinnon, Danny. 2012. "Beyond Strategic Coupling: Reassessing the Firm-Region Nexus in Global Production Networks." *Journal of Economic Geography* 12 (1): 227–45.

Mackinnon, Danny, Stuart Dawley, Andy Pike, and Andrew Cumbers. 2019. "Rethinking Path Creation: A Geographic Political Economy Approach." *Economic Geography* 95 (2): 113–35.

Markard, Jochen, Rob Raven, and Bernhard Truffer. 2012. "Sustainability Transitions: An Emerging Field of Research and Its Prospects." *Research Policy* 41 (6): 955–67.

McKenzie, Janetta, Scott McDougall, and Eyab Al-Aini. 2023. "Survival of the Cleanest: Assessing the Cost and Carbon Competitiveness of Canada's Oil." Calgary: Pembina Institute.

Mintz, Jack M., Ted Morton, and Tom Flanagan. 2020. *Moment of Truth: How to Think about Alberta's Future*. Toronto: Sutherland House.

Mordue, Greig. 2020. "Shifting Patterns in the Application of Industrial Policy." *International Journal of Automotive Technology and Management* 20 (1): 50–75.

Mordue, Greig, and Danish Karmally. 2020. "Frontier Technologies in Non-core Automotive Regions: Autonomous Vehicle R&D in Canada." *Canadian Public Policy* 46 (1): 73–93.

Mordue, Greig, and Brendan Sweeney. 2017. "The Commodisation of Automotive Assembly: Canada as a Cautionary Tale." *International Journal of Automotive Technology and Management* 17 (2): 169–89.

– 2020. "Neither Core nor Periphery: The Search for Competitive Advantage in the Automotive Semi-Periphery." *Growth and Change* 51 (1): 34–57.

Nelles, H.V. 1974. *The Politics of Development: Forests, Mines and Hydro-Electric Power in Ontario, 1849–1941*. Toronto: Macmillan.

OECD (Organisation for Economic Co-operation and Development). 2002. *OECD Territorial Reviews: Canada*. Paris: OECD.

Office of the Premier, Ontario. 2022. "Canada's First All-Electric Vehicle Manufacturing Facility Opens in Ontario." 5 December 2022. Toronto: Government of Ontario.

– 2023. "Volkswagen's New Electric Vehicle Battery Plant Will Create Thousands of New Jobs." 21 April 2023. Toronto: Government of Ontario.

Ohmae, Kenichi. 1995. *The End of the Nation State: The Rise of Regional Economies*. New York: Free Press.

Office of the Parliamentary Budget Officer (PBO). 2023. *Costing Support for EV Battery Manufacturing*. Ottawa, 17 November.

Perez, Carlota. 1983. "Structural Change and Assimilation of New Technologies in the Economic and Social Systems." *Futures* 15 (5): 357–75.

Pisano, Gary P., and Willy C. Shih. 2009. "Restoring American Competitiveness." *Harvard Business Review*, July–August 2009. https://hbr.org/2009/07/restoring-american-competitiveness.

– 2012. "Does America Really Need Manufacturing?" *Harvard Business Review*, March 2012. https://hbr.org/2012/03/does-america-really-need-manufacturing.

Proff, Heike. 2020. "Editorial." *International Journal of Automotive Technology and Management* 20 (4): 341–8.

RBC Economics. 2021. "Trading Places: Canada's Place in a Changing Global Economy." Toronto: RBC Economics. https://thoughtleadership.rbc.com/trading-places-canadas-place-in-a-changing-global-economy/,

Rea, K.J. 1985. *The Prosperous Years: The Economic History of Ontario, 1939–1975*. Toronto: University of Toronto Press.

Richards, John, and Larry Pratt. 1979. *Prairie Capitalism: Power and Influence in the New West*. Toronto: McClelland and Stewart.

Rodríguez-Pose, Andrés. 2018. "The Revenge of the Places That Don't Matter (And What to Do about It)." *Cambridge Journal of Regions, Economy and Society* 11: 189–209.

Sabel, Charles F., and David G. Victor. 2015. "Governing Global Problems under Uncertainty: Making Bottom-Up Climate Policy Work." *Climatic Change* 144: 15–27.

Sharpe, Ben, Nic Lutsey, Cedric Smith, and Carolyn Kim. 2020. *Power Play: Canada's Role in the Electric Vehicle Transition*. White Paper. Washington, DC: International Council on Clean Transportation.

Simeon, Richard, and Ian Robinson. 1990. *State, Society, and the Development of Canadian Federalism*. Collected Research Studies, vol. 71. Toronto: University of Toronto Press.

Stevenson, Garth. 1977. "Federalism and the Political Economy of the Canadian State." In *The Canadian State: Political Economy and Political Power*, edited by Leo Panitch, 71–100. Toronto: University of Toronto Press.

– 2009. *Unfulfilled Union: Canadian Federalism and National Unity*. 5th ed. Montreal and Kingston: McGill-Queen's University Press.

Storper, Michael. 1997. *The Regional World: Territorial Development in a Global Economy*. New York: Guilford.

Supreme Court of Canada. 2021. *References re Greenhouse Gas Pollution Pricing Act*, 2021 SCC 11.

Sweeney, Brendan A. 2020. *Canada's Automotive Industry: A Decade in Review*. London, ON: Trillium Network for Advanced Manufacturing.

Thompson, Lori. 2021. "Shifting Gears: Unprecedented Investments Driving the Change to a Greener Auto Sector in Ontario." *Toronto Star*, 10 February 2021. https://www.thestar.com/news/canada/shifting-gears-unprecedented-investments-driving-the-change-to-a-greener-auto-sector-in-ontario/article_95d3d6a9-d013-5cc6-915e-19f3b3a17177.html.

Trippl, Michaela, Simon Baumgartinger-Seiringer, Alexandra Frangenheim, Arne Isaksen, and Jan Ole Rypestøl. 2020. "Unravelling Green Regional Industrial Path Development: Regional Preconditions, Asset Modification and Agency." *Geoforum* 111: 189–97.

Trippl, Michaela, Simon Baumgartinger-Seiringer, Elena Goracinova, and David A. Wolfe. 2021. "Automotive Regions in Transition: Preparing for Connected and Automated Vehicles." *Environment and Planning A: Economy and Space*.

Varcoe, Chris. 2019. "NDP Doubling Down on Energy Subsidies a Risky Investment Bet." *Calgary Herald*, 21 March. https://calgaryherald.com/business/energy/varcoe-ndp-doubling-down-on-energy-subsidies-a-risky-investment-bet.

Wang, Jason, and Will Noel. 2023. *Investment Impact of Alberta's Renewable Energy Moratorium*. Calgary: Pembina Institute.

Weber, K. Matthias, and Harald Rohracher. 2012. "Legitimizing Research, Technology and Innovation Policies for Transformative Change." *Research Policy* 41 (6): 1037–47.

Wolfe, David A. 1978. "Economic Growth and Foreign Investment: A Perspective on Canadian Economic Policy, 1945–1957." *Journal of Canadian Studies* 13 (1): 3–20.

Woynillowicz, Dan. 2020. "Electric Vehicle Assembly Deals Put Canada in the Race." *Electric Autonomy*, 20 October 2020. https://electricautonomy.ca/2020/10/20/ev-supply-chain-canada/.

Yates, Charlotte, and John Holmes. 2019. *The Future of the Canadian Auto Industry*. Ottawa: Canadian Centre for Policy Alternatives.

Yergin, Daniel. 2020. *The New Map: Energy, Climate, and the Clash of Nations*. New York: Penguin.

Yeung, Henry Wai-chung. 2020. "Regional Worlds: From Related Variety in Regional Diversification to Strategic Coupling in Global Production Networks." *Regional Studies* 55(6): 989–1010. https://www.tandfonline.com/doi/full/10.1080/00343404.2020.1857719.

Zysman, John. 1994. "How Institutions Create Historically Rooted Trajectories of Growth." *Industrial and Corporate Change* 3 (1): 243–83.

– 1996. "The Myth of a 'Global' Economy: Enduring National Foundations and Emerging Regional Realities." *New Political Economy* 1 (2): 157–84.

9

A North American Electric Vehicle Supply Chain: What It Means for Canada's Vehicle Parts Manufacturing Industry

Bassel Kazzaz, Sarah Greene, and Charlotte Yates

Automotive manufacturing, including vehicle assembly and parts production, is Canada's second-largest export industry. In 2019, Canada exported over $59 billion of assembled motor vehicles and over $17 billion of motor vehicle parts (Industry Canada 2021). Because automotive manufacturing is a key contributor to Canada's economy, maintaining and expanding production and exports is essential. Going forward, vehicle electrification represents a significant disruption to Canada's automotive production and its supply chain. It is important that Canada prepare for the transition of its automotive manufacturing industry to electric vehicle (EV) production and its accompanying battery-manufacturing supply chain.

In recent years, EV purchases – specifically, purchases of battery electric vehicles (BEVs) – have taken a still small but growing share of global vehicle production in some of the world's largest vehicle markets. This process has been partially driven by the Government of Canada's attempts to meet climate change commitments after the Paris Agreement of 2015, prompting a transition away from internal combustion engine vehicles (ICEVs) towards BEVs. This process has been supported by a range of policies and regulations, including the offer of financial incentives for automotive original equipment manufacturers (OEMs) and consumers to adopt EV technology. Through this, several OEMs now pledge to foster an all-electric future: expanding their portfolios to enhance zero-emission propulsion technology, extend BEV driving range, and lessen charge times. Consequently, demand for batteries, specifically lithium-ion batteries (LIBs), and their components is growing rapidly.

This chapter explores the changing BEV-oriented automotive landscape, considering the implications of the transition for Canada's automotive manufacturing sector. It builds from Klier and Rubestein's contribution to this collection about the spatial distribution of automobile production in North America (chapter 4), as well as Wolfe and Lemphers's analysis of the economic and political implications of the energy transition for Canada's auto industry (chapter 7). It also provides context for aspects of chapter 3, which considers the consequences of the shift to electrification and green technologies in the Mexican automotive industry.

We start our discussion by providing an overview of the geographical distribution of the automotive supply chain as it applies to the production of vehicles and parts in North America. We consider how the combination of OEM strategy and government policy led North America's vehicle assembly plants and their suppliers to locate in the Great Lakes region between the 1960s and the late 1980s. We also discuss the role that previous trade agreements have had in shaping sectoral integration between Canada and the US. We explain that even though such integration has occurred, North America's automotive sector has also experienced a profound reallocation away from the traditional manufacturing epicentre, the Great Lakes region. Moreover, it is expected that under the US-Mexico-Canada Trade Agreement (USMCA), intra-regional manufacturing and supply chain integration will increase.

From there, we begin the process of examining the implications for Canada of the North American automotive supply chain's transition to EVs. As key actors, including policymakers, consumers, and manufacturers, undertake the gradual transition to EVs, the process of making vehicles – how they are made and where – is about to undergo significant alteration. For that reason, understanding key differences between ICEV and BEV automotive parts and production provides a foundation for exploration of the still nascent conversion. Therefore, we provide perspective on the potential repositioning of the geographic profile of North America's automotive manufacturing away from the Great Lakes region (including Canada). We also show how major powertrain components associated with traditional ICEV manufacturing will be altered or eliminated as the shift to BEVs occurs. This includes the effects of increased manufacturing of battery packs and other related components. As that occurs, new suppliers will join the sector. The upshot for many current manufacturers is that they will need to adapt to the new vehicle infrastructure; either that or become obsolete.

Certainly, the shift in the automotive supply chain, combined with the OEMs' need to secure access to materials and minerals required for batteries and electronic components, will influence future OEM decision-making strategies. OEMs will confront the tension between balancing the cost of abandoning sunk investments and the pull of repositioning their profile as they secure the parts and materials needed to produce EVs. Given these circumstances, this chapter also explores how the automotive supply chain will adjust in North America, including Canada. In particular, we consider how EV-centric manufacturing will shift North America's supply chain away from the Great Lakes region towards the US South, and possibly the West. We show how these adjustments will have significant implications for the Great Lakes region in general and Canada in particular. Moreover, we anticipate that the southward pull for investment, experienced most intensely since the advent of the North American Free Trade Agreement (NAFTA), will accelerate. As a result, we argue that Canada's ability to gain – as the introduction of this volume puts it – a "fair share" of North American automotive investment and production will be constrained.

BACKGROUND: SHIFTING SOUTH – AUTOMOTIVE SUPPLY CHAIN UNDER AN EVOLVING POLICY LANDSCAPE

Automobiles and their components account for the most significant percentage of all North American intra-regional product trade (Hufbauer and Schott 2005). Before the existence of any formal policy promoting trade integration within North America's automotive sector, American-owned automotive producers operated within the US, Canada, and Mexico (Rutherford and Holmes 2014). Even so, most automotive production was concentrated around the Great Lakes region, including the US states of Michigan, Ohio, Indiana, Illinois, and Wisconsin (Rutherford and Holmes 2014) and the Canadian province of Ontario (Klier 2019). Initially, production in Canada provided a basis for access to the broader Canadian market, and later became a launching point for access to Commonwealth markets. By the late 1950s, however, the Canadian automotive industry was experiencing challenges: many of the Commonwealth markets had established automotive manufacturing industries of their own, and European imports had started to occupy an increasing share of the Canadian market. Over several years a number of policy measures were put in place, culminating in the Canada-US Auto Pact of 1965, which effectively integrated the automotive manufacturing industries in Canada and the US. (For an overview of the Auto Pact, see the introduction of this compilation.)

Beyond heightened cross-border integration of the auto industries in Canada and the US, one of the outcomes of the Auto Pact was that aspects of the industry, particularly in Canada, became more specialized and efficient (Thomas 1997). Integration of US-Canada automotive trade was further enhanced in 1989 when the broader US-Canada Free Trade Agreement was put in place (Klier 2019). In 1994 those relations were affected again when Mexico was added to the continental trade agreement with the implementation of the NAFTA (Klier 2019). However, as Canada and the US already enjoyed (mostly) uninhibited access to the other's vehicle consumer market, NAFTA did little to promote further integration of Canadian and US automotive industries (Hufbauer and Schott 2005).

Following the signing of the NAFTA, Canada's automotive industry grew throughout the 1990s, an outcome of a growing market in North America overall, a beneficial mix of products, increasing productivity, good quality metrics, and lower (relative to the US) labour costs (Rutherford and Holmes 2014). By 2002, Canada's automotive trade with members of NAFTA had increased by 60% from 1993 levels, and an automotive trade surplus of $12 billion was recorded (Rutherford and Holmes 2014). By then (and still now), major OEMs with assembly plants in Canada included General Motors, Ford, Chrysler (now Stellantis), Honda, and Toyota. However, following a steady rise in vehicle production throughout the 1990s, Canadian production started to fall. In 1999, for example, Canadian assembly plants produced 3 million vehicles; by 2021, production had dropped to 1.1 million. Meanwhile, in the south of the US and in Mexico where lower wages and weak unions prevailed, production continued to grow (Klier 2019). (For a review of wages and labour patterns in Mexico see Covarrubias V. and Dufour-Poirer, chapter 13 of this work.) This shift is best exemplified by new assembly plant location decisions. Between 1993 and 2019, five new vehicle assembly plants were established in Canada (see Automotive Policy Research Centre, https://automotivepolicy.ca/database/); meanwhile, twenty-three plants were set up in Mexico and twenty-nine in the US. Twenty of the new US plants were set up outside the traditional Great Lakes region (Marklines 2021c).

Notwithstanding three decades of decline, the Great Lakes region (including Ontario) continues to represent the hub of the North American automotive industry. Sixty per cent of North American light vehicle production currently occurs in the Great Lakes region; 72% of all North American transmissions and 52% of engines are manufactured there (Rutherford and Holmes 2014). Even so, the shift of production to southern US states and Mexico is unrelenting, a consequence of lower total labour costs (Hufbauer and Schott 2005; Holmes 2015) and a southward shift of population growth and, thus, vehicle sales (Hill and Brahmst 2003).

It is likely that the USMCA will further influence regional (i.e., Canada-US-Mexico) investment decisions. Under the NAFTA 62.5% of local content was required, whereas the USMCA requires that at least 75% be sourced among its members. On top of that, the USMCA seeks to further influence the location of local content (and hence investment) within the three member states by including measures to reverse the attraction to Mexico. It does this by requiring that at least 40% of vehicles' content derive from facilities where workers earn an hourly wage of at least US $16. Beyond the USMCA, regional investment decisions have also been influenced by the US administration's Buy America policy. Policy instruments notwithstanding, the draw for US automotive investment continues to be influenced by long-standing structural certainties, including, for example, the size of its market and its hosting the headquarters of large automakers and Tier 1 suppliers (Mordue and Sweeney 2020).

VEHICLE ELECTRIFICATION TRANSITION

Besides adjusting to USMCA requirements, the automotive sector faces one of the most significant disruptions to automotive production in more than a century: the pressures of decarbonization, a consequence of the fact that transportation alone accounts for approximately 23% of all energy-related CO_2 emissions (Sims et al. 2014). Thus, an industry-wide transition towards production and sales of EVs, specifically BEVs, has taken hold. By 2030, under the current international policy landscape, the EV stock will grow at an average annual rate of approximately 30% (International Energy Agency 2021b). It is estimated that to stay on track for a net-zero scenario by 2050, approximately 60% of all new vehicle sales must be zero emissions by 2030 (McKerracher et al. 2021). To support the transition, governments are incentivizing automotive manufacturers to accelerate their electrification targets and increase their zero-carbon vehicle rosters (see International Energy Agency 2021b). In response, vehicle manufacturers are announcing increasingly ambitious electrification plans and commitments to capture the growing market for EVs and achieve carbon neutrality between 2040 and 2050 (General Motors 2021a; Ford Motor Company [hereafter Ford] 2021c; Stellantis 2021).

Of the world's top twenty automotive manufacturers, which accounted for approximately 90% of new vehicle registrations in 2020, eighteen have disclosed an intent to invest heavily in R&D, broaden their roster of electrified models, and scale up production of light-duty EVs (International Energy Agency 2021b). For example, GM has announced its intention to discontinue gas and diesel powertrains from its light-duty lineup by 2035 (General Motors 2021a). Ford says that 40% of its global sales will be fully electric by 2030 (Klayman 2021). It also claims that its European passenger vehicle line-up will consist of zero-emission, plug-in hybrid, or all-electric by 2026 (Ford 2021a). Stellantis (formerly Chrysler-Fiat) states that by 2025, 98% of its models will be either hybrid or electric (Krisher 2021).

Since the election of the Biden US administration in 2020, US government support for automotive production's electrification has increased. Specific measures include multi-billion-dollar funding for EV infrastructure, electric buses, and other modes of transportation (White House 2021b). Strategies have also been enacted to address vulnerabilities and opportunities within the US supply chain associated with the transition to EVs (US Department of Energy, 2021).

Measures are also being taken in Canada to support the transition. Its federal government has announced a mandatory target that all new light-duty vehicles and passenger trucks must be zero emission by 2035 (Transport Canada 2021). Although OEMs with manufacturing facilities within Ontario currently focus primarily on producing ICEVs, recently many of them have announced multi-billion-dollar investments towards electrification. The governments of Canada and the Province of Ontario have supported the assembly plants' transition, contributing, for example, a combined CDN $590 million towards Ford's CDN $1.8 billion investment in its Oakville, Ontario, assembly plant's transition to EV production (Prime Minister of Canada 2021). Other programs in Ontario and/or Canada focused on the EV transition include Ontario's $56.4 million commitment to its Ontario Vehicle Innovation Network (OVIN) to expedite EV development and a $10 million fund to support automotive suppliers to pivot their operations to support EVs (Invest Ontario, 2021).

FUNDAMENTAL CHANGES TO THE VEHICLE ASSOCIATED WITH THE EV TRANSITION

Vehicle electrification demands fundamental changes to the vehicle, its assembly, and the automotive supply chain. This section considers the changes to the vehicle this transition requires. There are four main types of electrified vehicles: (1) hybrid electric vehicles (HEVs); (2) plug-in hybrid electric vehicles (PHEVs); (3) battery electric vehicles (BEVs); and (4) fuel cell electric vehicles (FCEV) (Alternative Fuels Data Center 2021a, 2021b). This chapter mainly focuses on BEVs, which in 2020 accounted for two-thirds of all new electric car registrations and which are forecast to be the most common type of electrified vehicles (International Energy Agency 2021b). For example, it is predicted that by 2033 BEVs will make up 35% of global light vehicle sales and approximately 57% of all electrified vehicles (LMC Automotive 2021).

The shift will result in changes in how vehicles are manufactured as well as the underlying supply chain. Around 70% of EV parts are different from the parts of gasoline-powered vehicles. A BEV's powertrain has far fewer components than an ICEV and a lower number of moving and wearing pieces (Idaho National Laboratory 2020). With the shift to BEVs, several powertrain components are either altered or eliminated, and new predominantly electrical or electronic components are introduced (UBS Group 2017). Below, we explore the major differences between ICEVs and BEVs.

Engines

With vehicle electrification, the gasoline- or diesel-powered ICE is substituted with an electric motor. Unlike the ICE, which consists of pistons and a camshaft inside a cylinder block, the electric motor consists of magnetic rotors enclosed in a cylindrical-shaped case. Electric motors are less mechanically complex and have fewer moving parts, making them less susceptible to failure and requiring less maintenance (Idaho National Laboratory 2020). A study comparing the parts of a Chevrolet Bolt, a BEV, to the parts of a Volkswagen Golf, an ICEV, found that the Golf ICE contained 113 moving parts whilst the electric motor of the Bolt had only three (UBS Group 2017). Electric motors are also stronger, have a shorter response time and a wider usable revolutions per minute (rpm) range, and do not consume energy when running idle (UBS Group 2017). Additional components, such as a gearbox, clutch, and starter generator, are non-existent in an electric motor (UBS Group 2017).

Power Source (Battery)

The power needed to drive the electric motor is provided through an on-board battery pack, most commonly an LIB. The battery replaces the fuel tank as the energy source storage unit. The battery pack is a modular case assembly consisting of several connected battery modules, which in turn are made up of battery cells. The battery pack includes battery management and thermal management systems. High-voltage cables connect the battery pack, the electric motor, and other electrical and electronic components (UBS Group 2017). (We provide additional details on the structure and economics of EV batteries below.)

Transmissions

Electric cars do not require a multi-speed transmission. Unlike ICEs, which require multiple gears with different ratios for power output, electric motors produce a consistent amount of torque. Automotive manufacturers incorporate carefully calculated gear ratios to maximize efficiency for the electric motor without having to switch through gears (UBS Group 2017).

Other Powertrain Parts

Since EVs are powered by electricity from the grid and energy is stored in the battery pack, a converter is used to convert the electrical energy from alternating current (AC) to direct current (DC). Further, an on-board inverter is required to convert the electric supply from DC to AC to power the electric motor. The high-voltage power distribution unit (PDU) delivers power to all components within the EV system, including traction and auxiliary units (UBS Group 2017).

A SPLIT FROM THE TRADITIONAL SUPPLY CHAIN: A NEW BATTERY-FOCUSED SUPPLY CHAIN

The shift away from ICEVs to EVs will affect how automotive manufacturing supply chains operate. For an ICEV, engine and transmission capabilities are main sources of differentiation. The battery is a principal differentiation source for BEVs (Coffin and Horowitz 2018). It is estimated that the LIB battery pack accounts for 30–40% of the vehicle's total cost (Yu and Sumangil 2021). However, while an ICE and transmission are produced mainly in-house, automakers are increasingly reliant on new "non-traditional" suppliers for their battery inputs, including raw materials and battery cells (Harrison and Ludwig 2021). Additionally, most established battery producers are located in Asia; very few are headquartered in North America, and those that are, are quite small. Reliance on foreign suppliers for raw materials, battery technology, and cell and module production exposes North American automakers to supply chain risks, and so they are investing billions to diversify their suppliers and establish joint ventures and strategic partnerships to overcome those risks (Harrison and Ludwig 2021; Thielmann et al. 2020). (The implications of the changing power dynamics spawned by the advent of BEVs within automotive global value chains are discussed in the introduction to this collection.)

In order to be competitive against ICEVs and other EV manufacturers, automakers focus primarily on refining battery technology to enhance driving range, reduce charge times, and lower costs (Coffin and Horowitz 2018). It is suggested that EVs will compete with traditional ICEVs once battery pack prices are reduced to $100 per kilowatt-hour (kWh) (LeVine 2021). At this price point, automakers will manufacture and sell EVs at a comparable price to ICEVs in most markets, with similar profit margins (Bloomberg New Energy Finance 2020). Figure 1 shows the anticipated battery pack prices for the period 2021–25, extrapolated based on previous five-year battery price trends.

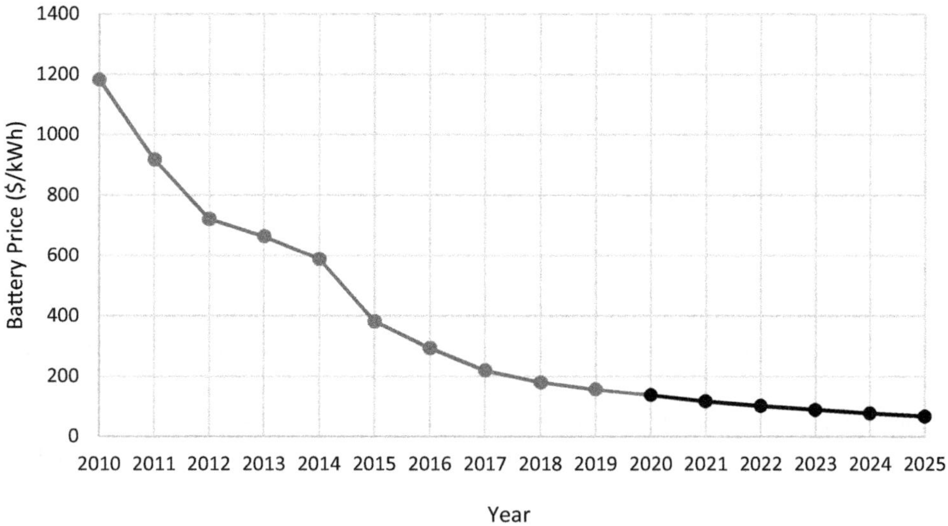

Figure 1. Projected Reduction in Battery Prices
Source: Bloomberg New Energy Finance (2020); Automotive Policy Research Centre.

There are three stages in the battery production process: (1) battery cell production; (2) battery module manufacturing; and (3) battery pack assembly. Manufacturing the battery cells accounts for 75% of the total battery cost, the module manufacturing stage accounts for around 11%, and battery pack assembly represents 14% of the overall cost of a finished LIB pack (Argonne National Laboratory 2021). Price modelling anticipates the average pack price dropping from the 2020 cost of $126/kWh to $101/kWh by 2023. However, real pricing tactics will differ by carmaker and location (Bloomberg New Energy Finance, 2020).

LIBs are the leading technology for EVs and are at the heart of the EV manufacturing supply chain evolution. Clearly, as demand for EVs increases, demand for ICEV-unique components and parts will consequently drop (PricewaterhouseCoopers 2019). Therefore, parts suppliers that rely on the production of ICEV parts will either alter their strategies and shift to EV components or disappear.

Common materials used in LIBs include lithium, aluminium, cobalt, graphite, manganese, and nickel. Of those, lithium, cobalt, and graphite face supply constraints (Coffin and Horowitz 2018). As demand for LIBs increases, it is forecast that 2025 lithium demand will triple from current levels to one million metric tonnes (MMT) of lithium carbonate equivalent (LCE – the first chemical in the lithium production chain) (Jones et al. 2021). By 2030, the available global lithium supply is expected to be 1.4 MMT LCE, yet the expected demand will be 1.8 MMT LCE (Jones et al. 2021). This leaves a supply gap of 0.4 MMT LCE, a risk of rising production costs due to material scarcity, and a slower-than-anticipated acceleration of EVs in the marketplace.

It is likely that under the USMCA, automakers will be encouraged to source and manufacture batteries within North America to meet the higher North American content requirement of 75% (Harrison and Ludwig 2021). By 2030, for example, battery production in North America is expected to grow in tandem with the market for EVs (see Harrision 2021; Coffin and Horowitz 2018; Thielmann et al. 2020).

The shift to electrified mobility is also altering the geographic profile of North American automotive manufacturing. Places outside of the traditional Great Lakes region have experienced significant increases in investment attention. Automakers such as Tesla and BYD Auto have built battery facilities and have announced continued investment in California, Nevada, and Texas. Reasons for doing so include access to raw materials and proximity to both domestic and foreign markets (BYD 2018). Traditional OEMs are also collaborating with lithium suppliers and battery manufacturers in these regions. For example, GM is partnering with Controlled Thermal Resources (CTR) in Imperial, California, to secure lithium hydroxide and lithium carbonate for its batteries (General Motors 2021b).

IMPLICATIONS OF THE BEV TRANSITION FOR CANADA'S AUTOMOTIVE MANUFACTURING INDUSTRY

The shift that is underway and starting to accelerate will have profound changes on supply chain dynamics. Here, we consider the implications of these changes for Canada's automotive manufacturing industry. We begin by considering Canada and the US's current automotive trade level and then examine, data and trends from the US EV and battery-manufacturing industries. From that, we suggest that the EV and battery-manufacturing industries' transition away from the Great Lakes region will disproportionately impact Canada.

Canada-US Automotive Trade Dynamics

Canada's automotive industry heavily relies on exports. In 2019, almost 50% (CDN $17.4 billion) of Canada's manufactured motor vehicle parts (North American Industry Classification System [NAICS] 3363) were exported, of which more than 91.2% of the exported parts were destined for the US (Industry Canada 2021). That year, Canada also imported CDN $28.21 billion worth of manufactured vehicle parts from the US (38.5% of total US manufacturing vehicle parts exports) (Industry Canada 2021).

Figure 2 shows that, by export value, gas engines and engine parts, and transmission and powertrain parts are the Canadian vehicle parts manufacturing industry's two most significant exports to the US. Combined, these two categories make up 45% of Canadian vehicle parts exports. Critically, it is expected that these two categories will be the ones most directly affected by the shift to EVs.

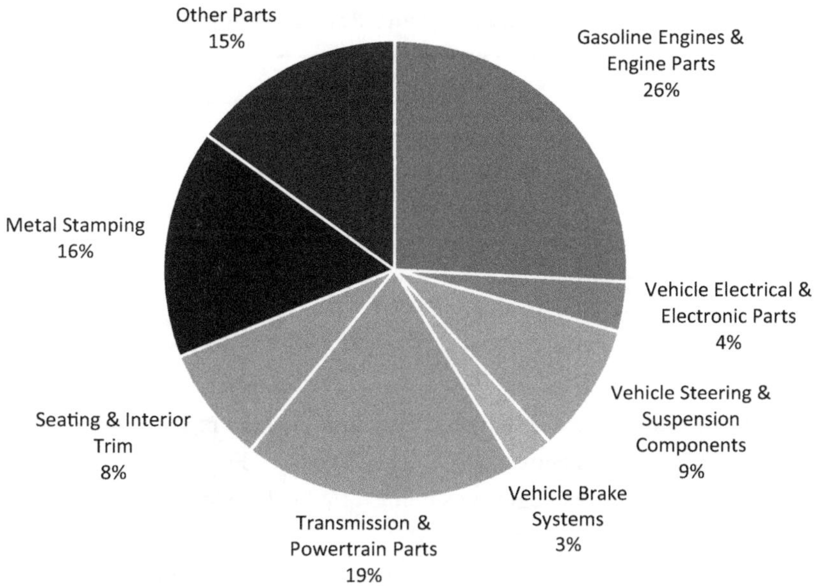

Figure 2. Distribution of Vehicle Parts Exports to the US, 2021
Source: Industry Canada (2021).

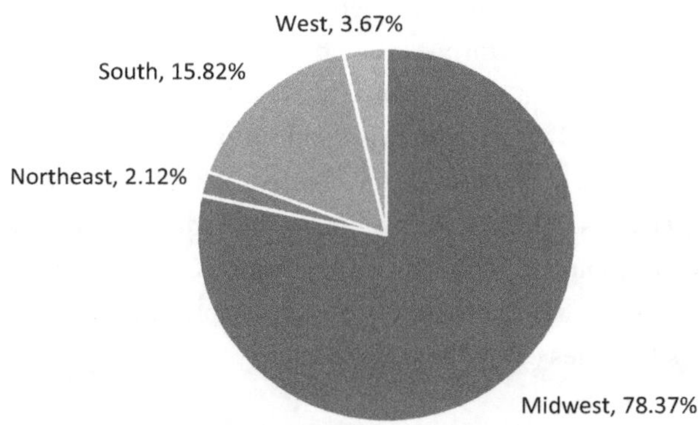

Figure 3. Distribution of Canada's Parts Exports to US Regions
Source: Industry Canada (2021).
Notes: The Northeast region comprises Connecticut, Maine, Massachusetts, New Hampshire, Rhode Island, Vermont, New Jersey, New York, and Pennsylvania. The Midwest region comprises Illinois, Indiana, Michigan, Ohio, Wisconsin, Iowa, Kansas, Minnesota, Missouri, Nebraska, North Dakota, and South Dakota. The South region comprises Delaware, Florida, Georgia, Maryland, North Carolina, South Carolina, Virginia, District of Columbia, West Virginia, Alabama, Kentucky, Mississippi, Tennessee, Arkansas, Louisiana, Oklahoma, and Texas. The West region comprises Arizona, Colorado, Idaho, Montana, Nevada, New Mexico, Utah, Wyoming, Alaska, California, Hawaii, Oregon, and Washington.

Table 1. Distribution of Vehicle Assembly and Parts Manufacturing in the US

Region	Midwest	Northeast	South	West
Number of assembly plants	39	2	25	6
Share of production capacity	63.33%	0.21%	33.3%	3.16%
Number (and percentage) of vehicle parts suppliers	2,212 (56.95%)	507 (13.05%)	657 (19.5%)	508 (10.5%)

Source: Marklines (2021c, 2021d).

Examining Canada's automotive parts exports to four main regions in the US showcases the automotive trade dynamics between Canada and the US. For the purpose of our analysis, we break down exports into four regions as defined by the US Census Bureau: the Northeast, the Midwest, the South, and the West.

The US Midwest is where most of that country's automotive manufacturing assets are located, and, as figure 3 indicates, it is where in 2019 78.4% of Canadian parts exported to the US went. Moreover, the importance of the Midwest has increased: over the past two decades, the portion of vehicle parts exported to the Midwest rose by almost 1%. The South region receives the second largest portion, approximately 16%, of Canadian parts exports to the US, while the West and Northeast account for less than 5% each (Industry Canada 2021).

As table 1 shows, based on seventy-two vehicle assembly plants in the US, 63.3% of US production capacity is housed in thirty-nine vehicle assembly plants in the Midwest, while 33.3% is in twenty-five plants in the South. The West hosts 3.2% of US vehicle production capacity (Marklines 2021c). Table 1 confirms that most parts facilities are also located in the Midwest (Marklines 2021d). Of relevance: the combination of data underpinning figure 3 and table 1 shows that Canada's automotive manufacturing industry is disproportionately reliant on the Midwest region. Figure 3 shows that the share of Canadian automotive parts exports to the Midwest (78.4%) exceeds the share of automotive production capacity (63.3%) and the share of vehicle parts facilities (57%) in that region.

THE US ELECTRIC VEHICLES SUPPLY CHAIN

As of 2019, EVs (BEVs, HEVs, PHEVs, ICEVs, FCVs) made up 4.2% of all US automotive sales (Marklines 2021b). While almost all EV sales in North America were hybrid vehicles pre-2011, BEVs have steadily gained popularity, a consequence of growing efficiency, increasing battery range and decreasing costs (Markines 2021c). As of 2021, twenty-five out of seventy-two vehicle assembly plants in the US produced at least one type of EV. Additionally,

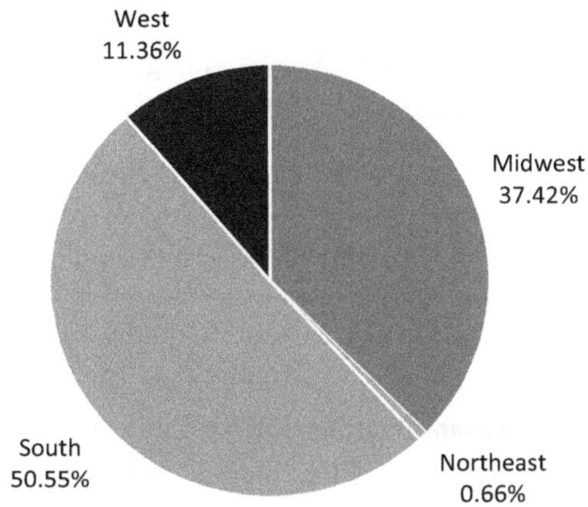

Figure 4. Distribution of Current and Planned BEV Assembly Plants by Production Capacity, 2021
Source: Marklines (2021c).

plans had been announced for another seventeen assembly plants to make EVs in the future. Out of the forty-two plants with current production or future EV plans, twenty-six facilities will be assembling BEVs with a total production capacity of 4.52 million vehicles (as of June 2021, nine automotive assembly plants were producing BEVs) (Marklines 2021c). Of the current and planned BEV production facilities, nine are in the Midwest, one in the Northeast, ten in the South, and six in the West. Figure 4 presents the current and planned production capacity distribution of BEV assembly plants across the US for a total production capacity of 4,516,000 units.

THE US BATTERY SUPPLY CHAIN

We now turn to recent trends and indicators from the US EV battery supply chain, including imports, the distribution of the supply chain, and the North American lithium mines and other battery material sources. Each section explores the implications of these trends and developments for both the US and Canadian automotive manufacturing industries.

Battery Parts and Components Imports

Over the past decade, the US EV industry has relied on the well-developed Asian battery supply chain to source EV battery parts. Given the high electrical and electronic component content in EV batteries, companies such as LG Chem, SK Innovation, Samsung Digital Interface (SDI),

Panasonic, Contemporary Amperex Technology Co., Limited (CATL), BYD, and Envision Automotive Energy Supply Corporation (AESC) emerged as major LIB manufacturers and suppliers (Asian Development Bank n.d.). These companies, headquartered in Japan, South Korea, or China, dominate the global EV battery industry (Tanaka et al. 2019). In 2019, they represented about 85% of the global EV battery output. While most EV battery production capacity is concentrated in Asia (Yu and Sumangil 2021), several battery companies have expanded their operations, establishing plants in Europe and North America. It is forecast that in 2025 Europe's LIB capacity will reach 25% of the global battery capacity (up from 6% in 2020), while the US will host only 6% of this global capacity, down from 8% in 2020 (Yu and Sumangil 2021). Meanwhile, Asian countries (mainly China) will continue to seize the majority of the global LIB capacity at 68% in 2025 (Yu and Sumangil 2021).

In 2019, only five battery manufacturers – all headquartered in Japan and South Korea – supplied the US EV market. These manufacturers were AESC, Panasonic, SDI, LG Chem, and SK Innovation. A recent study tracking the flow of products within the LIB supply chain for EVs in the US between 2010 and 2020 showed that in 2015, 79.5% of the battery cell capacity of vehicles sold in the US was imported from Japan and South Korea (Argonne National Laboratory 2021). However, the launch of a Panasonic/Tesla battery facility in Nevada in 2018 caused the share of battery cell imports from Japan and South Korea to fall to 29.7% in 2019.

While efforts to increase domestication of the North American battery supply chain continue, it is anticipated that reliance on imports will persist. The import of LIBs for use in EVs rose around 200% in 2020 with the rising demand for EVs (Hering and Holzman 2021). Further, more than 65% of the US battery component supply agreements between 2018 and 2022 (some agreements were set to start ahead of the date the data were collected) continue to be with Japanese and South Korean battery suppliers, while 31.25% of the agreements are with US-based battery manufacturing suppliers (Marklines 2021e).

As demand for EVs rises, a global shortage of EV battery capacity is forecast between 2025 and 2026 (see Desai and Nguyen 2021). We suggest that the combination of the current distribution of global battery production capacity and increased demand suggests that regions with well-developed battery supply chains (i.e., East Asia and Europe) will be advantaged over those that do not (i.e., North America). Thus, US-based OEMs will struggle to meet the aggressive targets for BEV proliferation to which they have committed.

Looking ahead, we anticipate that the development of the North American battery industry will adopt a geographic profile that diverts from the Midwest-centric pattern that has characterized the historical development of the US industry. We posit that the North American industry's combination of (1) high dependence on battery and battery component imports from Asia and Europe, and (b) the location of lithium mines and other battery material sources will cause battery production to be drawn to coastal locations. Indeed, a coastal proximity battery production strategy appears to have influenced the investment location decisions of a number of OEMs in the US, including Tesla's Fremont California factory, BMW's Spartanburg plant in North Carolina, and BYD's Lancaster plant in California (Marklines 2021a). Continued reliance on imported parts may cause the Midwest/Great Lakes Region to confront a lessening of its domination. Thus, while battery part imports may facilitate, even accelerate, the transition to EV production, that process may obstruct the historical domination of the centre. As that occurs, the Canadian automotive manufacturing industry – located almost exclusively in the Province of Ontario and therefore immediately proximate to the US Midwest/Great Lakes – can expect obstacles.

The Distribution of Battery Part Suppliers

Current and planned locations for US battery plants and components provide an early signal for the course that the US battery supply chain may adopt. By the end of 2021, the US had at least seventeen facilities capable of performing at least one of the three stages of battery manufacturing this chapter suggested earlier (cell manufacturing, module manufacturing, and pack assembly) (Marklines 2021c). US OEMs and battery manufacturers plan at least five additional battery manufacturing facilities, bringing the total to twenty-two. Current and planned battery facilities are distributed as follows: eight in the Midwest, eight in the South, and six in the West (Marklines 2021c). Additionally, the Midwest and West regions both host thirty-eight component suppliers. The South and the Northeast regions have thirty-two and twenty-one facilities, respectively (Marklines 2021d).

The current and planned distribution of battery manufacturing facilities and parts suppliers is inconsistent with the distribution of the traditional automotive parts manufacturing sector as it has evolved. In the traditional industry, the Midwest hosts the majority of the US parts facilities (2,213). However, the West and South are gaining a more important role as locations for battery manufacturing (Marklines 2021d). Therefore, even though the US battery industry is still taking shape, early geographic indicators point to an EV-inspired shift away from the traditional core of the Midwest towards the South and the West.

Lithium Mines and Other Materials

Several reports and studies about EV manufacturing discuss the influence and role of suppliers of the minerals and materials for batteries (see Coffin and Horowitz 2018; Clean Energy Canada 2021; Gallucci 2021). The availability of materials like lithium, cobalt, and graphite is essential. EVs are expected to be responsible for more than one-third of the global lithium demand by 2025, and demand will exceed supply at some point between 2025 and 2030 (Jones et al. 2021). Supply of cobalt is also considered to be precarious, with demand for it in EVs projected to increase at least ninefold by 2030 (International Energy Agency 2021a). OEMs like BMW and Tesla have responded by signing direct supply agreements with cobalt mining companies.

Over the past few years, sourcing LIB materials has been highly dependent on countries such as China, Australia, the Democratic Republic of Congo, and Chile. Given anticipated shortages from traditional sources, US-based companies are exploring opportunities to source materials directly from US and Canadian reserves (PR Newswire 2021). Securing domestic sources also furthers the compliance of firms operating in the USMCA region with the USMCA's rules of origin and helps avoid the associated tariffs. Indeed, it can be anticipated that the importance of these factors will escalate as EV demand and production rises.

US lithium deposits are located in two main regions: in Nevada, California, and Utah in the West and in Arkansas and North Carolina in the South (Fortier et al. 2019). In anticipation of increasing EV-related demand, mining companies have expanded their operations in these regions (Albemarle 2021). Among the leading lithium suppliers globally is Albemarle Corporation, which operates one of the largest US lithium mines in Clayton Valley in Nevada (Harrison and Ludwig 2021). Similarly, other American mining companies such as Lithium Americas Corp. and Schlumberger New Energy have established lithium extraction projects in Nevada. In the South, Piedmont Lithium operates in North Carolina (Schlumberger New Energy 2021).

Lithium mines in the US's western and southern regions have attracted several EV projects and battery-manufacturing plants to those regions. They include operations by Panasonic, KORE Power, and NeoLith Energy. Panasonic and NeoLith Energy are partners in an endeavour to optimize direct lithium extraction (Lasley 2021). Cobalt projects include First Cobalt's Idaho project, one of the first in the US (First Cobalt Corp. 2021).

The direct interest and involvement of automakers and battery-manufacturing companies in the mining industry represents an upstream expansion reminiscent of the approach Smitka reminds us of in chapter 5 of this collection: the vertical integration strategies of Henry Ford and William Durant enacted a century prior. These strategies highlight a new role for the mining industry, one that will influence and direct the future of EVs, the battery industry, and the geographic profile of the North American automotive manufacturing industry.

In Canada, lithium resources are present across the country, including in Quebec, Ontario, Alberta, and Manitoba (Canada Energy Regulator 2017). The biggest mining and battery material processing project in Canada currently under development is the Whabouchi Lithium Project in the James Bay area in central Quebec (Impact Assessment Agency of Canada 2020). Additionally, several global companies have also expressed interest in Canadian mining operations, including CATL, which acquired Canada's Millennial Lithium in 2021 (Reuters 2021). In chapter 1 of this collection, Mordue and Sweeney discuss one of Canada's key "industrial narratives," its "Mines to Mobility" narrative, which envisions a path for the Canadian automotive industry that leverages its resource riches to pursue an elevated role in battery and BEV manufacturing (see Canada 2020). Enthusiastic promotion of the "Mines to Mobility" narrative notwithstanding, Canada has so far failed to translate its critical-to-EV resource reserves into tangible battery-manufacturing investment.

TECHNOLOGICAL DEVELOPMENT AND ITS EFFECT ON ELECTRIC VEHICLE INVESTMENT PATTERNS

During the post-2000 period, the deployment of automotive electronics has expanded considerably (Fey and Shoshiev 2006), with such firms occupying an increasingly important role as drivers of automotive innovation (Deloitte 2013), including infotainment, ABS, vehicle safety, and connectivity. In many ways, important trends associated with the rise of electronics are also noted with respect to electrification. For example, non-traditional (i.e., "new") automotive suppliers of electronics, electrical, and related technology are poised to become core contributors to the automotive supply chain (Seattle Jobs Initiative n.d.). Meanwhile, suppliers of – and to – traditional ICEV components (e.g., engines, transmission, and fuel tanks) will either shift or contract.

It is well understood that the quantity and complexity of electrical content in EVs exceeds that of ICEVs (UBS Group 2017; Seattle Jobs Initiative n.d.), a condition that gives rise to the entry of new firms to the automotive space. The Chevrolet Bolt is illustrative: 56% of its content derives from LG Corporation, the parent firm of LG Chem (the Bolt's battery maker), a firm outside of the traditional Tier 1 automotive supply chain (UBS Group 2017). Beyond LG, the advent of electrification is ushering several new firms to the upper echelons of the automotive space, including Panasonic, SDI, and SK Innovation.

The geographic profile of the automotive industry is also shifting as traditional automotive actors reach for technological innovation from non-traditional sources. For example, major automotive OEMs are expanding their relationships with technology companies like Google, Apple, Cisco, and Intel, particularly on the US West Coast (California AutoTech Testing and Development Center 2018). Traditional automotive firms are also increasing their own footprints in the region, a means by which to access talent or facilitate collaboration with current or potential technology partners. All dominant US automakers have established divisions in the technology-dense San Francisco Bay area. For example, Ford, GM, Lucid, BMW, Volkswagen, Porsche, Hyundai, Volvo, and Mercedes-Benz have R&D centres there (NAIOP 2018) focused on electrification and advanced propulsion systems. Electrification is also triggering a shift southward. Ford, for instance, has established a partnership with SK Innovation to build the Blue Oval City and the Blue Oval SK Battery Park in Tennessee and Kentucky, respectively, for EV and battery production. These facilities will be proximate to SK Innovation's two battery plants in Georgia (Ford 2021b).

In Canada, some OEMs and parts-supplying companies maintain research and technology capabilities in or close to their production sites in Ontario and Quebec. Some of those resources are devoted to electrification and battery development (Automotive Policy Research Centre, https://automotivepolicy.ca/database/). However, as Mordue and Sweeney explain in chapter 1 in their discussion of core, semi-periphery, and integrated periphery countries, the mandates extended to these facilities pale compared to the work conducted closer to the headquarters of OEMs and parts-supplying companies in the US and other countries: core automotive countries (see also Mordue and Sweeney 2020).

DISCUSSION AND CONCLUSION

The shift to EV production brings with it significant changes to the vehicle and its manufacturing supply chain. As major powertrain components and parts are either altered or eliminated, several "traditional" automotive parts suppliers will be – and are being – affected. As this process accelerates, some vehicle parts manufacturers will be challenged for continuing relevancy, a consequence of their products' declining applicability. As that occurs, new "non-traditional" companies, primarily suppliers of electrical and electronic components, will emerge. Many of those firms will assume roles at the upper tier of the automotive value chain. This chapter has described the implications of that transition: for new entrants to the automotive space, for traditional suppliers, for regions and communities, and for policymakers.

As other chapters within this collection illustrate, single factors do influence investment decisions. Rarely, however, are they solely responsible (see Dziczek and Swiecki, chapter 6). That said, this chapter has demonstrated that the market's shift to EVs will affect, and is affecting, automotive investment decisions, including those related to research, the location of final assembly operations, and where any of the three stages of battery production will occur. It can be anticipated that incumbent regions and facilities (i.e., the US Midwest and communities hosting existing final assembly plants) hold a path-dependent advantage. Even so, this chapter has explained that other factors are at play and counterbalance the path-dependent status quo. For example, we have explained how aspects of the new USMCA will affect production location decisions for batteries and EVs in the North American region. In short, higher local content provisions within the USMCA suggest an urgency to localize key stages of battery production within North America overall. Beyond that, the USMCA's higher-wage requirements might also influence where in North America those investments ultimately land.

All of this will affect key aspects of the industry as it unfolds in Canada, including the development and award of research commissions and production mandates. Certainly, the effects of the transition have yet to find their final form. Even so, some trends – albeit nascent – offer clues. For Canada, some aspects are particularly troubling. First, this chapter has demonstrated that Canada's exports are disproportionately destined for the US Midwest, and that in recent years its preoccupation with the Midwest has accelerated. Concurrently, the automotive industry in the US South has grown, where Canadian exports are stable but low. Second, this chapter has shown that exports by Canadian automotive parts suppliers are disproportionately centred on engines and transmissions. Looking ahead, and assuming that elevated targets for electrified powertrains develop as OEMs foretell, Canadian firms will be disproportionately weakened. Third, this chapter has suggested that a combination of unique-to-BEV attributes – mineral reserves, access to the coast (and ports), the headquarters locations of emergent BEV makers – suggests that the automotive industries in the US South and West will grow disproportionately to that of other North American regions. If the Midwest, the traditional epicentre, continues to dissipate and the US West and South continue to grow, Canada's automotive industry – well removed from those latter locations – will be impaired.

These challenges aside, Canada does aspire to develop a significant role in alternative propulsion systems, encompassing battery supply chains as well as hydrogen fuel cells. Proponents point to Canada's potential role as a stable source of necessary metals (Clean Energy Canada 2021). It is also envisioned that the capabilities and infrastructure Canada has developed over one hundred-plus years of so-called traditional automotive manufacturing may be redeployed to battery plants and other actions associated with the industry's electrification. In chapter 1, however, Mordue and Sweeney refer to these aspirations as Canada's "Mines to Mobility" narrative and offer several reasons why, even though the narrative is appealing in the abstract, practical implementation will be problematic.

Regardless of the prognosis, effective policy is essential. So far, however, aside from the lofty narrative described above and the promise of incentives to anchor production, Canadian officials have engaged in limited policy intervention. By contrast, the US administration has been active in identifying gaps in the US battery supply chain, funding R&D projects and partnerships around advanced battery technologies, and providing financing for retooling to support battery-manufacturing operations (White House 2021a). Additionally, even though approval to provide incentives of up to $12,500 for union-made, US-produced EVs now seems unlikely, its inclusion in the Biden administration's Build Back Better agenda signalled the administration's ongoing and tangible support for the electrification of the US automotive manufacturing industry.

In the tightly integrated North American automotive supply chain, the implications of shifting industrial trends manifest in multiple manners and forms. For Canada, an expansion of its operations around battery manufacturing and EV assembly is seen as an essential instrument to help anchor its position in the Great Lakes automotive cluster. However, as the US systematically and aggressively moves to strengthen its capabilities around electrified mobility and its manufacture, Canada's vulnerabilities are increasingly exposed. This chapter has identified many of the still early trends that are developing as the industry, policymakers, and communities seek to affect the direction an electrified automotive industry takes. While the ultimate focus of this chapter has been the consequences of this transition for Canada and its automotive manufacturing industry, the trends identified here have application for stakeholders throughout the North American automotive ecosystem.

REFERENCES

Albemarle. 2021. "Albemarle Announces Expansion of Nevada Site to Increase Domestic Production of Lithium." Press release. https://www.albemarle.com/news/albemarle-announces-expansion-of-nevada-site-to-increase-domestic-production-of-lithium.

Alternative Fuels Data Center. 2021a. "Batteries for Electric Vehicles." US Department of Energy. https://afdc.energy.gov/vehicles/electric_batteries.html.

– 2021b. "Electric Vehicles." US Department of Energy. https://afdc.energy.gov/vehicles/electric.html.

Argonne National Laboratory. 2021. "BatPaC: Battery Manufacturing Cost Estimate." https://www.anl.gov/partnerships/batpac-battery-manufacturing-cost-estimation.

Asian Development Bank. n.d. "Lithium-Ion Battery Suppliers." 43207-PHI: Market Transformation through Introduction of Energy Efficient Electric Tricycles Project. https://www.adb.org/sites/default/files/projects/163994/lithium-ion-battery-suppliers.pdf.

Bloomberg New Energy Finance. 2020. "Battery Pack Prices Cited Below $100/kWh for the First Time in 2020, While Market Average Sits at $137/kWh" (blog). BloombergNEF, 16 December 2020. https://about.bnef.com/blog/battery-pack-prices-cited-below-100-kwh-for-the-first-time-in-2020-while-market-average-sits-at-137-kwh/.

BYD. 2018. "BYD Continues US Investment with New $5 Million Warehouse Facility." Press release. https://en.byd.com/news-posts/press-release-byd-continues-u-s-investment-with-new-5-million-warehouse-facility/.

California AutoTech Testing and Development Center. 2018. "The Automotive Sector in California & Silicon Valley." https://www.countyofmerced.com/3335/CATDC-at-Castle/.

Canada. 2020. *From Mines to Mobility: Seizing Opportunities for Canada in the Global Battery Value Chain: What We Heard Report*. https://publications.gc.ca/site/eng/9.891985/publication.html.

Canada Energy Regulator. 2017. "Market Snapshot: Growing Battery Demand Spurs Change in Global Lithium Markets." https://www.cer-rec.gc.ca/en/data-analysis/energy-markets/market-snapshots/2017/market-snapshot-growing-battery-demand-spurs-changes-in-global-lithium-markets.html.

Clean Energy Canada. 2021. *Turning Talk into Action: Building Canada's Battery Supply Chain*. Vancouver: CEC. https://cleanenergycanada.org/wp-content/uploads/2021/05/Turning-Talk-into-Action_Building-Canadas-Battery-Supply-Chain.pdf.

Coffin, David, and Jeff Horowitz. 2018. "The Supply Chain for Electric Vehicle Batteries." *Journal of International Commerce and Economics*. December 2018. https://www.usitc.gov/publications/332/journals/the_supply_chain_for_electric_vehicle_batteries.pdf.

Deloitte. 2013. "Trends and Outlook for the Auto Electronics Industry." Deloitte China Automotive Practice. https://www2.deloitte.com/cn/en/pages/manufacturing/articles/trends-and-outlook-of-auto-electronics-industry.html.

Desai, Pratima, and Mai Nguyen. 2021. "Shortages Flagged for EV Materials Lithium and Cobalt." Reuters. https://www.reuters.com/business/energy/shortages-flagged-ev-materials-lithium-cobalt-2021-07-01/.

Fey, Victor, and Alex Shoshiev. 2006. "Evolution of Automotive Electronics: A TRIZ Perspective." *Journal of Passenger Cars: Electronic and Electrical Systems* 115(7): 916–20. https://www.jstor.org/stable/44700125.

First Cobalt Corp. 2021. "First Cobalt Granted U.S. Department of Energy Funding for Idaho Cobalt Project." Cision. https://www.newswire.ca/news-releases/first-cobalt-granted-u-s-department-of-energy-funding-for-idaho-cobalt-project-880765925.html.

Ford Motor Company. 2021a. "Ford Europe Goes All-In on EVs on Road to Sustainable Profitability; Cologne Site Begins $1 Billion Transformation." Ford Media Center, Cologne Germany. https://media.ford.com/content/fordmedia/feu/en/news/2021/02/17/ford-europe-goes-all-in-on-evs-on-road-to-sustainable-profitabil.html.

– 2021b. "Ford to Lead America's Shift to Electric Vehicles with New Mega Campus in Tennessee and Twin Battery Plants in Kentucky; $11.4 Billion Investment to Create 11,000 Jobs and Power New Lineup of Advanced EVs." Ford Media Center, Dearborn Michigan. https://media.ford.com/content/fordmedia/fna/us/en/news/2021/09/27/ford-to-lead-americas-shift-to-electric-vehicles.html.

– 2021c. "Integrated Sustainability and Financial Report 2021." https://corporate.ford.com/microsites/integrated-sustainability-and-financial-report-2021/files/ir21.pdf.

Fortier, Steven M., Jane M. Hammarstrom, Sarah J. Ryker, Warren C. Day, and Robert R. Seal II. 2019. "USGS Critical Minerals Review." *Mining Engineering* 71(S5): 35–47. https://pubs.usgs.gov/publication/70206338.

Gallucci, Maria. 2021. "EVs Will Drive a Lithium Supply Crunch – Analysts Warn that Rising Battery Demand Will Constrain Supplies, Though There's Plenty Left to Mine." *IEEE Spectrum*, 5 May 2021. https://spectrum.ieee.org/evs-to-drive-a-lithium-supply-crunch.

General Motors Inc. 2021a. "General Motors, the Largest US Automaker, Plans to Be Carbon Neutral by 2040." GM Newsroom. https://media.gm.com/media/us/en/gm/home.detail.html/content/Pages/news/us/en/2021/jan/0128-carbon.html.

– 2021b. "GM to Secure US-Based Lithium for Next-Generation EV Batteries through Closed-Loop Process with Low Carbon Emissions." GM Newsroom. https://media.gm.com/media/us/en/gm/home.detail.html/content/Pages/news/us/en/2021/jul/0702-ultium.html.

Harrison, Daniel, and Christopher Ludwig. 2021. "Electric Vehicle Battery Supply Chain Analysis 2021: How Battery Demand and Production Are Reshaping the Automotive Industry." *Automotive Logistics*, 3 June 2021. https://shorturl.at/FJLXY.

Hering, Garrett, and J. Holzman. 2021. "US Lithium-Ion Battery Imports Jump as China Seizes Market Share." S&P Global Market Intelligence, 29 March 2021. https://www.spglobal.com/marketintelligence/en/news-insights/latest-news-headlines/us-lithium-ion-battery-imports-jump-as-china-seizes-market-share-63271388.

Hill, Kim, and Brahmst, Emilio. 2003. *The Auto Industry Moving South: An Examination of Trends*. Center for Automotive Research. https://www.cargroup.org/wp-content/uploads/2017/02/The-Auto-Industry-Moving-South-An-Examination-of-Trends.pdf.

Holmes, John. 2015. *Whatever Happened to Canada's Automotive Trade Surplus? A Preliminary Note.* Automotive Policy Research Centre. https://automotivepolicy.ca/wp-content/uploads/2018/05/aprc-canada-trade-deficit-holmes-report.pdf.

Hufbauer, G.C., and J.J. Schott. 2005. "The Automotive Sector." In *NAFTA Revisited: Achievements and Challenges*, edited by Gary Clyde Hufbauer and Jeffrey J. Schott, 365–93. Washington DC: Peterson Institute of International Economics. https://www.piie.com/publications/chapters_preview/332/06iie3349.pdf.

Idaho National Laboratory. 2020. "How Do Gasoline and Electric Vehicles Compare?" https://avt.inl.gov/sites/default/files/pdf/fsev/compare.pdf.

Impact Assessment Agency of Canada. 2020. "Whabouchi Mining Project." Compliance Promotion and Enforcement Unit. https://www.ceaa-acee.gc.ca/050/evaluations/proj/80021?culture=en-CA.

Industry Canada. 2021. "Import, Export and Investment." https://www.ic.gc.ca/app/scr/tdst/tdo/crtr.html?&productType=NAICS&lang=eng.

International Energy Agency. 2021a. "Annual Cobalt Demand for Electric Vehicle Batteries, 2019–2030." https://www.iea.org/data-and-statistics/charts/annual-cobalt-demand-for-electric-vehicle-batteries-2019-2030.

– 2021b. *Global EV Outlook 2021: Accelerating Ambitions Despite the Pandemic*. https://iea.blob.core.windows.net/assets/ed5f4484-f556-4110-8c5c-4ede8bcba637/GlobalEVOutlook2021.pdf.

Invest Ontario. 2021. "5 Reasons Ontario Is Poised to Lead the Future of Electric Vehicle Production." Government of Ontario. https://www.investontario.ca/spotlights/5-reasons-ontario-poised-lead-future-electric-vehicle-production.

Jones, Debbie, Corinne Blanchard, Luke Templeman, and Liam Fitzpatrick. 2021. "Is Lithium a 'Green' Alternative?" Deutsche Bank Research. https://shorturl.at/ELOPY.

Klayman, Ben. 2021. "Ford Boosts EV Spending, Outlines 2030 Sales Targets, Shares Near 5-Year High." Reuters, 26 May 2021. https://www.reuters.com/business/sustainable-business/ford-boosts-ev-spending-aims-have-40-volume-all-electric-by-2030-2021-05-26/.

Klier, Thomas. 2019. "North American Trade and the Auto Industry – A Primer." Paper presented at the 2019 Trade Protectionism, Regional Integration and Labor Disparities in the North American Automotive Industry International Workshop, Mexico City, 8 November.

Krisher, Tom. 2021. "Stellantis Says 98% of Models to Be Electric or Hybrid by 2025." *Manufacturing Business Technology*, 14 July 2021. https://www.mbtmag.com/home/news/21563374/stellantis-says-98-of-models-to-be-electric-or-hybrid-by-2025.

Lasley, Shane. 2021. "Panasonic Joins New Nevada Lithium Project." Metal Tech News, 10 June 2021. https://www.metaltechnews.com/story/2021/06/16/tech-metals/panasonic-joins-new-nevada-lithium-project/590.html.

LeVine, Steve. 2021. "The Goalposts Move: The New Lithium-Ion Standard Is an Astonishing $60 per kWh." *The Mobilist*, 27 April 2021. https://themobilist.medium.com/the-goalposts-move-the-new-lithium-ion-standard-is-an-astonishing-60-per-kwh-7153fa8ec328.

LMC Automotive. 2021. "Global Light Vehicle Powertrain Forecast." Production Forecast.

Marklines – Automotive Industry Portal. 2021a. "Automotive Sales – Vehicle Sales Data." Marklines Information Platform. https://www.marklines.com/en/vehicle_sales/index.

– 2021b. "Battery Plants – Plant Location." Marklines Information Platform.

– 2021c. "OEM Plants – Plant Location." Marklines Information Platform. https://www.marklines.com/en/global/.

– 201d. "Suppliers Database – 50,000 Database." Marklines Information Platform. https://www.marklines.com/en/supplier_db.

– 2021e. "Who Supplies Whom." Marklines Information Platform. https://www.marklines.com/en/wsw/search.

McKerracher, Colin, Aleksandra O'Donovan, Nick Albanese, Dr. Nikolas Soulopoulos, David Doherty, Milo Boers, Ryan Fisher, et al. 2021. "Electric Vehicle Outlook 2021." BloombergNEF. https://about.bnef.com/electric-vehicle-outlook/.

Mordue, Greig, and Brendan Sweeney. 2020. "Neither Core nor Periphery: The Search for Competitive Advantage in the Automotive Semi-Periphery." *Growth and Change* 51(1): 34–57. https://doi.org/10.1111/grow.12354.

NAIOP. 2018. "The Evolving Automotive Industry: Detroit Meets Silicon Valley." Commercial Real Estate Development Association. https://www.naiop.org/research-and-publications/magazine/2018/summer-2018/development-ownership/the-evolving--automotive-industry--detroit-meets-silicon-valley/.

PricewaterhouseCoopers. 2019. *Merging Ahead: Electric Vehicles and the Impact on the Automotive Supply Chain.* https://www.pwc.com/us/en/industrial-products/publications/assets/pwc-merge-ahead-electric-vehicles-supply-chain.pdf.

Prime Minister of Canada. 2021. "New Commitment to Battery-Electric Vehicle Manufacturing in Ontario." Government of Canada. https://pm.gc.ca/en/news/news-releases/2020/10/08/new-commitment-battery-electric-vehicle-manufacturing-ontario.

PR Newswire. 2021. "U.S. Looking to Canada for Lithium and Other Minerals to Build Electric Vehicles." 22 March 2021. https://www.prnewswire.com/news-releases/us-looking-to-canada-for-lithium-and-other-minerals-to-build-electric-vehicles-301252535.html.

Reuters. 2021. "Chinese Battery Maker CATL to Acquire Canada's Millennial Lithium." 28 September 2021. https://www.reuters.com/article/millennial-lithi-ma-catl-idUSL4N2QU467.

Rutherford, T.D., and J. Holmes. 2014. "Manufacturing Resiliency: Economic Restructuring and Automotive Manufacturing in the Great Lakes Region." *Cambridge Journal of Regions, Economy and Society* 7(3): 359–78. https://doi.org/10.1093/cjres/rsu014.

Schlumberger New Energy. 2021. "Schlumberger New Energy Venture to Launch a Lithium Extraction Pilot Plant in Nevada." Press release, 18 March 2021. https://www.slb.com/newsroom/press-release/2021/pr-2021-0318-sne-lithium-extraction-plant-nevada.

Seattle Jobs Initiative. n.d. *Amping Up Electric Vehicle Manufacturing in the PNW – Opportunities for Business, Workforce, and Education.* Seattle: SJI. https://www.seattle.gov/Documents/Departments/OSE/ClimateDocs/TE/EV%20Field%20in%20OR%20and%20WA_February20.pdf.

Sims, R., R. Schaeffer, F. Creutzig, X. Cruz-Núñez, M. D'Agosto, D. Dimitriu, M.J. Figueroa Meza, et al. 2014. "Transport." In *Climate Change 2014: Mitigation of Climate Change*, edited by O. Edenhofer, R. Pichs-Madruga, Y. Sokona, E. Farahani, S. Kadner, K. Seyboth, A. Adler, et al., 414–17. Contribution of Working Group III to the Fifth Assessment Report of the Intergovernmental Panel on Climate Change. Cambridge: Cambridge University Press.

Stellantis. 2021. "Stellantis: Building a World Leader in Sustainable Mobility." https://www.stellantis.com/en/news/press-releases/2021/january/stellantis-building-a-world-leader-in-sustainable-mobility.

Tanaka, Akito, Takashi Kawakami, and Yukihiro Omoto. 2018. "Battery Wars: Japan and South Korea Battle China for Future of EVs." *Nikkei Asia*, 14 November 2018. https://asia.nikkei.com/Spotlight/The-Big-Story/Battery-wars-Japan-and-South-Korea-battle-China-for-future-of-EVs.

Thielmann, Axel, Martin Wietschel, Simon Funke, Anna Grimm, Tim Hettescheimer, Sabine Langkua, Antionia Loibl, et al. 2020. *Batteries for Electric Cars: Fast Check and Need for Action.* Karlsruhe, Germany: Fraunhofer Institute for Systems and Innovation Research ISI. https://www.isi.fraunhofer.de/content/dam/isi/dokumente/cct/2020/Fact_check_Batteries_for_electric_cars.pdf.

Thomas, Kenneth P. 1997. "Capital Mobility and Trade Policy: The Case of the Canada-US Auto Pact." *Review of International Political Economy* 4(1): 127–53. http://www.jstor.org/stable/4177217.

Transport Canada. 2021. "Building a Green Economy: Government of Canada to Require 100% of Car and Passenger Truck Sales Be Zero-Emissions by 2035 in Canada." News release, 29 June 2021. https://shorturl.at/aefAY.

UBS Group. 2017. *UBS Evidence Lab Electric Car Teardown – Disruption Ahead?* UBS Evidence Lab, Global Research. https://neo.ubs.com/shared/d1wkuDlEbYPjF/.

US Department of Energy. 2021. "Biden-Harris Administration 100-Day Battery Supply Chain Review." Fact sheet, 8 June 2021. https://www.energy.gov/articles/fact-sheet-biden-harris-administration-100-day-battery-supply-chain-review.

White House. 2021a. "President Biden Announces Steps to Drive American Leadership Forward on Clean Cars and Trucks." Fact sheet, 5 August 2021. https://www.whitehouse.gov/briefing-room/statements-releases/2021/08/05/fact-sheet-president-biden-announces-steps-to-drive-american-leadership-forward-on-clean-cars-and-trucks/.

– 2021b. "President Biden Announces Support for the Bipartisan Infrastructure Framework." Fact sheet, 24 June 2021. https://www.whitehouse.gov/briefing-room/statements-releases/2021/06/24/fact-sheet-president-biden-announces-support-for-the-bipartisan-infrastructure-framework/.

Yu, Alice, and Mitzi Sumangil. 2021. "Top Electric Vehicle Markets Dominate Lithium-Ion Battery Capacity Growth" (blog). S&P Global Market Intelligence, 16 February 2021. https://www.spglobal.com/marketintelligence/en/news-insights/blog/top-electric-vehicle-markets-dominate-lithium-ion-battery-capacity-growth.

10

The Automobile Industry in Mexico and the Challenges of a New Era: A Perspective on Electric Vehicles and Green Technologies

Bertha Vallejo, Jorge Carrillo, Victor M. Cabral, and Humberto Garcia Jimenez

The literature on technological change in the automotive industry identifies increasing pressure to reduce carbon dioxide (CO_2) emissions in the transport sector as an essential factor behind technological change. It is also anticipated that policy-based endeavours to arrest the effects of transportation on climate change will be a necessary ingredient. Indeed, the influence of policy on transportation-related environmental outcomes was exemplified in the early 1990s when the United States (US) Clean Air Act resulted in modifications of the existing internal combustion engine (ICE) to satisfy the emission requirements. Examples of technologies introduced to meet those requirements include Honda's compound vortex controlled combustion engine (CVCC) and Chrysler's lean-burn engine (Lee et al. 2010; Dijk and Yarime 2010). However, these modifications to the ICE have failed to satisfy increasing emission reduction requirements.

Nevertheless, the automobile industry remains locked into the ICE as the dominant technology. Moreover, a branch of the empirical literature illustrates how automobile manufacturers are crucial in maintaining regime stability and opposing regime change (Wells and Nieuwenhuis 2012). In chapter 7 of this work, for example, Wolfe and Lemphers discuss the challenges confounding two subnational jurisdictions in Canada and the contrasting strategies they are employing to manage the transition to decarbonized energy sources and electrified transportation. They demonstrate how technology-push policies (i.e., technology-forcing regulations) play an important role in disrupting the path dependency of the sector and stimulating the development of cleaner technologies (Lee, Veloso, and Hounshell 2011; Lee et al. 2010; Meckling and Nahm 2018).

The increasing global pressure to reduce CO_2 emissions by 2035 and the institutional requirements for zero-emission vehicles (ZEVs) pose a major challenge for automobile manufacturers. Undoubtedly, more stringent environmental standards (and the financial packages to support them) have influenced the ongoing political discourse on the sector's transition to electric vehicles (EVs). Consequently, this new *path creation* has important consequences for the automotive and transportation sectors.

The automotive sector has a high level of technological complexity, which stimulates technological development and upgrading in its supporting industries. Therefore, technological disruptions originating in this sector will influence changes in many other industrial activities. These adjustments will alter dynamics associated with the automotive value chain and its employment. However, the transition towards a new *technological trajectory* is not a simple matter. As Kazzaz, Greene, and Yates describe in chapter 9, those shifts involve changes in the way that vehicles are produced: fewer components, fewer and more specialized suppliers, different types of infrastructure, and significant adjustments in the global automotive value chain.

This chapter explores how the ongoing technological transformation of the global automotive industry affects the integrated periphery. (For an explanation of automotive integrated peripheries, as well as core and semi-periphery automotive countries, see chapter 1.) It does so by using Mexico, the North American region's prototypical integrated periphery, as a case study.

The automotive industry hosts about 5% of the world's manufacturing employment, and for each direct job in the industry, about five indirect jobs are created (OICA 2006). Thus, it is one of the main providers of jobs in the integrated periphery. In Mexico, the industry had about 1.2 million employees in 2020, which is about 18.6% of total formal manufacturing employment (Mexico Industry 2018). Therefore, changes in its *technological paradigm* have important socio-economic and political implications. Pavlínek (2018, 144) defines automotive integrated peripheries as those countries geographically adjacent to a large market, integrated into a core automotive network through foreign direct investment (FDI), with low labour costs, and whose production and strategic functions are dependent on or controlled by foreign ownership. Thus, two important considerations in understanding the automotive integrated periphery are (a) its dependency on and vulnerability to the strategic decisions taken by core automotive countries (i.e., those hosting automotive headquarters), and (b) the weak links between foreign subsidiaries and domestic firms (Pavlínek 2018; Simonazzi, Sangines, and Russo 2020; Vallejo 2010).

Regulatory measures, changes in consumer habits and practices, and technological breakthroughs are factors Cowan and Hulten (1996) have identified for breaking ICE technologies' grip on the transportation sector's lock-in of ICE technologies. This chapter presents the changes in environmental discourse that have facilitated implementation of strong environmental policies, standards, and initiatives in core automotive countries pushing for zero-emission transportation and have enhanced the deployment of EVs in the international market. On the demand side, we present the findings from the literature on the factors influencing consumer choice of EVs over ICE vehicles. Then, by illustrating the trends in EV sales over time, we frame the Mexican context within the international trajectory regarding EVs.

Unfortunately, official data on the transition from ICE to alternative vehicles in Mexico is limited. Therefore, we have used information published in local and international reports, newspapers, and magazines to present an overview of the situation in Mexico on the EV-inspired technological transition that is underway. These sources are enhanced by the Economic Commission for Latin America and the Caribbean (ECLAC) report on electromobility (Carrillo, de los Santos Gomez, and Briones 2020).

This chapter considers three potential scenarios for cleaner vehicles described by Freyssenet (2011): diversity, progressiveness, and rupture. In the diversity scenario, countries favour specific technology or technologies because of the country's natural resources, interests, or commercial relations. The worldwide result is a diverse array of technologies and high costs for manufacturers (Freyssenet 2011). The diversity scenario is associated with a strategy of least-compliance, which minimizes the risks for firms (Wells and Nieuwenhuis 2012). The progressiveness scenario predicts a transition through different technological approaches and solutions until the process eventually results in the (gradual) adoption of EVs. This scenario requires stability in oil prices, weak climate change urgency, and slow progress in battery development. As early as 2011, Freyssenet was suggesting that this scenario was unlikely to prevail. Finally, the rupture scenario is one in which the industry adopts EVs, or EVs with an auxiliary ICE engine. This scenario requires governments and firms to develop the necessary infrastructure and financial conditions for mass adoption of EVs (Freyssenet 2011).

We start by presenting environmental regulations, considering how they have evolved over time and how they have affected technological change in the auto industry. We follow that with a discussion of how EVs have evolved worldwide. We then describe Mexico's participation in automotive production and its efforts to integrate into the EV value chain. We finish with a discussion of these matters and some concluding comments.

ENVIRONMENTAL REGULATIONS AND TECHNOLOGICAL CHANGE

Environmental regulations and the policies underpinning them have significantly influenced the automotive industry's technological development. For the past fifty years, policy initiatives have helped push the industry towards production of cleaner automobiles. In the early 1970s in the US, for example, the Clean Air Act (also known as the Muskie Act) required passenger vehicles to reduce tailpipe emissions by about 90% over five years (see Gerard and Lave 2005 for an overview of emission legislation from 1950 to 1975). The Muskie Act is considered an example of legislation serving as the impetus for technological change. Its passage also lent credibility to the US Environmental Protection Agency, the regulatory agency charged with enforcing its standards and creating competitive pressures to drive research and development (R&D).

Uncertainty about what technological developments would prove most effective as a means to meet the increasingly stringent regulatory environment pushed automotive assemblers to develop a variety of different engine types. These included the CVCC by Honda in 1972 and the three-way catalytic by Toyota and Nissan in 1981. (For descriptions of technologies emanating from these early-stage emissions regulations see Gerard and Lave 2005; Yarime 2009; and Yarime, Shiroyama, and Kukoki 2008.) By the late 1990s, increasing environmental concerns coupled with high fuel costs provided a foundation for development and commercialization of hybrid-electric engines (see Dijk and Yarime 2010; Aghion et al. 2016).

The complexity of portfolio planning in the automotive industry is exacerbated by increasingly strict CO_2 emissions laws and regulations, which require technologies to produce vehicles capable of satisfying elevated standards (Huls et al. 2020). During the United Nations Convention on Climate Change in 2005, an international effort was made to curb climate change. The outcome of that effort was the Kyoto Protocol, which legally obliged industrialized countries to avoid global temperature increases by setting targets for reducing greenhouse gases (GHGs), including CO_2 emissions during the period 2008–2012 (European Commission 2005). The United Nations Climate Change Conference in Paris in 2015 once again stimulated an international debate on targets for reducing CO_2 emissions.

Oki (2021) shows how the establishment of elevated expectations and standards has been an outcome of changing environmental discourse, the declining presence of opposing political coalitions, and the development of alternative technologies (i.e., EVs). He also shows that throughout that process, the European Union (EU) has played a determinant role in global climate negotiations, introducing an evolving, mostly complementary, and increasingly ambitious set of targets and initiatives to reduce the transportation sector's effect on climate change. For example, with the entry into force of the Kyoto Protocol, the EU, recognizing the need for mandatory approaches and regulatory frameworks to reduce CO_2 emissions, required that vehicle emissions be limited to 130 grams per kilometre (g/km). It also introduced several complementary technological measures, including more efficient air conditioning, tire pressure monitoring systems, gearshift indicators, and biofuels. The objective was to reduce emissions by a further 10 g/km by 2012 (Commission of the European Communities 2007). These measures were also supported by the EU's 2010 declaration of a long-term vision of reducing global GHG emissions by 80% by 2050, compared to 1990 levels (European Parliament 2014a, 2). Additionally, in 2014 the EU announced its intention to reduce GHG emissions by 40% by 2030, again using 1990 as the base. As this process unfolded, the EU consistently promoted electric vehicles and other low-emission innovations as essential (Oki 2021; European Parliament 2014b, 2019). Under the EU Green Deal, the European Union also set targets for a 55% reduction of emissions from cars by 2030 and the sale of only zero emission vehicles (ZEVs) by 2035 (IEA 2020b). Consistent with that, in 2017 several countries, firms, institutions, and NGOs endorsed the EV30@30 campaign to achieve a collective 30% market share for EVs by 2030 (IEA 2019). Within the EV30@30 campaign, countries collaborate on programs to support the introduction of advanced fuel cells, hybrid-electric vehicles (HEVs), battery-electric vehicles (BEVs), and other ZEVs.

Meanwhile, major investment by China in EV technologies has stimulated formation of new industries and jobs (Oki 2021). China is now the largest market for vehicle production and consumption, producing 25.2 million cars in 2020 (32.5% of total production worldwide) (OICA 2021). In 2021, China sold 3.4 million BEVs and plug-in hybrid-electric vehicles (PHEVs) (Irle n.d.). China's significant participation in the EV market is supported by extensive government incentive packages (Munoz 2021). Thus, policy measures in major markets are boosting the proliferation of low and ZEV transportation and accelerating CO_2 reduction plans: in China (via the Chinese Green Policy of 2018), in the US (via the 2021 measures announced by the Biden administration in 2021 and described by Kazzaz, Greene, and Yates in chapter 9), and in the EU (Munoz 2021; IEA 2021).

ALTERNATIVE POWERTRAINS AND TECHNOLOGICAL CHANGE

The automotive industry has traditionally been locked into ICE technology, partially due to the high costs involved in automotive production and the mass production volumes required in their manufacturing. Nevertheless, discussions about alternative powertrain technologies to meet the increasingly stringent environmental standards have been discussed since the late 1990s. Authors such as Brownstone and Train (1999), Holweg (2013), Train and Winston (2007), and Walther et al. (2010) present alternatives proposed and efforts made to substitute traditional ICE powertrains. Some of these alternatives are given in table 1.

One early-stage powertrain innovation to mitigate the effect of climate change was flexible fuel vehicles (FFVs), which entered the market in 2003. FFVs are ICE powertrains, fuelled by gas, biodiesel, or a blend of gasoline-ethanol of different ethanol percentages (E10, E50, E85, and E100). FFVs are considered alternative fuel vehicles under the US Energy Policy Act of 1992 (US Department of Energy, Alternative Fuels Data Center 2021). For vehicles firms, they limited cost and risk because they allowed vehicle makers to retain existing body-chassis technologies. They are also nearly identical to gasoline-only vehicles (except for the modifications to the engine). However, they helped mitigate climate-changing effects of transportation by generating less energy per volume (US Department of Energy, Office of Energy Efficiency and Renewable Energy 2021).

Table 2 presents FFVs' main characteristics and specifications.

Production of FFVs was and is concentrated in the EU, the US, Brazil, and Thailand. However, their proliferation has declined. In the US, for example, as recently as 2015 eighty FFVs were offered by eight different manufacturers; by 2020 only Ford and General Motors still offered them there (Biofuels International 2020). In the EU, FFVs and biofuels were popular in the early 2000s. However, they have been supplanted as a result of improved battery

Table 1. Descriptions of Powertrain Alternatives

Aim	Details	Low-carbon innovations
Improve the efficiency of conventional powertrain vehicles	- Reduce rolling resistance - Reduce air resistance - Downsize engine	- Advanced ICE based on improved fuel-injection systems, turbocharging, advanced value management, etc.
Change the fuel/powertrain used in vehicles	- Biofuel, natural gas - Partly electric: HEVs, PHEVs - Fully electric	- Biofuel and flex-fuel vehicles (FFVs) - BEVs - Fuel cell vehicles (FCV) - HEVs - PHEVs

Source: Vallejo (2015, 20), based on Walther et al. (2010, 242) and Penna and Geels (2015).

Table 2. Flexible Fuel Vehicle Characteristics and Specifications

Model	Characteristics	Representative models	Total energy efficiency (%) for the drivetrain	Details	Energy source
Flexible fuel vehicle	V8 Flex Fuel 5.7 Automatic (S6)	Citroen C4, Dacia Duster, Logan, and Sendero Fiat 500X Ford Focus, C-Max, Mondeo Peugeot 307 Saab 9-5 SEAT Leon Volvo C30 Toyota Sequoia, Tundra, Altis Honda Civic	8 cylinders 5.7 litres, on gasoline 15 gallons per 100 miles, on ethanol 85% (E85) 10 gallons per 100 miles	Four-wheel drive, six-speed shiftable automatic, 26.4 gallons FF, 381 HP @ 5,600 rpm	Uses a blend of gasoline and ethanol 85% (E85) (alcohol-based fuel)

Source: Based on information from United States Department of Energy, Office of Energy Efficiency and Renewable Energy, https://www.fueleconomy.gov/feg/noframes/40542.shtml.
Notes: HP = horsepower; rpm = revolutions per minute.

technology and the EU's shift to electrification (European Commission 2020). FFVs remain relevant in automotive integrated peripheries like Argentina, Brazil, and India (Argus 2021; HT Auto, 2021), as such technology aligns with those countries' long-standing promotion of biofuels in domestic sectors, with the Brazilian Alcohol Program providing one such example (see (Moreira and Goldemberg 1999; Goldemberg et al. 2004)

Notwithstanding its integrated periphery status, in Mexico no policies or regulations exist to incentivize the manufacture or commercialization of biofuel-based vehicles

Table 3. Changing Technologies (ICE Vehicles vs. EVs)

	ICE exclusive	Neutral	EVs exclusive
Parts and components	• Moving engine parts (i.e., pistons, flywheel, camshafts, crank) • Transmission • Differentials • Driveshaft • ICE engine parts • Clutch • Radiators • Gears	• Steering system • Brake lining • Brake pads • Shock absorbers • Seats • Headlights • Leaf springs • Gearbox • Tires and glass • Gaskets	• Electric motor • Inverter • Microprocessor • Battery

Source: Based on Chege (2021, 36) and Rodriguez (2021b).

(Riegelhaupt, Odenthal, and Janeiro 2016). As such, the market for them is almost non-existent (Paredes-Cervantes et al. 2020). Even so, Mexican automotive suppliers *do* manufacturer parts for FFVs (e.g., sensors) for export elsewhere in North American as well as the EU.

What the preceding section has shown is that the post-2000 (primarily) transition to less carbon-intensive transportation has been incremental, driven in large part by policy measures in core automotive locations (e.g., China, US, EU). So far, the transition to less carbon-intensive mobility, including electrification, has been characterized by automakers trying to maintain features and platforms similar – and often identical – to current platforms. However, the wider-scale transition to electric powertrains is about to give way to a more profound alteration. An ICE vehicle requires about two thousand functional parts, including thirty thousand parts manufactured by different-tier suppliers. They also require about ten million lines of software code. Electric vehicles require about 40% fewer parts and components (Rodriguez 2021b). Their engines are simpler: they require few moving parts and there is no need for a traditional transmission. Granted, many components are similar between ICEs and EVs; and some components are unique to EVs. Table 3 presents some of the changing technologies for EVs, as compared to ICEs.

The effects of this transition will not be benign. As table 3 shows, the type and quantity of parts required by EVs differs from those for ICE vehicles. Not only are fewer parts assembled; typically, the manufacture of EVs also has higher levels of automatization, blunting some of the low-cost labour advantage automotive integrated periphery countries currently enjoy. The sections that follow more fully explore these and other aspects associated with EV production as they apply to automotive integrated periphery countries like Mexico.

ELECTRIC VEHICLES WORLDWIDE

As preceding sections have implied, climate targets set for the automotive sector for the year 2030 present a challenge that cannot be met by improvements to the ICE alone. Thus, EVs will become increasingly relevant and necessary. (In this discussion, EVs include HEVs, BEVs, PHEVs, and FCVs.)

Since the 1990s, EV technology adoption has coincided with significant fiscal incentives and subsidies (IEA 2021; Levay, Drossinos, and Thiel 2017; Yang et al. 2016). In the EV industry's earliest years – the late 1990s and early 2000s – they represented a potentially useful but still indeterminate opportunity for newcomer manufacturers from previous non-core automotive countries (primarily Chinese) to position themselves in international markets (Freyssenet 2011). That said, table 4 dispels the notion that EV-related innovation has been the preserve of upstarts. In fact, the table shows that many of the most important EV products during the technology's nascent period arose from well-established OEM automotive firms from core automotive nations.

The evolution of EV technology from "niche" to near-"mainstream" status has not been straightforward or straight-line. The first attempts to promote EVs as an alternative to ICEs in the 1990s failed to achieve mass-market success, despite significant interest from well-established firms and enthusiastic promotion of electrified models (i.e., Renault Clio, Peugeot 106). By 2000, limited sales rendered them unfeasible (Dijk and Yarime 2010). As figure 1 shows, it was not until the 2010s that the market started to build. Between 2010 and 2014, global EV sales totalled 750,000. However, during the subsequent five-year period, 2015–19, global EV sales grew to 6.89 million. By then, according to Jetin (2020), volumes were sufficient to warrant mass production.

Figure 1 illustrates the main locations where global EV sales have occurred. It shows that China has become the most significant market, followed by Europe and the US. By 2019, those three regions/countries accounted for 93% of global EV sales. Despite this growth, the majority of which took place within the previous two to three years, by 2020 vehicles propelled by electric drivetrains accounted for only 3.1% of the global automotive market (Munoz 2021).

Research identifies that the adoption of EVs vehicles in the three primary markets (China, the EU, and the US) has been contingent on product-specific factors. These include: (1) battery and powertrain costs, (2) battery and powertrain design, performance, and manufacturing capacity; and (3) adaptation of new technologies and infrastructure to customer habits and practices (see IEA 2019; Strategy&, 2020; Righolt and Rieck, 2013). Beyond these direct product-related attributes, studies also identify several additional factors affecting EV demand: the availability of fiscal and tax incentives, gasoline prices, buyer's age and education, cost of electricity, and availability of charging stations (table 5).

Table 4. Characteristics of Different Forms of Electric Vehicles

Model	Characteristics[a]	Representative models[b]	Total energy efficiency (%) for the drivetrain[c]	Details[d]	Energy source[d]
Battery electric vehicle (BEV)	These are electric engines that require a battery for energy storage and an electronic engine controller (Dijk and Yarime 2010). BEVs run exclusively on electricity via onboard batteries that are charged by plugging into an outlet or charging station.	Nissan LEAF Fiat 500e Tesla Model S 2014 Mercedes B-Class	57	Storage capability acceptable range of 150 watt hours per kilogram (Wh/kg)	Lithium battery
Hybrid-electric vehicle (HEV)	These vehicles combine a gasoline engine with an electric motor. They have both an electric motor and battery, but cannot be plugged in and recharged. The batteries are charged from capturing energy when braking.	1997 Toyota Prius 2014 Honda Accord Hybrid	72	Combination of electric and combustion engine, automatic recharge, no need to plug in	Fuel for combustion and kinetic energy
Plug-in hybrid vehicle (PHEV)	These vehicles have both an electric motor and an ICE. PHEV batteries can be charged by plugging into an outlet.	2014 Ford Fusion Energy 2014 Chevy Volt	61	High potential for energy efficiency, zero tailpipe pollutants	Lithium battery
Fuel cells vehicle (FCV)	These vehicles have hydrogen fuel and air-processing energy to feed anode electronics. A low voltage is produced to a DC/AC converter to output electrical. The voltage via the fuel cell completes the second stage of the power processing unit, and power conditioning efficiency is higher than 80%.	2000 Daimler-Chrysler 1999 Ford P2000 (SUV) 2000 GM HydroGen 1 2000 Honda FCX-V3 1997 Toyota RAV-4 FCEV (SUV)	80	Acceleration of 0–50 km in 5 seconds, needs more infrastructure of hydrogen stations for refueling, repairs, and maintenance	Methanol hydrogen

Source: Column *a* from Dijk and Yarime (2010); column *b* from Goldman (2014); column *c* from Åhman (2001); columns *d* from Redelbach, Klotzke, and Friedrich (2012) and Thomas (2009).

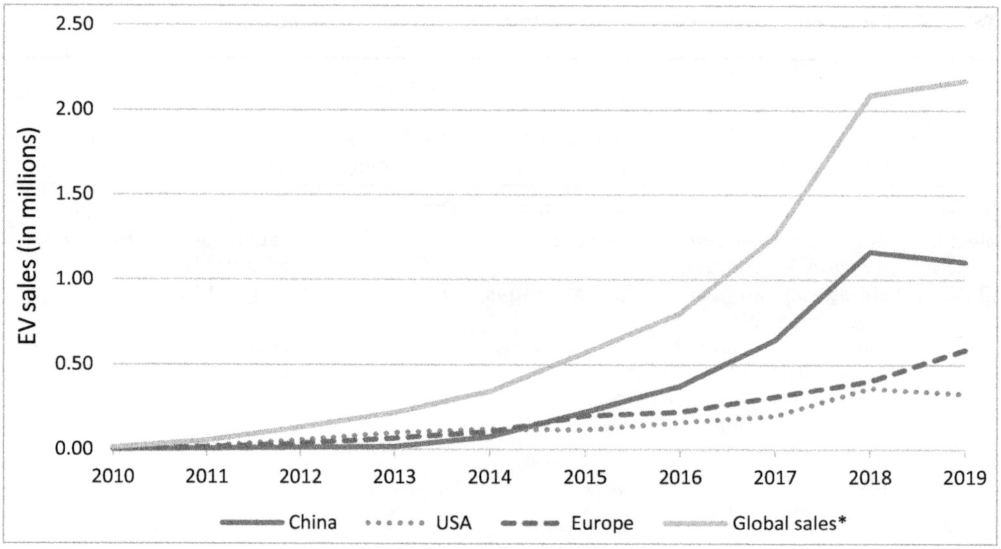

Figure 1. Global EV Sales by Key Markets, 2010–19
Source: Based on information from IEA (2020a).
Notes: Includes passenger and light-duty commercial vehicles.

Table 5. Factors Identified as Significantly Influencing Demand for EVs

				Effect	
Author	Method	Period	Location	Positive	Negative
Diamond (2009)	Panel data	2001–06	US	- Price of gasoline - Income - Government commitment to the environment	
Gallagher and Muehlegger (2011)	Fixed effects panel	2000–06	US	- Tax incentives - Income - Gasoline price	- Age of buyer
Mersky et al. (2016)	Linear regressions	2000–13	Norway	- Number of charging stations	
Sierzchula et al. (2014)	OLS	2012	30 countries	- Financial incentives - Infrastructure	
Vergis and Chen (2015)	OLS	2013	US	- Incentives - Charging infrastructure - Gasoline price - Education level of buyer	- Electricity price
Wee and La Croix (2018)	Panel data	2010–15	US	- Subsidies - Gasoline price	- Electricity price
Briseño, Ramirez-Nafarrate, and Araz (2021)	Multivariate analysis	2016–19	Mexico	- Gasoline price - GDP per capita	- Cost of vehicle - Family income - Electricity cost

Source: Drawn from from Briseño, Ramirez-Nafarrate, and Araz (2021).

Table 6. Worldwide Production of ICE Vehicles 2000–20 (Number of Units)

	2000	2005	2010	2015	2020	Change with respect to 2000 (%)
China	2,069,069	5,717,619	18,264,761	24,503,326	25,225,242	1,119.16
US	12,799,857	11,946,653	9,628,920	12,100,095	8,822,399	-31.07
Japan	10,140,796	10,799,659	7,743,093	9,278,238	8,067,557	-20.44
Germany	5,526,615	5,757,710	5,905,985	6,033,164	3,742,454	-32.28
South Korea	3,114,998	3,699,350	4,271,741	4,555,957	3,506,774	12.58
India	801,360	1,638,674	3,557,073	4,125,744	3,394,446	323.59
Mexico	1,935,527	1,684,238	2,342,282	3,565,469	3,176,600	64.12
Spain	3,032,874	1,684,238	2,387,900	2,733,201	2,268,185	-25.21
Brazil	1,681,517	2,530,840	3,381,728	2,429,463	2,014,055	19.78
Russia	1,205,581	1,354,504			1,435,335	19.06
Thailand	411,721	1,122,712	1,644,513	1,915,420	1,427,074	246.61
Canada	2,961,636	2,687,892	2,068,189	2,283,474	1,376,623	-53.52

Source: Based on information from Datosmacro.com (2021).

THE MEXICAN AUTOMOTIVE SECTOR

The automobile industry in Mexico got its start in 1925. Until the 1960s, production mostly consisted of assembling completely knocked down (CKD) kits. The automotive firms only gradually evolved production processes capable of higher levels of complexity (Carrillo and Contreras 2008). However, following implementation of the North American Free Trade Agreement (NAFTA) in 1994, the Mexican auto industry, responding to elevated requirements and manufacturing standards, commenced a quite rapid repositioning, eventually establishing itself as global player (Vallejo 2010). Since 1994, the Mexican auto industry has adapted to the production, organizational, and quality requirements established by auto assemblers worldwide, registering consistent and sustainable growth. Table 6 presents the evolution of the ten largest producers of vehicles worldwide during the post-2000 period. It shows that Mexico solidified its position among the top producers during that period. By 2020, for example, Mexico's vehicle production had climbed by 64.1% over 2000. Of the approximately 3.2 million units Mexico made that year, about 2.6 million units were exported, mostly to the US, Canada, and the EU (Metalmecanica 2021).

In addition to being the world's seventh-largest producer of automobiles, Mexico is the fourth-largest exporter of assembled vehicles and the fifth-largest exporter of auto parts (US International Trade Administration 2023). The automotive industry represents 3.6% of the nation's gross domestic product (GDP) and 18% of manufacturing GDP, and it employs over one million people (US International Trade Administration 2023).

Table 7. Mexican Regulations for Emissions

Standard	HC g/ bhp-hr	HCNM g/bhp-hr	CO g/bhp-hr	NOx g/bhp-hr	HCev g/test
A	1.1	n.a.	14.4	4.0	3.0
B	n.a.	0.14		0.2	1.75

Source: Torres González (2017).
Notes: HC = hydrocarbon; g/bhp-h = grams per brake horsepower-hour; HCNM = non-methane hydrocarbons; CO = carbon monoxide; NOx = nitrogen oxides (including nitric oxide and nitrogen dioxide); HCev = hybrid high-capacity electric vehicle.

Following the experiences of developed countries, Mexico was the first developing country to sign a climate change regulation in 2012, with that commitment giving rise to regulation ENER-SCFI-2013 published by the Ministry of Environment and Natural Resources (or SEMARNAT in Spanish) in June 2013. It set limits for CO_2, hydrocarbon, and carbon monoxide emissions from vehicles weighing a maximum of 3,857 kilograms (i.e., light vehicles) (Elizondo and Hernandez Amezcua 2018; González 2017), the specific standards for which are provided in table 7.

The main objective of the regulation was reduction of fuel use, improved vehicle performance, and, consequently, reduction of GHGs. In support of that, automotive manufacturers were also obliged to integrate designated technological packages. Subsequently, in an attempt to harmonize their approach with the US Environmental Protection Agency, the Mexican government also established progressive standards for CO_2 emission targets for 2025 (Elizondo and Hernandez Amezcua 2018), banning diesel vehicles from Mexico City (CDMX) in 2025, cutting emissions to 50% of 2000 levels by 2050, and increasing the use of renewable energy by 35% over 2000 levels by 2024.

CDMX (together with twenty other cities) also signed the C40 Fossil Fuel Free Streets Declaration, committing to procure only zero-emission buses from 2025 on and reach an all-EV fleet by mid-2030 (C40 Cities Finance Facility 2021). These measures have already sparked major adjustments in CDMX public transportation procurement. In 2019, for example, CDMX introduced sixty-three electric Yutong hybrid trolleybuses (Yutong 2019).

Following the model of the US, EU, and China, Mexico introduced a series of incentives, preferential tax rates, and tax benefits to stimulate firms' adoption of green technologies (Chargenow 2021). As part of that, EVs are exempt from the ISAN tax (federal tax on new vehicles). Meanwhile, some states have also provided tax benefits to promote the acquisition of EVs; the key instrument being a reduction or abolition of the ownership tax (Chargenow 2021).

As table 5 indicates, the literature notes that the availability of charging stations affects the propensity to acquire an EV. At the state level, some jurisdictions have instituted incentives to

Table 8. EV Sales in Mexico (Units)

	2016	2017	2018	2019	2020
HEV	7,490	9,349	16,022	23,964	22,139
PHEV	521	968	1,584	1,339	1,817
BEV	254	237	201	305	499
Total	**8,265**	**10,554**	**17,807**	**25,608**	**24,455**

Source: Developed by the authors with information from Statista (2022) and Paz (2021).

support the installation of charging stations at home (Congreso de la Union 2021). However, in so far as publicly available charging stations are concerned, even though the data tend to be inconsistent, there is a consensus that, on a nationwide basis, the infrastructure is underdeveloped and primarily available in large cities like CDMX, Monterrey, and Guadalajara (see US Department of Commerce 2020; Duran 2020; Zwaniger 2021). As table 8 shows, the number of EVs sold in Mexico has increased in the last few years. While HEVs are still the preferred model, BEVs and PHEVs are experiencing rapid growth. By 2021, several EV models were available in Mexico: Audi (e-tron), BMW (I13), Chevrolet (Bolt), Ford (Mustang Mach-E), Jaguar (I-Pace), Mercedes-Benz (EQC), Porshe (Taycan), and Renault-Nissan (LEAF, Twizy, and Kangoo Z.E.) (Garcia 2020). Honda announced its intention to sell its Prologue starting in 2024; production may occur at Honda's Ramos Arizpe assembly plant (Randall 2021b).

There have been several investment announcements concerning EVs in Mexico. For example, in 2021, GM announced an investment of over US $1 billion for EV production, and Ford announced its intention to manufacture the Mustang Mach-E in Mexico for the North American and European market (Blanco 2021). Ford also announced its plan to launch two more EV models by late 2022 (Kane 2021). In October 2021, Foxconn announced its intention to produce EVs in Europe, India, and Latin America, with Mexican production a possibility (Randall 2021a).

Future trends surrounding the electrification of transportation in Mexico will be influenced by a series of disparate factors. For example, the prevalence of 5G networks is said to be a fundamental ingredient for improved control, analysis, and overall EV performance (see Li 2020). Access to 5G is also necessary for reliable connectivity for EV charging stations, something fixed connectivity is unable to guarantee (see Stein 2021). At present, Mexico does possess elements of 5G capability that are being applied to EV production. For instance, Grupo Quimmco Autopartes y Maquinados, S.A. de C.V. (QUESTUM), a firm based in Monterrey, Mexico, is working with Next.e.GO Mobile (Germany) to establish a 5G-ready microfactory to supply BEVs for markets in Mexico and the US (Randall 2021c). Mexico also has the capability to provide backward integration in battery supply chains, a consequence of its having reserves of lithium. Under the Pena-Nieto administration

(2013–19), UK-based Bacanora Lithium received approval to extract lithium in the northern Mexico state of Sonora for use in EV batteries. However, in October 2021 the López Obrador administration declared lithium a strategic mineral, reserving its exploration and mining for the public sector only (Romero 2021). The administration's pronouncements notwithstanding, subsequent investments and overtures suggest that concessions granted to Bacanora Lithium will be respected (Ford 2021).

DISCUSSION AND CONCLUSION

The automobile industry is highly relevant when analysing innovation processes, an outcome of its deep integration and interrelations with other industrial activities and sectors. It is also true that the transportation sector, characterized by a long-standing adherence to ICE-propelled vehicles, has been shaped by its locked-in attachment to the ICE. Therefore, for many automotive actors – firms, policymakers, and consumers – the process of becoming unchained from its long-standing, well-established socio-technical regime has necessitated direct intervention from policymakers (Dyrhauge 2021; Oki 2021; Meadowcroft 2011).

To date, technology-push policies have been the main enabler for developing and deploying EVs worldwide. This chapter, for example, has noted that the introduction of technology-forcing regulations combined with new and elevated environmental standards, including ZEV mandates in the EU, China, and the US, has propelled EV development and acceptance in those places. We have also explained how fiscal incentives and making publicly accessible EV chargers available complemented those policies, further encouraging EV acquisition. The literature also shows that a major factor supporting the success of technology-forcing regulations is the credibility of the regulatory agency charged with overseeing policy. Specifically, the credibility of the agency charged with implementation and oversight tends to influence and determine the industry's response (Dijk and Yarime 2010). For that reason, the deployment of technology-forcing policies to achieve environmental objectives should be viewed as an exchange between regulators and the industry.

This suggests that the speed and trajectory of green and environmentally friendly transportation will be determined by a combination of policy decisions (Azar and Sanden 2011; Meckling and Nahm 2018, 2019) and the strategic business decisions that firms take, particularly in core automotive countries (i.e., China, the EU, and the US). Indeed, the policy discourse from this chapter consists of two central points. First, vehicles' emission reduction is an outcome of the introduction of robust standards and regulations. Second, vehicles' emission reduction is a consequence of pushes for technological development towards alternative sources of fuel and ZEVs. In fact, Dyrhauge (2021) suggests that the conjunction of these two discourses will cause a restructuring of the current regime, a restructuring of current institutions, and a shift in the socio-technological paradigm (Geels 2011) underpinning transportation.

The significant reforms to the energy sector undertaken from 2013 to 2019 explain the inclusion of Mexico in the EV market during that time. During those years, the policy discourse in Mexico favoured green initiatives. Regulations were put in place to reduce CO_2 emissions and accelerate the transition to smarter, less energy-intensive mobility. EV investment outcomes that accrued during that period demonstrated the key role of policy-business connections. However, the elevated and engaged discourse and direction that characterized the 2013–19 period has subsequently shifted. The López Obrador administration (2020–26) has moved away from policies supportive of green and renewable energy, reverting to an oil-based regime (i.e., refineries) (see Gross 2019). This discourse appears to be rooted in maintaining the structural power of two state actors: PEMEX, the Mexican state-owned petroleum company, and CFE, the Mexican state-owned electricity company. For this reason the ICE technological paradigm still endures.

The experiences of the EU, China, and the US confirm that the key element in a transition to EVs is the strength of governments' environmental discourse (IEA 2019, 2020b, 2021; Jetin 2020). This chapter has demonstrated that the credibility of public implementing agencies is also a critical component of successful technology-push policies in those places. Among the standard policies and incentives in these countries are clear emission standards, a ZEV mandate (in the case of China, the US, and the EU), incentives (purchase subsidies and tax deductions), and availability of charging infrastructure (IEA 2019, 2020b).

In the case of Mexico, the combination of political discourse redirected towards traditional carbon-based technologies, an ambivalent national plan for EVs, a reduction in incentives for green technologies, and increasing uncertainty among investors have discouraged Mexico's adoption of an EV pathway. Nevertheless, despite Mexico's hesitant political direction, the geographic location of the country and the USMCA regional content requirements to enter the broader North American market may provide the basis for a scenario in which Mexico maintains its role as a producer of ICE vehicles and FFV auto parts for other countries in the periphery and also develops niches in EV production (including batteries) for North American and European export markets.

The literature identifies technology-push policies and technology-forcing regulations as triggers to break technological path-dependency. However, in Mexico there is scant evidence of such factors, and thus Mexico's participation in the burgeoning EV market is at risk. The Mexican case also suggests that technological lock-in is not solely about the technology – it is also an outcome of the sociopolitical and institutional dependencies in place. In the end, the technological transition towards green transport on a global scale *is* moving quickly. That process is also accompanied by considerable sociopolitical changes. Paradoxically, in this case study, although technological expertise, investment interest, and key technological actors *are* present in the Mexican ecosystem, Mexico's failure to reform its sociopolitical context perpetuates a locked-in trajectory. This prevents new investment dedicated to EV production (and related services). It also disincentivizes investors already operating there. Looking ahead, market pressure *is certain to* alter the sociopolitical context for EV adoption in Mexico. Even so, questions linger about the extent to which those pressures will affect Mexico's underlying competitive advantage as a member of the automotive integrated periphery.

REFERENCES

Aghion, Philippe, Antoine Dechezlepretre, David Hemous, Ralf Martin, and John van Reenen. 2016. "Carbon Taxes, Path Dependency, and Directed Technical Change: Evidence from the Auto Industry." *Journal of Political Economy* 124 (1): 1–50. https://doi.org/https://doi.org/10.1086/684581.

Åhman, Max. 2001. "Primary Energy Efficiency of Alternative Powertrains in Vehicles." *Energy* 26 (11): 973–89. https://doi.org/https://doi.org/10.1016/S0360-5442(01)00049-4.

Argus. 2021. "Brazil Favoring Biofuels over EVs to Cut Emissions." 6 May 2021. https://www.argusmedia.com/en/news/2212635-brazil-favoring-biofuels-over-evs-to-cut-emissions.

Azar, Christian, and Bjorn Sanden. 2011. "The Elusive Quest for Technology-Neutral Policies." *Environmental Innovation and Societal Transitions* 1 (1): 135–9. https://doi.org/https://doi.org/10.1016/j.eist.2011.03.003.

Biofuels International. 2020. "Fewer Cars in US Offered as Flex Fuel Vehicles." https://biofuels-news.com/news/fewer-cars-in-us-offered-as-flex-fuel-vehicles/.

Blanco, S. 2021. "Ford Building More Mustang Mach-E EVs than Gas-Powered Mustangs." *Car and Driver*, 7 June 2021. https://www.caranddriver.com/news/a36651347/ford-mustang-mach-e-vs-gas-production/.

Briseño, Hugo, Adrian Ramirez-Nafarrate, and Ozgur M. Araz. 2021. "A Multivariate Analysis of Hybrid and Electric Vehicles Sales in Mexico." *Socio-Economic Planning Sciences* 76. https://doi.org/https://doi.org/10.1016/j.seps.2020.100957.

Brownstone, D., and K.E. Train. 1999. "Forecasting New Product Penetration with Flexible Substitution Patterns." *Journal of Econometrics* 89 (1–2): 109–29. https://www.sciencedirect.com/science/article/abs/pii/S0304407698000578.

Carrillo, Jorge, and Oscar Contreras. 2008. "The Historical Evolution of American Auto Firms in Mexico: Two Models of Local Development." *International Journal of Automotive Technology and Management* 8 (4): 382–400. https://www.inderscience.com/offers.php?id=20310.

Carrillo, Jorge, J. Saul de los Santos Gomez, and Julio Briones. 2020. "Hacia una electromovilidad publica en Mexico." Documentos de Proyectos (LC/TS.2020/115), Santiago, Chile, Comision Economica para America Latina y el Caribe (CEPAL).

C40 Cities Finance Facility. 2021. "Electrifying Bus Routes: Insights from Mexico City's Eje 8 Sur." https://c40cff.org/knowledge-library/electrifying-bus-routes-insights-from-mexico-citys-eje-8-sur.

Chargenow. 2021. "Learn about the Benefits for Electrified Vehicles in Mexico." https://www.chargenow.mx/incentivos-para-vehiculos-electricos-en-mexico/.

Chege, W. 2021. *The Electric Vehicle Ecosystem and Associated Value Chains: The Role the City of Cape Town Can Play in the Electric Vehicle Ecosystem.* Cape Town, South Africa: GreenCape. https://greencape.co.za/assets/The-Electric-Vehicle-Ecosystem-and-Associated-Value-Chains.pdf.

Commission of the European Communities. 2007. "Communication from the Commission to the European Parliament and Council – A Competitve Automotive Regulatory Framework for the 21st

Century. Commission Position on the CARS21 High Level Group Final Report – A Contribution to the EU's Growth and Jobs Strategy (COM 2007, 22 final)." https://eur-lex.europa.eu/EN/legal-content/summary/a-competitive-automotive-regulatory-framework-for-the-21st-century.html.

Congreso de la Union. 2021. "Ley Federal del impuesto sobre automoviles nuevos." https://www.diputados.gob.mx/LeyesBiblio/pdf/LFISAN.pdf.

Cowan, Robin, and S. Hulten. 1996. "Escaping Lock-In: The Case of the Electric Vehicle." *Technological Forecasting & Social Change* 53 (1): 61–79. https://doi.org/https://doi.org/10.1016/0040-1625(96)00059-5.

Datosmacro.com. 2021. "Vehicle Production." https://datosmacro.expansion.com/negocios/produccion-vehiculos?anio.

Diamond, David. 2009. "The Impact of Government Incentives for Hybrid-Electric Vehicles: Evidence from US States." *Energy Policy* 37 (3): 972–83. https://doi.org/https://doi.org/10.1016/j.enpol.2008.09.094.

Dijk, Marc, and Masaru Yarime. 2010. "The Emergence of Hybrid-Electric Cars: Innovation Path Creation through Co-evolution of Supply and Demand." *Technological Forecasting & Social Change* 77: 1371–90. https://doi.org/https://doi.org/10.1016/j.techfore.2010.05.001.

Duran, Itzel. 2020. "EV Ready busca electrificar a méxico" [EV Ready Seeks to Electrify Mexico]. *T21*, 14 April 2020. http://t21.com.mx/automotriz/2020/08/14/ev-ready-busca-electrificar-mexico.

Dyrhauge, Helene. 2021. "Discourses about EU Transport Decarbonisation: Towards a Paradigm Shift?" *The International Spectator* 56 (3): 71–86. https://doi.org/10.1080/03932729.2021.1962665.

Elizondo, Alejandra, and Thalia Hernandez Amezcua. 2018. "Regulacion de las emisiones de CO2 para vehiculos ligeros en Mexico" [Regulating CO2 Emissions for Light Vehicles in Mexico]. *Gestion y Politica Publica* 27 (2): 571–94. https://www.scielo.org.mx/scielo.php?script=sci_arttext&pid=S1405-10792018000200571

European Commission. 2005. "Winning the Battle against Global Climate Change." Memo /05/42. Brussels, 9 February 20005. https://ec.europa.eu/commission/presscorner/detail/en/MEMO_05_42.

– 2020. "Communication from the Commission to the European Parliament, the Council, the European Economic and Social Committee and the Committee of the Regions: Stepping Up Europe's 2030 Climate Ambition: Investing in a Climate-Neutral Future for the Benefit of Our People." Document no. 52020DC0562. Brussels. https://eur-lex.europa.eu/legal-content/EN/TXT/?uri=CELEX%3A52020DC0562.

European Parliament. 2014a. "Legislative Proposal to Amend Regulation (EC no. 443/2009) to define the modalities for reaching the 2020 target to reduce CO_2 emissions from new passenger cars (COM 2012, 0393 final)." Edited by Commission of the European Communities. https://eur-lex.europa.eu/LexUriServ/LexUriServ.do?uri=OJ:L:2009:140:0001:0015:EN:PDF.

– 2014b. "2020 Target to Reduce CO_2 Emissions from New Passanger Cars (Debate)." https://www.europarl.europa.eu/doceo/document/CRE-7-2014-02-24-ITM-017_EN.html?redirect.

– 2019. "Emission Performance Standards for New Passenger Cars and for New Light Commercial Vehicles (Debate)." Brussels.https://www.europarl.europa.eu/doceo/document/CRE-8-2019-03-26-ITM-018_EN.html.

Irle, Roland. n.d. "Global EV Sales for 2021." https://www.ev-volumes.com/news/ev-sales-for-2021/.

Ford, A. 2021. "Bacanora Lithium Comments on New Lithium Concession Proposals from the Mexican Government." *Proactive*, 4 October 2021. https://www.proactiveinvestors.co.uk/companies/news/962051/bacanora-lithium-comments-on-new-lithium-concession-proposals-from-the-mexican-government-962051.html.

Freyssenet, Michel. 2011. "Three Possible Scenarios for Cleaner Automobiles." *International Journal of Automotive Technology and Management* 11 (4): 300–11.

Gallagher, Kelly Sims, and Erich Muehlegger. 2011. "Giving Green to Get Green? Incentives and Customer Adoption of Hybrid Vehicle Technology." *Journal of Environmental Economics and Management* 61 (1): 1–15. https://doi.org/https://doi.org/10.1016/j.jeem.2010.05.004.

Garcia, G. 2020. "Estos son los 19 autos eléctricos a la venta en México, del más barato al más caro." *Motorpasion Mexico*, 22 December 2020. https://www.motorpasion.com.mx/industria/autos-electricos-a-venta-mexico.

Geels, Frank W. 2011. "The Multi-level Perspective on Sustainability Transitions: Responses to Seven Criticisms." *Environmental Innovation and Societal Transitions* 1 (1): 24–40.

Gerard, David, and Lester B. Lave. 2005. "Implementing Technology-Forcing Policies: The 1970 Clean Air Act Amendments and the Introduction of Advanced Automotive Emissions Controls in the United States." *Technological Forecasting & Social Change* 72: 761–78. https://doi.org/https://doi.org/10.1016/j.techfore.2004.08.003.

Goldemberg, Jose, Suani Teixeira Coelho, Plinio Mario Nastari, and Oswaldo Lucon. 2004. "Ethanol Learning Curve – The Brazilian Experience." *Biomass and Bioenergy* 26 (3): 301–4. https://doi.org/https://doi.org/10.1016/S0961-9534(03)00125-9.

Goldman, Josh. 2014. "Comparing Electric Vehicles: Hybrid vs. BEV vs. PHEV vs. FCEV." The *Equation* (blog), *Union of Concerned Scientists*, 20 September 2014. https://blog.ucsusa.org/josh-goldman/comparing-electric-vehicles-hybrid-vs-bev-vs-phev-vs-fcev-411/.

González, Elnatan Eder Torres. 2017. *Normatividad nacional e internacional de emisiones contaminantes para vehículos nuevos en planta.* Mexico City: UNAM.

Gross, S. 2019. "Order from Chaos: AMLO Reverses Positive Trends in Mexico's Energy Industry." Brookings. 20 December 2019. https://www.brookings.edu/blog/order-from-chaos/2019/12/20/amlo-reverses-positive-trends-in-mexicos-energy-industry/.

Holweg, Matthias. 2013. "Where Firm-Level Innovation and Industrial Policy Meet: Consensus Roadmaps for Low-Carbon Powertrain Technologies." *Journal of Product Innovation Management* 31 (1): 33–42. https://doi.org/https://doi.org/10.1111/jpim.12078.

HT Auto. 2021. "Flex-Fuel Engines to Get Mandatory for Carmakers in India, says Nitin Gadkari." https://auto.hindustantimes.com/auto/news/flexfuel-engines-to-get-mandatory-for-carmakers-in-india-says-nitin-gadkari-41624245028410.html.

Huls, Christoph, Christian Thies, Karsten Kieckhafer, and Thomas S. Spengler. 2020. "Limiting CO2 fleet emissions in the automotive industry - a portfolio planning approach." *International Journal of Automotive Technology and Management* 20 (4): 349–368.

IEA (International Energy Agency). 2019. "Global EV Outlook 2019: Scaling-Up the Transition to Electric Mobility." Paris, France. https://www.iea.org/reports/global-ev-outlook-2019.

– 2020a. "Global Electric Car Sales by Key Markets, 2010–2020." https://www.iea.org/data-and-statistics/charts/global-electric-car-sales-by-key-markets-2015-2020.

– 2020b. "Global EV Outlook 2020: Entering the Decade of Electric Drive." Energy Technology Policy Division, Paris, France.

– 2021. "Global EV Outlook 2021: Accelerating Ambitions Despite the Pandemic." Paris, France. https://www.oecd-ilibrary.org/energy/global-ev-outlook-2021_3a394362-en.

Jetin, Bruno. 2020. "Who Will Control the Electric Vehicle Market?" *International Journal of Automotive Technology and Management* 20 (2): 156–77.

Kane, M. 2021. "Rumor: Two EVs to Join Ford Mustang Mach-E Production Site in Mexico." *Inside EVs*, 18 March 2021.

Lee, Jaegul, Francisco M. Veloso, and David A. Hounshell. 2011. "Linking Induced Technological Change, and Environmental Regulation: Evidence from Patenting in the US Auto Industry." *Research Policy* 40 (9): 1240–52. https://doi.org/https://doi.org/10.1016/j.respol.2011.06.006.

Lee, Jaegul, Francisco M. Veloso, David A. Hounshell, and Edward S. Rubin. 2010. "Forcing Technological Change: A Case of Automotive Emissions Control Technology Development in the US." *Technovation* 30 (4): 249–64. https://doi.org/https://doi.org/10.1016/j.technovation.2009.12.003.

Levay, Petra Zsuzsa, Yannis Drossinos, and Christian Thiel. 2017. "The Effect of Fiscal Incentives on Market Penetration of Electric Vehicles: A Pairwise Comparison of Total Cost of Ownership." *Energy Policy* 105: 524–33. https://doi.org/https://doi.org/10.1016/j.enpol.2017.02.054.

Li, L. 2020. "5G and Its Big Bang Impact on the Auto Industry." In *Perspectives from Our Asia Pacific Junior Talents*, 7. Capgemini: Paris.

Meadowcroft, James. 2011. "Engaging with the Politics of Sustainability Transitions." *Environmental Innovation and Societal Transitions* 1 (1): 70–5. https://doi.org/https://doi.org/10.1016/j.eist.2011.02.003.

Meckling, Jonas, and Jonas Nahm. 2018. "When Do States Disrupt Industries? Electric Cars and the Politics of Innovation." *Review of International Political Economy* 25 (4): 505–29. https://doi.org/https://doi.org/10.1080/09692290.2018.1434810.

– 2019. "The Politics of Technology Bans: Industrial Policy Competition and Green Goals for the Auto Industry." *Energy Policy* 126 (470–479). https://www.sciencedirect.com/science/article/abs/pii/S0301421518307602.

Mersky, Avi Chaim, Frances Sprei, Constantine Samaras, and Zhen (Sean) Quian. 2016. "Effectiveness of Incentives on Electric Vehicle Adoption in Norway." *Transportation Research Part D: Transport and Environment* 46: 56–68. https://doi.org/https://doi.org/10.1016/j.trd.2016.03.011.

Metalmecanica. 2021. "Mexico enfrenta desafios para la produccion de vehiculos electricos." https://www.metalmecanica.com/es/noticias/mexico-enfrenta-desafios-para-la-produccion-de-vehiculos-electricos.

Mexico Industry. 2018. " El empleo en la Industria Automotriz." https://mexicoindustry.com/noticia/el-empleo-en-la-industria-automotriz.

Moreira, Jose R., and Jose Goldemberg. 1999. "The Alcohol Program." *Energy Policy* 27 (4): 229–45. https://doi.org/10.1016/S0301-4215(99)00005-1.

Munoz, F. 2021. "Q1 2021 EV Global Sales at the Same Level as 2017 Full Year Figures." *JATO* (blog), 7 June 2021. https://www.jato.com/q1-2021-ev-global-sales-at-the-same-level-as-2017-full-year-figures/.

OICA (International Organization of Motor Vehicle Manufacturers). 2006. "The World's Automotive Industry: Some Key Figures." https://oica.net/wp-content/uploads/2007/06/oica-depliant-final.pdf.

– 2021. "2021 Production Statistics." https://www.oica.net/category/production-statistics/2021-statistics/.

Oki, Takahiro. 2021. "European Fuel Economy Policy for New Passenger Cars: A Historical Comparative Analysis of Discourses and Change Factors." *International Environmental Agreements* 21: 165–81. https://doi.org/https://doi.org/10.1007/s10784-020-09510-7.

Paredes-Cervantes, Samantha A., Luis Felipe Barahona-Perez, Francisco G. Barroso-Tenoira, and Donny V. Ponce-Marban. 2020. "Biofuels and Their Potential in the Mexican Energy Market." *Revista de Economia* 37 (94): 35–56. https://doi.org/https://doi.org/10.33937/reveco.2020.128.

Pavlínek, Petr. 2018. "Global Production Networks, Foreign Direct Investment, and Supplier Linkages in the Integrated Peripheries of the Automotive Industry." *Economic Geography* 94 (2): 141–65. https://doi.org/https://doi.org/10.1080/00130095.2017.1393313.

Paz, K. 2021. "La venta de vehículos electrificados incrementó a 24 mil 343 unidades comercializadas en 2020." *JATO*, 20 April 2021. https://www.jato.com/mexico/la-venta-de-vehiculos-electrificados-incremento-a-24-mil-343-unidades-comercializadas-en-2020/.

Penna, Caetano C.R., and Frank W. Geels. 2015. "Climate Change and the Slow Reorientation of the American Car Industry (1979–2012): An Application and Extension of the Dialectic Issue LifeCycle (DILC) Model." *Research Policy* 44 (5): 1029–48. https://doi.org/https://doi.org/10.1016/j.respol.2014.11.010.

Randall, C. 2021a. "Foxconn Considers Manufacturing EVs in India, Europe and Latin America." Electrive, 21 October 2021.https://www.electrive.com/2021/10/21/foxconn-considers-manufacturing-evs-in-india-europe-and-latin-america/.

– 2021b. "Honda Reveals BEV Sales Targets for North America." Electrive, 21 September 2021. https://www.electrive.com/2021/09/21/honda-reveals-bev-sales-targets-for-north-america/.

– 2021c. "Next.e.GO Mobile to Enter Mexico." Electrive, 20 May 2021. https://www.electrive.com/2021/05/20/next-e-go-mobile-to-enter-mexico/.

Redelbach, Martin, Matthias Klotzke, and Horst E. Friedrich. 2012. "Impact of Lightweight Design on Energy Consumption and Cost Effectiveness of Alternative Powertrain Concepts." Paper presented at European Electric Vehicle Conference (EEVC), Brussels, 19–22 November 2012.

Riegelhaupt, Enrique, Jorge Odenthal, and Luis Janeiro. 2016. "Diagnóstico de la situación actual del biodiesel en México y escenarios para su aprovechamiento." https://www.gob.mx/cms/uploads/attachment/file/275444/Final_Report.pdf, Banco Interamericano de Desarrollo.

Righolt, H.C., and F. Rieck. 2013. "Energy Chain and Efficiency in Urban Traffic for ICE and EV." In *2013 World Electric Vehicle Symposium and Exhibition (EVS27)*, 1–7. Piscataway, NJ: IEEE. https://doi.org/https://doi.org/10.1109/EVS.2013.6914820.

Rodriguez, Ivet. 2021a. "Electrolineras: El gran negocio que se frenó por la contrarreforma eléctrica Electrolineras" [Electrolineras: The big business that was stopped by the electrical counter-reform]. *Expansión*, 17 May 2021. https://expansion.mx/empresas/2021/05/17/electrolineras-gran-negocio-freno-reforma-electrica.

– 2021b. "¿Habrá menos empleos automotrices con los autos eléctricos? La respuesta es sí" [Will there be fewer automotive jobs with electric cars? The answer is yes]. *Expansión*, 25 May 2021. https://expansion.mx/empresas/2021/05/25/empleos-automotrices-autos-electricos-mexico.

Romero, R. 2021. "Mexico Moves to Nationalise Lithium Production amid Potential Boom." *Diálogo Chino*, 17 November 2021. https://shorturl.at/flwZ1.

Sierzchula, William, Sjoerd Bakker, Kees Maat, and Bert van Wee. 2014. "The Influence of Financial Incentives and Other Socio-economic Factors on Electric Vehicle Adoption." *Energy Policy* 68: 183–94. https://doi.org/https://doi.org/10.1016/j.enpol.2014.01.043.

Simonazzi, Annamaria, Jorge Carreto Sangines, and Margherita Russo. 2020. "The Future of the Automotive Industry: Dangerous Challenges or New Life for a Saturated Market?" Institute for New Economic Thinking Working Paper no. 141. https://doi.org/10.36687/inetwp141.

Statista. 2022. "Número de vehículos eléctricos e híbridos vendidos en México desde 2016 a 2022" [Number of electric and hybrid vehicles sold in Mexico from 2016 to 2021]. https://es.statista.com/estadisticas/1114981/volumen-ventas-vehiculos-electricos-hibridos-mexico/.

Stein, Y. 2021. "How Can 5G Operators Enable an Electric Future?" *Automotive World*, 3 February 2021. https://shorturl.at/gKLZ1.

Strategy&. 2020. *Digital Auto Report 2020: Navigating through a Post-Pandemic World.* PwC. https://www.strategyand.pwc.com/de/en/industries/automotive/digital-auto-report-2020/digital-auto-report-2020-full-version.pdf.

Thomas, Carlton E. 2009. "Fuel Cell and Battery Electric Vehicles Compared." *International Journal of Hydrogen Energy* 34 (15): 6005–20. https://doi.org/https://doi.org/10.1016/j.ijhydene.2009.06.003.

Torres González, Elnatan Eder. (2017). "Normatividad nacional e internacional de emisiones contaminantes para vehículos nuevos en planta" [National and international regulations on polluting emissions for new vehicles in the plant]. Bachelor's thesis. National Autonomous University of Mexico, Mexico City. https://repositorio.unam.mx/contenidos/269956.

Train, Kenneth E., and Clifford Winston. 2007. "Vehicle Choice Behavior and the Declining Market Share of U.S. Automakers." *International Economic Review* 48 (4): 1469–96. https://www.jstor.org/stable/4542021.

US Department of Commerce. 2020. "Mexico Hybrid and Electric Vehicles." 10 March 2020. https://www.trade.gov/market-intelligence/mexico-hybrid-and-electric-vehicles.

US Department of Energy, Alternative Fuels Development Center. 2021. "Key Federal Legislation." https://afdc.energy.gov/laws/key_legislation.

US Department of Energy, Office of Energy Efficiency and Renewable Energy. 2021. "Flexible-Fuel Vehicles." https://www.fueleconomy.gov/feg/esflextech.shtml.

US International Trade Administration. 2023. Mexico Country Commercia Guide: Automotiver Industry. https://www.trade.gov/country-commercial-guides/mexico-automotive-industry

Vallejo, Bertha. 2010. "Learning and Innovation under Changing Conditions: The Auto Parts Industry in Mexico." PhD diss., Maastricht University.

– 2015. "The Emergence of Parallel Trajectories in the Automobile Industry: Environmental Issues and the Creation of New Markets." UNU-MERIT Working Paper Series no. 037. https://www.researchgate.net/publication/282011105_The_emergence_of_parallel_trajectories_in_the_automobile_industry_Environmental_issues_and_the_creation_of_new_markets.

Vergis, Sydney, and Belinda Chen. 2015. "Comparison of Plug-In Electric Vehicle Adoption in the United States: A State by State Approach." *Research in Transportation Economics* 52: 56–64. https://doi.org/https://doi.org/10.1016/j.retrec.2015.10.003.

Walther, Grit, Jorg Wansart, Karsten Kieckhafer, Eckehard Schnieder, and Thomas S. Spengler. 2010. "Impact Assessment in the Automotive Industry: Mandatory Market Introduction of Alternative Powertrain Technologies." *Research Policy* 44: 1029–48. https://doi.org/http://dx.doi.org/10.1016/j.respol.2014.11.010.

Wee, Sherilyn, and Sumner La Croix. 2018. "Do Electric Vehicle Incentives Matter? Evidence from the 50 U.S. States." *Research Policy* 47 (9): 1601–10. https://doi.org/https://doi.org/10.1016/j.respol.2018.05.003.

Wells, Peter, and Paul Nieuwenhuis. 2012. "Transition Failure: Undestanding Continuity in the Automotive Industry." *Technological Forecasting & Social Change* 79 (9): 1681–92. https://doi.org/Https://doi.org/10.1016/j.techfore.2012.06.008.

Yang, Zifei, Peter Slowik, Nic Lutsey, and Stephanie Searle. 2016. "Principles for Effective Electric Vehicle Incentive Design." Washington, DC: International Council on Clean Transportation.

Yarime, Masaru. 2009. "Public Coordination for Escaping from Technological Lock-In: Its Possibilities and Limits in Replacing Diesel Vehicles with Compressed Natural Gas Vehicles in Tokyo." *Journal of Cleaner Production* 17 (14): 1281–88. https://doi.org/https://doi.org/10.1016/J.JCLEPRO.2009.03.010.

Yarime, Masaru, H. Shiroyama, and Y. Kukoki. 2008. "The Strategies of the Japanese Auto Industry in Developing Hybrid and Fuel Cell Vehicles." In *Making Choices about Hydrogen: Transport Issues for Developing Countries*, edited by Lynn Mytelka and G. Boyle, 187–212. Ottawa: IDRC/United Nations University Press.

Yutong. 2019. "63 Yutong Dual-Source Trolleybuses Enter Mexico across the Ocean!" 14 October 2019. https://en.yutong.com/pressmedia/yutong-news/2019/2019JNOhRqN4yq.html.

Zwaniger, R. 2021. "EV Advances in Mexico." *Mexico Business News*, 7 April 2021. https://mexicobusiness.news/mobility/news/ev-advances-mexico.

PART 4

Wages, Workplace Democratization, and Collective Bargaining in a Regionally Integrated Industry

11

Collective Bargaining and Employment Relations in the North American Auto Industry: From Convergence to Marginalization?

Mathieu Dupuis

In fall 2019 the United Auto Workers (UAW) embarked on the longest strike in the Detroit Three's history of collective bargaining since the 1970s. The strikers' demands included, amongst others, a reduction in the gap between legacy workers and new hires, increased job security, and better pay. This conflict represented a curious burst of militancy within the UAW that started in 2015 and was surprising after decades of complacence about efforts to restructure plants in the industry. During the 2015 bargaining, Fiat Chrysler (FCA) workers – composed in large part of new hires with working conditions inferior to legacy workers – rejected a deal struck between the national bargaining committee and the firm on the basis that the agreement did not address workers' demands about the two-tier system, notably the demand to close the gap between legacy employees and new hires. Meanwhile, north of the border, the last two rounds of negotiations between the Detroit Three and Unifor in Canada were marked by demands related to investments. Faced with the largest contractions in the production in over a decade, in 2016 the union bargained under the banner of "Making History" to secure products in several plants, notably Ford Windsor and GM Oshawa. Similarly, in 2020 the union engaged in bargaining with the Detroit Three with the goal of securing the industry footprint in Canada. With Oshawa closed and Ford Oakville on the verge of losing its product lines, Unifor aimed to secure commitments from all the Detroit Three corporations, especially in the context of a shift to electrical vehicles (EVs). While some critics pointed out that commitments from the Detroit Three were volatile – for example, the reconversion of Ford Oakville to EV would materialize after the expiration of the actual collective agreement – Unifor called the end results a "home run" and, with the support of the state, achieved major investments at the three North American auto corporations.

From the point of view of industrial relations, this picture can be confusing. As clichés are persistent, we tend to conceptualize the two trajectories of auto unions from past understandings: faced with plant closures and a hostile institutional environment, the UAW engaged in cooperation and concession bargaining. Unifor (formerly CAW, Canadian Auto Workers), in a more worker-friendly environment and a vibrant democratic union, rejected concessions. In this chapter, I want to highlight major changes in collective bargaining and employment relations that have occurred over the last two decades and that shaped the understanding of unionized workplaces in the auto industry. In that regard, the chapter complements chapter 2 by A.J. Jacobs, which provides a description of the restructuring and rearranging that has occurred in the North American automotive industry during the same period.

As other authors have pointed out (e.g., Rutherford and Holmes 2013; Wells 1997; Mordue and Sweeney, chapter 1 of this collection), for Canada the passing of NAFTA, the disengagement of the state, and the ensuing shrinking of the Canadian auto industry have led to less favourable conditions for autoworker unions. In addition, the permanent restructuring of the industry (Siemiatycki 2012), particularly since 2000, and the direct intervention of government (Stanford 2010) have changed workplace governance in Canada. What I will illustrate is that these important transformations have led to a relative convergence with labour practices adopted in the United States.

Moreover, I argue in this chapter that the 2008–9 crisis represents a critical juncture for collective bargaining and the transformation of employment relations in the North American auto industry. As I will illustrate, employment relations and collective bargaining have been affected on three different fronts: (1) the rise of a multitier workforce in Canada and the US that departs from the Fordist norms; as well, changes in wages and benefits and work practices align unionized workplaces not only with foreign competitors, but also with the prevalent standards in the private sector; (2) the realization of lean practices and cooperation in all unionized workplaces; (3) a recentralization of industrial relations, particularly concerning investment dynamics, in which the local union's politics tend to assume a new role.

In consequence, labour and employment relations in the North American auto sectors have aligned their employment relationships with standards prevalent in the private sector – and to some extent the public sector – characterized through what Weil (2014) has called the "fissured workplace." As other scholars have pointed out (Holst 2014; Doellgast and Greer 2007; O'Brady 2021), the vertical disintegration of large firms and of institutional structures has not only led to the push of precarity towards external markets, but has also affected the so-called core that the unionized auto industry workplaces once represented. This has precipitated the rise of a workforce characterized by divergent status, fringe benefits tied to the market instead of guaranteed rights financed by corporations, and, for some parts of the workforce, a higher level of external flexibility. This model largely departs from Fordist standards and the "private welfare enterprise" that was the prevailing norm in the sector.

To support the argument, I first present a historical synthesis of labour relations trends in the North American auto sector and highlight major changes that occurred since the passing of NAFTA. Second, I develop the methodology and describe the data sources used for the empirical analysis. I then briefly illustrate how 2008–9 represents a critical period shaping the understanding of labour relations in the industry. Fourth, I present results concerning the three spheres of change in collective bargaining and employment relations. I conclude by analysing prospective scenarios for labour relations in the context of changes in transportation modes that have the potential to affect employment relations, level of jobs, and the labour process in industry unionized workplaces.

HISTORY AND THEORY: COLLECTIVE BARGAINING, LABOUR, AND EMPLOYMENT RELATIONS FROM THE 70S CRISIS TO POST-NAFTA

The structure of collective bargaining in North America's auto industry was introduced in the aftermath of the Second World War and was considered a "pace-setter" in the private sector for approximately three decades. The main parties were the Big Three (GM, Chrysler, Ford), followed by minor competitors. Workers in this industry have been represented by UAW in the United States and the UAW-Canada/CAW/now Unifor in Canada. Other unions are also present in the sector but tend to represent a minority of workplaces. These include the IUE in the Ohio region, which once represented the only non-UAW assembly plant in the US and is still present in parts manufacturing, and the Steelworkers, which represent a number of plants in the Canadian parts industry. From the sit-down strikes of the 1930s and the end of the Second World War through to 1979, the UAW and UAW-Canada represented almost the entire industry.

While the Wagner model of industrial relations is, by definition, based on decentralized bargaining, the overall system does not restrict parties from structuring their relationships through other forms. The auto industry has opted for a different type of bargaining from at least the end of the 1930s, in which wages and benefits have been negotiated at the company level, first between GM and the UAW. After 1945, the union attempted to bargain over certain management rights, such as an "open the book" policy at GM, but was vigorously rejected by corporations. As a compromise, the bargaining rounds of 1948 and 1950 (the latter christened by the press as the "Treaty of Detroit") established the basic contours of the structure of bargaining for the decades to come. This formula was not only a demand from the union, but also a push from management to control the production process and to ensure that workers would not interfere in their right to manage operations (Lichtenstein 1995). As a result, three elements can describe the bargaining structure and employment relations in the industry (Katz 1985). First is the *wage-formula*, tied to annual improvement factors and cost of living adjustments (COLA) to secure and stabilize the revenues of the workforce. In addition to this wage system, the union bargained over several aspects that created the model of the "private welfare enterprise": thirty-and-out pensions financed by corporations, medical coverage, off-days, and the like. Second is *connective bargaining,* which ensured that inter-plant variations were minimal (with wages and benefits negotiated at the corporate level and work rules at the plant level), but also that intercompany variations were virtually nonexistent, as pattern bargaining covered all corporations. The third element is *job control unionism* on the shop floor, enshrined in local agreements that codify job classifications and seniority rules for assignments and specify that the wage is attributed to the job and not to individual workers.

In Canada, workplaces in the auto sector were organized from the inception of the UAW in the 1930s with locals based in Windsor and Oshawa. Before the Auto Pact of 1965, Canadian branches of the Big Three tended to operate nationally and the industry was not tightly integrated (Holmes and Rusonik 1991). However, the passing of the Auto Pact led to the integration of the industry and also pushed the UAW to claim parity of wages between the two countries. In the 1970s, collective bargaining structures and employment relations in the industry were more or less similar, to the point that Chrysler workers in Canada and the US were covered by the same agreement (Holmes and Rusonik 1991). However, the two national unions developed divergent ideologies and different bargaining agendas (Yates 1993). The UAW purged the left from its union structures, was rapidly engaged in the turmoil of the Cold war, and stopped pushing for imaginative recruiting campaigns after the failed attempts of "Operation Dixie" in the 1930s and 1940s aimed at unionizing workplaces in the southern states. In Canada, the UAW regional section developed links with social groups, was part of the alliance in the socialist New Democratic Party (NDP), and, generally speaking, tolerated dissidence and activism at the local level more than its US counterpart (Yates 1993).

At the end of 1970s, the first cracks in the edifice of the collective bargaining structures started to appear (Holmes and Rusonik 1991; Katz 1985). The decade was a tremendous reversal of the pattern of economic growth that had characterized the post-war boom. The oil shocks of 1973 and 1979 led to stagnation in growth, but also to new standards for gas consumption that forced the Big Three to invest massively in R&D to conform to these regulations. Meanwhile, with galloping inflation, wages and benefits of workers, which would before have been internalized in car prices, began to be targeted by corporations and politicians as the main cause of the economic sickness. While previously vehicle sales were almost entirely dominated by the Big Three, new competitors from Germany and Japan entered the North American market with smaller cars. On the labour side, from 1968–75 rank-and-file rebellions in auto plants became the focus of national attention (Jones 2010), termed the "blue-collar blues" by the press. A new breed of younger workers that questioned authority and management prerogatives led to the famous wildcat strikes, such as the Lordstown, Ohio, conflict, that was directed against production standards (Aronowitz 1992). In Canada, similar factors affected labour relations as new plants were built and the average age of workers tended to be low.

In 1979, with Chrysler's bankruptcy and the ensuing period of restructuring that lasted until 1982, several aspects of collective bargaining and employment relations were modified. This period of change has been well documented; my goal here is to point to the major modifications that were introduced in the US. First, the UAW accepted major concessions over wages and benefits, one of the first retreats since the Second World War. Second, these concessions concerned primarily the wage rules to reduce the cost of production, the most visible part being the reduction of COLA and the introduction of profit-sharing schemes tying workers' destinies to corporations. Third, concessions on wage rules at the local level eventually led to the appearance of variations between plants. There were of course variations between plant practices before the 1980s, depending on the type of products manufactured or the technology utilized. But the tight control of the national over the local agreements prevented major variations between plant practices until that control was relaxed in the 1980s.

In Canada, while similar concessions were imposed, especially at Chrysler since the two unions shared the same agreement, the economic recovery of the industry after 1982 led to the crystallization of divergent strategies. Canadian workers rejected the extension of concessions via strikes, as a means to preserve the post-war pattern. Among other factors, the lower costs of the Canadian industry, the younger workforce, more recent plants and technology, a friendlier political system, and public-financed health care were the main political and economic factors in favour of the UAW-Canada branch's bargaining power. In the round of 1984, the unwillingness of the UAW international to authorize a strike against GM led to the creation of the Canadian Auto Workers the subsequent year (Gindin 1995; Holmes and Rusonik 1991). While some pointed at a simplistic "nationalism" explanation to understand this split, incompatible bargaining agendas regarding the restructuring of the industry, different ideologies, and divergent economic environments are better suited to explaining the creation of the CAW (Holmes and Rusonik 1991; Kumar and Holmes 1996; Yates 1993). As Holmes and Rusonik (1991) point out, after 1985 two patterns were identifiable concerning labour relations: in Canada, a traditional Fordist pact with arms-length relationships between management and the union; in the US, a new pattern of industrial relations marked with cooperative relationships between labour and the corporations.

Economic factors that were visible at the beginning of the 1980s became heavy trends at the end of the decade. First, foreign competitors, in hopes of grabbing market shares and circumventing tariffs on cars, began to invest massively in the US and Canada. These plants introduced new work practices and, more importantly, remained non-unionized, cracking the oligopolistic model of industry-labour relationships in which wages and benefits were taken out of the competition. In the US in particular, Japanese and German original equipment manufacturers (OEMs) located their greenfield plants in the southern states, a friendlier environment for corporations with lower taxes and flexible labour laws, which eventually led to the establishment of two different auto clusters, the Great Lakes and the South (Klier and Rubenstein, 2013). Second, the passing of the FTA (1988) and NAFTA (1994), to use Holmes's (2004) conceptualization, rescaled auto production in North America, but also labour relations in the industry. While auto production remains a process that is geographically rooted, and where a majority of suppliers must be located near the assembly plant for just-in-time practices, the inclusion of Mexico in the North American political economy would eventually give a new sourcing and auto investment option to the Big Three and put additional pressures on unions to accept concessions to retain jobs. Third, the arrival of Japanese auto producers and the prophetic assumptions that the era of "mass producing" was over (Womack, Jones, and Roos 1990) led to the popularization of lean production methods as a response to productivity and quality problems for the North American OEMs.

The 1990s were also marked by a "decentralization" of industrial relations that had several consequences for the model of the labour-management relationship in the industry (Katz 1993). While the wage formula remained centralized, experiments at the local level in the form of new work organization practices affected the job control unionism of the Fordist type of employment relations. In the US, the UAW embarked on many projects of "jointness" to establish new forms of labour-management cooperation. Amongst other things, the realization of this new culture and efforts to reduce costs were seen as a way of renewing competitiveness and saving plants from closures (Katz 1985). The union also bargained for several experiments that integrated features of the Japanese lean production with a North American flavour. NUMMI, the Californian joint venture between GM and Toyota, became a test case for the necessity of changing shop-floor relationships as it integrated the Toyota production system with the presence of a UAW local (Adler 1993). While some inside the union were convinced that this shift towards cooperation and worker involvement was the only way to save the North American auto industry and unionized jobs, other voices remained critical of this turn (Parker and Slaughter 1988). Perhaps the most striking example of this phase of experimentation was the negotiation between the UAW and GM for the establishment of the Saturn Corporation (Rubinstein and Kochan 2001). Designed in a joint effort and supposed to reconciliate lean practices with "industrial democracy" and union presence, Saturn was the emblematic case of worker involvement at every level of the corporation. Functioning with teamwork, multitasking, and workers' voices in business decisions, Saturn became the poster boy of the 1990s for changing labour relations and apparent success in involving unions.

In Canada, as Kumar and Holmes (1996) illustrated, the CAW approached the introduction of lean practices with scepticism. Perhaps the strong rebound of the industry in Canada explained this position, but the union also developed a comprehensive agenda against partnership and unilateral imposition of changes in work organization. The stronger labour movement in Canada, the independent agenda developed by the CAW, and lively rank-and-file militancy at the local level explained these divergent responses (Kumar and Holmes 1996). The CAW did bargain at the end of the 1980s over the CAMI initiative, a joint venture between GM and Suzuki incorporating Japanese production methods with the presence of unionized workforce outside of the pattern bargaining. However, as the ground-breaking study of the plant by Rinehart, Huxley, and Robertson (1997) illustrated, the diffusion of these practices was quickly accompanied by disenchantment of the union and the workers. CAMI workers eventually went on strike in 1992 to demand a contract similar to the CAW practices in other plants and the rollback of certain management initiatives. While on the surface the CAW remained opposed to the diffusion of lean practices and workers' involvement, with the changing nature of auto production in North American after NAFTA and as less favourable political economic conditions emerged, variations in work organization became discernable between certain plants. As Wells (1997) argued, these changing conditions, coupled with the decentralization of collective bargaining, led some locals to embark on concessions in work organization and cooperation with management.

In fact, even if Japanese production systems were publicized as the "one best way" to face the decline of North American OEMs and the solution to implement post-Fordist work practices, the 1990s were a period of divergence and experimentation in work organization and labour-management relations. Teamwork, quality circles, and workers' involvement were not diffused to every plant, even the modernized ones in the US (Milkman 1997). In the specific case of Ford (Cutcher-Gershenfeld, Brooks, and Mulloy 2015a), some local unions and managers began to establish new practices while others remained in traditional modes of labour relations. Even if the reduction of classifications and flexibility in the use of skilled trades workers was a long-standing demand from management (Katz 1985), the full realization of teamwork, multitasking, and functional flexibility was, as we will see below, far from being accomplished.

Another strong tendency that marked the auto industry after the passing of NAFTA was the vertical disintegration of the Big Three production systems. Divergence between firms always remained in their degree of integration – Chrysler, for example, has always been less vertically integrated than the two other Big Three – but the control of the overall value chain was perceived as a source of competitiveness and as a strategy to avoid uncertainties from at least the 1920s in the auto industry (Coase 2000). The consequence for labour relations is that unionized auto parts, especially those covered by master agreements in Canada and the US, enjoyed very advantageous working conditions and wages and benefits similar to those in the assembly plants. With the arrival of foreign competitors, especially the Japanese, these corporations built new networks of production with less in-house parts manufacturing. In addition, private consultants and the press pushed the idea that firms, to remain competitive, should now be focused on their "core competencies," which, in the case of the automotive sector, is to manufacture and market vehicles (Jacobides, MacDuffie, and Tae 2016).

The nature of auto production meant that OEMs should outsource a maximum of components and parts manufacturing to concentrate on the assembly of vehicles. The Big Three, especially at GM, led spectacular moves to reframe their production networks and, in consequence, to lower their manufacturing and labour costs. The spin-off of major axles plants and the founding of American Axle Manufacturing; the creation of Delphi in 1999, which was composed of 168 plants worldwide; and a similar move by Ford with the creation of Visteon reversed the vertical integration of North American OEMs. As the Flint strike of 1998 demonstrated, part of the explanation of this strategy was the corporations' desire to neutralize the power of unions to shut down the entire production system now running in just-in-time fashion. Ironically, this strategy backfired at GM when a strike at AAM held the corporation hostage, or when Delphi, under bankruptcy starting in 2005, threatened to collapse the entire firm's production system.

In Canada, because the focus of its automotive industry was on assembly (an outcome of the requirements of the Auto Pact, described in the introduction to this collection), the OEMs had never been vertically integrated in the same way as in the US. Nevertheless, similar trends were observable in the 1990s. The Big Three started to outsource parts, and the arrival of Japanese corporations with their own suppliers gave new sourcing options for OEMs. Additionally, the rise of Canadian-owned suppliers – mostly non-unionized even today – accelerated this changing pattern of sourcing in the Canadian industry (Anastakis 2013). In reaction to these trends, the CAW developed innovative bargaining agendas that were crystallized during a strike against GM in 1996, precisely on the topic of outsourcing (Holmes 2004). With the changing geography and patterns of auto production, the union reacted by demanding several protections against outsourcing or negotiated settlements that would either protect the workers or favour their unionization. Three strategies were used: satellite bargaining, in which the union bargains with the supplier and the customer (the OEM) as one entity; successor rights, which explicitly state that outsourcing production should be accompanied with unionization; and "work ownership, which contracted that the work performed by CAW members is their own and should not be outsourced unilaterally.

The beginning of the twenty-first century substantially changed the course of labour relations in the North American industry. I will treat the major shifts that occurred in the last twenty years further below, but some elements of context are needed to understand how the 2008–9 crisis changed the trajectory of labour relations in the sector. In the US, after a resurgence of Big Three sales due to the SUV boom of the late 1990s, Ford, Chrysler, and GM suffered major loss of market shares. This led to massive plans to close and consolidate that resulted in forced redundancies, mainly through early retirement (Katz, MacDuffie, and Pil 2013). For example, UAW membership at Ford fell from 102,907 in 2005 to 40,274 in 2009 (Katz, MacDuffie, and Pil 2013). In Canada, production of vehicles peaked in 1999; the ensuing decline eventually led to some restructuring. For example, GM closed its Sainte-Thérèse plant in 2002 while Ford closed its Ontario Truck plant in 2004. Tables 1 and 2 illustrate the restructuring of the assembly plants of the Detroit Three and their auto parts production over the years.

How to interpret these changes and their impact on labour relations? As Rutherford and Holmes (2013, 2014) point out, the integration of the Great Lakes auto industry into transnational global production networks has led to massive change in the workplace governance of both national industries. Still, this governance is influenced by differences in labour law, union strategies, and state strategies concerning the automotive sector. However, the rise of

Table 1. In-House Parts Plants in North America, Detroit Three

	Number of Plants		
Company	1988	2000	2019
FCA (Stellantis)	22	21	15
Ford	37	16	14
GM	62	31	22

Source: Various primary and secondary sources, author's compilation. 2019 includes in-sourced plants in other divisions.

Table 2. Number of Assembly Plants in North America, Detroit Three

	Number of Plants		
Company	2000	2011	2021
FCA (Stellantis)	14	9	8
Ford	19	10	9
GM	24	13	12

Source: Automotive News Market Data Book; companies' websites.

the Great Lakes auto cluster and its competition with the southern States and Mexico, producing vehicles in very different contexts, led to a recalibration of labour relations. The crisis of 2008–9 confirmed these trends as well as the constant diminishing of union density in the US and Canada. Between 1983 and 2016, union density in US "motor vehicle and equipment" manufacturing dropped from 59% to 17% (Hirsch and Macpherson 2003), while the collective share of the Detroit Three in the US market dropped from 74% to 44% (Ward's Automotive 2019). In Canada, membership density in OEMs fell from 73% (2005) to 58% (2014) and in parts manufacturers from 31% (2005) to 21% (2014) (Sweeney and Mordue 2017).

One could argue that these trends resulted in a shrinking core preserved by market pressures while flexibility and precarity have been pushed outside the OEMs boundaries. The trend in outsourcing during the 1990s tends to confirm this argument. Autoworkers made major concessions but the institutionalized pattern bargaining remained intact despite the influence of new foreign OEMs. However, replicating the types of employment relations typical of the southern cluster slowly became the norm, and state influence during 2008–9 vividly illustrated this change. The era of "permanent restructuring" in the industry pivoted unionized workplaces towards what is now the standard in the industry (Siemiatycki 2012).

While all these claims are correct, I want to highlight the need to disentangle the auto sector from specific industry trends, and put the changes in labour and employment relations in parallel with broader standards similar to the private sector that are the result of institutional changes in North America. As Doellgast and Greer (2007) have illustrated for Germany, the vertical

Table 3. Employment Relations in Unionized North American Auto Industry before 2008–9 Crisis

Object	US	Canada
Wage rule	Cost of living adjustments; profit-sharing	Cost of living adjustments; annual increases
Retirement	30-and-out; defined benefits	30-and-out; defined benefits
Employment protections	Supplemental unemployment benefits (SUB); job banks	Supplemental unemployment benefits (SUB)
Medical coverage	Employer-sponsored	Public insurance with complementary employer-sponsored benefits
Job control	Seniority; minor variations in wages between workers; number of classifications depends on plant	Seniority; minor variations in wages between workers; number of classifications depends on plant
Team work/quality circles/employee involvement	Implementation depends on plant; high variability, but jointness is massively adopted and supported by national union	Implementation depends on plant; high variability; cooperation and jointness are resisted at national level but sometimes adopted at plant level
Labour process	Lean production processes are implemented but highly variable from plant to plant; push from management to standardize practices	Lean production processes are implemented but highly variable from plant to plant; push from management to standardize practices

Source: Master and local agreements, UAW and CAW, various years; bargaining highlights, UAW and CAW, various years.

disintegration of firms has led to a disorganization of collective institutions and the adoption of new norms in subcontracted work that depart from standards of the visible labour relations system. Holst (2014) pushed this argument further by moving away from the distinction between "core" and "periphery." Vertical disintegration also affects lead firms that tend to copy practices that become perceived norms in their sector: "Vertical disintegration not only directly moves the core-periphery boundary; it also tends to establish cross-boundary competition between different segments of the workforce" (16). Workforces can be segmented both within and across firms, the degree of which is highly contingent on the institutional power of unions (O'Brady, 2021). From our point of view, these economic and political pressures in the North American auto sector have led to the adoption of common practices, which are now common in virtually every economic sector, that Weil (2014) has termed "fissured workplaces": the use of a flexible workforce and contingent forms of employment as well as outsourcing. Such practices have been adopted not only in the US but also in Canada, as many past studies have illustrated (Cranford, Vosko, and Zukewich 2003). We will present this argument in-depth in the empirical section.

Before we turn to the presentation of the methodology and the data and as a point of comparison, table 3 illustrates the major characteristics in employment relations before the 2008–9 crisis, in both Canada and the USA.

METHODOLOGY

To illustrate the changing patterns of labour and employment relations in the North American auto industry, I mobilize data from previous research (Dupuis 2018; Dupuis and Greer 2022) as well as new original materials coming from secondary sources. First, I have interviewed over one hundred individuals, including local, regional, and national unionists, actual and retired local/national managers, and industry experts from 2012 to 2019. These interviews have been conducted at different levels (corporations, national, local) and through sixteen case studies of local plants in the two countries. All interviews have been transcribed fully and analysed with the qualitative analysis software MaxQda.

The sample of plants analysed covers a wide range of possibilities in terms of unionized workplaces. To track the major changes in labour relations and union-management strategies, I investigated three types of plants: those that are covered by the master agreements; those that were formally owned by Detroit Three OEMs and were spun-off; and those that were spun-off and eventually insourced by the Detroit Three in separate divisions. For all three types, data were collected in both Canada and the United States. This sample enables one to compare different types of situations along the value chain and capture the extent to which the changes were diffused in every type of unionized plant in the sector.

In addition to the interviews, I collected secondary sources to investigate the nature of changes in employment relations. In particular, collective bargaining agreements (local, master agreements where they apply) were analysed to track changes across several aspects concerning labour relations. The sample includes all agreements divided into three categories: pre-crisis (before 2008), crisis (2008–2012), and post-crisis (2013 and onwards). The collective bargaining agreements (CBAs) contain information on numerous aspects of workplace governance, including wages and benefits, employment status, work rules, and union participation. In addition, I collected union materials (bargaining updates, policies, analysis, statements), corporation materials (annual report, statements, website), and press articles.

RECENT CHANGES IN LABOUR AND EMPLOYMENT RELATIONS IN UNIONIZED WORKPLACES: CONVERGENCE, FLEXIBILITY, AND RECENTRALIZATION

The entry into the twenty-first century has been a difficult one for unionized autoworkers in the US and Canada. Shrinking market shares, financial burdens of corporations, and overcapacity precipitated the restructuring of the Detroit Three production networks in both countries. Signs of turbulence were present even before the 2008–9 crisis. In the US, the UAW agreed from 2005 to 2009 to the closing of several plants and to diminishing their membership, mainly through early retirements (Katz, MacDuffie, and Pil 2013). Importantly, the bargaining round of 2007 introduced a new "in-progression" scheme (a "two-tier" structure) for new hires that departed from the "equal pay for equal jobs" principle that has guided the union's action for decades. A Voluntary Employee Benefits Association (VEBA) was also created to manage medical coverage of retirees, a large part of the financial burden for the corporations and, according to managers, a threat to their financial capacity. In Canada, the reopening of the GM agreement was a symbolic move from the CAW that included dispositions on outsourcing, early retirement, and changes to work rules. Sam Gindin (2006), the retired researcher of the CAW, called this opening "the end of the era" – a phrase that was correct at the time, but that would gain its real significance thirty-six months later. In 2008, just before the financial crash, the union also bargained a concessionary agreement that included a grow-in scheme for new hires at the three corporations. While technically not being a "genuine" two-tier system, since workers could achieve the top pay after the period, the concessions nevertheless represented a major blow to the CAW's traditional stance and to its ability to embody a union that made its image through rejecting concessions.

In the fall of 2008, when the Lehman Brothers' bankruptcy precipitated the financial crash, GM and Chrysler were in major financial trouble. The Bush administration agreed to grant emergency loans for the two corporations in exchange for new labour agreements. After the Obama administration was inaugurated, it soon moved to create an auto task force to manage the process of restructuring (Rattner 2010). It rapidly became clear that the use of taxpayers' money would be accompanied with major concessions from the UAW: the elimination of the job banks, the suspension of COLA, the suspension of lump sum increases, competitive work time, and flexibility to schedule work patterns were all targeted by the state (Cutcher-Gershenfeld, Brooks, and Mulloy 2015a). Symbolically, foreign producers would become the norm to follow in terms of labour costs. Several times, the Toyota plant in Kentucky, considered the most mature workplace with head cost at around $47 an hour, was mobilized as the model to justify concessions. In Canada, the Conservative administration of Stephen Harper tended to follow the US moves and adopted a similar stance against autoworkers. As Stanford (2010) argued, this involvement of the state in the auto sector in North America was quite exceptional, illustrating a different political economy and a strong bias against autoworkers despite the fact that labour represented – and still represents – only a fraction of overall auto production costs.

In spring 2009, the UAW and CAW reached deals with the Detroit Three on labour agreements and GM and Chrysler entered bankruptcy. In the US, concessions included a reduction in lines of demarcation between skilled trades, the extension of the two-tier system to all new workers, a defined-contribution retirement plan for the new hires, a percentage of utilization of this workforce, and a no-strike clause with binding arbitration. In Canada, the CAW made concessions on numerous benefits and the extension of the grow-in period. In exchange, governments injected funds into both "new" companies in exchange of shares and the UAW became co-owner of GM and Chrysler through its VEBA fund. Fiat, the Italian OEM, also became a shareholder of Chrysler with a fusion to be realized in the coming years that eventually became FCA. In a reversed pattern bargaining, concessions were also part of the Ford deal even though the corporation did not go into bankruptcy.

In retrospect, the 2008–9 crisis represented a critical moment in labour relations within the North American industry. How have these events concretely transformed employment relations in Canada and the US? I will first present these changes across different aspects of wages, benefits, and work rules. I then turn to the impact on local unions and investment dynamics.

THE RISE OF A MULTI-TIER WORKFORCE

As I have mentioned earlier, one of the guiding principles of the UAW since its inception – and by extension the CAW – has been "equal pay for equal work" on the line. For decades, these norms were part of collective bargaining agreements and few differences between jobs in plants were perceptible. Differences existed between skilled trades and production workers, but within these different categories, few variations were discernable between specific assignations or based on seniority. Moreover, external flexibility was hard for management to push as workers hired in plants were all benefiting from the same status. Seniority rules and job banks in the US ensured laid-off workers their job back following a downturn. As Katz, MacDuffie, and Pil (2013, 58) noted: "the Big Three auto companies, like other large U.S. manufacturing firms, have little flexibility in altering the labour use during the course of the year (short of layoff)." The UAW experimented in the 1980s with some forms of the two-tier system, but it was never fully realized or extended to all workplaces. The IUE pioneered this system during this decade, but the union's low influence in the industry prevented this scheme from being diffused as a norm in the sector. To gain flexibility, corporations generally used outsourcing or early retirement. The latter strategy became a burden as legacy costs exploded while the shrinking number of active workers paying for these benefits placed heavy pressures on corporations.

The 2008–9 crisis reversed these prevailing norms, and led to the rise of a multi-tier workforce. In the most spectacular case, as Dincer (2016) noted for an engine plant in the US, seven different hourly worker tiers coexisted in one workplace. Table 4 presents a comparison between the US and Canada based on different types of plants. For the majority of this sample, the system was introduced during the crisis period and has led to this multi-tier workforce. Differences between Canada and the US are negligible, as both countries tend to follow the same pattern. There is low variation between the different types of plant concerning employment status. The main differences are perceptible in hourly rates.

Interestingly, a third category, temporary workers, emerged during that period. The temps generally make the same wage as the tier 2 employees but, by definition, are not permanent workers and can be laid off easily. The introduction of this category is not negligible. For

Table 4. Starting Pay by Establishment Type and Tier (Hourly Wages, in Local Currency)

		Pre-crisis (2000–6)	Crisis (2008–12)	Post-crisis (2014–17)
Canadian establishments				
In-house covered by the master agreement	Skilled trades	29.85	40.58	40.84
	Production	21.60	33.90 (tier 1) 23.73 (tier 2)	34.15 (tier 1) 20.92 (tier 2)
	Temps		23.73	20.92
	Source (year)	*Local agreement (2000)*	*Ford-CAW bargaining highlights, master agreement (2008–9)*	*Ford-Unifor bargaining highlights, master agreement (2016)*
Spun-off	Skilled trades	29.85	26.33 (tier 1) 23.69 (tier 2)	27.95
	Production	21.60	19.50 (tier 1) 16.58 (tier 2)	16.58
	Source (year)	*Local agreement (2000)*	*Local agreement (2011)*	*Local agreement (2015)*
Insourced	Skilled trades	28.97	29.61	30.09
	Production	22.53	23.17 (tier 1) 16.22 (tier 2)	23.03 (tier 1) 16.12 (tier 2)
	Temps	22.53	16.22	16.12
	Source (year)	*Local agreement (2006)*	*Local agreement (2009)*	*Local agreement (2016)*
US establishments				
In-house covered by the master agreement	Skilled trades	28.99	32.34	32.81
	Production	25.93	28.24 (tier 1) 15.78 (tier 2)	29.33 (tier 1) 17.00 (tier 2)
	Temps		15.78	15.78
	Source (year)	*Local agreement (2003)*	*Local agreement; Ford-UAW contract highlights, master agreement (2011)*	*Local agreement; Ford-UAW contract highlights (2015)*
Spun-off	Skilled trades	23.68 (tier 1) 14.36 (tier 2)	21.60	25.25
	Production	20.01 (tier 1) 8.00 (tiers 2 & 3)	11.30 (tier 1) 10.30 (tier 2)	13.95 (tier 1) 12.95 (tier 2)
	Source (year)	*Local agreement (2002)*	*Local agreement (2008)*	*Local agreement (2017)*
Insourced	Skilled trades	24.94	32.34	32.81
	Production	21.40	16.29	16.25
	Temps		15.78	15.78
	Source (year)	*Local agreement (2000)*	*GM-UAW master agreement (2011)*	*GM-UAW master agreement (2015)*

Reproduced from Dupuis and Greer (2022)

example, Ford in the US reported that 6% of its hourly workforce was in that category in 2019 (Ford Motor Company 2019). By comparison, 43% were legacy workers (hired before 2007), 17% skilled trades, and 34% in-progression. In 2019, of the three corporations in the US, FCA made the more extensive use of in-progression (59%) and temp workers (13%) (Noble 2019). This gives more flexibility for corporations that tend to align their standards with transplants who are well known for extensively using contingent workers in the face of production fluctuations (Cutcher-Gershenfeld, Brooks, and Mulloy 2015b). There are no similar data for Canada, but investments in plants after the crisis have prompted the use of similar categories of workers. For instance, GM's 2020 investment in a pop-up plant in Oshawa led to the hiring of 1,700 workers, all in the grow-in status since it is considered a new plant and the older workforce has been pushed into retirement (Leah and Keetch 2020).

WAGES AND BENEFITS: FROM PRIVATE SOCIAL PROTECTIONS TO DIVERGENCE AND MARKETIZATION

One long-standing management demand in the sector has been the recalibration of labour costs to a "competitive" level. In the parts industry, this means an alignment with the prevailing standards in the non-unionized independent suppliers who compete with unionized plants not covered by master agreements. In the assembly sector, and to some extent in the in-house parts plants covered by master agreements, the prevailing norms, as previously mentioned, are represented by foreign transplants operating at a much more lower labour cost structure. Determining this gap is somehow confusing, since hourly rates, at least for the assembly sector, are not the main issue. Legacy costs and fringe benefits are usually the main drivers of divergence, as foreign producers face fewer financial burdens around these. At Ford, for example, the UAW calculated that its wage premium in 2005, compared to the average manufacturing rate, was 69% (Cutcher-Gershenfeld, Brooks, and Mulloy 2015, 205). Moreover, in 2005, the gap for all-in costs between a Ford worker and a transplant worker was $20.55 per hour ($64.88 compared to $44.33) (Cutcher-Gershenfeld, Brooks, and Mulloy 2015b). In Canada, a similar picture is discernable. In 2008 a CAW member could make up to CDN $35 an hour while the average manufacturing wage was $20.75 an hour (Gohier 2008). All-in costs were evaluated at $77 for a CAW member (Gohier 2008).

Table 5 illustrates the main changes in the wage formula and fringe benefits in the US and Canada during and after the 2008–9 crisis. Differences still remain between the two countries, especially in plants covered by the master agreements. CAW/Unifor has not agreed to profit-sharing, but stagnating COLA and annual raises, and the inclusion of lump sums, have altered the compensation mode in Canada. Major changes have occurred in all cases for the retirement schemes. New hires will now all be under a defined-contributions retirement plan, which is less costly for the employers. In the US, as I have specified earlier, the medical

Table 5. Wages and Benefits, Canadian and US Establishments

		Pre-crisis (2000–6)	Crisis (2008–12)	Post-crisis (2014–17)
Canadian establishments				
In-house covered by the master agreement	Wage formula	COLA, annual increases	COLA, lump sums payments, bonuses, grow-in for new hires	COLA, lump sums payments, annual increases, bonuses, grow-in for new hires
	Pension	DB[a]	DB	DB for legacy employees DC[b] for new hires
	Medical coverage	State provided, employer plan for certain coverages	State provided, co-payment for certain coverages	State provided, co-payment for certain coverages
	Source (year)	Ford-CAW bargaining highlights, *local agreement (2005)*	Ford-CAW bargaining highlights, *local agreement (2012)*	Ford-Unifor bargaining highlights, *local agreement (2016)*
Spun-off	Wage formula	COLA, annual increases	Annual increases, grow-in for new hires	Annual increases, grow-in for all employees
	Pension	DB	DC	DC
	Medical coverage	State provided, employer plan for certain coverages	State provided, co-payment for certain coverages	State provided, co-payment for certain coverages
	Source (year)	Ford-CAW bargaining highlights, *local agreement (2000)*	*Local agreement (2011)*	*Local agreement (2015)*
Insourced	Wage formula	COLA, annual increases, grow-in for new hires	COLA Grow-in for new hires	COLA, annual increases, grow-in for new hires
	Pension	DB	N/A	DC
	Medical coverage	State-provided, co-payment for ertain coverages	State-provided, co-payment for certain coverages	State-provided, co-payment for certain coverages
	Source (year)	*Local agreement (2006)*	*Local agreement (2009)*	*Local agreement (2016)*
US establishments				
In-house covered by the master agreement	Wage formula	COLA, profit-sharing, lump sums, bonuses	Profit-sharing, lump sums, bonuses, grow-in for new hires	COLA, profit-sharing, lump sums, bonuses, grow-in for new hires
	Pension	DB	DB for legacy employees, DC for new hires	DB for legacy employees, DC for new hires
	Medical coverage	Employer-provided	VEBA	VEBA
	Source (year)	Ford-UAW bargaining highlights, *local agreement (2003)*	Ford-UAW bargaining highlights, *local agreement (2012)*	Ford-UAW bargaining highlights, *local agreement (2016)*

(Continued)

Table 5. Continued

		Pre-crisis (2000–6)	Crisis (2008–12)	Post-crisis (2014–17)
Spun-off	Wage formula	COLA, lump sums, profit-sharing, bonuses, grow-in for new hires	Annual increases, bonuses, grow-in for new hires	Annual increases, bonuses, grow-in for new hires
	Pension	DB for legacy DC for new hires	DC	DC
	Medical coverage	Employer-provided	VEBA	VEBA
	Source (year)	*Delphi-IUE master agreement (2003), local agreement (2002)*	*Local agreement (2008), IUE-GM VEBA (2009)*	*Local agreement (2016), IUE-GM VEBA (2009)*
Insourced	Wage formula	COLA, lump sums, profit-sharing, bonuses, grow-in for new hires	Grow-in for all employees, profit-sharing	Grow-in for all employees, annual increases, profit-sharing
	Pension	DB	DC	DC
	Medical coverage	Employer-provided	VEBA	VEBA
	Source (year)	*Delphi-UAW master agreement (2003), local agreement (2000)*	*Delphi-UAW-GM agreement (2007), GM-UAW master agreement (2011), local agreement (2008)*	*GM-UAW master agreement* (2015), *local agreement (2016)*

[a] Defined benefits. [b] Defined contributions.

coverage is now administered by a VEBA at all three corporations. Moreover, and this is not illustrated in the table, some specific changes in fringe benefits were made in both countries, among them reduced insurance coverage, reduced off-days, the end of car vouchers for workers, and changes in work rules such as off-time.

The net result has been that overall labour costs are lower than they were before the Great recession. For UAW hourly members at Ford, which is extensible to the two other firms as variations are negligible, the wage premium compared to the average manufacturing sector was down to 33% in 2015 (Cutcher-Gershenfeld, Brooks, and Mulloy 2015a, 205) and the overall labour costs compared to transplants in 2010 was reduced to $6 ($58 compared to $52) (Cutcher-Gerschenfeld, Brooks, and Mulloy 2015b). In Canada, concessions granted in 2009 similarly reduced the overall labour costs. For example, it was estimated that the deal struck between the CAW and GM in May 2009 lowered labour costs by 15 to $16 an hour (Owram 2009). Outside the master agreements, these differences are difficult to measure as these plants are usually covered by individual agreements. and table 5 illustrates changes in the wage schemes in Canada and the US (some local unions even conceded in basic wages) and in fringe benefits that

Table 6. Classifications by Establishment Type and Worker Status, Canada and US

		Pre-crisis (2000–6)	Crisis (2008–12)	Post-crisis (2014–17)
Canadian establishments				
In-house covered by the master agreement	Skilled trades	20	8	7
	Production	36	12	11
	Source (year)	*Local agreement (2005)*	*Local agreement (2012)*	*Local agreement (2016)*
Spun-off	Skilled trades	33	2	2
	Production	231	5	16
	Source (year)	*Local agreement (2000)*	*Local agreement (2011)*	*Local agreement (2015)*
Insourced	Skilled trades	3	3	3
	Production	12	11	11
	Source (year)	*Local agreement (2006)*	*Local agreement (2009)*	*Local agreement (2016)*
US establishments				
In-house covered by the master agreement	Skilled trades	24	14	14
	Production	26	12	13
	Source (year)	*Local agreement (2003)*	*Local agreement (2012)*	*Local agreement (2016)*
Spun-off	Skilled trades	17	4	4
	Production	21	8	10
	Source (year)	*Local agreement (2002)*	*Local agreement (2008)*	*Local agreement (2016)*
Insourced	Skilled trades	27	8	6
	Production	93	45	34
	Source (year)	*Local agreement (2000)*	*Local agreement (2008)*	*Local agreement (2016)*

logically suppose a decrease in overall labour costs. In Canada, official data, including union and non-union workers, indicate that hourly nominal earnings in the auto parts sector dropped from 2006–13 ($24.23 to $22.31 an hour), while vehicle manufacturing hourly earnings rose modestly during the same period (from $32.87 to $35.37 an hour) (Statistics Canada, 2023).

WORK RULES AND THE LABOUR PROCESS: ACHIEVING FLEXIBILITY AND COOPERATION

For decades, the auto industry organized its labour process around Taylorist principles that included a strict division between management's right to direct and to conceive operations and workers' performance of manual labour. This division was enshrined in CBAs that included,

Table 7. Team Language by Establishment Type, Canada and US

		Pre-crisis (2000–6)	Crisis (2008–12)	Post-crisis (2014–17)
Canadian establishments				
In-house covered by the master agreement	Team language	Yes	Yes	Yes
	Source (year)	*Local agreement (2005)*	*Local agreement (2012)*	*Local agreement (2016)*
Spun-off	Team language	Yes	Yes	Yes
	Source (year)	*Local agreement, (2000)*	*Local agreement (2011)*	*Local agreement (2015)*
Insourced	Team language	Yes	Yes	Yes
	Source (year)	*Local agreement (2006)*	*Local agreement (2009)*	*Local agreement (2016)*
US establishments				
In-house covered by the master agreement	Team language	No	Yes	Yes
	Source (year)	*Local agreement (2003)*	*Local agreement (2012), interviews*	*Local agreement (2016), interviews*
Spun-off	Team language	Yes	Yes	Yes
	Source (year)	*Local agreement (2002)*	*Local agreement (2008)*	*Local agreement 2016)*
Insourced	Team language	No	No	Yes
	Source (year)	*Local agreement (2000)*	*Local agreement (2008)*	*Local agreement (2016)*

among other rules, complex job classifications governing tasks performed by production and skilled trades workers. As mentioned, starting in the 1980s management pushed to reduce job classifications in order to gain flexibility and productivity, and some plants embarked on cooperation and quality programs that implied workforce participation. Before 2008–9, however, these changes were far from finished: some plants were still operating with a high number of job classifications and lean work practices were not standardly diffused. One strong locus of change for lean practices has been the establishment of production systems in every Detroit Three corporation, which has had a strong standardizing effect in work practices, even among suppliers with direct relationships with OEMs that must also conform to these systems. In 1996 GM launched the Global Manufacturing System, which copied and further refined lean practices. Ford followed in 1999 with the Ford Production System and led a series of competitive operative agreements (COAs) in 2006–7 that rationalized work rules in most of its plants (Cutcher-Gershenfeld, Brooks, and Mulloy, 2015a). Chrysler adopted the World Class Manufacturing System in 2009 from Fiat. This structure includes lean standards and certification for plants and suppliers.

As illustrated in table 6, the sample indicates that these pressures for flexible work practices have been evenly distributed in the two countries and along the value chain. All classifications for skilled trades and production have been drastically reduced and all plants – except one where production work is characterized by a high variety of products to manufacture – operate with sixteen or less classifications. Aspects of teamwork, a contentious item in the 1980s and 1990s, are captured in table 7. The table shows that all plants in both the US and Canada now operate with a teamwork-based system. Concerning workers' involvement and quality standards, this item is less standardized and still varies from plant to plant. In theory, all these cases should at least have some form of involvement, as they are affected by the standards in OEMs' production systems. Language in CBAs exhibits strong variations. Nevertheless, similar topics were identified, such as "kaizen operator," "quality statement," "hourly and salaried workers cooperation," "quality team member," and so on. It's difficult to generalize from these items, as it would need a comprehensive observation of work practices in every plant. However, CBA analysis and qualitative interviews tend to confirm that local unions and managements have been engaged in one way or another in some kinds of practices that incorporate lean or quality improvement standards.

RECENTRALIZING INDUSTRIAL RELATIONS AND UNION POLITICS OVER INVESTMENT AND PRODUCTION

Another important result of the 2008–9 crisis has been its impact on the bargaining dynamics over investment and the implication for local union politics. As I have already mentioned, one strong trend in the 1990s was the decentralization of collective bargaining at the local level. The restructuring of unionized workplaces reversed this tendency and has, to a certain extent, recentralized the processes of bargaining, especially concerning investment decisions (Dupuis and Greer 2022).

First, the overall processes of restructuring have been rescaled. National unions, global corporations, and the state have all centrally negotiated to save the industry and to reduce labour costs (Rattner 2010; Stanford 2010).

Second, the trend towards outsourcing in the Detroit Three production networks stalled with the Great Recession. During that period, these corporations decided to insource work, including the repurchasing of plants, in an ad hoc fashion. In certain cases, trade unions played an active role through partnership or leverage to favour insourcing attempts. One important transformation in that regard has been the synchronizing of collective bargaining, platform development, and allocation of products in the Detroit Three production network. Historically, collective bargaining and investment in plants have been separate topics that were not clearly articulated.

In the US, the 2003 UAW-Detroit Three agreements introduced language over sourcing and created a "Business Review Team" in which unionists and salaried people would discuss sourcing decisions. Subsequent rounds of bargaining further refined this process in which the development of new vehicle models is now tied with union-corporation discussions. Two processes are at play: "allocation," in which certain plants are automatically allocated a product according to local capacity; and "bidding," in which plants can engage in a process of bidding, sometimes against outside suppliers, to attract investment and certain programs. In the case of bidding, this process can be highly politicized and can necessitate the establishment of coalitions between local actors and corporate actors in Detroit. Unifor does not have equivalent language in its agreements, but the union is nevertheless active in these processes. Local unions also lobby Detroit and participate in dialogue with corporate managers for product allocation. The shortening of the last agreements in Canada to coordinate their expiration with the UAW indicates that Unifor is motivated to consider the importance of sourcing decisions during bargaining rounds.

Finally, unions are engaged in different strategies at the local level to precipitate the in-sourcing of work. One common pattern is to use the skilled trades language to activate a negotiation over their utilization. I found this type of clause in most of the cases studied. This language specifies that both union and company should review the utilization of outside suppliers when it affects the work of skilled trades. During that process, unions may be able to retain work, according to different factors, and in particular based on costs. In certain cases I have analysed, local unions were incredibly imaginative in bringing work inside their plants: some lobbied the corporations in Detroit with the help of salaried people; others used partnership with managers to successfully attract investment; still others others crafted arguments around falling labour costs and use of grow-in schemes to convince Detroit to allocate products or investment in their plants. There were no strong differences between Canada and the US, as both unions engaged in one form or another of strategies to attract investment.

A LOOK AHEAD

In this chapter, I tracked the major transformations impacting collective bargaining and employment relations in the unionized North American auto industry. While some differences in labour relations persisted between the US and Canada before the twenty-first century, I illustrated that the 2008–9 crisis represents a critical moment that led to a relative convergence between the two countries. The restructuring of the Detroit Three, the vertical disintegration of firm production networks, and the intervention of the state during firm bankruptcies transformed labour and employment relations in three spheres: (1) working conditions that depart from past Fordist norms; (2) the introduction of flexible and lean work practices; and (3) the recentralization of industrial relations over investment dynamics. As I have argued concerning working conditions, these changes directly affect the so-called core workforce that once represented autoworkers, and have led to a model prevalent in the North American private sector that is characterized by a higher level of external flexibility for a certain part of the workforce, a high degree of internal flexibility, and fringe benefits associated with market fluctuations instead of guaranteed rights.

What to expect of labour relations in the coming years? First, the risk of complete marginalization of this model of industrial relations that has characterized the sector is plausible. Pattern bargaining is still in effect and is producing stable working conditions in plants covered by master agreements, but, as I have documented in this chapter, the differences between the Detroit Three unionized plants, foreign OEMs, and even general trends in the private sector are less and less discernable. In the US, the shrinking degree of unionization in both the assembly and parts sectors confirms this tendency. In Canada, the level of unionization is still higher, but the decline of the industry in the past twenty years, especially among the Detroit Three corporations and unionized suppliers, is a threat to the perpetuation of this model of labour relations.

Second, there will be continuing conflicts over employment status in the coming bargaining rounds. In the US, the rise of the multi-tier workforce has revealed tensions on the line between legacy and new workers that have emerged during two difficult bargaining rounds in 2015 and 2019. In Canada, opposition to this has been somewhat less vocal, partly because the rebound of the industry has been slower after the Great Recession, thus limiting the use of the grow-in schemes and temp workers. New investments announced in the past years could catch up to the union, as the use of these types of workers will grow. Unifor will certainly have to face the same pressures as the UAW and find ways to respond to the aspirations of this new workforce.

Finally, it is difficult to ignore the technological and environmental pressures that are sure to shape the auto industry in the coming decade. The seemingly inevitable shifts to Industry 4.0 and electrical vehicles are likely to be positive for unions. However, their effects on jobs and employment are not well known today, and some expect radical changes in work organization (Thibodeau 2019). Unions will then have difficult strategic dilemmas to overcome, including bargaining over new work rules but also over the shrinking of certain activities in their plants. While investments to preserve the industry and unionized jobs are welcome, they also come with risks regarding the future of autoworkers in North America.

REFERENCES

Adler, Paul S. 1993. "The 'Learning Bureaucracy': New United Motor Manufacturing, Inc." In *Research in Organizational Behavior*, vol. 15, edited by Larry L. Cummings and Barry M. Staw, 111–194. Greenwich, CT: JAI.

Anastakis, Dimitry. 2013. *Autonomous State: The Struggle for a Canadian Car Industry from OPEC to Free Trade*. Toronto: University of Toronto Press.

Aronowitz, Stanley. 1992. *False Promises: The Shaping of American Working-Class Consciousness*. Durham: Duke University Press.

Coase, Ronald. 2000. The Acquisition of Fisher Body by General Motors. *Journal of Law and Economics* 43 (1): 15–32. https://www.jstor.org/stable/10.1086/467446.

Cranford, Cynthia, Leah F. Vosko, and Nancy Zukewich. 2003. "Precarious Jobs: A New Typology of Employment." *Perspectives on Labour and Income* 4 (10): 16–26.

Cutcher-Gershenfeld, Joel, Dan Brooks, and Martin Mulloy. 2015a. *Inside the Ford-UAW Transformation: Pivotal Events in Valuing Work and Delivering Results*. Cambridge, MA: MIT Press.

– 2015b. *The Decline and Resurgence of the U.S. Auto Industry*. Briefing Paper no. 399, Economic Policy Institute. https://www.epi.org/publication/the-decline-and-resurgence-of-the-u-s-auto-industry/.

Dincer, Evren. 2016. "The Reindustrialization of the US: An Ethnography of Auto Workers in the Industrial Rust Belt." PhD diss., Cornell University.

Doellgast, Virginia, and Ian Greer. 2007. "Vertical Disintegration and the Disorganization of German Industrial Relations." *British Journal of Industrial Relations* 45 (1): 55–76.

Dupuis, Mathieu. 2018. "Crafting Alternatives to Corporate Restructuring: Politics, Institutions and Union Power in France and Canada." *European Journal of Industrial Relations* 24 (1): 39–54.

Dupuis, Mathieu, and Ian Greer. 2022. "Recentralizing Industrial Relations? Local Unions and the Politics of Insourcing in Three North American Automakers." *ILR Review* 75 (4). https://doi.org/10.1177/00197939211015191.

Ford Motor Company. 2019. *2019 UAW-Ford Negotiations Media Fact Guide*. https://media.ford.com/content/dam/fordmedia/North%20America/US/2019/07/uawford/uaw-ford-media-fact-guide.pdf.

Gindin, Sam. 1995. *The Canadian Auto Workers: The Birth and Transformation of a Union*. Toronto: Lorimer.

– 2006. "Concessions in Oshawa: The End of an Era?" *The Bullet*, 22 March 2006. https://socialistproject.ca/2006/03/b14/.

Gohier, Philippe. 2008. "Do Auto Workers Make Too Much?" *Maclean's*, 18 December 2008. https://www.macleans.ca/economy/business/auto-workers-make-a-lot-of-money-but-not-that-much/.

Hirsch, Barry T., and David A. Macpherson. 2003. "Union Membership and Coverage Database from the Current Population Survey: Note." *Industrial and Labor Relations Review* 56 (2): 349–54. https://www.jstor.org/stable/3590942.

Holmes, John. 2004. "Re-scaling Collective Bargaining: Union Responses to Restructuring in the North American Auto Industry." *Geoforum* 35 (1): 9–21.

Holmes, John, and Anthony Rusonik. 1991. "The Break-Up of an International Labour Union: Uneven Development in the North American Auto Industry and the Schism in the UAW." *Environment and Planning A: Economy and Space* 23 (1): 9–35. https://journals.sagepub.com/doi/10.1068/a230009.

Holst, Hajo. 2014. "'Commodifying Institutions': Vertical Disintegration and Institutional Change in German Labour Relations." *Work, Employment and Society* 28 (1): 3–20.

Jacobides, Michael G., John Paul MacDuffie, and C. Jennifer Tae. 2016. "Agency, Structure, and the Dominance of OEMs: Change and Stability in the Automotive Sector." *Strategic Management Journal* 37 (9): 1942–67.

Jones, A.C. 2010. "Rank-and-File Opposition in the UAW During the Long 1970s." In *Rebel Rank and File: Labor Militancy and Revolt from Below During the Long 1970s*, edited by Aaron Brenner, Robert Brenner, and Calvin Winslow, 281–310. London: Verso.

Katz, Harry C. 1985. *Shifting Gears: Changing Labor Relations in the US Automobile Industry*. Cambridge, MA: MIT Press.

– 1993. "The Decentralization of Collective Bargaining: A Literature Review and Comparative Analysis." *Industrial and Labor Relations Review* 47 (1): 3–22.

Katz, Harry C., John Paul MacDuffie, and Frits K. Pil. 2013. "Crisis and Recovery in the US Auto Industry: Tumultuous Times for a Collective Bargaining Pacesetter." In *Collective Bargaining under Duress: Case Studies of Major North American Industries*, edited by Howard R. Stanger, Paul F. Clark, and Ann C. Frost, 45–79. Ithaca: Cornell University Press.

Klier, Thomas, and James M. Rubenstein. 2013. "Restructuring of the U.S. Auto Industry in the 2008–2009 Recession." *Economic Development Quarterly* 27 (2): 144–59. https://journals.sagepub.com/doi/abs/10.1177/0891242413481243.

Kumar, Pradeep, and John Holmes. 1996. "Change, but in What Direction? Divergent Union Responses to Work Restructuring in the Integrated North American Auto Industry." In *Social Reconstructions of the World Automobile Industry*, edited by Frederic C. Deyo, 159–99. London: Palgrave Macmillan.

Leah, Tony, and Rebecca Keetch. 2020. "General Motors Returns to Oshawa – But Offers Only Second-Tier Jobs in a 'Pop-Up' Plant." *Labor Notes*, 25 November 2020. https://labornotes.org/2020/11/general-motors-returns-oshawa-offers-only-second-tier-jobs-pop-plant.

Lichtenstein, Nelson. 1995. *The Most Dangerous Man in Detroit: Walter Reuther and the Fate of American Labor*. New York: Basic Books.

Milkman, Ruth. 1997. *Farewell to the Factory: Auto Workers in the Late Twentieth Century*. Berkeley: University of California Press.

Noble, Breana. 2019. "Temps, Former Tier 2 Biggest Challenge for FCA in Labor Talks." *Detroit News*, 17 November 2019. https://www.detroitnews.com/story/business/autos/chrysler/2019/11/17/temporary-progression-employees-biggest-challenge-uaw-talks-fiat-chrysler/2519484001/.

O'Brady, Sean. 2021. "Fighting Precarious Work with Institutional Power: Union Inclusion and Its Limits across Spheres of Action." *British Journal of Industrial Relations* 59 (4): 1084–1107. https://doi.org/10.1111/bjir.12596.

Owram, Kristine. 2009. "CAW Members Vote in Favour of Cost-Cutting Deal with GM." *CP24*, 25 May 2009. https://www.cp24.com/caw-members-vote-in-favour-of-cost-cutting-deal-with-gm-1.401575.

Parker, Mike, and Jane Slaughter. 1988. *Choosing Sides: Unions and the Team Concept*. Boston: South End.

Rattner, Steven. 2010. *Overhaul: An Insider's Account of the Obama Administration's Emergency Rescue of the Auto Industry*. Boston: Houghton Mifflin Harcourt.

Rinehart, James, Christopher Huxley, and David Robertson. 1997. *Just Another Car Factory?: Lean Production and Its Discontents*. Ithaca: ILR.

Rubinstein, Saul A., and Thomas A. Kochan. 2001. *Learning from Saturn: Possibilities for Corporate Governance and Employee Relations*. Ithaca: Cornell University Press.

Rutherford, Tod D., and John Holmes. 2013. "(Small) Differences That (Still) Matter? Cross-Border Regions and Work Place Governance in the Southern Ontario and US Great Lakes Automotive Industry." *Regional Studies* 47 (1): 116–27.

– 2014. "Manufacturing Resiliency: Economic Restructuring and Automotive Manufacturing in the Great Lakes Region." *Cambridge Journal of Regions, Economy and Society* 7 (3): 359–78.

Siemiatycki, Elliot. 2012. "Forced to Concede: Permanent Restructuring and Labour's Place in the North American Auto Industry." *Antipode* 44 (2), 453–73.

Stanford, Jim. 2010. "The Geography of Globalization and the Politics of Auto Bailouts." *Cambridge Journal of Regions, Economy and Society* 3 (3): 383–405.

Statistics Canada. 2023. "Table 14-10-0206-01: Average Hourly Earnings for Employees Paid by the Hour, by Industry, Annual." https://doi.org/10.25318/1410020601-eng.

Sweeney, Brendan A., and Greigory D. Mordue. 2017. "The Restructuring of Canada's Automotive Industry, 2005–2014." *Canadian Public Policy* 43 (S1): S1–S15.

Thibodeau, Ian. 2019. "Shift to Electric Vehicles Will Radically Change Auto Factories." *Detroit News*, 5 September 2019. https://www.detroitnews.com/story/business/autos/2019/09/05/shift-electric-vehicles-radically-change-auto-factories/2208961001/.

Unifor. 2020. "Unifor Reaches Tentative Agreement with Ford Motor Company." 22 September. https://wardsintelligence.informa.com/.

Ward's Automotive. 2019. "US Total Vehicle Sales Market Share by Company." https://wardsintelligence.informa.com/datacenter.

Weil, David. 2014. *The Fissured Workplace*. Cambridge, MA: Harvard University Press.

Wells, Donald M. 1997. "When Push Comes to Shove: Competitiveness, Job Insecurity and Labour-Management Cooperation in Canada." *Economic and Industrial Democracy* 18 (2): 167–200.

Womack, James P., Daniel T. Jones, and Daniel Roos. 1990. *The Machine That Changed the World*. New York: Rawson Associates.

Yates, Charlotte. 1993. *From Plant to Politics*. Philadelphia: Temple University Press.

12

Prometheus Bound? Technology and Labour in the North American Automotive Industry

Tod Rutherford

In his magnum opus *The Unbound Prometheus* (1969) David Landes argued that the Industrial Revolution was driven by dynamic synergies between the division of labour and technology. Landes was optimistic that entrepreneurs and markets would produce optimal economic, if not social, outcomes. Today, we have entered an arguably less sanguine period in which disruptive technologies are heralded, yet concerns are raised regarding not only job loss and displacement but a more permanent secular and technological stagnation in which Prometheus is increasingly constrained (Brynjolfsson and McAfee 2014; Gordon 2016; Storm 2019). Recently, some observers have also argued that the automobile industry, which for over a century has been in the forefront of new manufacturing technology, may also produce employment dislocations or be subject to technological restraints (Groshen et al. 2018; Pardi, Krzywdzinski, and Luethje 2020), a pattern that other chapters within this collection build upon. For example, in chapter 9 Kazzaz, Greene, and Yates discuss the disruptions associated with the advent of electrification; in chapter 6 Dziczek and Swiecki assess the effect of evolving content rules on automakers' investment strategies.

Such concerns establish the context for this chapter: an examination of technological change and labour in the North American automotive industry, focusing on processes for manufacturing technologies. Shifts in product technology – such as ongoing innovations in lightweighting as well as the advent of connected and electric vehicles (EVs) – are impacting work technology and organization. In fact, the automotive industry has long been in the vanguard of process technological adoption, including mass and lean production and now, according to some pundits, Industry 4.0. I argue that this process has not simply been determined by the immanent or inherent qualities or potential of technology itself, but has also been shaped by management cultures, institutional factors including state policies, and in particular the role played by labour. As such, labour in the automotive industry has not only been affected by technology introduction, it has shaped technological change itself. This chapter also underlines that the relationship between labour and technological change has been both antagonistic and cooperative. That, along with the factors above, has meant that the geography of technological change, while subject to strong convergence pressures, has also been geographically uneven, both between and within the US, Canada, and Mexico.

This chapter is structured as follows. First, I examine debates over the technology-labour relationship, emphasizing its role at both the macro-economic and micro-workplace scales. While workers and their representatives in North America seldom have formal input into technological adoption, they have been important actors in three ways: (1) in their role, following more heterodox economics arguments, as collective macro-agents, including via state intervention, and wage or cost push factors in technology adoption; (2) in how concerns over labour control and productivity play a role in technology design; and (3) in their role in post-adoption *technological or work system governance*, including overall employment levels, maintenance, and other, often informal interventions that are critical to technology's actual performance. Following this overview, I outline the twentieth-century uneven adoption of Fordist mass production in the US, Canada, and Mexico. I examine the ambivalence towards mass production by workers and trade unions around work intensification and concerns over the employment impacts of automation. The chapter also reviews the adoption of lean production, an innovation that addressed slowing productivity and which after 1970 represented an alternative to largely failed automation experiments, especially in final assembly operations. Finally, this chapter will examine current debates around the adoption of Industry 4.0 as a digital technology-led advanced manufacturing paradigm. Despite its apparent promise, Industry 4.0 adoption is being impeded by a range of technical problems, supply chain power asymmetries, and Fordist/Taylorist managerial philosophies. The effect is that, so far, Industry 4.0 is being only partially implemented.

THE TECHNOLOGY-LABOUR RELATIONSHIP IN CONTEXT

The study of technology and labour has a long history (Marx [1867] 1971; Mumford 1934; Landes 1969; Noble 2011). Context for understanding that history is provided on three levels. The first concerns how the technology-labour relationship is conceptualized. Many mainstream or conventional studies of technology often "fetishize" it as a thing in which its effects are given or immanent in the technology itself (Edwards and Ramirez 2016). In fact, even Marx was criticized for accepting Andrew Ure's perspective that Industrial Revolution machinery had completely subordinated, if not eliminated, the need for workers (Edwards 2001). Yet far from possessing given effects, technologies are subject to, and shaped by, complex socio-spatial forces, including those involving labour-management relations (Noble 2011; Arboleda 2017). Predicting technology's impacts is also difficult because, even though technologies have some immanence effects that follow from their physical or artefactual aspects, especially in their early adoptive stages, they are also shaped by overall market conditions, public policies, and workers and their representatives (Edwards and Ramirez 2016, 111–12).

The second aspect of technology is the macro and micro impacts of labour legislation and unions on technological adoption and overall firm and economic performance (Freeman and Medoff 1984; Betcherman 2012; Addison 2014; Stelzner and Cerrutti 2018). Neoclassically influenced research argues that union "rent seeking" and state intervention leading to higher wages and costs reduce the capital available for firms to invest in technology or R&D (Hirsch 2010). However, heterodox approaches contend that trade unions and state intervention favouring workers are important factors in wage or cost push investment by firms in new technology (Betcherman 2012; Gordon 2016; Storm 2019). By closing off lower wage options, stronger labour legislation and worker power enhance technological investment (Stelzner and Cerrutti 2018).

The third aspect of technology-labour study is more micro or workplace-centred and examines both the types of labour involved in technological adoption and technology's impacts on worker conditions. In this perspective, workers' "voice" – especially collective – plays a critical role (Freeman and Medoff 1984). However, this varies considerably over different skill levels and stages of technological innovation. Thus, engineering and managerial labour have considerable influence on the conceptual and artefactual design of technology. Yet even in European economies with co-determination institutions, shop-floor employee input typically occurs only very late in the adoption process (Clark et al. 1988; Bosch and Schmitz-Kießler 2020).

Micro-level studies, then, explore how labour and the employment relationships inform the technological adoption processes. Technological development cannot be reduced to labour control or cost issues, but such concerns are never far from the minds of engineers and managers. First, despite constituting a declining share of manufacturing and especially automotive industry, total costs of direct labour still represent a significant share of value added in an industry often characterized by relatively low profit margins (Williams et al. 1995). Second, workers themselves have complex attitudes towards new technology. On the one hand, they fear its potential to erode skill, quality of work life, and job security. On the other, they welcome technological investment as a sign of a firm's continuing commitment to the viability of their establishment (Daniel 1987). Finally, there can be a significant difference between technology's potential and actual performance in terms of uptime, quality, and reliability, and as such, technological adoption can involve considerable "learning by doing," which can open it up to worker influence (Edwards and Ramirez 2016). Thus, even if the intent is to control or displace labour, technological change may have unintended consequences, including the reliance it engenders on shop-floor worker interventions in order for firms to achieve operational goals. As such, shop-floor labour plays an important role in both the *informal governance* of technology and, where unions are present, in its *formal governance*. This can include bargaining over labour allocation, training, and health and safety.

These latter considerations are illustrated in Noble's (2011) study of the adoption of numerical control (N/C) machinery by General Electric (GE) in the 1950s. By being centrally programmed, N/C machinery could bypass skilled unionized workers and put control into the hands of management. However, N/C machinery's actual performance was very uneven – its quality was erratic, and it was prone to expensive downtime. To work effectively, N/C ultimately required the cooperation of the skilled workforce in its *technological governance* that GE had sought to displace. Employee informal and formal governance roles, then, point to the continued salience of production labour in the adoption of new technology. Furthermore, because such governance roles are influenced by a range of factors, including establishment-specific labour-management relations and overall employment and industrial relations laws, how governance affects technological adoption is subject to significant geographic variation (Rutherford and Holmes 2007).

FROM MASS PRODUCTION TO LEAN MANUFACTURING: TECHNOLOGICAL DEVELOPMENT OF THE TWENTIETH-CENTURY NORTH AMERICAN AUTOMOTIVE INDUSTRY

New technology adoption in the twentieth-century automobile industry illustrates many of the above points. Mass production initiated in Henry Ford's Highland Park plant in 1913 was subject to significant challenges, failures, and transformations. While Ford's decision to adopt the assembly line was mostly based on wanting to produce a mass-market car cheaply, he inevitably confronted significant issues surrounding labour. Like other automobile manufacturers, Ford initially relied on the skill of craft workers. The introduction of the assembly line presented an opportunity to wrest control from such employees (Meyer 1981).

While Ford's assembly line gets the majority of attention, his innovations also included interchangeable parts and specialized rather than general-purpose machinery (Hounshell 1984). In addition, many of his initial productivity gains were generated by taking out indirect labour, as only 15% of the employees worked on the assembly line (Williams, Haslam, and Williams 1992). Furthermore, while Ford's mass production system was more flexible than some observers maintain, its highly centralized structure focused on the Model T reached its limits by the mid-1920s, when more decentralized competitive rivals such as General Motors introduced greater product ranges and variety. GM also emphasized the rapid reconfiguration of general-purpose machinery, significantly reducing the time for model changes and ultimately forcing Ford to follow suit (Hounshell 1984).

Another major challenge was the habituation of semi-skilled labour to the demands of assembly systems. Workers, largely unaccustomed to major increases in work intensity incumbent in assembly production work, quit. In 1914, immediately following assembly-line introduction, daily absenteeism reached 10% while employee turnover soared to 370%, meaning that Ford needed to hire 52,000 workers in one year to keep the 14,000-employee plant operating (Meyer 1981). To address this, Ford introduced the Five Dollar Day. While this program was partially based on profit-sharing, it represented a doubling of the average industrial wage. Moreover, the Five Dollar Day was contingent on each worker passing a six-month probation and submitting their personal and domestic lives to investigation by Ford's sociological department (Meyer 1981).

Ford's new "high-wage" strategy, however, was not copied during the 1920s by GM and Chrysler, who continued to use piece rates (Gindin 1995). Nor did Ford and other automotive manufacturers avoid significant wage cuts and layoffs when the Depression began in 1929. The formation of industrial unionism – most notably the United Auto Workers (UAW) in Detroit in 1935 – and the subsequent strikes in both the US and Canada were significant challenges to automobile manufacturers. While strikes were principally around union recognition, they also featured shop-floor struggles to gain greater worker control over the labour process and technological governance, including assembly-line speed-ups and workload (Wells 1995). However, in the initial post-war period, both the US and Canadian UAWs increasingly recognized management workplace rights, while union strategies became increasingly focused upon higher wages and benefits (Gindin 1995). Nonetheless, as worker wages became linked to productivity and increased New Deal labour standards were adopted in the post-war period, this gave a strong incentive for manufacturers to invest in technology (Stelzner and Cerrutti 2018; Storm 2019).

Post-war union bargaining thus moved away from a direct challenge to management's control over technology and assembly processes. However, during the 1950s and 1960s the UAW under Walter Reuther became increasingly concerned over the employment impacts of a new wave of automation in which formerly discrete production operations of handling, fabricating, and moving individual parts were linked by interlocking "transfer" machines (Meyer 2004). This development marked an extension of assembly processes into component parts and displaced shop-floor employment. The UAW viewed automation as having a clear anti-labour and anti-union intent (Steigerwald 2010). Union concerns, though, did not translate into technological issues assuming greater priority in collective bargaining. Rather, the union favoured federal government policy action by the Democratic Kennedy and Johnson administrations.

Another factor shaping mass production in North America was the impacts of differing markets and public policies, especially in Canada and Mexico. Between the initial development of the Canadian automotive industry around the Second World War until 1965, Canadian public policies were largely based on the 1879 National Policy tariffs designed to protect domestic industry (Anastakis 2005). This led to American firms such as Ford and GM establishing branch plants to serve Canadian and British Empire markets. However, due to the relatively small size and segmentation of the Canadian market, plants had problems achieving economies of scale (Holmes 1983). Furthermore, American assemblers imported components from the United States. The effect of this was that by the late 1950s Canada was running a substantial deficit in automotive trade (Anastakis 2005). To resolve this crisis, in 1965 Canada negotiated a conditional free trade agreement with the United States permitting the continental integration of components and assembly operations. This allowed Canadian plants to achieve improved economies of scale and secure both US and Japanese investment, a policy framework that endured until the WTO overturned the Auto Pact in 2001.

Such US-Canadian differences were also evident in industrial relations. By 1937, Canadian automobile workers were represented by the US-based UAW. However, in the post-war period the Canadian union was relatively autonomous, less centralized, and more democratic than its US counterpart (Gindin 1995). The Canadian UAW also moved away from direct shop-floor challenges to managerial prerogatives over technology use (Wells 1995). Nonetheless, the union secured more concessions around technological governance than its US counterpart (Yates 1993).

Mass production technology adoption and labour relations in Mexico were also shaped by unique national circumstances. The Mexican automobile industry was established mostly in the Mexico City region in the 1920s and 1930s and, as in Canada, was part of US assembler international expansion programs and a response to tariff protection offered to local assembly operations (Middlebrook 1989, 71). Original equipment manufacturers (OEMs) based in Mexico were located there to serve the local market. However, the high costs associated with annual model changes, combined with high-scale economies in some production phases such as stampings, meant these firms also needed to export to the rest of Latin America (Bennett and Sharpe 1979, 182).

In 1962, Mexico adopted import substitution policies mandating that 60% local content be purchased from independent Mexican suppliers. While this made foreign OEMs develop full production capacities, it also led to increasing trade deficits that ultimately caused Mexico to adopt a more export-oriented strategy in the 1970s. At that point, Mexico lowered local content rules and established the maquiladora program in northern Mexico near the US border, shifting the geographical centre of the auto industry away from Mexico City. This export focus intensified after Mexico's 1982 economic crisis and led to its joining with the US and Canada in the 1994 NAFTA agreement (Klier and Rubenstein 2017).

One factor underlying this spatial shift was the geography of Mexican collective labour organizing. As Middlebrook (1989) explains, the post-1962 growth of the Mexican automotive industry spurred the development of independent, democratic unions, especially in the Mexico City area. These unions pushed back against manufacturers' arbitrary movement of workers and "quickly won greater control over the production process. This included input on production rates, in-plant workforce distribution, increasing equalization of wage categories, and the establishment of occupational health and safety measures" (Middlebrook 1989, 85). However, union advances were undermined by export-oriented production regimes centred on the maquiladoras, where both OEMs and component manufacturers reasserted shop-floor control by recruiting in greenfield, low-wage rural areas and circumventing independent unions by signing contracts with compliant, government-sanctioned unions (Wenten 2017). (See Covarrubias V. and Dufour-Poirier's chapter 13 in this collection for a more expansive discussion of Mexican labour union proclivities.)

The availability of a low-wage labour workforce was not the only factor underlying the Mexican automotive industry's rapid post-NAFTA expansion (Swieki and Menk 2016). Nonetheless, the availability of low-cost quality engineering and semi-skilled assembly workers contributed a distinctive NAFTA spatial division of labour in which Mexico specialized principally in labour-intensive small car production assembly for export to the rest of North America (Klier and Rubenstein 2017).

MACHINES VS. LEAN: TECHNOLOGICAL DEVELOPMENT AND LABOUR, 1980–2010

As described above, post-war technological adoption in the automotive industry was modified by national circumstances and worker and union influence. Such automation was largely the incremental extension of Fordism. Besides the use of transfer machines, this included the first applications of industrial robots by GM in 1970 focused primarily on engine production, "body in white" areas (including welding and painting), and sub-assembly production, rather than final assembly "where most of the variety and complexity of the assembly process converged, was still manually intensive and concentrated over 60% of the total employment in the factories" (MacDuffie and Pil 1997, 247). Addressing this final assembly "bottleneck" was a critical element of automotive technological strategies after 1980.

By the mid-1970s, not only was productivity stagnating and labour costs increasing but, induced by higher energy prices, North American OEMs were confronting increasing offshore competition, especially from Japanese small car imports (Holmes 1987). This intensified North American manufacturers' motivation to address the crisis of productivity and costs via an intensive adoption of new technology. The strategy was premised on the latest computer-based technologies being able to cope with the complexities of variation of, especially, final assembly, and to monitor and control feedback, including identifying and rectifying overall production system errors (Pardi, Krzywdzinski, and Luethje 2020; Kopp, Howaldt, and Schultze 2016). As Pardi, Krzywdzinski, and Luethje (2020, 7) sum up:

> The result of these massive efforts was extremely expensive factories with a high level of final assembly automation like the Fiat Cassino plant, the GM Hamtramck plant and the VW's Hall 54 in Wolfsburg, whose performances were overall disappointing due to frequent machine stops, which affected productivity and quality, and low flexibility, which constrained and slowed down the introduction of new models.

Such high-tech solutions thus proved expensive and ineffective. However, a low-technology alternative – the Toyota Production System (TPS) or lean production – soon became hegemonic. As Williams, Haslam, and Williams (1992) note, TPS represented a return to aspects of Ford's original strategy of removing indirect labour. However, TPS extended this principle: minimize resource waste via the use of multiskilled workers, quick set-ups and changeover, and kaizen or continuous quality-improvement techniques. Thus, as Krafcik (1988, cited in Yin, Stecke, and Li 2018, 850) argued, lean manufacturing requires the use of less of everything throughout the production of the product, including less labour, space, tools, investments, and time, which can lead to keeping less inventory and achieving few inventory defects, resulting in variety and greater production.

Lean manufacturing was a less technology-intensive option, but it nonetheless had significant implications for the types of technologies deployed and how they were used. It involved "hard" technologies such as computer-aided design and manufacturing (CAD-CAM), especially in components manufacturing, and the use of cellular manufacturing (Yin, Stecke, and Li 2018, 851). It is principally an organizational innovation focusing "soft" technologies such as quality analysis and benchmarking to improve production processes. It also involves flatter managerial hierarchies and greater employee and team autonomy in work design and performance and task rotation (Aghazadeh and Seyedian 2004; Lippert et al. 2014).

By the mid-1980s, because of the high work intensity of lean production, Japanese automotive producers, encountering recruitment difficulties, began to adopt "human-fitting" technologies in the most stressful work areas (Pardi, Krzywdzinski, and Luethje 2020, 7). Based on lean production, Japanese automotive producers achieved significant reductions in labour hours per vehicle and superior quality compared to North American producers (Womack, Jones, and Roos 1990). Furthermore, Japanese manufacturers successfully transferred lean production to their North American transplant operations (Kenney and Florida 1993). Thus, by the early 1990s North American automotive OEMs and their suppliers were forced to emulate TPS methods.

Importantly, because of its emphasis on teamwork, lean production had significant implications for North American labour utilization. Union observers questioned whether it broke with Taylorism/Fordism or intensified it. The process of kaizen and teamworking required renegotiation of collective agreements, especially over work rules, with both the UAW and the newly established Canadian Auto Workers (CAW; after 2012, Unifor), which broke away from the UAW in 1985 (Gindin 1995). Due to overcapacity, model mix, and plant performance, the UAW was in a weaker position than the CAW and quickly accepted lean production – and most notably teamworking (Cutcher-Gershenfeld, Brooks, and Mulloy 2015). The CAW had a stronger structural position and a more assertive union culture; it opposed lean production and established the Department of Work Organization in 1993, the only North American union to have such an office (Gindin 1995). Thus, in a notable strike against the GM-Suzuki CAMI plant, it sought concessions around lean production, including insisting on the election of team leaders (Rinehart, Huxley, and Robertson 1997). Eventually, however, the CAW shifted to a strategy of engagement that encouraged "productiveness" (Yates 1993). The union proved pragmatic around individual plant's relative competitive positions, a situation that led to greater adoption of teamworking at some establishments (Wells 1997). Furthermore, both the CAW/Unifor and UAW negotiated contracts around overall production standards and the right to have ergonomics technicians negotiate work norms and mitigate the often high levels of repetitive strain injuries associated with lean production, practices that were explored by Rutherford and Frangi (2020) as well as Dupuis in chapter 11 of this collection.

Thus, the main impact of Canadian and US unions on lean production centred on its technological governance. In Canada, the relative strength of the CAW/Unifor meant that its credible threat to unionize Japanese transplant operations led the latter to adopt more union-substitution practices than in the United States, including practices associated with wages and shift systems (Rutherford 2001). In Mexico, unions were mostly government controlled and significantly weaker. Nonetheless, Wenten (2017) found that Mexican unions had negotiated considerable amendments to shift-and-pay systems, the use and deployment of teams, and the ability of workers to influence the organization of work and time in production areas. Despite this governance role, from the mid-1990s onwards North American unions did not directly oppose or offer any real alternatives to lean production (Rutherford and Frangi 2020). The success of (comparatively) low-technology lean production systems meant that more technology-focused alternatives were largely abandoned. Its success meant that even though more flexible robots were introduced in paint and body shops, by 2000 the rate of automation in assembly had not progressed significantly since the late 1980s (Pardi, Krzywdzinski, and Luethje 2020, 8).

There were several other reasons why automation levels did not advance. First, at a global scale, some of the wage pressures that had pushed manufacturers to adopt new technology during the 1980s had mostly abated after 1990, as the global labour force increased due to the fall of the Soviet Union and the further integration of China and India into the world market. Second, while manufacturers sought to increase standardization by adopting global platforms and using common components between models, this was offset by intensified market segmentation and accompanying model variety, which, especially in final assembly, depressed automation levels. Finally, the ongoing greening and interconnectedness of the automobile demanded considerable capital for product investment, thus leaving less funds for automation. The impact of these factors in North America will be explored below.

ROBOTS, AI, AND ALL THAT: TOWARDS AN INDUSTRY 4.0/SMART MANUFACTURING PARADIGM?

By the mid-1990s, lean production or TPS had become the paradigmatic form of automotive production, both in final assembly and in components manufacture (Lippert et al. 2014).

However, after the 2008–9 economic crisis, a new paradigm began to emerge, initially in Germany as Industrie 4.0 and in North America as Smart Manufacturing (Pardi, Krzywdzinski, and Luethje 2020). Industry 4.0 refers to the digitally driven integration of manufacturing (Rainnie and Dean 2020, 18). This includes technologies such as robotics automation, sensors, artificial intelligence, big data, cloud computing, virtual reality (VR), augmented reality (AR), and additive manufacturing (i.e., 3D printing). These tools are creating new forms of human-machine interaction or "cyber-physical" production systems, including touch interfaces, augmented-reality systems, and "big-data" analytics (Edwards and Ramirez 2016, 110).

The introduction of Industry 4.0 also brought with it a strong managerial discourse, primarily as a German response to increasing competitive challenges from China (Pfeiffer 2017). As such, national and sectoral context matters to the interpretation of Industry 4.0. In Germany, for example, it is viewed as a critical enabler of a deeper transformation, not only in manufacturing but in all sectors of the economy (Rainnie and Dean 2020, 20). In the automotive sector, Industry 4.0 interest reflects several intersecting pressures and opportunities. The first are the perceived limitations of lean manufacturing. For example, Yin, Stecke and Li (2018, 851) document that while lean manufacturing was able to reduce demand variability in volume and variety dimensions, it was less successful with mixed-product assembly lines in reducing the time dimensions. Such apparent limits is one reason why OEMs have shown renewed interest in advanced forms of automation. As the International Labour Organization (ILO 2020, 16) summarizes, these reasons include the need

> to reduce lead times and increase customization. Furthermore, digitalization is disrupting the entire automotive supply chain, from product design to the sale of automobiles. Technological advances are also enabling manufacturers to offer new products and services, such as EVs and automated vehicles (AVs).

Another factor influencing Industry 4.0 adoption in the automotive industry is shifting product strategies, especially for electric vehicles (EVs). EVs currently constitute only 2% of all US vehicle sales, but rapid advances in battery and other technologies are significantly lowering vehicle costs so that by 2035 all car and truck sales could be electric (Phadke and Abhyankar 2021). As the ILO (2020, 21) suggests, Industry 4.0 technologies promise greater manufacturing streamlining, which can reduce the parts required to produce vehicles, especially EVs:

> OEMs and parts suppliers have primarily adopted 3D printing to lower the costs of specialized equipment (such as moulds, jigs and fixtures) and to reduce pre-production model design time. Yet on-demand 3D printing also holds the potential to facilitate the in-house production of parts and could save manufacturers considerable time and resources,

reconfiguring the automotive value chain in the process. In 2014, United States-based Local Motors produced the world's first 3D-printed EV, consisting of only 50 individual parts, compared to almost 30,000 in a traditional vehicle.

The application of digital sensors on discrete production operation both within and between plants and firms also promises the ability to lower costs, reduce lead times, and allow end-to-end analytics of the supply chain (ILO 2020, 22). Digitalization, then, is viewed as critical for allowing effective communication and coordination of machines, workers, and managers (Pardi, Krzywdzinski, and Luethje 2020).

Robots are another important facet of Industry 4.0. While robots have been used in the North American automotive industry for over fifty years, their capabilities have grown considerably in recent years. This includes improvements to their full running costs, including the cost of maintenance (Helper, Martins, and Seamans 2018). By 2019 in the US, automotive manufacturing accounted for 39% of all robot installations. Globally, the automotive sector is the largest user of robots among manufacturing industries, accounting for 30% of total installations (ILO 2020, 21). Innovations in robotic technology such as lightweight mobile co-bots are being deployed in both parts and final assembly operations. At Canadian suppliers Magna and Linamar, for example, co-bots are used mainly for visual inspection of parts or picking out components on an assembly line, repetitive tasks that are often linked with the highest rates of employee turnover (Simone 2020). A related innovation is the development of self-moving chassis, which allow automotive assembly to move away from conventional fixed routes and permit a greater range of models to be manufactured in a single plant (Peters et al. 2014, 6–7). Technological innovation is also being applied to workers directly via wearable technologies such as Google Glass and augmented reality devices, effectively integrating production operators into the digital loop of information (Peruzzini, Grandia, and Pellicciari 2020).

Therefore, there has been increasing media and scholarly interest in Industry 4.0 technologies in the North American automotive industry (Groshen et al. 2018; Simone 2020). This has occurred while there have been significant new rounds of investment in new plant and equipment by manufacturers. Thus, between 2009 and 2019 firms invested $147.9 billion at North American sites. The great majority of this occurred in the United States ($114.5 billion), with $24.7 billion (17%) in Mexico and $8.7 billion (6%) in Canada (Swiecki 2020).

While these investments are important to local and regional automotive manufacturing ecosystems, it is not certain if they will usher in a qualitative shift towards Industry 4.0. As noted earlier, new product development such as EVs may be supported by Industry 4.0 processes. However, they can also be facilitated by existing technologies. Moreover, even before the COVID pandemic began in 2020 overall sales and production were falling. Total North American vehicle production peaked in 2016 at 18 million and declined to around 17 million by 2019. In the United States this decline was even more significant, with production falling from 12.18 million to 10.87 million during same period while total sales fell from 14.13 million in 2015 to 13.68 million in 2019 (US Bureau of Transportation Statistics). Alexander and Keyler (2020) suggest that a less positive environment had caused firms to rethink some of their advanced automation investments. Even in 2016, for example – when automotive profit margins were the highest in a decade – the top ten OEMs averaged only a 4% return on invested capital, barely covering their borrowing costs (Parkin and Wilk 2017).

Importantly, there remains a significant gap between the promise and the performance of Industry 4.0 technologies. Manufacturers are confronting significant challenges in adopting digital technologies in the comprehensive, integrated way suggested by the purveyors of Industry 4.0. Thus, despite US manufacturers spending over $330 billion on digital projects in 2018, there was a reported failure rate of 84% on digital transformation projects (Groden-Morrison 2019). Due to technical challenges, many firms remain in "pilot purgatory," with only 30% able to capture value from Industry 4.0 technologies at scale (Garms et al. 2019). There are also important limitations to many Industry 4.0 technologies. Take, for example, co-bot technology. Even though co-bots are faster to reprogram than industrial robots and have a smaller footprint, they are slower, the amount of payload they can carry is limited, and they are not as durable (Simone 2020).

The technical limitations of robotic technologies mean that they have remained largely excluded from final assembly operations. For example, Honda's Marysville Ohio assembly plant has 342 robots for manufacturing the Accord, but these are found almost exclusively in painting and welding operations; only 20 are in final assembly (Lippert 2018). In fact, according to the International Federation of Robots (IFR 2019), between 2016 and 2018 car manufacturers' investment in robotic automation fell by 26%. Thus, among OEMs, final assembly operations remain labour intensive:

> Today, final assembly lines in automotive series production are characterized by dozens of well-defined workplaces rowing up in one fixed route. Each station has a fixed work program and a more or less fixed number of employees which can be smoothed by the so called "drifting" of single workers. The cars move along the lines and are assembled in a strict sequence at the stations. The material is delivered to the stations in the order of processing ... robots are only used very little and only in fixed positions and for specific tasks in final assemblies. (Peters et al. 2014, 6–7)

There is also substantial evidence that even when automotive firms adopt new technology, they are still informed by Taylorist mass production paradigms. For example, a survey of US automotive manufacturers by Fiorelli, Dziczek, and Schlegel (2019) found that companies are not taking advantage of the potential benefits and capabilities that new machines offer. This is especially the case with data analysis, where less than 8% of respondents used the sensors on machines to send data to unified corporate business systems (e.g., ones integrating data from other operations, HR, finance, and sales), with one firm reporting that the "company is using its new equipment in much the same way as it used old machines" (Fiorelli, Dziczek, and Schlegel 2019, 13).

Additionally, implementation of Industry 4.0 in automotive manufacturing is affected by asymmetric interest and capabilities. Specifically, increased technological investment is confined mostly to the top tier of suppliers and coexists with existing machinery. As the ILO (2020, 20) finds:

> Digital technologies are interacting with existing technologies, such as welding robots, that have been utilized in vehicle manufacturing for decades. Nevertheless, access to these technologies is not evenly distributed throughout the supply chain. Advanced digital technologies used by OEMs and large parts suppliers often coexist with legacy technologies in many SMEs in lower segments of the supply chain.

In the United States these findings are confirmed by Kuan, Snow, and Helper's (2015, 3) study showing that independent small and medium-sized enterprise (SME) suppliers confronting downward pressures on prices and profits were "performing less innovative activity and specific asset investment, producing lower value products, and somewhat avoiding investment altogether." This was especially the case for single plant operations employing fifty or fewer workers that had sustained themselves, especially after the 2008–9 recession, by investing below-average amounts in R&D and using older technology.

This means that amongst US suppliers, Industry 4.0 technology adoption is uneven and segmented. A similar situation confronts Canadian- and Mexican-based suppliers. As noted above, while larger first tier suppliers in Canada (e.g., Magna and Linamar) *are* investing in Industry 4.0 automation, smaller Canadian-owned plants are less engaged. Canada also has fewer policy tools in place to facilitate technology transfer to SMEs (Holmes, Rutherford, and Carey 2017), a problem replicated in Mexico (Guthrie 2017). Additionally, the Mexican auto industry relies heavily on foreign direct investment (FDI) (Klier and Rubenstein 2017). Associated with that, key technological innovations in Mexico are mostly imported, causing low levels of development of that country's domestic value chain (Simonazzi, Carreto Sanginés, and Russo 2020, 17). The result is that overall automotive automation rates are lower in Mexico than either the US or Canada.

Uneven – and mostly limited – Industry 4.0 proliferation over the last decade has coincided with increased debate over employment losses linked to advanced technology adoption (Brynjolfsson and McAfee 2014; Acemoglu and Restrepo 2017). However, past experience of technological adoption's effect on employment levels suggests that the most significant challenge associated with it is the displacement of existing workers as occupations and jobs are restructured (Autor 2015). Nonetheless, the relationship between technological adoption and labour is complex and is an outcome of technology's labour-saving propensities and its countervailing labour-generating effects. As Acemoglu and Restrepo (2017, 32) argue, labour-generating effects have been too weak to offset technology's labour-saving tendencies. The effect of this is that labour's share of income has declined, a turn of events that has caused further inequality.

The trend of technology-inspired labour displacement poses challenge to both firms and government (Groshen et al. 2018). That challenge is exacerbated by the fact that so far, the uptake of robotic technology appears associated with skill polarization in the labour force. For example, a recent Statistics Canada report concluded: "Firms adopting them [robots] tend to hire more, not fewer, workers. But they hire fewer managers to oversee them, and tasks and responsibilities shift within the firm. Turnover increases for all types of workers, but middle-skilled workers appear to fare worse than both their high and low skilled counterparts" (Dixon 2020, 1).

Some of the challenges captured above are masked by the fact that adjustments are occurring during a time of overall automotive industry employment growth. In North America, for example, direct employment increased 47% between 2009 and 2017, led by Mexico, where automotive employment almost doubled. Since that time, however, auto industry employment has entered a period of uncertainty. While this uncertainty is due partly to Industry 4.0 challenges (and opportunities), more relevant factors include increasing trade tensions, a global slowdown in vehicle production and sales, and the climate change–induced shift to EVs. Indeed, the latter presents a considerable challenge, a consequence of the fact that EVs require fewer parts than internal combustion engines. This has led to concerns that an EV transition will be accompanied by considerable employment loss, with estimates ranging from 35,000 union jobs by the US UAW to 400,000 in the German auto industry over the next five to ten years (Dawson, Naughton, and Coppola 2019; ILO 2020).

Certainly, technology affects employment and wages (see, for example, Acemoglu and Restrepo 2017). However, other scholars put less emphasis on technology as a factor contributing to declining wages (Gould 2019). Indeed, they argue that since the 2008–9 recession, the automotive industry has experienced a slowing pace of advanced automation adoption. The suggestion is that technology proliferation has slowed due to wage suppression and outsourcing (Gordon 2016; Stelzner and Cerrutti 2018; Moody 2018; Fiorelli, Dziczek, and Schlegel 2019). One contributor to this is the availability of significantly cheaper Mexican labour. It is also a function of growing production in non-union locations in southern US "right to work" states (Rothstein 2016).

Especially since the 2008–9 crisis firms have secured lower entry-level wages and benefits in unionized establishments. While the Canadian Unifor union has been able to negotiate grow-in periods, new hires can take more than ten years to achieve standard full-time rates. This has led to multiple tiers of workers, and in some unionized US plants, there are up to ten levels of workers performing similar jobs. Labour costs have also been lowered through the increasing use of temporary workers. In some unionized plants, temporary workers represent between 10 and 25% of the total workforce (Lepadata and Janoski 2018). Additionally, since the year 2000 unionized automotive OEMs have increased outsourcing, augmented in part by their spinning off of their formally captive suppliers like GM-Delphi (Upjohn Institute 2020). Finally, automotive firms have a long history of reducing labour costs via work intensification using such measures as decreasing cycle time, deploying alternative shift systems, and reducing break times (see Rothstein 2016; Moody 2018).

Such wage-suppression strategies have had a dramatic impact both on labour's share of total automotive production costs and on worker wages. In the 1990s and early 2000s labour costs ranged between 10 and 15% of total production costs. By 2019, they had dropped to 5 % (Cody 2015; Drizek 2019). Furthermore, Drizek (2019) shows that while nominal wages for US workers in the auto-manufacturing sector increased by 6% from $28.49 in 2002 to $30.20 in 2018, real wages fell by 23.5%. Indeed, real wages have also fallen for skilled workers even when there are shortages (Fiorelli, Dziczek, and Schlegel 2019). Similarly, over the same time Canadian assembly and parts real wages stagnated and declined for significant segments of both unionized and non-unionized Canadian automotive (Auto Labour Market Information Project 2019, 16). In Mexico, estimated total labour compensation (wages, social benefits, etc.) is 18% of the US average, and despite significant employment growth and skill shortages there has been no increase in real wages since the signing of NAFTA in 1994 (Swieki and Menk 2016, 32). Moreover, there is debate about the extent to which the USMCA will alter that pattern.

According to Moody (2018) and Pardi, Krzywdzinski, and Luethje (2020), lack of wage and labour cost pressures in the North American automotive industry has reduced incentives for firms to invest in Industry 4.0. In fact, the Bureau of Labor Statistics (BLS) reports limited gains in capital productivity in US manufacturing, including automotive manufacturing. It is suggested that any productivity gains achieved have been a function of outsourcing and work intensification, not capital investment (Brill, Chansky, and Kim 2018). As Fiorelli, Dziczek, and Schlegel (2019, 6) explain: "Firms who are adopting this technology do not seem to be using the equipment to its full capability. Instead, companies tend to use automation to substitute for the shortage of workers they are unable to find at wages they are willing to pay."

In the Mexican case, real wage stagnation and decline is an outcome of both weaker labour market institutions – including a lack of independent unions *and* automation effects. As UNCTAD (2017:57) concluded:

> Unit labour costs declined faster on average in activities relying more on robotic automation than in industries with low robot density. As a result, such automation mostly rewarded capital and contributed to the downward trend in labour income share in Mexico, which declined by about 10 percentage points during the period 1995–2014. Moreover, real wages in the highly automated automotive sector dropped by 1.6 per cent between 2011 and 2015, while real wages expanded by 1.5 per cent in manufacturing as a whole.

We can conclude, with Pardi, Krzywdzinski, and Luethje (2020), that advanced Industry 4.0 automation in the North American automotive industry is characterized by more of an incremental path-dependent series of experimentations consisting of the adoption of discrete advanced technologies than a wholesale shift towards Industry 4.0.

North American patterns regarding wages, productivity and technological investment are not unique. In Germany, automotive OEMs pay wages that are higher, on average, than US assembly plants. Since 2000, German workplaces have been marked by overall wage suppression. On top of that, automation in German automotive factories has been stagnant since the 1990s, and only marginal increases in productivity have been registered. The OECD (2018) reveals that the average rate of annual labour productivity growth in German manufacturing since 2006 has deteriorated and is now well below that of most of its advanced economy competitors. More generally, the European Central Bank (2017) has also noted how wage suppression via the delinking of wages from productivity growth has contributed to a European-wide problem of low levels of technological investment.

Therefore, whether an Industry 4.0 transition is ongoing involves the question of labour's role. As described, the issue is near universal. In that regard, several North American and European researchers have argued that integration of Industry 4.0 technologies must be accompanied by significant involvement of employees, especially shop-floor workers and their representatives (Totterdill 2015; Edwards and Ramirez 2016; Groshen et al. 2018). In North America, some OEMs *have* recognized the need to reform labour's governance role to better confront Industry 4.0 challenges. For example, the UAW has negotiated with GM to have skilled trades workers run 3D printing rooms as part of what Helper, Martins, and Seamans (2018) term "worker-enhancing" strategies. In both Canada and the United States unions have the right to negotiate over the employment effects of technological change, including securing rights to notice of technological change and facilitating training to prevent contracting out of work (UAW 2019a, 58). Also with GM, concerns over the introduction of Industry 4.0 technologies led to the 2019 UAW-GM contract establishing a joint National Committee on Advanced Technology. It meets quarterly to discuss how GM plans to implement new technologies such as EVs, autonomous vehicles, and 3D printing, and what impact they might have on UAW jobs (Noble 2019). Both the UAW and Unifor believe they maximize their influence around Industry 4.0 through collective bargaining agreements, which "means keeping workers at the centre of decision-making when it comes to technological change [including] that workers deserve to have early notice of upcoming technological changes, the right to participate in and benefit from new opportunities, and the right to negotiate new language arising from those changes" (Unifor 2018, 17).

In the end, the ability of North American automotive unions to play a significant role in shaping advanced automation and its governance remains open to question, a consequence of there being a lack of institutional support for direct forms of employee voice within an industrial relations system that has traditionally been adversarial in nature (Lippert et al. 2014). In the wake of the 2008–9 crisis some North American OEMs *were* granted UAW board representation. However, on balance, North American firms have been reluctant to grant workers and unions a co-determination role based largely on anticipation that doing so would be accompanied by higher wage demands (Helper, Krueger, and Wial 2012). (Canada's Unifor has remained resistant to formal co-management relations.)

Beyond ambiguity surrounding labour-related technological process governance, these trends have arisen during a period when union density within the North American automotive industry has declined. For example, the US share of union-manufactured light vehicles fell from 75% in 2004 to just over 50% in 2012. Declines in Canada have been similar; in 2016 union density was 48% (Unifor 2018). In Mexico, many auto workers are unionized but tend to have little autonomy. While more assertive independent Mexican unions have emerged, their coverage remains limited (Ramírez and Marinaro 2019).

In addition to the contradictory approaches described above in terms of governance between countries and unions, there are also inconsistent attitudes and tactics between firms. As mentioned above, GM did agree to discussion and governance surrounding certain aspects of technological introduction and how it affects the workplace. At Ford – despite its official commitments to negotiating worker upskilling around Industry 4.0 – the 2019 UAW Ford contract saw the union agree to a Taylorist strategy, allowing the firm to deploy digital video recording and path-mapping technologies to surveil and better control worker movements (Brooks 2019). Typically, unions face deep challenges in negotiating new technology. Despite legal and contract rights to advanced notification over new technology, their involvement occurs late in the adoption process; they have little input into the design of technology itself. Furthermore, shop-floor representatives often lack the technological expertise to bargain effectively around advanced automation (Rutherford, 2021). Even German unions and works councils, which have modified co-determination to obtain greater involvement in technology adoption, confront difficulties. Similar to the experience in North America, these challenges include lack of knowledge of works councillors and firms' resistance to sharing powers over technology (Bosch and Schmitz-Kießler 2020).

CONCLUSION

Framing a chapter about technology and labour in the North American automotive industry around the question "Prometheus Bound?" might seem unexpected. After all, for at least a century the automobile industry has been a byword for technological innovation and prodigious output. Yet as has been argued, such innovation has never been just a "technical" issue, but one inextricably bound up in the employment relationship between labour and capital. This relationship has involved both conflict and cooperation. Indeed, technological adoption has never been simply about labour costs and control. Even so, such concerns do influence managerial decisions, including the governance of new technology. This chapter traced this relationship over the course of the twentieth century, arguing that a combination of converging pressures around issues like quality and cost, as well as contrasting state policies and approaches to labour relations, have meant that the US, Canada, and Mexico have followed interlinked – but differentiated – paths.

Such patterns are also evident in debates surrounding Industry 4.0 within the North American automotive industry. The industry has long been at the vanguard of technological advancement, including most recently the development of EVs and autonomous vehicles. It has also employed technologies associated with digitally linked process automation (including co-bots, AI, and wearable technologies). However, a more thorough deployment of Industry 4.0 instruments has been impeded by narrowing profit margins, sluggish sales, and uneven production. This has caused the final assembly operations of automotive OEMs, as well as the operations of smaller suppliers, to remain relatively unautomated. Advanced automation investment in the North American automotive manufacturing industry has also been suppressed by wage suppression and work intensification strategies. On top of that, greater influence of workers in both technology design and governance has been hindered by an overall weakening of unions and the continued influence of Taylorist managerial philosophies.

The North American automotive industry's technology-labour relationship seems a Janus-faced Prometheus. Viewed from its technological side, its innovative and productive capacities are undeniable. Yet its labour perspective appears contradictory and less sanguine. As the evidence around Industry 4.0 advanced automation illustrates, its contemporary role is constrained. That said, it is important to remember that the Prometheus myth was also a metaphor for unintended consequences. Such asymmetries constraining labour may also be bound by any Industry 4.0 transition.

REFERENCES

Acemoglu, Darron, and Pascual Restrepo. 2017. "Robots and Jobs: Evidence from U.S. Labor Markets." Working Paper no. 23285, National Bureau of Economic Research. http://www.sipotra.it/wp-content/uploads/2017/04/Robots-and-Jobs-Evidence-from-US-Labor-Markets.pdf.

Addison, John T. 2014. "The Consequences of Trade Union Power Erosion." *IZA World of Labor*. https://wol.iza.org/articles/consequences-of-trade-union-power-erosion/long.

Aghazadeh, Seyed-Mahmoud, and Mojtaba Seyedian. 2004. "The High-Performance Work System: Is It Worth Using?" *Team Performance Management* 10 (3/4): 60–4. https://doi.org/10.1108/13527590410545054.

Alexander, Jason, and Lawrence Keyler. 2020. "For Auto Suppliers, Reassessing Capital Spending Is Key for Innovation." *RSM,* 13 November 2020. https://rsmus.com/insights/industries/manufacturing/for-auto-suppliers-reassessing-capital-spending-is-key-to-innova.html.

Anastakis, Dimitri. 2005. *The Auto Pact: Creating a Borderless North American Industry*. Toronto: University of Toronto Press.

Arboleda, Martin. 2017. "Revitalizing Science and Technology Studies: A Marxian Critique of More-than-Human Geographies." *Environment and Planning D: Society and Space* 35 (2): https://doi.org/10.1177/0263775816664099.

Auto Labour Market Information Project. 2019. *Automotive Industry Labour Market Analysis: Wage Report*. Toronto. https://automotivepolicy.ca/wp-content/uploads/2019/12/Wage-Report.pdf.

Autor, David. 2015. "Why Are There Still So Many Jobs? The History and Future of Workplace Automation." *Journal of Economic Perspectives* 29 (3): 3–30. https://www.jstor.org/stable/43550118.

Bennett, Douglas, and Kenneth E. Sharpe. 1979. "Transnational Corporations and the Political Economy of Export Promotion: The Case of the Mexican Automobile Industry." *Industry International Organization* 33 (2): 177–201. https://www.jstor.org/stable/2706609.

Betcherman, Gordon. 2012. "Labor Market Institutions: A Review of the Literature." Policy Research Working Paper no. 6276. Washington, DC: World Bank. https://openknowledge.worldbank.org/handle/10986/16382.

Bosch, Gerhard, and Jutta Schmitz-Kießler. 2020. "Shaping Industry 4.0 – An Experimental Approach Developed by German Trade Unions." *Transfer: European Review of Labour and Research* 26 (2): 189–206. https://journals.sagepub.com/doi/10.1177/1024258920918480.

Brill, Michael, Brian Chansky, and Jennifer Kim. 2018. "Multifactor Productivity Slowdown in U.S. Manufacturing." *Monthly Labor Review*, July 2018. Washington, DC: US Bureau of Labor Statistics. https://doi.org/10.21916/mlr.2018.19.

Brooks, Chris. 2019. "Why Did the UAW Agree to Let Ford Expand Its Surveillance Technology for Assembly Workers?" *Jacobin*, 11 November 2019. https://bit.ly/3svw8xY.

Brynjolfsson, Erik, and Andrew McAfee. 2014. *The Second Machine Age: Work, Progress, and Prosperity in a Time of Brilliant Technologies*. New York: Norton.

Clark, John, Ian McLoughlin, Howard Rose, and Robin King. 1988. *The Process of Technological Change: New Technology and Social Choice in the Workplace.* Cambridge: Cambridge University Press.

Cody, John. 2015. *How Labor Manages Productivity Advances and Crisis Response: A Comparative Study of Automotive Manufacturing in Germany and the US.* Global Labour University Working Paper no. 32. Geneva: International Labour Organization.

Cutcher-Gershenfeld, Joel, Dan Brooks, and Martin Mulloy. 2015. "The Decline and Resurgence of the U.S. Auto Industry." Economic Policy Institute Briefing Paper no. 399, 6 May 2015. Washington, DC: Economic Policy Institute. https://www.epi.org/publication/the-decline-and-resurgence-of-the-u-s-auto-industry/.

Dawson, Chester, Keith Naughton, and Gabrielle Coppola. 2019. "Auto Workers Fear EVs Will Be Job Killers." *Automotive News*, 27 September 2019. https://canada.autonews.com/labour/auto-workers-fear-evs-will-be-job-killers.

Daniel, William. 1987. *Workplace Industrial Relations and Technical Change.* Shaftesbury, UK: Francis Pinter.

Dixon, Jay. 2020. *The Effects of Robots on Firm Performance and Employment*. Statistics Canada Catalogue no. 11-626-X, no. 126. Ottawa: Statistics Canada. https://www150.statcan.gc.ca/n1/pub/11-626-x/11-626-x2020024-eng.htm.

Dziczek, Kristen. 2019. *The Issues in 2019 UAW-FCA, Ford, & GM Negotiations*. 9 September 2019. Ann Arbor, MI: Center for Automotive Research. https://www.cargroup.org/the-issues-in-2019-uaw-fca-ford-gm-negotiations/.

Edwards, Steve. 2001. "Factory and Fantasy in Andrew Ure." *Journal of Design History* 14 (1): 17–33.

Edwards, Paul, and Paulina Ramirez. 2016. "When Should Workers Embrace or Resist New Technology?" *New Technology, Work and Employment* 31 (2): 99–113.

European Central Bank. 2017. "The Slowdown in Euro Area Productivity in a Global Context." ECB Economic Bulletin no. 3. https://www.ecb.europa.eu/pub/economic-bulletin/html/eb201703.en.html#IDofArticle1.

Fiorelli, Terni, Kristin Dziczek, and Trishi Schlegel. 2019. *Automation Adoption & Implications for the Automotive Workforce.* Ann Arbor, MI: Center for Automotive Research.

Freeman, Richard, and James Medoff. 1984. *What Do Unions Do?* New York: Basic Books.

Garms, Florian, Christian Jansen, Christoph Schmitz, Stefan Hallerstede, and Andreas Tschiesner. 2019. *Capturing Value at Scale in Discrete Manufacturing with Industry 4.0.* Report. Frankfurt, Germany: McKinsey & Company. https://mck.co/3sykL8y.

Gindin, Sam. 1995. *The Canadian Autoworkers: The Birth and Transformation of a Union.* Toronto: Lorimer.

Gordon, Robert. 2016. *The Rise and Fall of American Growth: The US Standard of Living since the Civil War.* Princeton: Princeton University Press.

Gould, Elise. 2019. "State of Working America Wages 2019: A Story of Slow, Uneven and Unequal Growth over the Last 40 Years." 20 February 2019. Washington, DC: Economic Policy Institute. https://www.epi.org/publication/swa-wages-2019/.

Groden-Morrison, Amy. 2019. "The Missing Link in Industry 4.0: Employee Engagement." Alpha Software. https://www.alphasoftware.com/blog/the-missing-link-in-industry-4.0-employee-engagement.

Groshen, Erica, Susan Helper, John-Paul MacDuffie, and Charles Carson. 2019. "Preparing U.S. Workers and Employers for an Autonomous Vehicle Future." Upjohn Institute Technical Report no. 19-036. Kalamazoo, MI: W.E. Upjohn Institute for Employment Research. https://bit.ly/3qyqxVZ.

Guthrie, Amy. 2017. "Trump Talk Aside, Auto Manufacturing and Automation Are Booming in Mexico." *MIT Technology Review*, 12 July 2017. https://www.technologyreview.com/2017/07/12/242345/trump-talk-aside-auto-manufacturing-and-automation-are-booming-in-mexico/.

Helper, Susan, Timothy Krueger, and Howard Wial. 2012. *Why Does Manufacturing Matter? Which Manufacturing Matters? A Policy Framework.* Metropolitan Policy Program at Brookings, Brookings Institute, Washington, DC, February 2012. https://www.brookings.edu/wp-content/uploads/2016/06/0222_manufacturing_helper_krueger_wial.pdf.

Helper, Susan, Raphael Martins, Robert Seamans. 2018. *Value Migration and Industry 4.0: Theory, Field Evidence, and Propositions.* Paper presented at the Torino RENIR Workshop, Turin, 19–20 February 2018.

Hirsch, Barry. 2010. "Unions, Dynamism, and Economic Performance." IZA Discussion Paper no. 5342. Forschungsinstitut zur Zukunft der Arbeit/Institute for the Study of Labor, Bonn, Germany, November 2010. https://www.econstor.eu/bitstream/10419/52094/1/670019674.pdf.

Holmes, John. 1983. "Industrial Re-organization, Capital Restructuring and Locational Change: An Analysis of the Canadian Auto Industry in the 1960s." *Economic Geography* 59: 51–71.

– 1987. "Industrial Restructuring in a Period of Crisis: An Analysis of the Canadian Automobile Industry, 1973–1987." *Antipode* 20 (1): 19–51.

Holmes, John, Tod Rutherford, and Jeff Carey. 2017. "Challenges Confronting the Canadian Automotive Components Industry: What Role for Public Policy?" *Canadian Public Policy* 43 (1): 75–89.

Hounshell, David. 1984. *From the American System to Mass Production, 1800–1932.* Baltimore: Johns Hopkins University Press.

International Federation of Robots (IFR). 2019. *World Robotics 2019 Preview*. Frankfurt Main, Germany: IFR. https://ifr.org/downloads/press2018/IFR_World_Robotics_Outlook_2019_-_Chicago.pdf.

International Labour Organization (ILO). 2020. *The Future of Work in the Automotive Industry: The Need to Invest in People's Capabilities and Decent and Sustainable Work*. Issues paper for the Technical Meeting on the Future of Work in the Automotive Industry, Geneva, International Labour Office, Sectoral Policies Department, 4–8 May 2020.

Kenney, Martin, and Richard Florida. 1993. *Beyond Mass Production: The Japanese System and Its Transfer to the U.S.* Oxford: Oxford University Press.

Kim, Jaewon, John Paul MacDuffie, and Frits K Pil. 2010. "Employee Voice and Organizational Performance: Team versus Representative Influence." *Human Relations* 63 (3): 371–94.

Klier, Thomas, and Robert Rubenstein. 2017. "Mexico's Growing Role in the Auto Industry under NAFTA: Who Makes What and What Goes Where." *Economic Perspectives* 41 (6): 1–29. https://www.chicagofed.org/publications/economic-perspectives/2017/6.

Kopp, Ralf, Jürgen Howaldt, and Jürgen Schultze. 2016. "Why Industry 4.0 Needs Workplace Innovation: A Critical Look at the German Debate on Advanced Manufacturing." *European Journal of Workplace Innovation* 2 (1): 7–23.

Kuan, Jennifer, Daniel Snow, and Susan Helper. 2015. "Supplier Innovation Strategy: Transactional Hazards and Innovation in the Automotive Supply Chain." Social Science Research Network (SSRN). https://ssrn.com/abstract=2567536.

Landes, David. 1969. *The Unbound Prometheus: Technological Change and Industrial Development in Western Europe from 1750 to the Present*. Cambridge: Cambridge University Press.

Lepadata, Darina, and Thomas Janoski. 2018. "Just-in-Time Workforce? Temporary Workers as a Structural Aspect of Lean Production in the US Auto Industry." *International Journal of Automotive Technology and Management* 18 (2): 160–79.

Lippert, Inge, Tony Huzzard, Ulrich Jürgens, and William Lazonick. 2014. *Corporate Governance, Employee Voice, and Work Organization: Sustaining High-Road Jobs in the Automotive Supply Industry*. Oxford: Oxford University Press.

Lippert, John. 2018. "Human vs. Robots: The Car Production Debate." *Bloomberg News*, 23 January 2018. https://www.bnnbloomberg.ca/humans-vs-robots-the-car-production-debate-1.976017.

MacDuffie, John Paul, and Frits Pil. 1997. "From Fixed to Flexible: Automation and Work Organization Trends from the International Assembly Plant Study." In *Transforming Assembly: Experience in Automation and Work Organization*, edited by Koichi Shimokawa, Urlick Jürgens, and Takahiro Fujimoto, 238–54. Berlin: Springer.

Marx, Karl. [1867] 1971. *Capital: A Critique of Political Economy*. Moscow: Progress.

Meyer, Stephen. 1981. *The Five Dollar Day: Labor Management and Social Control in the Ford Motor Company, 1908–1921*. Albany: SUNY Press.

– 2004. "The Automobile in American Life and Society: The Degradation of Work Revisited: Workers and Technology in the American Auto Industry, 1900–2000." http://www.autolife.umd.umich.edu/Labor/L_Overview/L_Overview.htm.

Middlebrook, Kevin. 1989. "Union Democratization in the Mexican Automobile Industry: A Reappraisal." *Latin American Research Review* 24 (2): 69–93.

Moody, Kim. 2018. "High Tech, Low Growth: Robots and the Future of Work." *Historical Materialism* 26 (4): 3–34.

Mumford, Lewis. 1934. *Technics and Civilisation*. New York: Harcourt, Brace.

Noble, Breana. 2019. "UAW-GM Deal Adds Tech Committee to Address Industry Changes." *Detroit News*, 23 October 2019. https://bit.ly/3bMxeQ3.

Noble, David. 2011. *Forces of Production: A Social History of Industrial Automation*. New York: Routledge.

OECD (Organisation for Economic Co-operation and Development). 2018. "OECD Economic Surveys: Germany." Report. Paris: OECD. https://www.oecd.org/economy/surveys/Germany-2018-OECD-economic-survey-overview.pdf .

Pardi, Tomasso, Martin Krzywdzinski, and Boy Luethje. 2020. *Digital Manufacturing Revolutions as Political Projects and Hypes: Evidences from the Auto Sector*. International Labour Organization Working Paper no. 3. Geneva: ILO.

Parkin, Rich, and Reid Wilk. 2017. "The Automakers' Dilemma: Getting More Impact from Innovation Capital." *strategy+business,* 27 July 2017. https://www.strategy-business.com/blog/The-Automakers-Dilemma-Getting-More-Impact-from-Innovation-Capital?gko=cc676.

Peruzzini, Margherita, Fabbio Grandia, and Marcello Pellicciari. 2020. "Exploring the Potential of Operator 4.0 Interface and Monitoring." *Computers & Industrial Engineering* 1 (39): 1–19.

Peters, Steven, Gisela Lanza, Jun Ni, Jin Xiaoning, Yi Pei-Yun, and Marcello Colledani. 2014. "Automotive Manufacturing Technologies – An International Viewpoint." *Manufacturing Review* 1 (10): 1–12. https://re.public.polimi.it/handle/11311/969002.

Pfeiffer, Sabine. 2017. "Industry 4.0 in the Making – Discourse Patterns and the Rise of Digital Despotism." In *The New Digital Workplace: How New Technologies Revolutionize Work*, edited by Abigail Marks, Kendra Briken, Shiona Chillas, and Martin Krzywdzinski, 21–42. London: Macmillan Palgrave.

Phadke, Amol, et al. 2021. *2035 Report: Plummeting Costs and Dramatic Improvements in Batteries Can Accelerate Our Clean Transportation Future*. 21 April 2021. Goldman School of Public Policy, University of California, Berkeley.

Rainnie, Al, and Mark Dean. 2020. "Industry 4.0 and the Future of Quality Work in the Global Digital Economy." *Labour & Industry: A Journal of the Social and Economic Relations of Work* 30 (1): 16–33.

Ramírez, Cirila, and Paolo Marinaro. 2019. "The Remaking of the Mexican Labor Movement in the Automotive Industry." *Labor and Society* 22 (1): 9–23.

Rinehart, Jim, Chris Huxley, and David Robertson. 1997. *Just Another Car Factory?: Lean Production and Its Discontents*. Ithaca: ILR.

Rothstein, Jeffrey. 2016.*When Good Jobs Go Bad: Globalization, De-unionization, and Declining Job Quality in the North American Auto Industry*. New Brunswick, NJ: Rutgers University Press.

Rutherford, Tod. 2001. "Mutual Adaptation: Japanese Automobile Transplants in North America and the Restructuring of Buyer-Supplier Relations." *Environments* 29 (3): 73–89.

– 2021. "'Negotiate the Algorithm': Labor Unions, Scale and Industry 4.0 Experimentation." In *Revaluing Work(ers): Toward a Democratic and Sustainable Future*, edited by Tobias Schulze-Cleven and Todd E. Vachon, 79–100. Labor and Employment Relations Association Series. Ithaca: Cornell University Press.

Rutherford, Tod, and Lorenzo Frangi. 2020. "Is Industry 4.0 a Good Fit for High Performance Work Systems? Trade Unions and Workplace Change in the Southern Ontario Automotive Assembly Sector." *Relations Industrielles/Industrial Relations* 75 (4): 751–73.

Rutherford, Tod, and John Holmes. 2007. "'We Simply Have to Do that Stuff for Our Survival': Labour, Firm Innovation and Cluster Governance in the Canadian Automotive Parts Industry." *Antipode* 39 (1): 194–221. https://onlinelibrary.wiley.com/doi/abs/10.1111/j.1467-8330.2007.00512.x.

Simonazzi, Annamaria, Jorge Carreto Sanginés, and Margherita Russo. 2020. "The Future of the Automotive Industry: Dangerous Challenges or New Life for a Saturated Market?" Working Paper no. 141, Institute for New Economic Thinking, 24 November 2020. https://www.ineteconomics.org/uploads/papers/WP_141-simonazzi-carreto-russo.pdf.

Simone, Rose. 2020. "Human-Like Robots Arrive, Creating a New Industry within the Automotive Industry." *Automotive News Canada*, 25 February 2020. https://canada.autonews.com/technology/human-robots-arrive-creating-new-industry-within-auto-industry.

Steigerwald, David. 2010. "Walter Reuther, the UAW, and the Dilemmas of Automation." *Labor History* 51 (3): 429–53.

Stelzner, Mark, and Enzo Cerrutti. 2018. "Workers and Technological Change in the United States." *Labor History* 59 (6): 657–75.

Storm, Servaas. 2019. "The Secular Stagnation of Productivity Growth." Working Paper no. 108, Institute for New Economic Thinking, 12 December 2019. https://www.ineteconomics.org/uploads/papers/Storm-WP-108-The-Secular-Stagnation-of-Productivity-Growth.pdf.

Swiecki, Bernard. 2020. "North American Auto Manufacturing Challenges during a Global Pandemic." Center for Automotive Research, Ann Arbor, MI, 3 April 2020. https://www.remi.com/event/bernard-swiecki-north-american-auto-manufacturing-challenges-during-a-global-pandemic/.

Swiecki, Bernard, and Debbie Maranger Menk. 2016. *The Growing Role of Mexico in the North American Automotive Industry: Trends, Drivers and Forecasts.* Center for Automotive Research, Ann Arbor, Michigan. https://www.cargroup.org/wp-content/uploads/2017/02/The-Growing-Role-of-Mexico-in-the-North-American-Automotive-Industry-Trends-Drivers-and-Forecasts.pdf.

Totterdill, Peter. 2015. "Closing the Gap: The Fifth Element and Workplace Innovation." *European Journal of Workplace Innovation* 1 (1): 55–74.

Unifor. 2018. *The Future of Work Is Ours: Confronting Risks and Seizing Opportunities of Technological Change.* Unifor Toronto. https://www.unifor.org/resources/our-resources/future-work-ours-confronting-risks-and-seizing-opportunities-technological.

United Auto Workers. 2019a. "2019 Proposed Resolution: Special Convention on Collective Bargaining." 11–13 March 2019. Detroit: United Auto Workers. https://uawfca.wordpress.com/2019/03/15/2019-uaw-special-bargaining-convention-update/.

– 2019b. "UAW-General Motors Contract Summary: Hourly Workers." 7 October 2019. Detroit: United Auto Workers. https://uaw.org/wp-content/uploads/2023/11/56100-UAW_hourly-1.pdf.

United Nations Conference on Trade and Development (UNCTAD). 2017. *Trade and Development Report 2017 – Beyond Austerity: Towards a Global New Deal.* Report by the secretariat of UNCTAD. New York: UN. https://unctad.org/system/files/official-document/tdr2017_en.pdf.

Upjohn Institute. 2020. "Automotive Industry." W.E. Upjohn Institute for Employment Research, Kalamazoo, MI. https://www.upjohn.org/major-initiatives/outsourcing-impacts-us-workforce/research/automotive-industry.

US Bureau of Transportation Statistics. 2022. "Annual U.S. Motor Vehicle Production and Domestic Sales." https://www.bts.gov/content/annual-us-motor-vehicle-production-and-factory-wholesale-sales-thousands-units.

Wells, Don. 1995. "Origins of Canada's Wagner Model of Industrial Relations: The United Auto Workers in Canada and the Suppression of 'Rank and File' Unionism, 1936–1953." *Canadian Journal of Sociology/Cahiers canadiens de sociologie* 20 (2): 193–225.

– 1997. "When Push Comes to Shove: Competitiveness, Job Insecurity and Labour-Management Cooperation in Canada," *Economic and Industrial Democracy* 18: 167–200.

Wenten, Frido. 2017. "Does It Matter What Workers Do? The Role of Workers' Relational Agency in the Hybridisation of TNC Subsidiaries in China and Mexico." *International. Journal of Automotive Technology and Management* 17 (2): 190–207.

Williams, Karel, Colin Haslam, and John Williams. 1992. "Ford vs. Fordism: The Beginning of Mass Production?" *Work, Employment and Society* 6 (4): 517–55.

Williams, Karel, Colin Haslam, John Williams, Sukdev Johal, Andy Adcroft, and Robert Willis. 1995. "The Crisis of Cost Recovery and the Waste of the Industrialised Nations." *Competition and Change* 1 (1): 67–93.

Womack James, Daniel Jones, and Daniel Roos. 1990. *The Machine That Changed the World: The Story of Lean Production.* New York: Free Press.

Yates, Charlotte. 1993. *From Plant to Politics: The Autoworkers Union in Postwar Canada.* Philadelphia: Temple University Press.

Yin, Yong, Kathryn E. Stecke, and Dongni Li. 2018. "The Evolution of Production Systems from Industry 2.0 through Industry 4.0." *International Journal of Production Research* 56 (1–2): 848–61.

13

The USMCA and Third-Generation Labour Arrangements: From Previous Experience in Latin America to Probable Scenarios in Mexico

Alex Covarrubias V. and Mélanie Dufour-Poirier

A new regulatory framework has emerged in the North American region, aimed at reformulating the terms of trade and investment between Canada, Mexico, and the United States. It also aims to influence labour relations in and between the three countries. Under the precept of "America First," the United States lobbied strongly to replace the North American Free Trade Agreement (NAFTA), viewing the NAFTA as a vessel to drain jobs and investment away from the US towards Mexico and the low wages that country offered. To achieve its aims, the new treaty – the United States-Mexico-Canada Agreement or USMCA of 2020 – increased the regional value-content rule in strategic industries such as the automotive industry and introduced a labour value content rule. It also introduced a comprehensive description of workers' rights directed at Mexico, including a prohibition of the practice of undermining labour rights to attract investment, a prerequisite for the US's signing of the treaty.

Both by mandate of the USMCA and by the historical internal demands of workplace democracy, the Mexican government of Andres Manuel López Obrador introduced a new federal labour law in May 2019 that placed new limitations on and regulations around the practice of subcontracting. It also granted increases to the minimum wage in the first three years of López Obrador's government. The cumulative total of those increase was a 60% hike. Another 22% increase was included for 2022. The overall effect: the minimum wage climbed from $88 pesos per day in 2018 to $172.9 pesos per day in 2022.

These changes have planted the notion that Mexico is in the process of enacting a new labour model: one where fundamental labour rights, free negotiations, collective bargaining agreements, and union democracy prevail. Such adjustments constitute a radical transformation: a sharp contrast to the old corporate model based on protection contracts, coupled with politicized and patronizing control structures, features that made Mexico a paragon of downplayed and discounted labour. So-called protection contracts have been a prominent feature of Mexican workplaces. These are contracts negotiated and signed between companies and union leaders behind workers' backs, even before companies started operations; they were a cornerstone of Mexico's old labour system (see Cook 2007; Bensusán Areous and Middlebrook 2013; Covarrubias V. and Bensusán Areous 2022; Covarrubias V. and Ramirez 2020; Covarrubias V. 2020b, 2020c, 2021). In exchange for perks, money, and workers' fees, union leaders would regularly sell the idea of workplace peace, decrease wages, pare away at working conditions, and ensure the suppression of worker protest. It has been suggested that between 60 and 90% of labour contracts were of the "protection" variety (see Covarrubias V. and Bouzas 2017; Secretaria del Trabajo y Previsión Social n.d.).

This study will assess the extent to which Mexico's new labour model will take hold. It draws from the work of Bensusán Areous, Covarrubias V., and Nicolas (2022), Covarrubias V. and Bensusán Areous (2022), and Covarrubias V. (2020b, 2020c, 2021). It also builds from the report on the legitimization of collective contracts of the Maquila Solidarity Network (2021). As will be shown, the legitimization of collective agreements is one of the central components of Mexico's new labour law. This includes a direct and secret vote for workers, aimed at providing them with an elevated sense of workplace democracy.

We base our analysis on a reconstruction of the effects on labour of free trade agreements previously signed by the United States with countries in Latin America and the Caribbean. To do so, we examine six free trade agreements signed by the US with eleven countries in those regions. Through this examination, we assess whether the optimism prevalent in some circles regarding the direction of the Mexican labour transition is warranted. Our study is supported by an extensive review of documents relevant to labour aspects of those free trade agreements. It is also informed by interviews we conducted over the last five years with union leaders from Latin America and North America as well as officials from the International Labour Organization (ILO). We also conducted interviews about labour reform in Mexico with union leaders, workers, and labour authorities.

We begin with the premise that the changes produced so far are limited, focused primarily on strategic transnational industries, including automotive manufacturing. We consider the automotive industry's central role in debates surrounding the shape of the USMCA, including the USMCA's chapters on labour. We also examine the effects the new framework has on Mexico's micro, small, and medium enterprises (MSMEs), firms and sectors typically outside the radar of transnational control mechanisms and the interests of union organizations in the United States and Canada.

MSMEs constitute the majority of Mexican workplaces and most of its workers, and for that reason Bensusán Areous, Covarrubias V., and Nicolas (2022) and Covarrubias V. and Bensusán Areous (2022) anticipate that Mexico's corporate and protection unionism may be able to bury, or at least delay, much of the labour transformation envisaged. This, coupled with labour institutions' lack of resources to supervise and encourage transformation (Covarrubias V. 2020b; Covarrubias V. 2020c; Covarrubias V., 2021), including the limitations associated with support resources provided by the United States, are important variables that may cause overall labour reforms in Mexico to progress in a more limited manner than initially advertised.

We postulate that sustained labour relation transformation will only occur if the legislative changes are supported and processed by the stakeholders involved. In other words, we suggest that an orchestration from below is necessary, one that is supported and extended by civil society, the premise being that adjustments at the local level will translate to legitimacy (ILO 2017; Martin, Dufour-Poirier, and Villanueva 2021; Rennie et al. 2017). Thus, the success of what we describe as the third generation of labour-oriented trade agreements – and the possibility of an effective transition to a new labour model for Mexico – will depend on the ability of organizations from civil society, including unions, to develop an agency that allows them to mobilize and optimize the new opportunities that were anticipated when they were put in place.

This chapter contains four sections. The first section reconstructs the history of free trade agreements signed by the United States with Latin American countries. Our aim here is to explain how the USMCA jump-started the development of new labour arrangements in Mexico. In the second section we describe some of the results of that process and explain outstanding labour issues with partner countries. The third section evaluates progress in Mexico with respect to labour reform and the labour rules detailed by the USMCA, the third generation of labour arrangements. The fourth section provides a summary along with probable labour scenarios in the future.

THE TURN TOWARDS WORK IN THE FREE TRADE AGREEMENTS: THE CREATION OF WORKING ARRANGEMENTS

The United States has negotiated six trade agreements with Latin American and Caribbean countries: the USMCA, the CAFTA-DR signed in 2004 with six Central American countries and the Dominican Republic, and agreements with Chile (2003), Colombia (2006), Peru (2006), and Panama (2007). Dewan and Ronconi (2014) outline four stages or generations in the evolution of the labour provisions introduced by the United States in their trade negotiations with Latin American countries. In the first, corresponding to the original free trade agreement with Mexico (and Canada) in 1994, the United States negotiated a parallel agreement to deal with workplace arrangements. The second stage occurred during the free trade agreements with Chile and with countries of Central America and the Dominican Republic. These included a chapter on labour and also touched upon facets associated with "capacity building." The third stage corresponds to the free trade agreement between the United States and Peru: it used language that purported to make every effort to ensure the adoption, maintenance, and application of labour-oriented laws. The fourth stage corresponds to the United States-Colombia free trade agreement, which also obliged Colombia to sign an extensive binding document called the Labour Action Plan. Contrary to Dewan and Ronconi, we maintain that up to the time the USMCA was signed only two generations can be properly identified: the first corresponds to NAFTA and the second can be seen in common elements weaving through the remaining agreements.

FIRST GENERATION: THE LABOUR AGREEMENT PARALLEL TO NAFTA

The first-generation trade agreement affecting labour was the NAFTA (1994). The labour provisions in the NAFTA appeared as a mechanism to gain approval from the United States Congress (a consequence of concerns about Mexico's low wages and labour standards). However, labour-related dispositions were hemmed in by language outside the central body of the treaty proper and the binding mechanisms the treaty stipulated (cf. Compa and Brooks 2015). Specifically, in the original 1994 NAFTA signatories acknowledged that complaints about labour issues had to be exclusively trade related to be considered relevant and therefore actionable (Orbie, Van den Putte, and Martens 2017).

The inadequacy of the NAFTA in so far as management and enforcement of labour standards are concerned is demonstrated by the Labour Cooperation Commission. The commission was created as an outcome of the NAFTA negotiations and was headed by the ministers of labour and a secretariat assisted by National Administrative Offices (NAOs). The commission established a complicated process of consultation, arbitration, and conflict resolution. NAFTA also subjected the commission to a double lock: first, to cases where there was a "persistent pattern" of violations related to safety and health, child labour, and minimum wages; and second, to those violations dealt with by domestic laws. The ineffectiveness of these mechanisms was demonstrated by the fact that a few years after the NAOs were put in place, they simply disappeared.

SECOND-GENERATION LABOUR ARRANGEMENTS

The second generation of trade-inspired labour agreements corresponds with the free trade agreements signed by the United States in the first decade of this century. In the 2004 agreement between the United States and Chile, for example, a chapter on labour was introduced within the body of the treaty itself. It was from that point on that the disposition of the United States towards the creation of labour laws began to change. Chapter 18 of the treaty established that "each party must endeavour to ensure that the principles of the 1998 Declaration of the International Labour Organization are recognized and protected by its domestic law"

(United States Trade Representative 2004). In the agreement, the fundamental rights claimed by the ILO were specified in terms of acceptable working conditions with respect to minimum wages, working hours, and occupational health and safety. It was also agreed that financial penalties would be levied for violations of any of the ILO-based categories. Additionally, inspection capacities were enhanced and the institutions charged with their administration and oversight were strengthened.

After the US-Chile agreement, subsequent trade pacts the United States reached with countries of the region were distinguished by five labour-related characteristics:

1 Each started by recognizing that lack of compliance (enforcement) of labour laws and regulations was problematic, and that restoring faith in labour institutions was key (Martin, Dufour-Poirier, and Villanueva 2021).
2 Consistent with the previous point, strengthening labour inspection institutions in Latin American and Caribbean countries was deemed essential in providing the means to supervise labour laws and create a culture of compliance.
3 Actions were taken and resources committed by the parties involved – from the United States Department of Labor and the respective ministries of labour or equivalents – to build capacities to support labour inspection and ensure inspection services had sufficient funds and autonomy to achieve objectives in accordance with the provisions included in the free trade agreements.
4 While some variation occurred between agreements, the labour provisions were placed in parallel agreements (as was the case with NAFTA), and action plans were established whereby governments were obliged to undertake actions before the agreements could commence (which might have included considerable adjustments in labour laws). Conflict-resolution mechanisms that could lead to fines and suspension of tariff benefits were also created.
5 The ILO's 1998 "Declaration on Fundamental Principles and Rights at Work" was established as the minimum standard. (However, in Peru, for example, the rights at issue already formed part of their constitution, making this point redundant.) The four categories of interest were freedom of association and recognition of the right to collective bargaining; elimination of forced or compulsory labour; abolition of child labour; and elimination of discrimination in respect to employment and occupation.

These elements came about, in part, as the result of protests by the American Federation of Labour and Congress of Industrial Organization (AFL-CIO) against the unrestricted promotion of trade agreements, without qualms about their implications for labour. The AFL-CIO emphasized the importance of ensuring a satisfactory level of union acceptability to justify ratification. They were also motivated to avoid aspects of the NAFTA, where labour matters were confined to a parallel agreement (the "labour side agreement") that was largely ineffective.

For the United States, securing an agreement with Colombia was of strategic importance, a consequence of the problem of drug trafficking as well as US interest in mining, flowers, ports, sugar, and palm oil. A US agreement with Panama was seen as helping US companies compete in major projects (e.g., expansion of the Panama Canal and in the communications and transportation industries).

THE USMCA: THIRD GENERATION OF LABOUR ARRANGEMENTS

A third generation of labour provisions underpins key facets of the USMCA of 2020 and builds on trade pacts that preceded it. These provisions encouraged a comprehensive amendment to Mexico's Federal Labour Law, capping two decades of partial reforms in Mexico. They also provide a strengthened set of mechanisms for monitoring, reporting, and resolving disputes – framed by a rapid-response mechanism – aimed at exerting considerable pressure on Mexico's labour institutions. The USMCA also includes two bilateral rapid response work methods: one between the US and Mexico and the other between Canada and Mexico.

The USMCA comprises thirty-six chapters. For our purposes, the most important are chapter 4 (which regulates the rules of origin), chapter 5 (origin procedures), and chapter 23 (labour issues). Chapter 4 (article 7) also contains a labour value content (LVC) rule requiring vehicle manufacturers to certify that a minimum 40% (passenger cars) and 45% (trucks) of vehicles' value are produced by workers who earn $16 an hour or more (for a vehicle to cross borders without tariffs). The regulations also include requirements of a 70% regional content for steel and aluminium. (For a comprehensive discussion of these provisions see Bensusán Areous, Covarrubias V., and Nicolas 2022; Bensusán Areous 2020.)

While chapter 23 covers labour provisions, Annex II covers collective rights, stipulating that the ILO's fundamental conventions (1998–2008) should be met. Here, the signing parties commit to recognizing the role of workers' organizations. They also agree to respect freedom of association, the right to strike, and the right to collective bargaining. The USMCA requires parties to only trade in goods that have been manufactured respecting those rights. Additionally, it required Mexico reform its federal labour laws, which goal was achieved in May 2019. The most important aspects of this reform were:

- Strengthening of the principles of freedom of association and collective bargaining;
- Assuring the democratic rights of union members, including freedom of affiliation or disaffiliation; freedom to engage in union participation; and the exercise of individual, free, direct, and secret votes. Gender equality regulations were also provided, including proportional gender representation;

- Ensuring the right to *not* be forced to join a union. However, a pre-entry closed shop – under which the employer agrees to hire union members only – remains as a possibility. It was also ruled that a union's disciplinary sanctions on workers may not affect her/his job;
- Stipulating autonomy in relation to government. This included (a) a new procedure to register unions and committees under the principles of autonomy, equity, democracy, legality, transparency, certainty, immediacy, impartiality, and respect for union freedoms and their guarantees; (b) the creation of the Federal Centre for Conciliation and Labour Registry – decentralized from the executive branch, eliminating the division between federal and local jurisdictions;
- Providing democratic guarantees, including worker consultation procedures for the approval of collective agreements, a measure that opened the possibility of ending employer protection contracts;
- Incorporating accountability and transparency provisions, including rules granting workers access to information about the management of union assets;
- Adding certificates of representativeness and legitimization of collective agreements. This involved requirements to obtain certificates of representativeness (support of 30% of the workers covered) for the purposes of requesting the negotiation of a collective agreement, as well as its approval by a majority vote. A process of validation of the will of the majority to legitimize the already-existing collective agreements was also included, which was to take place a maximum of four years from the implementation of reform;
- Eliminating Tripartite Conciliation and Arbitration Councils, replaced by Independent Centers for Conciliation and Labour Tribunals.

The main rupture of the USMCA with its predecessor NAFTA involved the monitoring mechanisms and the resolution of complaints to enforce compliance with Mexico's Federal Labour Law. In fact, they were the most rigorous binding mechanisms contained in any of the trade agreements in the Americas, as evidenced by two provisions. First, a complaint mechanism and system for rapid resolution of labour disputes was introduced. If a complaint is made that a Mexican plant is breaching a labour regulation – without any requirement to prove that violation – Mexican authorities have forty-five days to respond. If there is a violation, they have ten days to resolve it. If the Mexican authorities find that no violation has occurred, the complainant can convene a verification panel comprised of panelists from each country. Mexico then has seven days to accept the panel and thirty additional days to conduct a review. The panel of experts is given 80 to 120 days to arrive at a determination; however, the US is allowed to request a determination within 30 days. The determinations of the panel are binding. The USA and Canada may suspend the preferential tariff arrangements and/or block the entry of goods from plants that fail to comply.

Second, in the American government process implementing the USMCA, various committees were established, made up of representatives of US government agencies, as well as committees of experts and five labour attachés in the embassy that monitor compliance with the labour commitments contracted by Mexico. The US dedicated $240 million to monitoring compliance.

RESULTS OF THE LATIN AMERICAN EXPERIENCE

Our assessment of labour issues and standards emanating from the USMCA is also informed by observance of fundamental labour rights as they have unfolded in previous free trade agreements. Doing so establishes benchmarks to improve understanding of how the evolution of the labour commitments contained in the USMCA will unfold.

Implementation of free trade agreements with Central America, as well as those signed with Colombia, Chile, and Peru, was – and continues to be – difficult. This is because these countries have faced repeated violations of labour rights, killings of trade unionists and militants, and ongoing use of child labour (which at times becomes forced labour). León Palencia (2012) suggests that the perpetuation of such conditions suggests ongoing shortcomings associated with the underlying laws and enforcement mechanisms in those countries. The inference is that the sanctions for non-compliance are inadequate – that the commercial advantage of violation is greater than the penalty. Consistent with that, labour provisions associated with the Chilean trade agreement were not matched by resources necessary to support compliance.

ILO officials we interviewed agreed that access to union representation and collective bargaining continues to be complicated in the Andean states. They also point out that fear of reporting anti-union violence persists and that workplace cultures have proven insufficient to support the collection of evidence and making of complaints. This has occurred despite provisions in free trade agreements and despite the existence of reinforced inspection systems. One interviewee observed:

> Let's say that at the regional level, there is a climate that is quite hostile to unionization. For example, with very high rates of unionization in mining in Chile and Peru in the seventies and eighties, people were systematically dumped, not to say physically eliminated, and this type of outsourcing practices was created to weaken the union movement. With the free trade agreements, people began to go to the Ministry of Labour and say to the trade unionists: what do you need? This with the aim to document and teach unions how to document because unfortunately, we have not had the habit of doing it. So there is a very bad taste but there is not a habit of systematic documentation, and that is very important. Because if you don't do it, neither in the free trade agreements nor with the problems that the national justice [system] has, nor in the international justice [system], nor in the international complaints system, a complaint can't be made. For all that, you need to build evidence, which is very difficult given the scarcity of resources of many unions and the informality of the economy in Latin America.

In the case of Peru, observers note that some progress was made, the result of a commitment to adjust labour institutions to support new, elevated legal requirements (Dewan and Ronconi 2014). As part of that, Peru modified its Law on Collective Labour Relations, introduced incentives for companies that respect the law and promote fundamental workers' rights, and approved plans to eradicate forced labour and child labour. Despite the legislative measures, challenges persist. For example, the existence of thirty-nine parallel labour regimes in Peru has made it difficult to apply uniform labour regulations at the national level on freedom of association and gender discrimination (Confederación Sindical Internacional 2019). Also, the prevalence of special work regimes without any agreement by occupation (in the agriculture sector, for example) or status (permanent or temporary) continues to legitimize differential treatment between workers (Pacheco-Zerga 2010). Additionally, Dewan and Ronconi (2014) found that four years after the signing of the free trade agreement with the United States, the number of labour inspectors in Peru had not increased and that the system was non-existent in some regions, deficiencies that were echoed by the US Department of Labor.

Peru also introduced more comprehensive language governing the resolution of disputes. It was established that if one of the parties, offended or complaining, was not attended to in a timely manner, it could withdraw commercial benefits or be compensated via the payment of a fine. It could also demand that funds be allocated to force the offending party to comply with their commitment. However, these provisions often turned out to be more theoretical than real, as the collective labour relations law reached few workers. This situation was perpetuated by the persistence of a "no-complaint" culture.

In the case of Colombia, a binding Labour Action Plan was issued that included a range of measures the Colombian government promised to implement before the treaty was approved by the US Congress. Columbia's pledge included introducing legislation to satisfy the fundamental rights outlined by the ILO, hiring additional labour inspectors, establishing systems to mediate conflicts and investigate labour rights, toughening penalties for the crime of attacks against trade union association, and expanding resources for the protection of trade unionists. Though the agreement was approved in 2006, it was not ratified until 2011. Discussions lingered around the violent targeting of union leaders and human rights defenders, the impunity with which violence was carried out, and the non-application of labour laws. Reports in subsequent years detailed continuing challenges associated with the protection of trade unionists and labour rights, including anti-union violence (Confederación Sindical Internacional 2019; International Labour Organization 2017)

THE IMPLEMENTATION OF LABOUR REFORM AND THE PROVISIONS OF THE USCMA IN MEXICO

Mexico's revamped labour model – an outcome of the USMCA negotiations – includes three milestones: adjustments to the labour justice system, the promotion of heightened workplace democracy, and legitimization of collective bargaining.

First, as the previous conciliation and arbitration boards were extinguished, a labour justice and conciliation system was introduced. This step included the November 2020 creation of the Federal Centre for Conciliation and Labour Registration (CFCRL). The CFCRL was given responsibility for monitoring procedures supporting union democracy and ensuring the legitimacy of labour organizations. It was also given oversight of collective bargaining, including monitoring the process of union registration, ratification of union elections, and verification of collective agreements. As that was being put in place, the process of instituting state-level conciliation centres and labour courts also commenced, occurring via a three-stage process. Those practices unfolded starting in November 2020 (as did the creation of the CFCRL) and were due for completion by May 2022, by which time all states were expected to have joined.

The second milestone was the adaptation of union statutes to pave the way for union life to be based on the principles of democracy, transparency, gender equality, and accountability. Between eight and twelve months were allocated for that process starting in May 2018 (the day the new labour law entered into force). According to the Ministry of Labour and Social Welfare, as of November 2021, 95.65% of 2,160 active federal jurisdiction unions had adapted their statutes. However, at the local level only 48.5% – 5,480 of 11,285 active unions – had done so.

The third milestone was the legitimization by workers of the content of their collective bargaining agreements, a process achieved through personal, free, direct, and secret voting. That milestone was scheduled to roll out over a period of no more than four years. The aim was to guarantee free collective bargaining as well as put an end to the protection contracts that plagued union life in Mexico, a situation where contracts were regularly signed and negotiations conducted with little transparency. By the end of 2021, the Ministry of Labour and Social Welfare reported that a total of 2,556 collective contracts had been legitimized comprising 1.1 million workers (Secretaria del Trabajo y Previsión Social n.d.). However, gaining an exact measure of the spread of this milestone is a challenge. For example, assuming there are 27,500 collective bargaining agreements registered with the Federal Conciliation and Arbitration Board and 532,469 with the locals (totaling 559,969 agreements), only 0.45% of the total have been legitimized. However, it is possible that about 25% of union members have legitimized their contracts, given that the number of unionized workers is about 4.4 million (INEGI 2019; Independent Mexico Expert Labor Board 2020). Despite this, as of November 2021, the CFCRL reported that only 0.06% of contracts reviewed had been rejected by the workers (Más Reforma Mejor Trabajo 2021), implying that most corporate unions – and therefore most protection contracts – *are* being approved by workers. The Maquila Solidarity Network (2021) attributes these results to weaknesses in the design of the collective bargaining legitimation process: claiming control of organizing, and conducting and reporting on legitimization votes, are entrusted almost entirely to the incumbent union. Other shortcomings include insufficient monitoring by state institutions of the actions of employers and unions prior to authentication votes, lack of access to information on voting results, and inadequate transparency about findings of investigations into allegations of irregularities.

To date there have been only two shake-ups of the corporatist union system in Mexico. Significantly, both occurred in the automotive sector: at the GM Silao assembly plant (in

Guanajuato) and Tridonex in the state of Tamaulipas in the country's north-east region. In the case of GM Silao, the US raised concerns about "serious violations of workers' rights to free association" associated with an April 2021 vote on a collective bargaining agreement. The US used the new rapid response mechanism described earlier. As the system requires, the Mexican government rapidly accepted the complaint and agreed on a remediation plan to protect workers' rights, including a new vote in August 2021 that workers rejected. Importantly, the union and the contract had been controlled by Tereso Medina, general secretary of the Miguel Trujillo López union, affiliated with the business-friendly Confederation of Mexican Workers or CTM (see "Workers" 2021; DiMaggio and Feliz Leon 2022).

At the Tridonex auto parts company, a subsidiary of the US firm Cardone, the Independent National Union of Workers in Industries and Services Movement 20/32 (SNITIS) filed a claim for ownership of the collective agreement with the Federal Conciliation and Arbitration Board (JFCA). After firings, threats to union representatives, and complaints about violations of worker's rights to free association and collective bargaining, the US Trade Representative (USTR) filed a complaint, also under the rapid response mechanism. In August 2021, the USTR announced that it had reached an agreement with Tridonex. As part of that agreement, Tridonex agreed to provide compensation and back pay to the workers, as well as commit to neutrality in future union elections (USTR 2021).

On other fronts – and in contrast to the cases described immediately above – the leadership of the CTM, CROC, and CROM unions reported compliance with the new processes and expectations. Tereso Medina, for example, reported that GM Silao was the only misstep of the 180 collective contracts that his union, CTM, holds with automotive companies. Similarly, in the Bajio region (the central-north region of Mexico), the SITIMM (Sindicato de Trabajadores de la Industria Metal Mecánica, Automotriz, Similares y Conexos de la República Mexicana), a union with 60,000 members across Guanajuato, San Luis Potosi, Querétaro, and Jalisco, reported a process of adaptation of statutes and legitimation of contracts without setbacks.

In Sonora, on the northern border, the regional leader of CTM, Javier Villarreal, reported that more than 90% of his union's 120,000 members had legitimized contracts with approvals of 95 to 99% (Moreno 2021). At BMW's San Luis Potosi assembly plant, for example, its members voted 90% in favour of legitimization (N.L. Hernández 2021). The BMW case is significant because many observers portray it as a typical protection contract, a consequence of its wages for production workers starting at $1.10 per hour with a top wage of $2.53 (see Covarrubias V. 2020c; Rubin 2022).

It should be emphasized that to date most disputes have occurred in the automotive sector, where the US government and the USCMA placed greatest emphasis. This suggests that in the sectors not subject to the scrutiny of the mechanisms contemplated by the USMCA (e.g., large state-owned companies or the thousands of small businesses), progress related to union democracy and independent unionism is more challenging. Consider, for example, unions known for the power and wealth of their leaders (e.g., the 89,000-worker Mexican Oil

Workers Union [Sindicato de Trabajadores Petroleros de la República Mexicana]). As of late 2021, the dominant structures have been victorious in most of that union's regional elections.

The fact that traditional unions are transitioning to increased worker legitimization of their contracts – including those of the "protection" variety – without significant setback points to what the Maquila Solidarity Network (2021, 7) describes as "the weaknesses of the design of the CBA [collective bargaining agreement] legitimization process." Moreover, as anticipated by Bensusán Areous, Covarrubias V., and Nicolas (2022) and Covarrubias V. and Bensusán Areous (2022), corporate unionism and protection continue to show a large capacity for adaptability, a capacity that allows them to "weather the storm" and make changes so as *not* to change.

Labour institutions' lack of resources to monitor and encourage transformation is key. A study by Covarrubias V. (2020a) on labour inspection in Mexico describes the weak capacity of labour institutions to inspect, and ultimately enforce, application of the law on four fronts: numbers, capacities, resources, and competencies of the inspection process. For context: the Secretaria del Trabajo y Previsión Social has 450 inspectors for a working population of 36.4 million – one inspector per 80,000 workers; and field studies by the authors indicate that inspection coverage barely reaches 2–3% of companies and in rural areas is almost non-existent (Covarrubias V. 2020a). Given these limitations, it is foreseeable that the Secretaria del Trabajo y Previsión Social and the Federal Center for Conciliation and Federal Registry do not have the capacity to monitor and inspect the union contract legitimization processes, even though the law and associated protocols empower them to do so.

DISCUSSION AND CONCLUSIONS

Free trade agreements in the Latin American and Caribbean region have had limited effect on labour, notably at the local level (United States-Peru Trade Promotion Agreement 2015). Although the Office of the US Trade Representative asserts that some Latin American countries (e.g., Chile, Colombia, Panama, and Peru) did adjust labour laws to meet international norms following ratification of trade agreements with the US, those jurisdictions do not uniformly enforce their laws and regulations. Thus, to date, trade agreements have not led to definitive improvements in labour rights enforcement or working conditions (Aaronson 2010). In addition, the US has not uniformly backed up its trade agreements with funds sufficient to build capacity for enforcement or help policymakers in partner countries gain expertise.

Negotiation and implementation of the USMCA has had the effect of bringing to light abuses endemic in the previous Mexican labour model. Those exploitations were particularly visible in the automotive industry, a consequence of government and union interests in the US and their shared attention to advancing labour and union rights beyond US borders. In keeping with that, the third generation of labour arrangements that the USCMA encouraged provided the foundation for a comprehensive and binding framework of labour obligations among its three signatory countries, most notably Mexico.

Even though the USMCA has caused various facets of labour governance in Mexico to change, like the rest of Latin America where agreements were signed, labour reforms and regulations still have a long way to go before they are translated into a new labour model: one supported by the pillars of institutionalized realities and accreditation of participating actors. The future effect on industry and workers of the new Mexican labour laws will depend on the actions of opposing forces. It can be anticipated, for example, that institutional forces such as USMCA and the new labour institutions in Mexico will be opposed by the presence of a powerful system of political corporatism that today, as ever, hinders reform.

Certainly, the USMCA has caused aspects of the labour model in Mexico to evolve. That said, a lack of resources and the limited capacity of labour institutions to implement change undermines progress. As the ILO explains, problems related to continued violations of labour rights in targeted countries are attributable to, among other factors, weak domestic institutions. In this regard, the strengthening of important civil society actors is one of the most important drivers for achieving lasting and deeply entrenched change (ILO 2017; Martin, Dufour-Poirier, and Villanueva 2021; Maquila Solidarity Network 2021; Covarrubias V. 2020a).

The complicated evolution of the processes of union legitimization in Mexico and the statutes underpinning them underlines corporate unions' capacity for resistance and adaptation (Bensusán Areous, Covarrubias V., and Nicolas 2022). This together with the fragmentation, weakness, and divisionism of independent unions has further impeded the capacity of the labour provisions of the Mexican Federal Labour Law and the USMCA to cause change of the magnitude and sort its proponents have sought.

The experiences of other Latin American countries in this regard are overwhelming. In frameworks enacted during times of dictatorship, hampered their capacity to establish alliances with other actors from civil society. The same situation unfolded between unions representing permanent workers versus unions of outsourced and/or subcontracted workers (Manky 2017). These factors impeded attempts to level up labour standards. This was especially evident during the periods following the signing of free trade agreements (Dufour-Poirier 2022).

Processes and evolutions can be even more complicated (and limited) within small and medium-sized industries, which are not considered to be transnationally strategic, and with large domestic companies and government entities. Here, labour practices and governance are not subject to the attention of inspection bodies provided by the USCMA, nor do they fall under the eye of unions located elsewhere in North America.

The scenarios and challenges identified in this chapter lend content and gravity to our underlying premise: that a substantive transformation of labour relations will only occur if legislative changes are supported and processed by more stakeholders, an outcome that we suggest demands an *orchestration from below*. By this, we mean that actions and outcomes facilitated at the local level will eventually translate into a strengthened and broader-based legitimacy (ILO 2017; Martin, Dufour-Poirier, and Villanueva 2021; Rennie et al. 2017). As the ILO (2017) highlights, when it comes to involving stakeholders in trade agreements, US-demanded mechanisms *have* increased public awareness of labour issues, a situation facilitated by the provision of detailed information about specific cases (which have been supported by US trade agreements).

While commitments to provide feedback are present in trade agreements made by Canada and the United States, there is a lack of formal feedback mechanisms (ILO 2017). Hence, the success of the third generation of labour arrangements and the possibility of an effective transition to a new labour model will depend on the capacity of civil society, including unions, to mobilize their forces (including rank-and-file membership) and thus to make optimal use of the new opportunities at the labour-political level.

This study has considered a series of factors affecting the establishment of a new labour model in Mexico, considering its potential impacts on industry and work. We posit that the development of a new labour model in Mexico serves the interests of all three USMCA signatory countries. We also suggest that a greater balance of trade in the region will cause positive knock-on effects on employment and investment in the United States and Canada. This would in turn cause wages to improve in Mexico and stimulate its internal market. Through this, both workers and the industries in the three countries would achieve gains. The overall effect would be a normalizing of transnational solidarity between Mexican, Canadian, and American unions. From that would flow a new and elevated model of labour institutionalization.

REFERENCES

Aaronson, S.A. 2010. "Is the Wedding of Trade and Human Rights a Marriage of Convenience or a Lasting Union?" *Human Rights and Human Welfare* 10 (13). https://ciaotest.cc.columbia.edu/journals/hrhw/v10i0/f_0021088_17524.pdf.

Bensusán Areous, G. 2020. *The Transformation of the Mexican Labour Regulation Model and Its Link to North American Economic Integration*. ILO Working Paper no. 15. Geneva: ILO. https://www.ilo.org/static/english/intserv/working-papers/wp015/index.html.

Bensusán Areous, Graciela, and Alex Covarrubias V. 2016. "Relaciones labourales y salariales en la IAM: ¿Vendrá el cambio de fuera?" In *La industria Automotriz en México: Relaciones de empleo, culturas organizacionales y factores psicosociales*, edited by A. Covarrubias V., A. Arteaga, G. Bensusán Areous, and S. Sandoval, 197–223. Mexico City: Red ITIAM: COLSON-CIAD-AM Editores-CLAVE.

Bensusán Areous, Graciela, and Kevin Middlebrook. 2013. *Sindicatos y política en México: Cambios, continuidades y contradicciones*. UAM-CLacso-Flacso. https://biblioteca.clacso.edu.ar/clacso/coediciones/20130708125012/SindicatosypoliticaenMexico.pdf.

Bensusán Areous, Graciela, Alex Covarrubias V., and I.G. Nicolas. 2022. "The USMCA and the Mexican Automobile Industry: Towards a New Labour Model? *International Journal of Automotive Technology and Management* 22 (1): 128–44. https://ideas.repec.org/a/ids/ijatma/v22y2022i1p128-144.html.

Bureau of Labour Statistics (BLS). 2018. "Occupational Employment Statistics." Accessed 12 July 2019. https://www.bls.gov/oes/current/naics4_336100.htm.

Camarillo, Vanessa. 2020. TradeTankMX. 30 June 2020. https://tradetankmx.com/wp-content/uploads/2020/06/TradeTankMx-Editorial-T-MEC-Perspectivas-de-cambio.pdf.

CFCRL (Centro Federal de Conciliación y Registro Laboral). 2021. *Acuerdo por el que se Aprueba el Protocolo para el Procedimiento de Legitimación de Contratos Colectivos de Trabajo Existentes*. Mexico City. http://www.dof.gob.mx/2021/CFCRL/Protocolo_Legitimacion_ContratosColectivos.pdf.

Compa, Lance, and Tequila Brooks. 2015. *NAFTA and the NAALC: Twenty Years of Trade-Labour Linkage in the Americas*. Alphen aan den Rijn, Netherlands: Wolters Kluwer.

Confederación Sindical Internacional. 2019. "Informe sobre las violaciones de los derechos sindicales." Revised 6 July 2021. https://survey.ituc-csi.org/?lang=es.

Conference Board. n.d. "International Labour Comparisons." Accessed 15 June 2017. https://www.conference-board.org/ilcprogram/.

Cook, Maria Lorena. 2007. *The Politics of Labour Reform in Latin America: Between Flexibility and Rights*. University Park, PA: Pennsylvania State University Press.

Coordinadora nacional de derechos humanos en el Perú. 2014. *Del TLC Perú-Estados Unidos: Cuando la competitividad se basa en la reducción de los derechos labourales*. Lima: Pontificia Universidad Católica del Perú.

Covarrubias V., Alex. 2019. "La ventaja competitiva de México en el TLCAN: Un caso de dumping social visto desde la Automotriz." *Norteamérica* 14 (1): 89–118. https://www.scielo.org.mx/scielo.php?pid=S1870-35502019000100089&script=sci_abstract.

Covarrubias V., Alex. (2020a). "The Boom of the Mexican Automotive Industry: From NAFTA to USMCA." In *New Frontiers of the Automobile Industry: Exploring Geographies, Technology, and Institutional Challenges*, edited by Alex Covarrubias V. and Sigfrido M. Ramírez Perez, 323–48. Palgrave Macmillan Cham.

– 2020b. "El T-MEC: Escenarios probables para el trabajo y la industria automotriz regional." Fundación Friedrich Ebert. Mexico: Cuadernos de Trabajo.

– 2020c. *La inspección del trabajo en México. Propuestas para un modelo basado en el imperio de la ley*. Red de Mujeres Sindicalistas. Mas Reforma Mejor Trabajo. Fundación C&A.

– 2021. "El T-MEC y la tercera generación de arreglos laborales: Los escenarios probables para el trabajo y la industria regional." *Norteamérica* 16 (1). https://www.scielo.org.mx/scielo.php?script=sci_arttext&pid=S1870-35502021000100147.

Covarrubias V., Alex, and Graciela Bensusán Areous. 2022. "Editorial." In "The North American Auto Sector: From Nafta to USMCA, the Road Ahead," special issue of *International Journal of Automotive Technology and Management* 22 (1). https://www.inderscience.com/info/inarticletoc.php?jcode=ijatm&year=2022&vol=22&issue=1.

Covarrubias V., Alex, and Alfonso Bouzas. 2017. "Employment and Labour Policies in the Auto Industry in Mexico." In *The Automotive Sector in Emerging Economies: Industrial Policies, Market Dynamics and Trade*, edited by Rudolf Traub-Merz, 163–86. Berlin: Friedrich-Ebert Stiftung.

Covarrubias V., Alex, and Sigfrido Ramirez, eds. 2020. *New Frontiers of the Automobile Industry: Exploring Geographies, Technology, and Labour Challenges*. London: Palgrave-Macmillan.

Dewan, Sabina, and Lucas Ronconi. 2014. "U.S. Free Trade Agreements and Enforcement of Labour Law in Latin America." Inter-American Development Bank Working Paper Series no. 543. https://papers.ssrn.com/sol3/papers.cfm?abstract_id=2559639.

Di Caro, A., and L. MacDonald. 2021. ¿El tratado comercial entre México, Estados Unidos y Canadá dará lugar a una nueva época de protecciones labourales en América del Norte? Los métodos laborales del T-MEC representan un laboratorio de pruebas para la protección de los trabajadores en América del Norte. *The Monitor*, 30 July 2021. https://www.dol.gov/agencies/ilab/our-work/trade/los-derechos-laborales-y-el-tratado-entre-m%C3%A9xico-los-estados-unidos-y-canad%C3%A1-t-mec.

DiMaggio, D., and L. Feliz Leon. 2022. "In a Landslide Victory, Mexican GM Workers Vote In an Independent Union." *Labor Notes*, 4 February 2022. https://labornotes.org/2022/02/landslide-victory-mexican-gm-workers-vote-independent-union.

Dufour-Poirier, M. 2022. *Building North-South Trade Union Solidarity: Putting Collective Identities at Stake*. Entreciencias: Diálogos en la Sociedad del Conocimiento, vol. 10, no. 4. https://www.academia.edu/79546492/Building_Cross_Border_Trade_Union_Solidarity_in_the_Americas_Putting_Organizational_Identities_at_Stake.

El Financiero. 2020. "Hasta 85% de los contratos colectivos existentes se firmaron a espaldas de los trabajadores: Alcalde." 7 January 2020. https://www.elfinanciero.com.mx/economia/ hasta-85-de-los-contratos-colectivos-existentes- se-firmaron-a-espaldas-de-los-trabajadores-alcalde/.

El Sol de Leon. 2021. 2021. "Cumple SITIMM 50 años de velar por derechos de obreros." 2 December. https://www.elsoldeleon.com.mx/local/cumple-sitimm-alejandro-rangel-segovia-50-anos-de-velar-por-derechos-de-obreros-7557198.html.

Hernández, Gerardo. 2021. "Reforma laboral en México: Un cambio de 728 millones de dólares … hasta ahora." *El Economista*, 11 June 2021. https://www.eleconomista.com.mx/capitalhumano/Reforma-laboural-en-Mexico-un-cambio-de-728-millones-de-dolares...-hasta-ahora-20210610-0121.html.

Hernández, N.L. 2021. "Legitima CTM contrato colectivo de trabajo en BMW San Luis Potosí." *El Universal San Luis Potosi*, 7 September 2021. https://sanluis.eluniversal.com.mx/cartera/legitima-ctm-contrato-colectivo-de-trabajo-en-bmw-san-luis-potosi.

Independent Mexico Expert Labor Board. 2020. *Interim Report*. 15 December 2020. https://shorturl.at/izIV7.

Industriall. 2021. "Workers at General Motors' Silao Plant Secure Historic Win." 23 August 2021. https://www.industriall-union.org/workers-at-general-motors-silao-plant-secure-historic-win.

INEGI (National Institute of Statistics and Geography). 2019. "Tasa de sindicalización: Derechos sindicales: Recepción del derecho." https://datos.gob.mx/busca/dataset/tasa-de-sindicalizacion-derechos-sindicales-recepcion-del-derecho.

International Labour Organisation (ILO). 2017. *Handbook on Assessment of Labour Provisions in Trade and Investment Arrangements*. Chap. 1: "Trends in Labour Provisions in Trade Arrangements," 11–16; chap. 4, "Assessing the Effects of Labour Provisions in Trade Agreements," 37–43. In the Matter of Guatemala – Issues Relating to the Obligations under Article 16.2.1(a) of the CAFTA-DR Final Report of the Panel 14 June 2017 (37–75 and 167–201). Geneva: ILO. https://www.ilo.org/wcmsp5/groups/public/---dgreports/---inst/documents/publication/wcms_564702.pdf.

Kay, T. 2005. "Labour Transnationalism and Global Governance: The Impact of NAFTA on Transnational Labour Relationships in North America." *American Journal of Sociology* 111 (3): 715–56.

– 2011. *NAFTA and the Politics of Labour Transnationalism*. Cambridge: Cambridge University Press.

León Palencia, I. 2012. "Análisis de las clausulas labourales en los TLC de Canadá y USA con Colombia, su impacto y realidad material en el mundo del trabajo." Universidad libre de Bogotá, Facultad de derecho, Centro de investigaciones sociojurídicas.

Manky, Omar. 2017. "Part-Time Miners: Labour Segmentation and Collective Action in the Peruvian Mining Industry." *Latin American Perspectives* 45 (5), 120–35. https://www.researchgate.net/publication/316950049_Part-Time_Miners_Labor_Segmentation_and_Collective_Action_in_the_Peruvian_Mining_Industry.

Martin, Isabelle, Mélanie Dufour-Poirier, and Francisco Villanueva. 2021. "Against, Before, or With Corporate Social Responsibility? Unions' Perception and Mobilization of CSR Regulation in Transnational Mining Enterprises." *Canadian Labour & Employment Law Journal* 23 (1): 37–70.

Maquila Solidarity Network. 2021. *Legitimating Collective Bargaining Agreements in Mexico: What Have We Learned to Date?* Toronto: MSN. https://www.maquilasolidarity.org/sites/default/files/attachment/Legitimating_CBAs_in_Mexico_Dec_2021.pdf.

Más Reforma Mejor Trabajo. 2021. 11 November 2021. https://www.masreformasmejortrabajo.mx/index.php/entorno-laboural/reforma-laboural/item/9094-solo-0-6-de-los-contratos-colectivos-de-trabajo-sometidos-a-legitimacion-son-rechazados-por-trabajadores. (Site no longer in existence.)

McGinnis, Devon. 2018. "What Is the Fourth Industrial Revolution?" *The 360 Blog*, 5 July 2023. https://www.salesforce.com/blog/2018/12/what-is-the-fourth-industrial-revolution-4IR.html.

Moreno, A.L. 2021. "Avanza legitimación de contratos colectivos: CTM." *Ehui*, 2 December 2021. Ehui. https://ehui.com/2021/12/avanza-legitimacion-de-contratos-colectivos-ctm/.

Moreno-Brid, Juan Carlos, Rosa Gómez Tovar, Joaquín Sánchez Gómez, and Lizzeth Gómez Rodríguez. 2021. "Trade Agreements and Decent Work in Mexico: The Case of the Automotive and Textile Industries." ILO Working Paper no. 26. https://www.ilo.org/global/publications/working-papers/WCMS_808957/lang--en/index.htm.

Muller, Joan. 2016. "America's Car Capital Will Soon Be … Mexico." *Forbes*, 20 August 2016. https://www.forbes.com/sites/joannmuller/2014/08/20/americas-car-capital-will-soon-be-mexico/#18ed986948ce.

Oficina Internacional del Trabajo. 1998. *Declaración de la OIT relativa a los principios y derechos fundamentales en el trabajo y su seguimiento*. Adoptada por la Conferencia Internacional del Trabajo en su octogésima sexta reunión, Ginebra, Colombia,18 June 1998. https://www.ilo.org/declaration/thedeclaration/textdeclaration/lang--es/index.htm.

– 2019. *Trabajar para un futuro más prometedor – Comisión Mundial sobre el Futuro del Trabajo*. Ginebra, Colombia: OIT. https://www.ilo.org/wcmsp5/groups/public/---dgreports/---cabinet/documents/publication/wcms_662442.pdf.

Orbie, J., L. Van den Putte, and D. Martens, D. 2017. "The Impact of Labour Rights Commitments in EU Trade Agreements: The Case of Peru." *Politics and Governance* 5 (4): 6–18.

Osler Hoskin & Harcourt LLP. 2017. "Canada Unveils Its Top Priorities for NAFTA Renegotiations." 15 August. https://www.lexology.com/library/detail.aspx?g=fb8f4acf-f8ff-4dc0-a6cc-ec9bf3387551.

Pacheco-Zerga, L. 2010. "La legitimidad constitucional de los regímenes laborales especiales." In *Sociedad Peruana de Derecho del trabajo y de la Seguridad Social*. Trabajo presentado en el IV Congreso Nacional de la SPDTSS: Retos del derecho del trabajo peruano: Nuevo proceso laboral, regímenes especiales y Seguridad y Salud en el trabajo, 803–16. Cusco: SPDTSS.

Powell, Naomi. 2019. "Half of Canadian Executives Say Old NAFTA Better for Our Economy than USMCA." *Financial Post*, 22 February 2019. https://business.financialpost.com/news/economy/half-of-canadian-executives-say-old-nafta-better-for-canadian-economy-than-usmca.

Rennie, S., T. Connor, A. Delaney, and S. Marshall. 2017. "Orchestration from Below? Trade Unions in the Global South, Transnational Business and Efforts to Orchestrate Continuous Improvements in Non-State Regulatory Initiatives." *UNSW Law Journal* 40 (3): 1287–1309. https://doi.org/10.53637/XUSU1796.

Rubin, J. 2017a. "How Has Canadian Manufacturing Fared under NAFTA? A Look at the Auto Assembly and Parts Industry." 8 August 2017. https://www.cigionline.org/publications/how-has-canadian-manufacturing-fared-under-nafta-look-auto-assembly-and-parts-industry/.

– 2017b. “How NAFTA Has Hurt Canadian Auto Jobs.” *Toronto Star*, 8 August 2018. https://www.thestar.com/opinion/commentary/2017/08/08/how-nafta-has-hurt-canadian-auto-jobs.html.

– 2018. “The Future Looks Bleak for Ontario’s Manufacturing Sector.” *Globe and Mail*, 12 May 2018. https://www.theglobeandmail.com/report-on-business/economy/the-future-looks-bleak-for-ontarios-manufacturing-sector/article16132219/.

– 2022. *The Expendables: How the Middle Class Got Screwed by Globalization*. Toronto: Vintage Canada.

Secretaria del Trabajo y Previsión Social. n.d. “Nuevo modelo laboral.” Accessed 15 December 2021. https://reformalaboral.stps.gob.mx/nuevo_modelo_laboral.

Tole, J. 2013. “Los TLC de Estados Unidos con países latinoamericanos: Un modelo de integración económica “superficial” para el continente americano.” *Revista Derecho del Estado*. https://revistas.uexternado.edu.co/index.php/derest/article/view/3525/3536.

US Department of Labor. 2019. *United States-Mexico-Canada Agreement (USMCA)*. Labour Rights Report. Washington, DC: Bureau of International Labour Affairs.

US International Trade Commission. 2019. *US-Mexico-Canada Trade Agreement: Likely Impact on the U.S. Economy and Specific Industry Sectors*. Publication no. 4889. Investigation no. TPA 1-5-003. Washington, DC: ITC.

United States Trade Representative. 2004. “Final Text United States Chile Free Trade Agreement.” https://ustr.gov/sites/default/files/uploads/agreements/fta/chile/asset_upload_file853_4012.pdf.

– 2017. “Summary of Objectives for the NAFTA Renegotiation.” 17 July 2017. Washington, DC: Executive Office of the President.

– 2021. “United States Reaches Agreement with Mexican Auto Parts Company to Protect Workers’ Rights.” 10 August 2021. Washington, DC: USTR. https://ustr.gov/about-us/policy-offices/press-office/press-releases/2021/august/united-states-reaches-agreement-mexican-auto-parts-company-protect-workers-rights.

United States-Peru Trade Promotion Agreement. 2015. Public Report of Review of US Submission 2015-01 (Peru). Washington, DC: US Department of Labor, Office of Trade and Labor Affairs.

Conclusion

Greig Mordue and Dimitry Anastakis

Over the course of thirteen chapters, this collection has sought to elevate understanding of the adjustments that have ensued since the implementation of the NAFTA almost three decades ago. We have explored questions about the economic profiles and industrial policy measures affecting the firms, segments, workers, regions, and supply chains that make up the NAFTA region's three member nations. We have done so from the perspective of political science, labour studies, trade policy, geography, business, and engineering. In doing so, our intention has also been to provide a platform for questions and debates about the history of the North American automotive industry as well as its trajectory going forward.

While the NAFTA's implementation in 1994 coincided with a shift in profiles of the automotive industries in its three signatory nation members, this was not the only factor at play during this period. For example, Mordue and Sweeney's chapter 1 demonstrates the extent to which *all* semi-periphery automotive countries, represented in North America by Canada, have struggled, describing how automotive investment, jobs, and the "fair" allocation of each have increasingly coalesced around core and integrated periphery countries, represented in North America by the United States and Mexico respectively. They suggest that the NAFTA merely reinforced the inevitability of that pattern. Their interpretation of the effect of 1994's NAFTA is consistent with that of Dziczek and Swiecki, who argue in chapter 6 of this collection that since the USMCA came into effect in 2020, automotive investment decisions have been only partially affected by the new agreement's contents.

Looking ahead, we suggest that the local, regional, national, and continental profiles of the automotive industry will continue to be buffeted by myriad factors. Thus, while trade policy considerations can be expected to influence automotive investment patterns, such matters will also be influenced by technological, labour, and resource availability, geopolitical constraints, and various industrial policy measures as well as firm-level issues and dynamics. In the paragraphs that follow, we describe three issues that may unsettle the industry – locally, regionally, and globally – in new and profound manners. For emphasis: trade policy will be contributory, not dominative.

First, it is now accepted that the proliferation of electric drivetrains will disrupt – in fact, *is* disrupting – automotive industry actors in firms, policymaking roles, transportation and infrastructure planning, and economic development in myriad ways. For example, most key stages of the development and manufacture of the internal combustion engine (ICE) have long resided almost exclusively within the direct oversight of the automotive industry's original equipment manufacturers (OEMs). Indeed, powertrains have been integral to automotive brand-building. However, the rise of electrification will engender an unprecedented revamp of power dynamics within automotive global value chains. To start, in contrast to the situation with ICEs, existing automotive OEMs own none of the largest global battery makers. Therefore, notwithstanding OEM–battery-maker joint ventures and various forms of vertical integration, responsibility for large portions of the vehicle (at least 30% of a vehicle's value comes from the powertrain) will devolve to new actors – away from traditional automotive OEMs, towards battery makers. Until recently, most of those battery makers were uninvolved in automotive value chains (see Covarrubias V. and Ramírez Pérez 2020; Harrison and Ludwig 2021). Additionally, major battery firms are headquartered outside of North America, removed from the hegemony of the Detroit Three. Combined, these features mean that power within North American automotive value chains as traditionally experienced by its industry actors will transform, becoming more functionally diluted and geographically dispersed. However, it is also conceivable that over an even longer period the rate of battery-related development will decelerate. As that occurs, battery costs will decline, the result being that batteries may drift to near-commodity status, an outcome that might cause power within automotive global value chains to revert to OEMs.

As the macro-level adjustments described above unfold, and as the geographic reprofiling of the industry and the shifting power dynamics play out, electrification will also strike at more local, immediate, and personal levels. Chapter 4 by Klier and Rubenstein, for example, catalogues sixty-four engine and transmission plants in North America, each under the ownership of an incumbent automaker. As well, the industry has already demonstrated a tendency to operate battery plants at a scale that is different and larger than those for engines and transmissions (see Rhys 2004 for a discussion of scale economies for various automotive processes, including powertrain machining and assembly; see Harrison and Ludwig 2021 for comments about the size of automotive battery plants). What happens to those sixty-four plants, the people who work there, and the regional economies those plants support during the transition from traditional ICE drivetrains to battery electric vehicles (BEVs)? How many, if any, of those engine or transmission plants will be retooled to perform operations capable of supporting the transition to BEVs? Will foreign-owned battery makers supply North American assembly plants from local (i.e., North American) battery plants? If they do, will they locate them in traditional automotive manufacturing locations or do BEVs portend a(nother) new economic geography for the North American automotive industry? Even if one accepts the inevitability of a wholesale conversion to BEVs, the transition will without question be chaotic and prolonged for all actors, including labour, policymakers, and incumbent OEMs. The foregoing are fundamental, foundational questions that have profound implications for the broader economy, for technology, for work, and for the notion of "fair share."

Second, even though descriptions of the automotive industry as we know it are often prefaced with the adjective "global," in practice the preponderance of manufacturing operations of major OEMs have evolved as a series of regional nodes. In other words, for major OEMs with a global footprint, their high-volume vehicles have tended to be made in the region(s) in which they are sold (e.g., North America or Europe), a consequence of higher-volume vehicles' capacity to support viable economies of scale (see Rhys 2004) and a desire by OEMs to avoid the political/public relations–related hazards that arise when firm-level regional value added occurs at levels that are viewed by policymakers as an underperformance relative to sales. While the practice is rooted in the long-standing politics of the notion of "fair share" as this collection has described, it became further entrenched in North America in the 1980s when Japanese-based firms such as Nissan, Honda, and Toyota responded to external pressures and established assembly plants there (Cohen 2000; Dryden 1995; Mordue 2020). Through this, local/regional suppliers provide most of the parts and components and therefore much of each locally assembled vehicle's content (including NAFTA-cum-USMCA compliant levels of content, which in the latter case is 75%).

This well-established pattern notwithstanding, it is conceivable that events may eventually conspire to disturb the regionalized nature of automotive investment and development as it has come to be known. For example, it is possible that OEMs from the narrow group of automotive countries concurrently holding traits associated with both core automotive countries (a consequence of their hosting the headquarters of their own home-grown automakers) and attributes connected to the integrated periphery (an outcome of their offer of low labour costs) will disrupt the long-standing "build where you sell" protocol. China, for example, straddles both (see chapter 1 of this collection, figure 2, p. 23). To date, its OEMs have neither made nor sought meaningful, disruptive forays into the North American marketplace with high-volume vehicles. However: China's automotive manufacturing capacity is now well established as the world's largest; it hosts most of the world's leading lithium battery cell manufacturers; unlike other core automotive countries, its home-grown OEMs offer products, including BEVs, across all classes; and its assembly plants have systematically narrowed quality levels with global brands (JD Power 2021). From this, three questions emerge: (When) will Chinese-based firms enter the North American marketplace with high-volume (presumably, battery electric) vehicles? Will those Chinese firms feel compelled, as Japanese firms like Toyota, Honda, and Nissan did in the 1980s, to follow high-volume sales with local (i.e., North

American) production? Alternatively, will Chinese-based OEMs ignore the "build where you sell in volume" protocol, seeking profile and sales devoid of a commensurate manufacturing footprint?

The third question above has major ramifications for the geographic organization of the automotive industry as we understand it as well as for contemporary rules and conventions associated with the governance of trade. Some historical context is helpful. When the Japanese-based OEMs listed above announced North American assembly plants in the 1980s, they did so as a consequence of a series of propositions, overtures, beratings, and enticements from their then North American rivals (some aspects of which are discussed by Jacobs in chapter 2 of this collection). Indeed, many of the industrial policy instruments deployed by American and Canadian policymakers to entice Japanese automotive investment to North America, while permissible at the time, are now non-compliant with the rules governing global trade as they have subsequently evolved. As a result, 1980s-era tools like export restraints, import ceilings, port blockages, and trade-related production incentives – controversial now, though de rigueur at the time – no longer comply with the post-NAFTA standards established by trade governance bodies like the WTO. What happens in the future if an OEM, presumably from a low-cost integrated periphery/core country, enters the North American automotive marketplace with no intention of reciprocating with manufacturing investment, prepared instead to absorb the tariffs imposed on imported vehicles that do not meet USMCA regional content requirements? While a combination of browbeating and investment incentives remain, obstinance by the OEM, unlike in the 1980s, is now a permissible rejoinder.

While it *is* possible to anticipate a response by policymakers in such circumstances of acquiescence, it is also conceivable that a greater level of truculence by certain policymakers might ensue, dependent, of course, on the United States administration and its proclivities. After all, the automotive industry remains iconic: providing well-paying direct and indirect jobs, playing an oversized role in economic development, wielding considerable political influence. How might an overriding strategy of truculence arise? How far might policymakers go to protect the most recognizable symbol of North America's industrialism? Ultimately, what are the implications for the rules and structures governing global trade?

Admittedly, elements of the scenarios presented and the questions posed above tilt to the fanciful. The point, however, is this: the automotive industry – including its products, its factories, and its workers – continues to occupy a place at the nexus of North American and global sentiments. As such, one can expect industrial policy measures to be floated and debated that are reflective of the industry's outsized status. Indeed, as the history of the USMCA chapter of the North American automotive industry unfolds, it can be anticipated that issues of this nature will continue to occupy the attention of those seeking a "fair share" of the considerable spoils that designing, making, distributing, and selling vehicles confers.

REFERENCES

Cohen, Stephen. 2000. *The Route to Japan's Voluntary Export Restraints on Automombiles: An Analysis of the US Government's Decision-Making Process in 1981*. Working Paper no. 20. Washington: School of International Service, American University.

Covarrubias V., A., and S.M. Ramírez Perez. 2020. "Introduction: Changing Geographies and Frontiers of the Automotive Industry." In *New Frontiers of the Automobile Industry: Exploring Geographies, Technology, and Institutional Challenges*, edited by Alex Covarrubias V. and Sigfrido M. Ramírez Perez (1–38). London: Palgrave Macmillan Cham.

Dryden, S. 1995. *Trade Warriors: USTR and the American Crusade for Free Trade*. New York: Oxford University Press.

Harrison, D., and C. Ludwig. 2021. *Electric Vehicle Battery Supply Chain Analysis 2021: How Battery Demand and Production Are Reshaping the Automotive Industry*. London: Ultima Media.

JD Power. 2021. "Newly Launched New-Energy Vehicle Models in China Have Fewer Quality Problems in Smart Features, J.D. Power Finds." Press release, 22 July 2021. https://china.jdpower.com/press-release/2021-china-NEV-IQS.

Mordue, G. 2020. "Shifting Patterns in the Application of Industrial Policy." *International Journal of Automotive Technology and Management* 20(1): 50–75.

Rhys, D.G. 2004. "The Motor Industry in an Enlarged EU." *The World Economy* 27(6): 877–900.

List of Contributors

Dimitry Anastakis is a professor and the L.R. Wilson and R.J. Currie Chair in Canadian Business History in the Department of History and the Rotman School of Management at the University of Toronto, Toronto, ON.

Victor M. Cabral is a doctoral candidate at El Colegio de Chihuahua, Cd. Juárez, Chihuahua, Mexico.

Jorge Carrillo is a professor emeritus, El Colegio de la Frontera Norte, Tijuana, Baja California, Mexico.

Alex Covarrubias V. is a professor at El Colegio de Sonora, Hermosillo, Sonora, Mexico.

Mélanie Dufour-Poirier is an associate professor in the Faculty of Arts and Sciences, School of Industrial Relations, Montreal, QC.

Mattieu Dupuis is an associate professor, Department of Industrial Relations, Faculty of Social Sciences, Laval University, Quebec City, QC.

B. Kristin Dziczek is the first senior vice president, Center for Automotive Research, Ann Arbor, MI.

Humberto Garcia Jimenez is a research professor at El Colegio de la Frontera Norte, Nogales, Sonora, Mexico.

Elena Goracinova has a doctorate in political science from the University of Toronto, Toronto, ON.

A.J. Jacobs is a professor at East Carolina University, Greenville, NC.

Bassel Kazzaz is the director of research at the Automotive Policy Research Centre, Toronto, ON.

Thomas Klier is a senior economist and economic advisor with the Federal Reserve Bank of Chicago, Chicago, IL.

Nathan Lemphers is an adjunct professor in the Department of Political Science, University of Waterloo, Waterloo, ON. He was formerly a postdoctoral researcher with Smart Prosperity Institute at the University of Ottawa, Ottawa, ON.

Greig Mordue is an associate professor and the ArcelorMittal Dofasco Chair in Advanced Manufacturing Policy in the W Booth School of Engineering Practice and Technology in the Faculty of Engineering at McMaster University, Hamilton, ON.

Sarah Greene is a research associate at the Automotive Policy Research Centre, Toronto, ON.

James Rubenstein is a professor emeritus of geography, Miami University, Oxford, OH.

Clemente Ruiz Durán is a professor in the Graduate School of Economics, Ciudad Universitaria División de Posgrado Facultad de Economía, Universidad Nacional Autónoma de México, Coyoacán, Ciudad de México.

Tod Rutherford is a professor in the Department of Geography and the Environment, Maxwell School of Citizenship and Public Affairs, Syracuse University, Syracuse, NY.

B. Mike Smitka is a professor emeritus of economics, Washington and Lee University, Lexington, VA.

Brendan Sweeney is the managing director of Trillium Network for Advanced Manufacturing, Western University, London, ON.

Bernard Swiecki is the vice president mobility and research, Detroit Regional Partnership, Detroit, MI.

Bertha Vallejo is a visiting researcher at INGENIO (CSIC-UPV), Universitat Politècnica de València, Spain.

David Wolfe is the co-director of the Innovation Policy Lab and professor of political science at the University of Toronto, Toronto, ON.

Charlotte Yates is the president and vice-chancellor of the University of Guelph. She is also a faculty member in the Department of Political Science.